Unmentionable

CUISINE

Calvin W. Schwabe is Professor of Epidemiology in the Schools of Veterinary Medicine and Medicine at the University of California, Davis. He serves on the International Committee for the Anthropology of Food and Food Habits and was a member of the National Academy of Science Committee on Agricultural Production Efficiency and the Subcommittee on Animal Health, World Food, and Nutrition Study.

WESTERN MAN, DESPITE HIS FREQUENT

TEMPTATION TO CLAIM *HIS* FOODWAYS ARE BASED

ON RATIONAL CONSIDERATIONS,

IS NO MORE RATIONAL IN THIS THAN

OTHER MEN, FOR IT MAKES NO BETTER

SENSE TO REJECT NUTRITIOUS

DOGFLESH, HORSEFLESH, GRASSHOPPERS

AND TERMITES AS FOOD THAN TO REJECT

BEEF OR CHICKEN FLESH.

— FREDERICK SIMOONS

CALVIN W. SCHWABE

Unmentionable

CUISINE

University Press of

VIRGINIA

Charlottesville

THE UNIVERSITY PRESS OF VIRGINIA
Copyright © 1979 by the Rector and Visitors
of the University of Virginia

First published 1979

Library of Congress Cataloging in Publication Data

Schwabe, Calvin W
  Unmentionable cuisine.

  Bibliography: p.
  Includes indexes.
  1. Animal food. 2. Food habits. I. Title.
TX371.S38   641.6′6   79-15957
ISBN 0-8139-0811-6

  Printed in the United States of America

To Cathy and Christopher

FOR BEING SUCH GOOD-SPIRITED

ADVENTURERS

CONTENTS

Acknowledgments

COLLECTING these and similar recipes has been an enjoyable spare-time activity during the thirty years our family has lived and traveled around the world, partially in more direct efforts to improve its food supply. "Guinea pigs" for a cause have been the numerous guests at our table who have helped us sample many of these new items of diet and have good-naturedly accepted from us in the process some rather uncommon fare. In thanking those who have assisted more specifically, I wish first to acknowledge lovingly my wife's very special contribution. Her students and mine abroad and our foreign students in the United States have helped us locate or verify many of these recipes. Very special thanks are also due to Man Tat Yan for securing in mainland China several unusually difficult-to-obtain recipes and to Marjorie Weston-Roth and Joyce Adams for much help with assembling the manuscript, as well as with the library research. Two of my colleagues at the University of California, Professors Rose Marie Pangborn of the Department of Food Science and Technology and Frederick Simoons of the Department of Geography have been especially interested in and supportive of this whole venture. Dr. Simoons's *Eat Not This Flesh* is the standard English-language work on the geography and anthropology of meat prejudices in the Old World, and, like all students of this subject, I am much in his debt.

Unmentionable

CUISINE

Food for Thought

BECAUSE OF PREJUDICE or ignorance, we Americans now reject many readily available foods that are cheap, nutritious, and good to eat. Though we unhesitantly criticize Indians because *they* refuse to eat beef, the more appalling fact that a majority of *us* refuse to eat equally valuable foods rarely receives even passing notice. Such obviously biased distinctions between the irrationalities of others and our own will become more difficult for us to make as the long-range consequences of our rapidly changing land-use, agricultural, and food-marketing practices become more widely understood.

Unmentionable Cuisine is a book about foods seldom eaten by Americans though standard fare for others. It is meant to be a practical guide to help us and our children prepare for the not too distant day when the world's growing food-population problem presses closer upon us and our overly restrictive eating habits become less tolerable. I do not think this prospect need portend disaster, for opening our minds about foods and educating our palates to receive new and varied taste experiences could prove as enjoyable an experience as it will be a necessary one. To suggest how, I have assembled a sampler of receipes for foods of animal origin which most of us do not now eat but which millions of other people do. To increase the prospects for their fair trial, I have included a variety of uses for most of them.

This "unmentionable cuisine" for our future intentionally focuses upon foods of *animal* origin that are already available in the United States, or could be. This is because proteins of high biological value—for which animals are our principal sources—are now less plentiful and more poorly distributed worldwide than are other foods and because Euell Gibbons and others have written already about plant foods present in the United States though seldom eaten.

A doubt in some persons' minds that must be dispelled at the outset, therefore, is whether in the future Americans and others should eat meat or any animal foods at all. This question is one being raised increasingly by many socially concerned and well-meaning individuals. It is, however, a question beclouded by at least as much ignorance and misinformation as obscures the related issue of food avoidances which this book addresses.

The seriousness of the world food problem demands as much balanced judgment as each of us can bring to it. Above all, it is too serious a problem for catchy phrases or ideological biases. Such widely quoted statements as Dumont's, that "by consuming meat, which wastes the grain that could have saved them, last year we ate the children of the Sahel, Ethiopia, and Bangladesh," are not only sweepingly simplistic but patently false in their implications.

While I have no quarrel with the personal preferences of philosophic vegetarians, it should be made clear that the consequences of lifetime *strict* vegetarianism—through the reproductive cycle—have never been scientifically assessed. Recent clinical observations in the United States warn, however, of the risks of severe anemic and neurologic manifestations of vitamin B_{12} deficiency to infants nursed by vegetarian mothers, since foods of animal origin provide our only source of this essential vitamin. Aside from that problem and equally important practical difficulties in obtaining a dietary balance of essential amino acids solely from plant proteins, advocates that mankind cease eating animal foods totally disregard many other vital facets of the world food problem. Perhaps the most important is that, of the 15 billion hectares of the earth's land surface not covered by ice, most authorities agree that only about 1.5 billion, most of them now under plow, could be cultivated practically. On the other hand, the vegetation on about 3 billion additional hectares of nonarable lands is utilizable to feed man through the grazing and browsing activities of animals that harvest under their own power and convert highly scattered or otherwise inaccessible plant life to the highest-quality human food. About 60 percent of the world's annual animal-protein production of 30 million metric tons now comes from such nonarable lands. Thus herbivorous animals provide the *only* vehicle for exploitation of immense land areas for food production.

Beyond this, promoters of vegetarianism also overlook the fact that plant and animal agriculture are naturally complementary. The uniqueness and, perhaps, impermanence of our highly fossil-fuel–dependent, tractor-powered agriculture cause this relationship to escape notice by many in our present generation. Yet cattle, buffaloes, horses, camels, yaks, and llamas still provide about 75 percent of the world's draft power, much of it irreplaceable. In the not atypical situation of India, cattle alone produce 54 percent of the energy used for crop production. In fact, cattle generate fully 33 percent of the energy consumed in rural India for *all* purposes (16.3 percent of it from burning their dung and 14 percent from their work). In many other countries cattle dung is also a primary source of cooking fuel. To replace the manure produced by one cow per year if it is burned as fuel would require 2.7×10^6 kcal of fossil-fuel equivalent. To replace its fertilizer value would require 0.9×10^6 kcal of fossil fuel, and, with new technology, animal manures can yield methane gas for burning and still be used for fertilizer. Unless significant new sources of cheap energy are discovered, meat and milk will continue in most countries to be important by-products of these primary uses of animals in plant agriculture and rural economy.

Moreover, the excessive feeding of grains to ruminant livestock, as is now the American practice, is unnecessary. Beef grading U.S. Good is produced in Argentina almost solely on grasses and other forages, and a 25 to 30 percent saving in grain consumption by beef cattle could be realized readily in the United States simply by finishing animals to "good" rather than "choice" grade. At the same time most nutritionists agree that meat grading "good" is better for you. Among nonruminants, meat-producing chickens can now be fed at an efficiency level such as to offer nearly a straight choice to the consumer of eating grains directly or in the form of meat. China maintains four times the swine population of the United States almost solely by recycling wastes. And so on. For these and other equally valid reasons, meat and other foods of animal origin remain vital to man's future, and it behooves us all not to contribute to their undersupply, maldistribution, or cost by wasting or not utilizing to best advantage those available to us.

Though helping to avoid such food wastage in the future is this book's goal, I have intentionally excluded from consideration the meat of ecologically threatened wildlife like whales. Instead, I have emphasized our eating of other wild animal species that are now destructive pests.

Finally, some mention needs to be made of animal fats, particularly of cholesterol, an essential metabolite synthesized by man, as well as by other animals. Epidemiological studies have very clearly associated increased risks of certain forms of heart disease with cigarette smoking, excessive body-weight, and high blood serum cholesterol, particularly when these factors are combined. In addition to being produced by our own bodies from other substances, our chief sources of cholesterol are from animal fats in our diet. Recent research has shown that, while most people's bodies handle this dietary cholesterol well, the cholesterol transport mechanisms of a minority of people are defective to the extent that increased serum levels and other metabolic changes result. The reason for this is poorly understood, but these individuals for whom high cholesterol diets are a special health hazard can be identified medically.

The commonness of overweight problems among Americans testifies to our currently excessive consumption of calories generally. This is another reason for us to begin to finish our food animals to less fatty "good" rather than "choice" grades and to reduce our consumption of food overall, particularly of fats and carbohydrates. It also recommends that the protein in our diets come from food sources balanced in amino acids yet relatively low not only in fats but in carbohydrates too. Most of the recipes in this book are for foods that fit those needs admirably.

For each food animal considered, the recipes have been organized systematically wherever possible, starting first with recipes for the whole carcass, which is by far the most economical way to purchase any meat animal. Next follow recipes for the head and its parts; the skin, neck, feet (or wings), and tail; the bones and their marrow; the visceral organs, including the various glands; and finally blood and scraps. Recipes using several parts of an animal have been listed under only one, but the general index cross-references all of them; there is also a special index by country that includes the foreign language name for each recipe. I have included a glossary of less common culinary terms; these are keyed in text by printing the terms glossed in SMALL CAPITALS. Where appropriate and where informa-tion has been obtainable, I have commented too upon a food item's availability, its nutritional value, any general steps required for its prepara-tion, and any special health precautions necessary.

I hope that this book contributes in some measure to a better understand-ing by Americans of the global food problem to which people's prejudices and ignorance add significantly—and that it proves a source of enjoyment at the same time. *Bon appétit.*

Part One

MEAT

MEAT

Kila nyama nyama tu—every meat is meat.

SWAHILI SAYING

A
N IMMENSE GAP separates this Swahili conception of what consti-
tutes edible meat from the experience of today's average Ameri-
can family. And this gap will probably widen further before a combination of
circumstances causes it to begin to narrow again. Only a generation ago,
even in our cities, the whole beef or pork or lamb carcass was dissected
before the eyes of the housewife by her local butcher, and our many farm
families did the job themselves. Today few younger Americans have had
either experience, and it is not surprising for surveys to show that many of
our urban youth now make no association between the fast-food ham-
burger or plastic-wrapped supermarket steak and a live farm animal. Ac-
celerating promotion and acceptance of high-cost processed foods make the
future likelihood of such associations even more remote. Swift, Armour,
and others of our largest meat-packers are now owned by conglomerates
that are very actively pressuring their managements to convert higher and
higher proportions of the meat the United States produces into processed
and prepackaged foods on which the profits are far higher than they are on
fresh meats. Few Americans any longer recognize, therefore—much less
eat—the full range of edible products even our most common food animals
can supply, and gastronomic possibilities necessarily become more limited
for the average American family. Eating is tending in many American
homes to be a mere "tanking up" exercise on a narrower and narrower

range of fast foods, fad foods, and precooked dinners, so much so that one perceptive European feels our national motto should now be "gobble, gulp, and go."

The result of this whole process is that potentially valuable cheap meats that could add variety, goodness, and balance to our diets are overlooked and wasted entirely as human food or are overprocessed to the lowest common denominator of taste and, sometimes, of nutritional value. Ironically, it is largely the well-to-do in America, persons who can readily afford expensive TV dinners and processed meats nightly, who are beginning to rediscover the joy and creative satisfaction of selecting and preparing from scratch real foodstuffs.

So much for how social changes and ignorance have contributed to our currently unimaginative utilization of flesh foods. What about the other matter of prejudice? Prejudice implies the holding of an opinion or the making of a judgment without sufficient grounds. Few of us like admitting to prejudice in any sphere because it reflects irrational behavior and a closed mind.

Food dislikes are not prejudices if they are based upon a sufficient range of experiences and a willingness to recognize that tastes may change or palates be educated. There are rational explanations, for example, for children disliking particular foods more commonly than adults do—but parental permissiveness is surely not one of them.

Nor is it unnatural, and surely not uncivilized, for a child or an adult not to relish the idea that a living animal, particularly a familiar animal, might have to be killed to supply him with food. This necessity—and the pain it may cause us—has been a part of the experience of living for all previous generations, and it need not stimulate callousness, inhumaneness, or a disrespect for life. It requires of us as husbanders of animals, however, to make the lives of those that serve us as pleasant, and their deaths as painless and free of fear, as we possibly can.

Prejudices against flesh foods commonly result from recognition of an animal as being of a species that is especially liked. For other animals, however, revulsion rather than sentiment may be the basis of prejudice and may result from the live animal's unattractive appearance, its habits, or some other real or fancied association in the mind of the prospective preparer or consumer. Beyond these two common sources of food prejudices many other factors may also assert themselves. For example, the moist appearance of uncooked meat, particularly the presence of blood, is unappealing to many who then translate these feelings to the finished dish. To the preparer a particular meat's slippery feel or its uncooked smell may similarly prejudice him or her against its fair trial.

None of these kinds of restrictions upon dietary variety have anything to do with a dish's taste, its nutritional value, or our enjoyment of it, and they can all be outgrown with little effort. One reason we probably seldom make the effort, however, is that surveys have repeatedly shown that American women, who generally select and prepare our food, have more numerous food aversions than do American men. For example, it is probably the rare American household today where game or fresh-caught fish will even be prepared unless the man of the house does the cleaning, skinning, or scaling.

More difficult for both men and women to handle are religious or other strong *cultural* obstacles to experimental eating of particular animals or particular organs. These are things we readily see as irrational in the behavior of others but completely overlook in ourselves. Such prejudices may relate to conscious or unconscious unwillingness or reluctance to be like some other class of people. For example, prejudices against eating a certain food may result from associations of its eating with a detested or enemy people, as was probably the origin of pork avoidance, then abhorrence, by Jews and other nomadic peoples. Eating certain other foods may be regarded as a sign of poverty as only the destitute in a particular culture will eat them. These food avoidances, of whatever cultural or historical origin, lead to unfamiliarity with particular flavors or other sensations associated with the avoided foods. This then becomes a cyclical process of reinforcement because the unfamiliar tends to be avoided for that reason alone.

Finally, "fear of germs" is a major cultural source of Americans' food prejudices. When Americans travel abroad it is often in terms of "germs" that they rationalize a wide range of food prejudices. To be sure, there are health risks involved in preparing or eating many types of foods, particularly if we are not aware of them. For example, the digestive tracts of most animal species may harbor pathogenic or potentially pathogenic micro-organisms such as salmonellae and clostridia, just as many food plants contain poisonous principles like cyanide or goiterogens. With a little knowledge of such risks, we realize, for instance, that rubber gloves must be worn when cleaning or handling an animal's digestive tract preparatory to its being cooked or pickled in brine; similarly, that the handling of these organs should be done in such a manner and place as not to contaminate surfaces on which other foods are to be kept or prepared, utensils used for other foods, or other foodstuffs directly. Simple things like these plus thorough cooking and thorough cleaning up will protect against most germs potentially transmissible through foods. Such reasonable precautions and unreasonable avoidance of the new are, however, two quite different things. Other types of food prejudices will be commented upon as examples present themselves in the text.

The first part of this book is about "meat," in its usual cookbook sense of *mammalian* meat. I have begun with some of the less familiar cuts of our most familiar animals and have gone from there to other edible mammalian meats that are available in America yet are seldom eaten by us.

1

Beef

O,NE REASON to begin our exploration of unmentionable cuisine with cattle is that "in America, steak is to meat what Cadillac is to cars" (Harris and Ross, 1978). Beef is America's favorite meat by far and constantly becomes more so. We eat 110 percent more beef today per person than we did in 1925, though our total per capita meat-consumption rate has remained fairly constant. And this despite the fact that beef prices have risen 550 percent in the interval! *Our* beef prejudices might come then as some surprise, but we must understand that our use for food of even this very popular species is now virtually limited to hamburger, steaks, and roasts, a fact that goes a long distance to explain their high costs. We show little interest in the many other edible parts of cattle, preferring to dispose of most of them in that culinary abomination the supermarket hot dog, in dog and cat foods (now a $2.5 billion per year industry), in livestock feeds, or in other industrial by-products not even indirectly destined for the table. These are not always the highest or most valuable uses for these cattle meats.

THE ORIGINS OF BEEF EATING

POORLY understood by most Americans is the relative peculiarity of our beef-eating habits. Beefsteaks and prime ribs are seldom eaten by people outside of the United States and a few other affluent countries. Even the idea of raising cattle expressly for meat was a comparatively recent invention of the British upper class, and the very word *beefsteak* is a loanword from English in many European languages. In the words of a seventeenth-century English author, "We conquered France by [other means] than by any odds of our . . . Beef-eaters, as the French were then scornfully pleas'd to terme us." In the rest of Europe cattle meat is still largely a by-product of the dairy industry. This less tender meat of old bulls and cows is enjoyed in a great variety of interesting stews, ragouts, goulashes, and sauerbratens. Surplus male calves are not fattened on grains but harvested almost entirely as highly relished milk-fed veal. And people *eat* the innards of both—and enjoy them.

BEEF AVOIDANCE

WE are all well aware that India maintains about one-fifth of all the world's cattle, though Hindus will not eat beef, a practice most of us find easy to condemn. Yet before British financial interests helped provide impetus to large-scale beef production on the vast prairies of North America and the South American pampas, cattle had been throughout history a species whose other relationships to man were usually too valued for them to be raised expressly for meat. And this pattern persists not just in India but in many other populous countries where cattle remain a principal source of rural power and producers of milk or also serve a central religiocultural function.

In fact, cattle were probably domesticated first for religious reasons in virtually all of the most ancient civilizations. The now extinct aurochs, or wild bull, standing up to six feet at the shoulder, was the animal held in greatest fear and awe by ancient peoples as diverse as the Egyptians, Mesopotamians, Greeks, Persians, and Indians. Because of its strength, bravery, swiftness, and much admired libido, the mature bull was venerated by early man, and among these earliest organized societies and others it eventually assumed the role of a chief god associated with fertility. In many cultures he was conceived of as a great rain god in the heavens, the constellation Taurus, who sometimes resided too in the sun or moon and, with his heavenly herd, nightly traversed the cattle path in the sky, the Milky Way. The thunder was this bull-god's bellow, the lightning his ejaculate, and the rain his fertilizing semen, which brought forth the crops of the earth. His mother and consort became the holy cow-mother goddess in each of these civilizations, and this role as an earth mother was reinforced when, following domestication, she produced offspring that made possible the plow and served as wet nurse to man's own children.

Pharaohs and other kings for thousands of years claimed descent from these originally bovine gods and goddesses. The prime test for proving manhood was to match wits with the bull, as is *still* the case in some Mediterranean countries. It is unsurprising, therefore, that the first civilizations all arose in the period from 4000 to 2000 B.C., in the astrological Age of Taurus, in which the sun rose each day in this bull constellation.

While it was illegal to kill cows in most of the ancient world, surplus bulls provided the highest form of sacrifice in kind to the gods and were often consumed in communion meals. Hindu priests once performed such rites. Thus the protective attitudes present-day Hindus display toward cattle, which most Americans now regard as aberrant and deplorable, are deeply ingrained and merely reflect the unique survival of ideas once believed by the ancestors of almost all of us. Gandhi has said that "the real essence of Hinduism lies in the protection of the cow, the embodiment of the pre-human world, the giver of riches, the basis of agriculture, the mother of the people."

While such ideas are not easily changed, few Americans would disagree that the restraints that these ancient and anachronistic beliefs provide on the rational use for human food of India's surplus calves and cattle whose productive life has ended must eventually cease. But all of these expressions of dismay and concern on our part can carry little force until *we* begin to eat our own cattle more efficiently by casting off far less well founded aversions to eating brawn, tripe, kidneys, brains, and other equally nutritious and tasty cuts of beef. Forty years ago a study of American university students (Hall and Hall, 1939) found that even then almost 40 percent of these young people already had a strong aversion to eating such meats. That this percentage is now much higher among their grandchildren is readily demonstrable.

CHEAPER BEEF

MOST Americans are unable to raise their own cattle, but many of us do have access to freezing facilities. Buying a whole beef, particularly buying at auction an animal on the hoof, is by far the most economical way to eat. To appreciate the extent to which this is so, consider these comparative prices for beef purchased in different forms. In the autumn of 1978 the auction price of a 1,000-lb. choice beef steer in California was about $550. Such an animal would dress to a carcass weight of about 600 lbs. If it were home butchered (Romans and Ziegler, 1977, provide detailed instructions), the hide would return $53, reducing the cost of the carcass plus head, extremities, and all innards to $497. (Should you wish to sell them, too, the wholesale price of these latter parts would be another $60.)

If you had the steer custom butchered, however, the charges (including cutting and freezer wrapping) would be $120 (plus the hide) for a total freezer-ready cost of the carcass plus the head, extremities, and innards of $670.

If, instead of buying a live animal, you chose to buy the whole 600-lb. carcass cut, wrapped, and freezer-ready from the custom butcher, the cost of the *carcass alone* would be $672; that is, by buying it alive and doing nothing else yourself you get free extras worth at least $60. Either way you would have the following quantities of meat that were available retail at that time at the prices indicated: 36 lbs. of porterhouse, T-bone, and club steaks (retail cost $116); 40 lbs. of sirloin steak (retail cost $121); 66 lbs. of round steak (retail cost $158); 48 lbs. of rib roast (retail cost $115); 25 lbs. of boneless rump (retail cost $62); 102 lbs. of chuck (retail cost $153); 112 lbs. of stew meat (retail cost $169); 45 lbs. of ground beef (retail cost $72); and 126 lbs. of bones and scraps (retail cost $38).

Assuming that you bought the steer alive and had it butchered, cut, and wrapped for you, the difference in cost from the retail price would mean, for example, that you would get *free* 25 lbs. of boneless rump roasts, 45 lbs. of ground beef, 112 lbs. of stew beef, about 100 lbs. of bones and scraps, 35 lbs. of blood, the head, tail, and feet, 10 lbs. of liver, 4 lbs. of heart, 2.5 lbs. of tongue, the brain, lungs, tripe, sausage casings, spleen, pancreas, membranes (and some garden manure).

However, even if you do not have a large freezer, you need not forego these organ meats. The local butchers we still have in many towns can readily provide them—and even the supermarket's meat department will obtain on request most of the organ meats considered here that it does not stock. In fact, they will regularly stock those for which any local demand is created. Compared to an autumn 1978 retail price per pound of $3.00 for bone-in sirloin steak and $2.09 for a boneless rump roast, the bone-free retail prices alone per pound of beef liver ($0.98), heart ($0.98), tongue ($1.29), brains ($1.09), sweetbreads ($1.29), kidneys ($0.59), tripe ($0.79), and spleen ($0.29) should encourage their purchase.

For comparing the nutritional contents of each of these parts of the beef animal in the text, the nutritional value of U.S. Choice grade T-bone steak has been selected as a familiar standard. (Nutritional data used refer to the raw "edible portion" only.) Thus, a U.S. Choice T-bone steak consists of protein 14.7 percent, fat 37.1 percent, calcium 0.008 percent, phosphorus 0.135 percent, iron 0.0022 percent, sodium 0.065 percent, potassium 0.355 percent, vitamin A 70 I.U./100 grams, thiamine 0.006 percent, riboflavin 0.00013 percent, and niacin 0.0035 percent (plus water and other substances).

No unusual health hazards are associated with the preparation or eating of most of the cattle organs considered, although a general warning about handling animals' digestive tracts was given in the introduction to this part. The only part of cattle commonly eaten raw or undercooked is the usual muscle meat of beef. The principal risk in the United States from not cooking muscle beef thoroughly is infection with the beef tapeworm, *Taenia saginata*. Its larval stages (cysticerci, or beef measles) localize primarily in muscle meat, including the heart and tongue, of infected cattle. These larvae appear in raw meat as pale oval bodies about 1/4 inch in length. Infected cattle in the United States are seen mostly in southern California, where they are usually diagnosed in the slaughterhouse during veterinary inspection. Lightly infected beef carcasses are frozen to kill these parasites, while heavily infected ones are condemned. Toxoplasmosis has also been contracted by eating rare or raw beef, though that is not its chief means of transmission to people.

The Whole Carcass

Since the head of the ox is customarily removed before roasting, prejudices against cooking and eating an ox whole should be minimal.

However, as festive as the once common English ox-roast must have been, because of the beef animal's size it probably remains a practical possibility today only for the politician seeking office or for some exciting community occasion. Even then a so-called baby beef carcass would be easiest to manage, and the risk of spoilage, because of the long cooking time required, markedly reduced.

Roasted Ox / England

A large hardwood fire should be built against a heat-resistant reflecting surface, such as an ordinary brick, refractory brick, or stone wall. After the fire has burned several hours, a whole spitted steer carcass (or a half, baron, or quarter of beef) is set up alongside the fire with a drip pan placed underneath. Basting with a generous quantity of suet and drippings should be carried out regularly. The slow roasting of a 750-lb. steer may take up to 3 days, but proportionately less time is required for a baby beef carcass or for portions of carcasses. The desired doneness should be monitored carefully with 6 to 8 meat thermometers inserted throughout the carcass into its most heavily and more lightly muscled portions.

MUSCLE MEAT

BEEF muscle meat is so commonly consumed in the United States that the only two recipes I will give are for jerky and corned beef, both methods, in addition to freezing, for preserving meat. Oddly, however, cattle meat that strays even that far from just plain beef will already begin to elicit some American food prejudices. In one survey of university students, for example, an amazing 61 percent said they either refused to eat even corned or dried (chipped) beef or had never tried them.

The Hawaiian name for jerky is *pipikaula*, and nowadays it is very commonly served as an hors d'oeuvre at Island parties.

JERKY *(Pipikaula)* / HAWAII

Cut beef into long, thin, 1-in.-wide strips. Sprinkle with coarse salt and marinate in soy sauce (with or without garlic) for several hours or overnight. Hang the well-separated strips to dry in the hot sun (preferably in a screened area) for one or more days or until they are thoroughly dry.

This really delicious meat can be eaten broiled over charcoal or fried in hot oil.

Before commercial refrigeration, much of the beef consumed in the United States was dried like this as jerky or cured in brine, which is another way many families could preserve portions of a whole or half beef carcass purchased for economy reasons.

CORNED BEEF / UNITED STATES

Pack boneless pieces of chuck, brisket, plate, and round not more than 3 in. thick in a wooden barrel or tub or a stone crock. Cover with a chilled pickle. Weight the meat with a board upon which a heavy stone or other nonmetallic weight has been placed. After 14 days the meat will be corned and may then be removed from the pickle barrel as needed.

Before we leave beef muscle meat as such, a word or two about veal is also in order. Annual per capita consumption of veal (calf meat) in the United States has now dropped to 1.7 lbs., whereas in much of Europe it is the most preferred meat. In fact, the real white-meat milk-fed veal of Europe is now rarely obtainable in this country. The deep-pink to red meat often sold as veal here, although calf meat, would not pass as veal in Europe. This is the main reason some classic veal recipes cannot easily be duplicated in the United States. White veal, like foie gras, is in a sense a pathological meat, though certainly not dangerous to consume. It is obtained from calves that are maintained to veal weight exclusively on a milk diet and thus often develop a pronounced iron-deficiency anemia. This accounts for the white meat. This diet, when prolonged, makes the animals more susceptible to infections. Vealers, therefore, are difficult to raise. This, in turn, contributes to genuine veal's high cost. If this anemia is treated with iron compounds, an effect is noted on the muscle pigment, or myoglobin, too. The resulting meat is pink and in Europe does not command the premium price paid for white veal.

HEAD

CATTLE heads are seldom served as such, so prejudices against their use for food *should* be limited entirely to aesthetic objections on the part of some cooks to the head's uncooked appearance. Thus, though calf's head is often prepared at Texas barbecues, decorum now dictates that it usually not be displayed on the table. The skinned beef or calf head consists largely of muscle meat and bone, plus the brain and sensory organs. The head meat per se is like any carcass meat, but because it is readily removed only after cooking, it is eaten most commonly as so-called headcheeses, or brawns, or is used as a sausage ingredient.

Headcheeses are made by pressing the cooked meat into a mold or wrapping it tightly in cloth. Because the head's bones, cartilages, and ligaments yield a gelatin-rich stock when it is boiled, the headcheese sets as it cools, hence its name. Headcheese can be easily sliced, therefore, and its mosaic appearance is attractive on the plate. My recipe is for a traditional English version, but interesting modifications for tasty, colorful, and nutritious cold luncheon or supper dishes merely await the cook's imagination. Headcheeses, as usually prepared, have a slightly higher protein content than T-bone steak with only about two-thirds of its fat.

HEADCHEESE, OR OXHEAD BRAWN / ENGLAND

Soak a split, skinned beef head in brine overnight, then rinse and trim it well. Put it into a large kettle and add peppercorns, salt, desired herbs, and vegetable trimmings, with water to cover. Simmer until the meat falls from the bones. Concentrate the gelatin-rich stock. Chop the meat, season it with pepper and preferred herbs, and add the liquid gelatin. Press into a mold, place a weight on top of the brawn, and chill it well in the refrigerator. Unmold onto a platter and garnish with parsley; slice and serve with pickles and boiled potatoes.

Other miscellaneous bony, cartilaginous, or tendinous cuts can also be used for making brawn, and hot dishes based upon beef head meat are also to be found in a number of cuisines. Devizes pie is one English Wiltshire dish made from calf head, and these two others suggest some of the possibilities.

FRIED CALF'S HEAD (*Kirántott borjútej*) / HUNGARY

Simmer a skinned and washed calf's head 3/4 hour in salted water containing onions, celery, and parsnips and allow it to cool. Bone and slice it, salt the slices, dredge them in flour, dip each into beaten egg, and then into breadcrumbs. Fry the meat slices in a generous amount of lard until nicely browned. Serve with baked potatoes and tartar sauce.

CALF'S HEAD WITH BRAIN FRITTERS / 19TH-CENTURY NEW ENGLAND

Simmer a skinned and washed calf's head in salted water only and cool it. Remove and slice the meat. Put the brain through the fine blade of a food chopper and mix it with a beaten egg, 1 T flour, 3 T milk, and some nutmeg. Fry the brain mixture as fritters. Place the slices of head meat in some leftover beef gravy that has been seasoned with pepper, mace, cloves, herbs, onions, and cayenne and simmer them 10 minutes. Remove the meat, strain the sauce, and add some sautéed sliced mushrooms. Return the meat to the sauce and reheat. Surround the head meat on a platter with the brain fritters and fried bacon.

TONGUE

THE tongue is the only part of the cow's or steer's head seen in American markets, but even it is not commonly eaten. This is surprising because tongue, like heart, consists only of very lean, boneless muscle meat and is surely one of the cheapest sources of beef. A beef tongue contains slightly more protein than T-bone steak with less than half its fat.

The American prejudice against eating tongue seems to derive entirely from its readily recognizable appearance in the market and from its being served whole. In fact, rather surprisingly, in one U.S. survey tongue ranked with kidneys as foods university men most commonly refused to eat. At our family's pre-Christmas caroling suppers each year, it amuses me to see how a whole cold poached tongue to be sliced and eaten with mustard, mayonnaise, or aïoli sauce may remain all evening virtually untouched, while the pot of tongue spread next to it (see below) will have to be refilled. Thus one time-tested tactic for breaking down prejudices against inadequately experienced foods or ones against which recognition prejudices exist is to serve them first in disguised forms, only revealing the new food item's identity after it has been eaten and, one hopes, enjoyed.

Basic Preparation

Unless indicated, fresh beef tongue is soaked first in cold water for several hours, trimmed of cartilage and fat, and simmered in boiling salted water with celery, onions, and carrots (and any other indicated ingredients) until it is tender. Then it is cooled in its stock and skinned (a tongue may be skinned before it is poached, but not easily). Pork, sheep, or deer tongue can also be prepared by these recipes for beef tongue.

TONGUE SPREAD / ORIGINAL

Combine a finely ground poached beef tongue, chopped BLANCHED almonds, and chopped pimento-stuffed green olives with enough mayonnaise to achieve spreading consistency. Season with salt, pepper, and crushed garlic and serve with party rye bread or crackers or on bread rounds as canapés garnished with a strip of pimento or an olive slice.

A next step for introducing tongue might well be this hearty beef tongue salad, which combines interesting tastes and textures. Since the Danes are already highly regarded in the United States for their "sensible" and straightforward yet imaginative cuisine, their recipe for new meats may prove good vehicles for many first efforts.

TONGUE SALAD *(Tunge salat)* / DENMARK

Mix a JULIENNE of boiled beef tongue and cooked beets, diced apples, and sliced hard-cooked eggs. Dress with mayonnaise or oil and vinegar.

If they have now gone that far with tongue, the family is probably ready for any of these others. The next two recipes are for different versions of sweet-and-sour tongue, a dish served around the world. In fact, this first Polish recipe suggests by its ingredients a Middle Eastern origin; it probably entered Poland through the Balkans with Turkish influence or via the Tartars. Perhaps the tongue's role as the organ of taste provided the original sweet-and-sour inspiration.

BEEF TONGUE *(Ozór na szaro)* / POLAND

Simmer a beef tongue as above (basic preparation) with some bay leaves and peppercorns added. Slice the skinned tongue thinly, reserving the stock. Caramelize about 3 t sugar and 3 t water. Add 1 T butter, then 1 T flour and about 3 C of the stock. Bring to a boil and add generous amounts of chopped BLANCHED almonds and raisins, a little grated lemon rind, a little lemon juice, and a glass of wine. Add the sliced tongue, return to a boil, and serve. This is a good luncheon dish.

Another more unusual version of sweet-and-sour tongue is this robust Italian recipe, possibly again a recipe adopted during Arab rule in Sicily, although the use of chocolate betrays a Mexican influence, probably via Spain. The Italians, because of their central location in the Mediterranean and past trading prowess, have readily absorbed into their cuisine many diverse foreign influences, modifying them through necessity and true culinary genius to suit local tastes.

Sweet-and-Sour Tongue *(Lingua dolce forte)* / Italy

Slice a poached beef tongue. Fry chopped onion, chopped carrots, chopped celery, and chopped parsley in olive oil over medium heat until soft. Stir in a little tomato paste, some finely chopped candied lemon or orange peel, raisins, a little sugar and flour, and some chopped unsweetened chocolate. Add wine vinegar (2 T per T of sugar) and 1 C of the poaching stock. Bring to a boil and then remove from the heat. Salt the sauce to taste. Alternate layers of sliced tongue and sauce in a shallow casserole. Add a top layer of pine nuts and bake covered in a 325°F oven for about 45 minutes.

The Chinese BRAISE in dark soy sauce all red meats and dark-fleshed fowl such as duck. They call this process red-simmering.

Red-simmered Beef Tongue *(Hom pao nio shuh)* / China

Cover a parboiled, skinned tongue with fresh water, add some scallions cut in large sections, a few slices of fresh ginger root, a generous quantity of dark soy sauce, some sherry, and a little salt. Simmer, covered, until tender. Add sugar to taste, correct the salt, and simmer a bit longer. Allow the tongue to cool. Slice and serve it cold or quickly reheated in the cooking stock.

Plain boiled rice is sufficient accompaniment for red-simmered tongue or for this Filipino tongue, sausage, and ham stew.

Tongue *(Lengua)* / Philippines

Prepare a poached beef tongue and reserve the stock. In another pot add to the tongue one chorizo de Bilbao or other firm sausage, a little sliced Chinese ham or a similar meat, some soy sauce, a can of tomato sauce, some ground pepper, and 1 t fermented fish sauce (or Worcestershire sauce with a bit of anchovy paste). Add 4 C of the stock, which has been well thickened with a flour-and-butter ROUX. Add fancily cut carrots and green and red peppers and some mushrooms and peas. Cook for a few minutes or until the carrots are barely done. To serve, slice the tongue and garnish it with slices of chorizo and/or ham, some fried bananas (preferably plantains), and the cooked vegetables. Cover the meat with some of the sauce and pass the rest.

Tongue is also a traditional accompaniment of cabbage in several cultures. Below are two very different recipes, the first for a dish popular in Germany and central Europe, as well as Alsace, the second for a cheap version of corned beef and cabbage.

ALSATIAN BEEF TONGUE (*Langue de boeuf à l'alsacienne*) / FRANCE

Add a BOUQUET GARNI to cooking liquid and poach a beef tongue until half done. Drain off the liquid, skin the tongue, surround it with sauerkraut, and finish the cooking as for *choucroute garni*. Serve with boiled new potatoes.

CORNED BEEF TONGUE AND CABBAGE / IRELAND

Soak a skinned tongue (previously parboiled 5 minutes) in cold water and drain. Prick the entire surface deeply with a cooking fork and rub with a mixture of salt and sodium nitrate. Put it into an earthenware crock or wooden tub and cover with cooled pickling brine. A suitable brine is made from 1 lb. coarse salt dissolved in a quart of boiling water to which 1 oz. saltpeter (sodium nitrate), 1/2 C brown sugar, and preferred pickling herbs and spices have been added. An alternative curing brine (in a quantity sufficient for 100 lbs. of meat) is made by dissolving 8 lbs. salt, 3 lbs. sugar, 5 oz. baking soda, 3 oz. sodium nitrate, and 1/4 oz. sodium nitrite in 4 gallons of boiling water. Add pickling spices as desired.

Allow the tongue to remain in the brine for at least 14 days. Soak corned tongue in cold water several hours before poaching it for about 2–1/2 hours. Add quartered cabbages and peeled potatoes the last hour.

And this last is a tasty dish for a backyard cookout or Sunday night supper.

DEVILED BEEF TONGUE (*Langue de boeuf à la diable*) / FRANCE

Cut a poached beef tongue into thick slices, coat them with freshly prepared mustard, then melted butter and bread crumbs. Sprinkle with more melted butter and grill them over charcoal, being careful not to burn the coating. Serve with diable sauce.

The muzzle, cheeks, and palate of beef are even cheaper cuts that can be cooked like tongue.

These are three other interesting possibilities for inexpensive eating "straight from the cow's mouth."

OX PALATES AND CHICKEN / 18TH-CENTURY ENGLAND

Simmer 10 beef palates until tender. Skin them and cut into squares. Season 2 or 3 cut-up chickens with salt, nutmeg, and thyme. Brown them in butter until golden. Put the chicken and palates in a kettle, add some beef or chicken velouté sauce (incorporating the chicken drippings), and simmer until the chicken is tender. Thicken the sauce with several egg yolks beaten in a glass of white wine and finish with a piece of butter and some cream. Garnish the dish with grapes.

SLIVERS OF OX PALATE (*Allumettes de palais de boeuf*) / FRANCE

Boil some ox palates. Skin and cut them into match-sized strips. Marinate them in the refrigerator in vinegar with added salt, parsley, and chopped green onions. Drain and put them into a thick creamy batter prepared from flour mixed with a little oil into which beer is beaten a little at a time (or blend the 3 ingredients in an electric blender). Fry the battered palate strips in deep oil until golden brown. These may be simply garnished with deep-fried parsley or served with a tomato sauce.

OX PALATES IN BROWNED SAUCE (*Palais de boeuf au gratin*) / FRANCE

Boiled and skinned palates are sliced, arranged in a flat mound on a heat-proof serving dish, covered with a duxelles sauce, sprinkled with bread crumbs and melted butter, and browned in a slow oven.

EYES

BEFORE leaving the culinary possibilities for beef heads, I offer, hesitantly, two variations on a more exotic French dish which I confess not to have tried. It would probably make excellent Halloween party fare and immediately establish the culinary reputation for any truly venturesome cook.

STUFFED CALF'S EYES (*Des yeux de veau farcis*) / FRANCE

Soak some calf's eyes in cold water for several hours and then BLANCH them. Remove the corneas, lenses, and irises with a sharp knife or small curved scissors. Fill the cavities with pieces of truffle or small mush-rooms. Dip the stuffed eyes in beaten eggs and fine bread crumbs and deep-fry them in oil. Serve with small braised onions and mushroom caps.

Stuffed eyes may also be put in gratin dishes, covered with a mixture of sieved hard-cooked eggs, fine herbs, and melted butter, or with grated Gruyère or Parmesan cheese, butter, and fine herbs and baked in a hot oven until the top is nicely browned.

Shall we quickly move on?

BRAINS

Many people are put off by the appearance of the whole brain, especially uncooked, or by the very idea of eating it. In a list of 143 foods presented to one sample of Americans, brains, together with tripe and kidneys, were overwhelmingly rejected. In another survey brains headed the list of "disliked foods." Twenty-eight percent of university students surveyed had never tried them; an additional 40 percent had, but refused to try them again. Yet brain is a delectable meat of good texture and a mild flavor to which few who give it a fair trial could honestly object. Calf's (or lamb's) brains are such delicacies, in fact, that they should be prepared very simply. Brains of mature animals receive somewhat fancier treatment. While the protein content of brains is slightly less than for T-bone steak, their fat content is only about one-fourth. Their fat is, however, rich in cholesterol.

Basic Preparation

Unless indicated otherwise, brains are treated initially as follows: soak them in ice water for about 4 hours, then remove the membranes and clots of blood. Some cooks then BLANCH brains—that is, simmer them in salted water containing a little vinegar or lemon juice, some sliced carrots and onions, and a BOUQUET GARNI for 15 to 20 minutes depending on the size. (I think that some of the delicate flavor of calf's brains is lost in the blanching process. So if the brains are to be cooked further anyway, blanching may not be necessary. If they are blanched, they should be immersed im-mediately afterwards in ice water, allowed to cool, then drained and dried.)

France has produced one of the greatest and most experimental and assimilative cuisines in the world (the three qualities seem inseparable). An excellent introduction to brains, therefore, is this good French dish borrowed from the Romans.

FRIED BRAINS ROMAN STYLE *(Cervelle à la romaine)* / FRANCE

Slices of prepared brains are marinated in a mixture of olive oil, lemon juice, salt, pepper, and chopped parsley. Then they are dipped in lightly beaten eggs, then fine bread crumbs, fried in hot deep oil, and drained. Arrange the slices in a ring, fill the hollow with cooked chopped spinach mixed with butter, garnish each brain slice with a rolled anchovy fillet, and sprinkle them with some lightly browned butter.

In fact, spinach goes unusually well with brains, as these brain fritters also attest.

BRAIN FRITTERS *(Subrics de cervelle)* / FRANCE

Mix small cubes of poached brains, chopped buttered spinach, a crepe batter (1:1:1), salt, and pepper. Fry spoonfuls in hot oil until browned on both sides.

Or they may be batter-fried without the spinach, as in this recipe.

BATTER-FRIED BRAINS *(Beignets de cervelle)* / FRANCE

Sliced brains are marinated in a mixture of lemon juice, olive oil, and chopped parsley. Dip the slices into a thin TEMPURA-type batter and deep-fry them. Mesentery, sweetbreads, tongue, and other meats may be prepared by this same recipe.

Equally good are brain cakes of various kinds.

BRAIN CAKES / ENGLAND

Mash some poached brains with beaten egg yolks, a little flour, salt, cayenne, finely chopped parsley, sage, mace, and a little grated lemon rind. Fry as small cakes in butter until lightly browned.

BRAIN CROQUETTES *(Crépinettes Reine-Jeanne)* / FRANCE

To a thick béchamel sauce add diced poached brains, diced ham, chopped onions, and mushrooms. Roll spoonfuls of this mixture in squares of pork omentum, or mesentery. Dip into beaten egg white and bread crumbs, fry in butter or oil, and serve with lemon wedges.

Other simple recipes for either breakfast or supper are for brains and eggs. The result of either of these two Austrian versions is an excellent combination of delicate and complementary flavors.

CALF BRAINS AND EGGS *(Kalbshirn mit Ei)* / AUSTRIA

Fry some chopped onions in butter until golden. Add chopped un-blanched brains and fry them briskly until they firm up. Stir in seasoned eggs beaten with cream and cook slowly until the eggs are soft and creamy. Serve on hot croutons.

Alternatively, an unblanched brain is cut into a small dice. Some finely chopped onions are sautéed in lard until golden, the brains and some chopped parsley are added, the mixture is seasoned with salt, pepper, and a little marjoram and cooked with occasional stirring for about 5 minutes. The heat is reduced and lightly beaten eggs are added to the pan. The ingredients are agitated with a spatula until the eggs are of the desired consistency.

Specially suitable for filling VOL-AU-VENT or crepes are either of these two simple concoctions.

CREAMED BRAINS AND SPINACH *(Cervelles en chausson)* / FRANCE

A mixture is prepared of brain cubes, chopped spinach, and a little béchamel sauce cooked only until the brains are done.

CREAMED BRAINS *(Purée de cervelle)* / FRANCE

Blend a poached brain with béchamel sauce in an electric blender. Heat, correct the seasoning, and use in *vol-au-vent* or as a sauce for poached eggs served on croutons. Ham or sautéed mushrooms are sometimes added, and this same type of purée may be prepared from sweetbreads.

More exotic recipes of the same generic type are this sweet-and-sour brain dish with dill, from Russia, and spicy brains in coconut cream, from Indonesia.

Brains in Lemon Sauce *(Mozgi pod limonym sousom)* / Russia

Prepare a butter-and-flour ROUX, stir in veal stock, and cook to make a smooth velouté sauce. Add a generous amount of grated lemon rind, a little lemon juice and sugar (1:1), salt and pepper, and simmer a bit. Add sliced parboiled brains and chopped dill, bring to a boil, and serve.

Brains in Coconut Cream *(Gulai otak)* / Indonesia

Brown a chopped onion in oil and add a BLANCHED brain cut into large pieces. Also add ground pepper, tumeric, salt, and chopped mint; cover with coconut cream. Simmer about 20 minutes.

Besides frying or serving in a cream sauce or with eggs, brain pâtés can be used to make dumplings to be served as is or in broth.

Brain Dumplings *(Hjerneboller)* / Norway

Put a BLANCHED brain through the finest blade of a food chopper with half its weight of white bread. Mix in crushed garlic, an egg, lemon juice, chopped parsley, salt, and pepper. Form into small dumplings and poach.

Or brains may be used as the basis for an excellent soup itself, as in this Swabian recipe.

Brain Soup *(Hirnsuppe)* / Germany

Fry some chopped onions in butter until golden. Add diced brains and simmer for 5 minutes. Stir in enough flour to form a smooth ROUX and then beat in with a whisk a generous quantity of hot beef stock. Simmer for about 10 minutes. Add some white wine, salt, pepper, and some egg yolks previously beaten with cream. Stir in chopped parsley and serve without reboiling.

Brains also combine well with other meats. These are but two easy-to-prepare examples, both from Austria.

Calf's Liver and Brains *(Kalbsleber mit Hirn)* / Austria

Fry finely chopped onions in butter until golden. Add liver cut into small pieces and quickly stir-fry it a bit. Season with pepper and marjoram, add diced brains, and stir-fry until they are firm. Add salt, lemon juice, and chopped parsley and serve.

KIDNEYS WITH BRAINS *(Nieren mit Hirn)* / AUSTRIA

Fry finely chopped onions in butter until golden. Cut kidneys into small slices and add to the onions. Stir in salt, pepper, some ground caraway seeds, and stir-fry a few minutes. Sprinkle with a little flour, add some stock, and stir some more to produce a smooth sauce. Add a chopped brain and lemon juice and cook a few minutes longer. Sprinkle with chopped parsley before serving.

This final recipe for calf brains is for a simple Colombian "graduation" dish for the fully liberated brains eater.

CALF'S BRAIN WITH TOMATOES *(Sesos en tomate)* / COLOMBIA

Fry some chopped onion in olive oil until golden, add chopped to-matoes, continue to cook, add beef stock seasoned with salt and pre-ferred herbs, boil for 10 minutes, and strain, reserving the liquid. Pour this thin sauce over halved brains, bring them to a boil, and simmer for about 15 minutes or until done.

FEET

SOME people regard animals' feet as dirty and therefore inedible, yet the feet of animals provide other very cheap sources of meat that can only be removed easily from the bones after the feet have been boiled. Like head meat, the meat of the feet and the stock prepared from them are rich in gelatin, which gives them particular body. This French recipe is a good beginner for a hearty main dish.

CALF FEET PROVENCE STYLE *(Pieds de veau provençale)* / FRANCE

Simmer calves' feet until very tender in boiling salted water containing a BOUQUET GARNI, carrot slices, a clove-studded onion, and some pepper-corns. Remove the meat from the bones and serve it hot with an aioli or other provençal sauce.

A fancier calf's-foot stew interestingly flavored with peanut butter comes from the Philippines. That ingredient betrays the influence of Peru; this dish probably originated during the course of Spanish trade between the two colonies.

CALF'S-FOOT STEW *(Kari-karing pata)* / PHILIPPINES

Cut a cleaned calf's foot and lower leg into pieces, cover them with water, and boil until tender. Reserve the stock. Sauté an ample amount of crushed garlic and sliced onions in a little oil. Brown the meat in the same pan. Return all to the stock pot and bring to a boil. Add 1 finely sliced banana tree blossom (or sliced bamboo shoots), and when it is almost tender add about 30 cowpeas cut into 2-in. lengths, some eggplant cut into pieces, and a number of sliced radishes. Soak 2 T ANATTO seeds in 1/2 C water and add this red-colored water to the meat pot. Thicken with 1/3 C powdered toasted rice or rice flour (previously mixed until smooth with a little of the liquid) or cornstarch and about 1/2 C peanut butter and stir thoroughly. Pass with this dish some *bagoong* sautéed with pork.

This simpler English stew is also hearty and flavorful, though plainly titled.

COW HEEL / ENGLAND

Split a cleaned cow's foot lengthwise and cut it into pieces. Do the same for a beef shin. Put the meat in a kettle and add some peppercorns, mace, parsley, salt, and pepper. Cover with beef stock and simmer for about 4 hours. Add a glass of sherry and thicken the stock with a butter-and-flour ROUX. Garnish with toast triangles and parsley.

In giving the recipe for cow's headcheese, I mentioned that similar molded brawns could be prepared from other gelatin-rich meats. This one is particularly attractive when sliced.

NEAT'S-FOOT BRAWN / ENGLAND

Split and clean 2 cow's feet. Lightly salt for a few hours tongues and cheeks of 2 cows. Rinse the salted meat and arrange it and the feet in a heavy kettle. Add some onions, celery, carrots (and other vegetables as desired), some peppercorns, and a large stick of cinnamon. Cover with water and simmer all day. Strain the broth through muslin and reduce it well at a rapid boil. Skin and trim the tongues and remove the meat from the feet and cheeks. Stand the 2 tongues (root to tip) in a tall cylindrical container. Pack the other meat about the tongues and fill the mold with the reduced stock. Allow the brawn to set well in the refrigerator and unmold to serve. Serve with a cold sauce made by melting lard and blending into it as much flour and dry mustard (1:1) as it will take up. Cook this *roux* well and make a smooth sauce by stirring in some milk to cool it.

Their high gelatin content also makes cow's feet a good basic ingredient for rich soups.

QUEEN SOUP *(Királyné leves)* / HUNGARY

Boil a cleaned calf's foot, some meaty beef bones, a dismembered stewing hen, and 1/2 C rice in salted water for about 4 hours. Strain the stock and reserve it; pick the meat from the bones and put it and the rice through the fine blade of a food chopper twice. Add the stock, stir, and strain again, pressing the meat and rice mixture with the back of a spoon through the sieve. Bring the soup to a boil, correct the seasoning, and garnish with croutons.

TAIL

OXTAILS are sometimes seen in American supermarkets, and canned oxtail soup is readily available. Like cow's feet, tail yields gelatin-rich stock together with considerably more well-flavored meat than do the feet. It is excellent for rich stews or soups. This simple Roman recipe is a good introduction to the use of this cheap, versatile meat.

OXTAIL ROMAN STYLE *(Code di manzo alla romana)* / ITALY

Brown a skinned and disjointed oxtail in lard in a soup kettle with some chopped bacon, sliced onion, a clove or more of garlic, chopped carrot, and chopped parsley. Salt and pepper. Add a cup or so of dry red wine, some tomato paste, and sufficient water to cover the meat. Cover the pot and simmer 4 to 5 hours. Add some celery cut in large pieces and cook 20 minutes longer.

Slightly fancier is this central European stew.

OXTAIL RAGOUT *(Ökörfarok ragú)* / HUNGARY

Salt 2 disjointed oxtails, dredge them in flour, and brown in lard in a shallow casserole. Add crushed garlic, chopped onions, a generous amount of paprika, and some chopped tomatoes. Cover and simmer about 2 hours, adding a little water if required. Pull the meat to the center of the casserole and arrange about it, in separate areas, small white onions, carrot sections, olive-sized balls cut from potatoes, and button mushrooms. Add a little water, cover, and simmer until the vegetables are done.

Generically related is a French oxtail stew that combines contrasting flavors of cheap beef and pork cuts in another attractive one-dish meal.

OXTAIL IN A FIREPOT *(Queue de boeuf en hochepot)* / FRANCE

In a soup kettle place a disjointed oxtail, 2 cleaned and cut-up pig's feet, and a pig's ear. Cover with water and simmer for about 2 hours, removing the accumulated scum. Add a large dice of turnips and carrots, some small white onions, and a sectioned cabbage and simmer for about 2 hours more. Arrange the pieces of oxtail and pig's feet in a deep serving dish, mound the cooked vegetables on top, and surround them with grilled sausage links and the pig's ear cut into strips.

For many oxtail recipes the meat is removed from the bones and combined with other ingredients. For this variant of *Sauerbraten*, the tail may be marinated several days beforehand in the vinegar water and spices.

SOUR OXTAIL WITH DUMPLINGS *(Savanyú ökörfarok gombóccal)* / HUNGARY

Cover a disjointed oxtail with water and vinegar (1:1), a bay leaf, a few onion slices, some peppercorns, and salt. Simmer, covered, until the meat falls from the bones. Add more water if necessary. Remove the tail, discard the bones, thicken the stock with a lard-flour ROUX, return the meat and simmer for a while. Stir in sour cream before serving over potato dumplings.

This is also a delicious central European beef dish with its tartness provided by some lemon juice and an excellent sauce of currants or cranberries.

STEAMED OXTAIL *(Geduensteter Ochsenschlepp)* / AUSTRIA

Brown some seasoned, disjointed oxtails in butter and lard and remove them. Fry some sliced onions, chopped carrots, chopped turnip, chopped celery root, and chopped parsley in the same pan. Salt and pepper and sprinkle in some flour and brown it lightly. Add a generous amount of red wine and reduce it somewhat over a brisk fire. Return the meat to the pan and add a BOUQUET GARNI containing a slice of lemon peel. Add water to barely cover and simmer for about 3 hours or until the meat falls easily from the bones. Cool the pan, skim off the congealed fat, and separate the meat from the bones, putting it in a separate dish. To the defatted stock add some red currants or cranberries and bring them to a boil. Remove the *bouquet garni* and blend the currants or cranberries and stock in an electric blender. Return the meat, heat well, thicken if necessary, stir in a little lemon juice, and serve the stew with dumplings.

Oxtail soup of European origin is common fare in good restaurants, and recipes for it are readily available. This soup is much more unusual and makes a fine first course for a company dinner. The fruits are obtainable in most oriental specialty stores.

OXTAIL AND PEANUT SOUP *(Nio weh hwa sen tan)* / CHINA

Parboil a disarticulated oxtail, drain, and wash the pieces. Brown them quickly in peanut oil in a WOK. Boil several cups of water in another pan, add the oxtails, some skinned raw peanuts, some Chinese red dates, a piece of presoaked dried tangerine peel, and a few slices of fresh ginger. Boil, skim, and reduce the heat. Cover the pan, simmer for about 2 hours, and season with salt just before serving.

BONES

BONY pieces of the carcass from which scraps of muscle meat are removed with difficulty are commonly used for preparing soups and stocks. Joints, in particular, contain cartilage, tendons, and ligaments that partially solubilize as gelatin when subjected to prolonged boiling. Bones thus yield the rich stocks that form the bases of many classic sauces, as well as such flavorful by-products as their marrow.

BASIC VEAL STOCK

Break veal marrow bones with some meat attached. Place them and a cut onion in an ovenproof casserole and brown them well in the oven. Add water to cover, some white wine, a tomato, a carrot, a stalk of celery, a clove or two, and a BOUQUET GARNI. Bring to a boil, skim, simmer in the oven for several hours, and filter. Stock may be prepared too from beef bones or a mixture of beef and veal bones. Large quantities may be divided into convenient portions and frozen for future use.

The following sauces based upon veal stock are used elsewhere in this book.

Velouté Sauce

Melt butter in a saucepan and with a whisk blend in enough flour to take up the butter and form a smooth ROUX. Stir and cook gently a few minutes to remove the raw flour taste. Then vigorously whisk in boiling veal, chicken, fish, or other stock, as the case may be, not adding too much at first. Stir and simmer until the sauce is thick and smooth. Control its thickness by the addition of more stock or more *roux*. Pass through a fine strainer.

Velouté sauce is the basis for béchamel, allemande, and mornay sauces.

Allemande Sauce

Also sometimes called parisienne sauce, this is most often merely a velouté or béchamel sauce into which egg yolks and cream are beaten with a wire whisk.

Espagnole Sauce

This is the basic brown sauce and is related to a veal velouté sauce. Prepare a thin velouté sauce and add to it a MIREPOIX made as follows: sauté finely chopped vegetables (usually turnips, leeks, celery, fennel, onions and/or carrots), some thyme, and bay leaves in lard until the vegetables are golden. Pour off all the fat and add this *mirapoix* to the sauce. DEGLAZE the pan with white wine and add this too. Add sprigs of parsley and rosemary and, if desired, a ham bone and/or beef shin bone with meat attached. Boil, skim, simmer in the oven for several hours, and strain the sauce through a fine strainer. Simmer further if necessary to thicken more.

Ragout Sauce

This basic French brown sauce, a substitute for the more tedious espagnole sauce, is prepared by browning trimmings and/or giblets of the particular meat base of the sauce in rendered fat from the same meat, or in oil or clarified butter, then removing the meat and making a well-cooked brown ROUX with added flour. To this is beaten in with a wire whisk the appropriate boiling meat stock (and wine if desired). The seasoning is corrected and the sauce is cooked and beaten until smooth. It improves with prolonged simmering.

Another substitute sauce for many purposes may be prepared from the partially degreased pan drippings from an appropriate roast. In this case the trimmings or giblets may usually be omitted.

Chaud-froid Sauce

For brown chaud-froid sauce, blend espagnole sauce with some much reduced liquid in which mushrooms have been cooked, some aspic, and cream. For a white chaud-froid sauce, use chicken or fish velouté rather than the espagnole.

Diable Sauce

To an espagnole sauce add finely chopped shallots and fresh herbs plus some white wine and vinegar and simmer until the shallots are soft.

Bourguignonne or Bordelaise Sauces

DEGLAZE the drip pan from a roast or the pan in which meat has been sautéed or baked with a generous amount of the appropriate red wine. Add to it some finely chopped shallots sautéed until golden in a little butter. Reduce this sauce considerably and add a little rich veal stock or espagnole sauce; thicken if desired with some blended flour and butter.

Duxelles Sauce

This sauce is now usually prepared by sautéing finely chopped mush-rooms and onions, which have been seasoned with salt, pepper, and nutmeg, in butter until the water is completely evaporated. This duxel-les is mixed with white wine (4 T to 1 C) and cooked until most of the wine has evaporated. Then stir in about 1–1/2 C rich beef gravy or demi-glace or concentrated ragout sauce and 1 C tomato purée and simmer for about 5 minutes. Add some chopped parsley at the end.

Chasseur Sauce

This does not differ appreciably from duxelles sauce in that it contains chopped mushrooms and shallots sautéed in butter, white wine, beef stock, or veal concentrate, which are reduced, a little tomato purée, and at the last minute some chopped parsley.

Beef bones yield marrow also, itself a highly nutritious meat. This marrow recipe is probably the simplest recipe in the book but, in my opinion, one of the best. Beef marrow is among the most delicious of foods, and this dish could well provide the nucleus about which a medieval or renaissance dinner party could be constructed.

Baked Marrow Bones / England

The fresh femurs or humeri of a choice beef animal are cut into fourths and the cut ends plugged and capped with dough. They then are baked. The baked bones are wrapped individually in napkins, served with salt, pepper, and toast (or on trenchers) and eaten with a long marrow spoon.

A classic European variant of this simple recipe is *osso buco*. The incorporation of anchovies suggests their replacement of the original Roman GARUM and supports the belief that this dish has been a Mediterranean favorite for a long time. Its ease of preparation further recommends it.

Stewed Veal Shins Milanese Style (*Osso buco milanese*) / Italy

Select veal shin bones with all the meat attached and have the butcher cut them into 4-in. sections. Dust them with flour and brown well in butter in a deep frying pan. Add dry white wine and water (1:2), cover, and simmer for about 1 hour. Add some chopped parsley, crushed garlic, some thin strips of lemon peel, and a chopped anchovy fillet. Turn the bones and cook about 2 to 3 minutes more. Add a little water or stock and some butter, stir well, correct for salt, and serve.

In a French version of *osso buco (jarret de veau à la provençale)*, the marrow bones, usually not floured, are fried in olive oil. Some chopped tomatoes are substituted for the lemon peel and anchovies, and a little brown veal gravy or espagnole sauce may be substituted for the stock. The parsley and lemon peel are omitted sometimes.

Marrow removed from beef bones lends itself to many other flavorful and interesting treatments of which the following provide good examples.

MARROW CANAPES (*Canapés à la moelle*) / FRANCE

Marinate slices of beef marrow in a mixture of olive oil, lemon juice, salt, pepper, and chopped parsley or a French salad dressing. Coat with a TEMPURA or CHILIS RELLENOS BATTER and deep-fry in hot oil. Drain and garnish with fried parsley.

MARROW CANAPÉS (*Canapés à la moelle*) / FRANCE

Spread poached and drained beef marrow on toast. Salt and pepper. If desired, sprinkle with fine bread crumbs and melted butter and brown under the broiler.

Marrow fillings are also excellent for VOL-AU-VENT or mushroom caps. For a simple one, poach diced beef marrow and mix it with a concentrated veal or beef stock (or a suitable gravy). Add some chopped onions or shallots which were cooked in butter and white wine. Simmer until the liquid is almost evaporated.

Finally, marrow can be the unusual ingredient for very flavorful dumplings that are eaten as such or served in a clear soup or broth.

MARROW DUMPLINGS (*Pulpety*) / POLAND

Remove the marrow from 2-in. to 3-in. sections of good beef marrow bones and finely chop it. Add 4 eggs and 2 cups of bread crumbs to each pound of marrow. Add salt and enough flour to knead into a heavy dough. Roll between the hands into cylinders the diameter of a cigar and about 1–1/2 inches long. Drop them into boiling salted water and remove with a slotted spoon when they rise to the surface.

HEART

THE heart and lungs of an animal are called the pluck—but it really takes none at all to eat and enjoy them both. They make up part of the so-called offal, or visceral organs. This rather sinister-sounding collective name is a corruption of the word *off-fall*, a butcher's term for what falls out when he opens and guts the carcass of an animal. Offal often euphemistically masquerade in the United States under the daintier name "variety meats." In contrast to many types of muscle meat, which are improved in tenderness and taste by aging, the visceral organs used for food should be bought as fresh as possible. Hearts are almost all muscle meat with slightly more protein than T-bone steaks and very little connective tissue or fat (one-tenth that of steak) or other waste. They are also a good source of B vitamins. As very active muscles, however, they do tend to toughness in older animals and are often marinated before cooking to make the meat more tender. Hearts are conveniently made for stuffing and invite a creative cook to experiment.

Basic Preparation

Trim out the major blood vessels, fat, and heart valves.

Hearts are particularly good and inexpensive barbecue fare, and I've never met a person who didn't like them this way. In a simple Italian recipe, a thinly sliced beef heart is marinated for several hours in olive oil, salt, and pepper. The meat then is grilled over charcoal and served with lemon wedges.

The really classic beef heart barbecue, however, is the Peruvian *anticucho*. The most exciting version of this dish is served at sidewalk stands outside of the *futbol* stadium in Lima. This recipe is that of my former student Dr. Elva Lopez-Nieto.

Barbecued Hearts (*Anticuchos*) / Peru

Cut a beef heart into approximately 1-in. cubes. Marinate the heart overnight in the following mixture: 1/4 C ground chili peppers, 1/2 C finely chopped chili peppers, 1/2 t ground cumin seed, 1/2 t ANATTO, 1 t salt, and 1/2 t black pepper, with enough vinegar to cover the meat. Skewer the meat and broil over charcoal, basting frequently with a mixture of more ground chili peppers fried in a generous amount of oil and some of the marinade.

A delicious variation of plain *anticuchos* is *anticuchos mixtos*. Here a good marinade consists of much crushed garlic, powdered cumin, marjoram, salt, black pepper, ground fresh chili peppers, ground *anatto*, and enough vinegar to cover pieces of beef heart. About an hour before cooking, add shelled tails of large shrimp, scallops, and cubes of a firm-fleshed marine fish. Mix well to cover thoroughly with the marinade. Alternate the hearts and seafood on skewers and broil them slowly over charcoal, basting frequently with the marinade, which is kept at the boil in a pot on the edge of the grill.

Serve *anticuchos* on a bed of shredded lettuce with sections of boiled sweet potatoes and corn and a relish which consists of sliced onions and chili pepper strips, salted and pickled in lemon juice and to which some oil is mixed in at the last minute.

The Chinese also have their ways to use heart.

STIR-FRIED HEART *(Nan chow sin)* / CHINA

Trim a beef or pork heart and cut into a 1/8-in. JULIENNE. Marinate it and some sections of scallions in a mixture of cornstarch in cold water, a little soy sauce, some sherry, sugar, salt, and minced ginger. Drain the meat and vegetables and stir-fry them in medium-hot oil. (If *pork* heart is used, it should be *thoroughly* cooked through.)

Both of these Italian recipes are also good with plain boiled rice or as an accompaniment of pasta.

BEEF HEART WITH MUSHROOMS *(Cuore di manzo con funghi)* / ITALY

Soak some dried mushrooms; rinse and drain well. Salt and pepper and brown them lightly in a little olive oil. Add a couple of spoonfuls of tomato paste and some water, cover, and cook over medium heat for 45 minutes. Brown a thinly sliced beef heart in olive oil and season it with salt and pepper. Add the tomato-mushroom sauce, heat through, and serve.

BEEF HEART IN ANCHOVY SAUCE
(Cuore di manzo in salsa di acciughe) / ITALY

Brown some garlic in olive oil. Add a thinly sliced beef heart and brown it quickly on both sides. Add some chopped anchovy fillets and cook for 1 minute. Remove from the heat, add a little lemon juice and some chopped parsley, and salt and pepper to taste.

This is a poor Englishman's Christmas dinner.

Mock Goose / England

Simmer a washed beef heart overnight in salted water with a little vinegar and some peppercorns. Cool it in the broth and skim the fat. Stuff the heart with a mixture of bread crumbs, some of the skimmed fat, chopped onions, sage, salt and pepper, beaten egg, and heart broth. Sew up the heart, flour it, LARD it well with strips of bacon, and roast it, basting frequently. Garnish the "goose" with sausages and roasted potatoes and serve it with apple sauce.

Like most innards, heart is also combined with other organs in flavorful soups or other dishes. This is one example. Other mixed-organ dishes containing beef heart are listed in the index.

Cowboy Soup (*Gulyásleves*) / Hungary

Brown chopped onions in lard. Add a beef heart, some beef, and some beef liver all cut into small cubes and brown them in the fat. Then add some sliced carrots, green peppers, tomatoes, chopped parsley, salt, and quite a bit of paprika. Cover with water, cover the pan, and simmer the stew until the meat is very tender. Add some diced potatoes and cook until they are done. Serve over buttered noodles.

LUNGS

MAMMALIAN lungs are sometimes called lights in English. They are probably the cheapest organ meat, contain slightly more protein than T-bone steak, and only 6 percent as much fat. Their vitamin content, except for niacin, is low compared to most other organs.

In 1971 the U.S. Wholesale Meat Act was amended to declare lungs unfit for human consumption. This is an example of unenlightened legislation completely out of tune with world food needs.

Basic Preparation

Beat the lungs with a mallet or flat side of a cleaver to expel most of the air. Trim out the main bronchi and cartilaginous parts.

Sheep and pork lungs may be prepared by these same recipes.

This first recipe is for a typical provençal treatment of lungs. It is a good recipe for those who have not previously eaten lungs because similar recipes for other meats and seafoods are widely enjoyed.

CALF LUNG PROVENCE STYLE (*Mou de veau à la provençale*) / FRANCE

Cut beaten calf's lungs into thin pieces and poach them for 30 minutes in salted water. Drain and dry them. Dredge with seasoned flour. Add them to a pan containing chopped onions fried in oil until golden and cook together until the lungs begin to brown. Add chopped tomatoes, chopped parsley, crushed garlic, salt, pepper, and a generous amount of white wine. Simmer for a half hour.

A generically similar Hungarian recipe substitutes some of the classic flavorings of that country.

CALF'S LUNG AND HEART IN PAPRIKA SAUCE (*Savanyú malac tüdö és sziv pörkölt*) / HUNGARY

Boil the heart and lungs of a calf in salted water until tender and cut them into thin strips. Sauté some chopped onions in lard until golden, add 1 t or so of paprika, a little tomato purée, a generous amount of crushed garlic, and a bit of marjoram. Stir a few minutes, then add the meat, salt, and a little of the stock. Cover the pan and allow it to simmer about 15 minutes. Add some chopped tomatoes and chopped celery leaves. Thicken with a few bits of flour blended with lard and continue to simmer for another 10 minutes.

And an Italian recipe incorporating kidney beans yields an equally tasty and even heartier dish.

CALF'S LUNGS AND BEANS (*Polmoni di vitello con fagioli*) / ITALY

Brown a sliced onion, some diced salt pork, some crushed garlic, chopped parsley, and chopped celery in a mixture of olive oil and lard. Add cubed calf's lungs and brown them thoroughly. Add a wineglass or so of white wine, some peeled tomatoes, salt and pepper, and cook about a half hour. Add a generous quantity of previously cooked kidney beans and a little water, cover, and simmer for about an hour. Add some chopped sweet basil the last few minutes of cooking.

This German peasant recipe combines lungs with other cheap cuts as the basis for another filling meal.

CALF'S-HEAD CASSEROLE *(Töttchen)* / GERMANY

Simmer a boned-out calf's head, a calf lung and heart, an onion stuck with cloves, and a bay leaf in water to cover until the meats are tender. Cut the meat into pieces. Fry chopped onions in butter until golden, stir in some flour, and then enough of the strained stock to make a smooth sauce. Add some white wine and a little sugar. Reheat the meat in butter, pour the sauce over it, and serve with mustard and black bread.

Most often lungs are used to provide the principal ingredient or one of the ingredients for inexpensive stews. Three quite different lung stews are included here as examples. The second and third are central European recipes, the first of them slightly sweet, the latter rather sour.

CALF LUNG STEW *(Civet de mou de veau)* / FRANCE

Salt and pepper pieces of lungs and fry them in butter until well browned. Sprinkle with flour, stir well, and cook for a few minutes more (or thicken with blood). Cover with dry red wine or a mixture of wine and stock. Add a BOUQUET GARNI and some crushed garlic. Cover and bake in a moderate oven for 1–1/2 hours. Transfer the pieces of lung to a shallow baking dish and add some chopped and fried bacon, sliced or whole mushrooms, and a number of small onions (and/or carrots) fried in butter or with the lean bacon. Cover with the strained cooking liquid and return to the oven for an additional 30 minutes. Garnish with croutons.

Lamb's or pig's lungs may be prepared the same way.

LUNG STEW *(Lungen rayots)* / JEWISH

Lightly brown chopped onions and crushed garlic in oil. Add a cow's lung and some lean beef cut into cubes and brown them. Add chopped, peeled tomatoes, several tablespoons of brown sugar, salt, and pepper; cover the pan and simmer until the meat is done. Part way through the cooking process add diced potatoes, carrots, or other vegetables if desired, and a little water if needed. If thickening is required, this may be done with a butter-and-flour ROUX.

CALF-ORGAN STEW *(Beuschel)* / AUSTRIA

Put the lungs and heart of a calf into a soup kettle and barely cover with water. Add sliced carrots, an onion, a bay leaf, thyme, cloves, peppercorns, and a generous amount of salt. Simmer until the meats are tender. Prepare a lightly browned butter-and-flour ROUX and brown in it a pinch of sugar. Add some of the stock and beat into a smooth sauce. Add a mixture of chopped anchovies, lemon peel, capers, gherkins, garlic, onion, and parsley. Simmer for about 20 minutes. Add the heart and lungs cut into thin strips and heat through. Add some prepared hot mustard and lemon juice. Correct the salt, pepper, and sugar. Stir in some sour cream and serve with dumplings.

This last lung dish is clearly an Eastern recipe modified for German tastes. Sheep lung would probably be an even more suitable basic ingredient for an authentic lung curry.

LUNG STEW *(Lungenragout)* / GERMANY

Cut a calf's lung and heart in pieces and put them, a stalk of celery, a parsnip, and a carrot in a kettle. Add some salt, pepper, and any desired herbs. Cover with water and simmer until the meats are tender. Discard the vegetables. Fry some chopped onion in butter and add some uncooked rice and curry powder. Stir-fry for several minutes. Add the strained stock and cook until the rice is done. Mix into the rice the heart and lungs, which have been cut into small pieces. Reheat and serve.

LIVER

I debated whether to include beef liver in this book at all because it is eaten in the United States, although quite unimaginatively and by only a minority of Americans. Liver is one of the most nutritionally valuable foods available to man. It contains one-third more protein that T-bone steak and only one-tenth of its fat. It is also an excellent source of vitamin A, thiamine, riboflavin, niacin, pantothenic acid, biotin, and iron.

While most would acknowledge that there is liver and there is liver, many persons who claim to dislike this excellent meat have only experienced liver of poor quality or have experienced it overcooked. One survey of University of Nebraska students showed 22 percent unwilling to eat liver, while in another study of students in three universities, 30 percent avoided beef liver and 28 percent calf's liver too.

Both the flavor and texture of beef liver vary according to the age of the animal slaughtered, the liver's freshness, the size of the piece purchased, and, obviously, its method of preparation. The liver of young animals is more delicate in flavor; the amount of connective tissue, therefore the toughness, increases with age. Preslicing of liver, which is common to American supermarkets, is another enemy of texture because sliced liver "bleeds," or weeps, excessively and is less moist and tender after cooking than liver that is sliced just before it is prepared. Another problem with slicing and prepackaging meats like liver is fraud. A common practice of supermarket butchers is to slice higher-priced "calf liver" from the small end of a 10- to 12-lb. *beef* liver. The quantity of real calves' liver available is limited and corresponds to the amount of veal available. Since Americans eat less than 2 lbs. of veal per capita yearly and much real calf liver goes to restaurants and small butcher shops, the conclusion is obvious. To avoid the possibility of this fraud, you should ask to see the whole 2- to 5-lb. calf liver and have it cut in your presence.

Good-quality calf's liver is such a delicately flavored and textured meat that it is enjoyed best by connoisseurs very simply prepared, preferably by quickly grilling it in pieces over hot coals or by browning thin slices very quickly on each side in sizzling butter. Calf's liver cooked in either manner merely has its surfaces seared with the juices all sealed in. The inside is pink and moist. While some persons prefer that liver slices be lightly dusted with flour before searing, heavy dredging in flour is detrimental to texture, as is slow cooking in insufficiently hot butter or repeated turning of the liver slices in the pan. I am of the school that does *not* salt liver before cooking, because this also contributes to the weeping process and toughens the meat.

In keeping with my pattern of trying to introduce most items in a somewhat disguised form, the first liver recipe is for *crostini,* a classic pâté that enjoys wide acceptance on initial exposure.

LIVER PASTE FLORENTINE STYLE *(Crostini alla fiorentina)* / ITALY

Fry chopped onions, celery, and carrots in 1/2 C olive oil until soft. Add cubed calf's liver and continue to cook about 5 minutes. Add butter (1/4 C per lb. of liver), melt it, and add some chopped anchovy fillets. Blend this mixture in small amounts in an electric blender. Stir or blend in chopped capers and salt and pepper to taste. Serve the paste hot or cold on toast, garnished with chopped parsley and capers.

This generically related, less-known Polish recipe is one example of many other European liver loaves and liver sausages.

LIVER PÂTÉ *(Pasztet)* / POLAND

Soak some sliced calf's liver in milk overnight. Cut up an equal weight of mixed meats (1/3 veal, 1/3 pork, 1/3 duck or lamb) and a little bacon. Put all but the liver in a kettle, add some celery, onions, carrots, parsley, parsnips, some diced mushrooms, a bay leaf, a little marjoram, and a number of juniper berries. Cover with water and simmer for 3 hours (the drained calf's liver is added for the last hour only). Strain the meat and vegetables and blend them in small amounts in an electric blender or pass them repeatedly through the fine blade of a food chopper or pound them in a mortar to a smooth paste. Moisten quite a bit of dry bread with a little stock and add it and some Madeira to the meat paste. Beat in some eggs (2 for every pound of meat used) one at a time. Season with salt and pepper. Pack this paste in a buttered mold which is coated with bread crumbs and then lined with bacon strips. Bake in a 350°F oven for about 1/2 hour. Slice the loaf and serve hot or cold.

Similar pastes may also be shaped into dumplings to be eaten as a meat dish, as described below, or served in a clear beef broth.

LIVER DUMPLINGS *(Leberknödli)* / GERMAN SWITZERLAND

Put beef liver and bacon (4:1) through the fine blade of a food chopper (it may then be put through the electric blender, if desired). Blend in some sautéed chopped onions and parsley, beaten egg (1 large egg per lb. of liver), salt, pepper, and enough fresh bread crumbs to take up much of the moisture. Allow this mixture to stand awhile and then shape it into small dumplings. Simmer them, covered, in boiling salted water for 7 minutes or so. Drain and serve covered with grated Gruyère cheese and melted butter. Applesauce is a usual side dish.

Another excellent recipe for the person who claims not to like liver is this flavorful German Swiss one in which liver is grilled with two of its most traditional accompaniments, onions and bacon.

SKEWERED LIVER *(Leberspiessli)* / GERMAN SWITZERLAND

Wrap finger-sized pieces of calf's liver with some sage leaves in strips of lean bacon. Prepare a bed of chopped onions sautéed until golden in butter in a large frying pan. On it place the liver pieces, which have been threaded several to a skewer, and cook them over a moderate heat until the bacon begins to crisp. Season and serve the skewered liver and bacon on a bed of buttered green beans.

Liver also goes well with dairy products, and several European cuisines have their quite different versions, for example, of liver in sour cream.

LIVER IN SOUR CREAM *(Pechenka v smetane)* / RUSSIA

Dust slices of calf liver with seasoned flour, fry them in hot butter, and transfer to a shallow casserole. Fry sliced onions until golden in the same pan and add them and the pan scrapings to the liver. Add sour cream and veal or chicken stock (1:1) and simmer, covered, for about half an hour. Serve sprinkled with chopped parsley.

Fresh cream is also the basis of liver sauces seasoned with horseradish or with dill or other herbs.

CALF LIVER WITH HORSERADISH *(Kalbsleber mit Kren)* / AUSTRIA

Dust slices of calf's liver with flour and pepper and fry quickly in hot butter. Remove to a hot dish and in the same pan fry some chopped onions until golden. Add a little veal stock or water, stir well, and reduce to a smooth sauce. Add a generous amount of cream and cook a few minutes. Correct the seasoning. Remove from the heat and stir in some finely grated horseradish. Pour this sauce over the salted liver slices.

And, more unusually, cheese may be a constituent of a cream-based sauce.

CALF'S LIVER WITH GOAT CHEESE (*Kalvlever med getost*) / SWEDEN

Soak a whole calf's liver in ACIDULATED cold WATER for about an hour and wipe dry. LARD well with slivers of salt pork. Roll and tie the liver, rub it with salt and pepper, and brown it well in hot bacon fat. Put it in a sauce pan, add some veal stock, and simmer, covered, for 15 minutes. Add cream and more stock to almost cover the meat and simmer for another 30 minutes. Add finely crumbled Scandinavian (or *feta*-type) goat cheese and thicken if necessary with a ROUX made of bacon fat and flour. Serve sliced with crisp bacon and mashed potatoes.

For another whole class of liver dishes, wine replaces milk as a prominent ingredient. The use of juniper berries in this recipe suggests a middle European home.

MARINATED CALF'S LIVER / Unknown Origin

Put a large piece of calf's liver in a bowl and cover with some sliced onion, a few crushed juniper berries, a generous amount of freshly ground white pepper and allspice, a bay leaf, several cloves, and a piece of thyme. Cover all with a dry red wine and marinate one day in the refrigerator, turning several times. Drain the liver well and brown it in butter in a casserole. Add about a cup of the marinade, put in a 350°F oven and bake uncovered for about an hour. Add a little more marinade now and then to maintain about a cup of liquid. Thicken sauce with a butter-and-flour ROUX and finally add an equal volume of cream to the sauce. Slice the liver, pour some of the sauce over it, and pass the rest.

Wine-based sauces also readily accommodate the complementing flavors of fruits, many of which go unusually well with liver.

CALF'S LIVER WITH PRUNES *(Kalbsleber mit Dörrzwetschgen)* / GERMANY

In a shallow casserole cover a layer of fried bacon with pieces of lightly floured calf's liver that have been quickly browned in hot bacon fat and then seasoned with salt and pepper. Cover with another layer of bacon and a well-heated sauce prepared by simmering pitted prunes in red wine with cinnamon, lemon juice, and sugar and finally blending this cooked mixture in an electric blender. Heat through quickly in the oven and serve.

The numbers of other types of sauces in which beef liver may be prepared are merely suggested by these three very different dishes.

BEEF LIVER FLORENTINE STYLE *(Fegato di manzo alla fiorentina)* / ITALY

Dust thinly sliced beef liver with flour. Fry in olive oil containing chopped garlic and several sage leaves. Remove liver from pan and add a little oil and some tomato purée and cook for several minutes. Salt and pepper liver and return to the sauce for reheating.

CALF'S LIVER SAUTÉ *(Piritott borjúmáj)* / HUNGARY

Brown chopped onions in bacon fat. Stir in a generous amount of paprika and an equal amount of tomato paste. Add thinly sliced calf's liver, cover, and cook over a low heat until done, turning the liver only once. Salt and serve.

BATTER-FRIED LIVER *(Kahn juhn)* / KOREA

Boil a piece of beef liver, drain, trim it, and cut it into 1/8-in. slices. Dip them in egg beaten with a little water, then in flour, and back into the egg. Fry quickly in hot sesame oil and cut into strips 1 in. by 2 in. Serve with a vinegar-SHOYU sauce and KIM CHEE.

For some other sauced liver dishes, vegetables are included, as in these two oriental recipes. The Filipino dish illustrates the interesting and unique blend of oriental, European, Spanish, and American influences that contribute to the varied but too little known cuisine of the Philippine Islands.

BEEF LIVER *(Nio kan)* / CHINA

Cut beef liver in 1/2-in. cubes. Marinate 15 to 30 minutes in a mixture of soy and sherry (1:1) and some salt. Dust the drained liver cubes with flour, deep-fry in a basket in hot oil until brown, and drain. In a WOK stir-fry diagonally cut sections of BLANCHED celery, asparagus or broccoli, and sliced onions. Add the liver and stir-fry to reheat.

LIVER AND PORK STEW *(Fritada)* / PHILIPPINES

Marinate thinly sliced beef liver in soy sauce. Add vinegar, salt, and crushed garlic to cubed pork meat (about twice as much pork as liver) and cook until tender and the sauce is thick. In another pan sauté garlic, sliced onions, and sliced tomatoes. Add a green pepper cut in strips and a number of quartered potatoes. Cover and simmer until the potatoes are almost done. Add to these vegetables the pork meat, salt to taste, more vinegar, some soy sauce, and enough stock to cover. Bring to a rapid boil and simmer a few minutes. Add the liver, turn the heat up high, and serve when the sauce thickens.

And as for most other food items considered, I have tried wherever possible to include at least one soup.

LIVER DUMPLING SOUP *(Leberknödelsuppe)* / AUSTRIA

Fry finely chopped onions and parsley in butter until soft. Cool. Mix in some beaten egg and raw liver that has been passed through the finest blade of a food chopper. Soak some crustless white bread in milk and squeeze it dry. Mash enough of this bread into the liver-egg mixture to make a workable forcemeat. Mix in a little salt, pepper, and marjoram and some toasted fine bread crumbs. Form into dumplings, simmer them in salted boiling water for about 12 minutes, and serve them in hot consommé.

Having experienced and liked several of these more complicated liver preparations, the "liver-hater" is probably now ready for the simpler treatments that do full justice to calf liver's delicate flavor and texture.

GRILLED CALF'S LIVER

Grilling, preferably over charcoal, is the simplest and one of the best ways to prepare calf's liver. Variations include simply brushing slices first with butter, with or without a light dusting with flour; or grilling *en brochette,* alternating thick squares of liver on the skewer with similarly sized pieces of lean bacon and brushing both with butter. Grilled liver may be served with mâitre d'hôtel butter, aïoli sauce, or with any other sauce appropriate for grilled meat. An experienced American barbecue chef could, of course, easily think of many interesting variations of such liver kebabs.

For a more formal presentation, calf's liver may also be grilled or roasted whole, then sliced at the table.

ROAST CALF'S LIVER *(Foie de veau rôti)* / FRANCE

An entire calf's liver, or a large piece, is LARDED with strips of fat bacon, seasoned with pepper (and other spices, if desired), sprinkled with chopped parsley and some brandy, wrapped in presoaked omentum (or caul), tied well, and roasted in a hot oven or on a spit for 13 to 15 minutes per pound. The liver is sauced with the pan drippings diluted with either white wine or veal stock.

FRIED CALF'S LIVER

Similarly good is equally plain fried calf's liver in which thin, lightly floured slices are seared quickly on each side in very hot butter and removed to a warm serving dish. Some lemon juice is added to the butter and pan juices, which are agitated with a fork to detach the browned flour, and the liver slices are sauced with this mixture.

There are many national and regional variations on the theme of fried liver, only a sampling of which can be mentioned.

CALF LIVER ENGLISH STYLE *(Foie de veau à l'anglaise)* / FRANCE

This is prepared as for frying but the liver is sprinkled too with chopped parsley and served with slices of bacon. The English, in whose style the French ostensibly prepare this version, often omit both the lemon juice and the parsley.

CALF LIVER LYON STYLE *(Foie de veau à la lyonnaise)* / FRANCE

This recipe calls for the liver to be cut in strips, lightly floured, fried briskly in butter (or butter and oil), and sauced with a little vinegar added to the pan juices (in place of the lemon juice). In the manner of Lyon, the liver then is covered with sliced onions sautéed in butter to which a little rich veal stock is added at the end. The whole is sprinkled with chopped parsley.

The Venetians are well known for a very similar treatment. However, they *brown* quite a bit of chopped onion in olive oil, then add sliced calf's liver, brown it quickly, season with salt and pepper, and serve. In another Hungarian variation on this liver-and-onions theme, sliced onions are fried in lard until golden and a little black pepper and marjoram are added. Slices of calf's liver are browned quickly in the same pan, some paprika is stirred in, the liver is seasoned with salt, and served with mashed potatoes that have been sautéed with chopped onions blended into them.

Liver is also deep-fried or stir-fried in Chinese cookery.

DEEP-FRIED LIVER *(Tsa kan)* / CHINA

Marinate 1/2-in. cubes of calf's or beef liver in a mixture of soy sauce, sherry, ginger, salt, and a little crushed garlic; drain and dust with flour or cornstarch; then deep-fry until just brown. Drain thoroughly. In some hot peanut oil in a WOK stir-fry some sliced onion and sliced BLANCHED celery. Sprinkle these vegetables with a little sugar and soy sauce, add the liver cubes, quickly heat through, and serve.

STIR-FRIED CALF LIVER *(Nan chow nio kan)* / CHINA

Cut the liver into a 1/4-in. JULIENNE. Heat some peanut oil in a WOK and stir-fry until lightly brown the white part of leeks, which have been split and cut into thick slices. Add the liver to the hot pan and stir-fry it momentarily. Add a little sherry and quickly evaporate it. Stir in a little light soy sauce, heat through, and serve.

Beef or pork liver may be substituted.

SPLEEN

SPLEEN, also called melt by butchers, is commonly seen in American supermarkets labeled "pet food." This very cheap, blood-rich organ, which is often bright red on its cut surface, is most frequently incorporated in sausages or similar preparations though it can be eaten as is. Beef spleen contains one-fourth more protein than a T-bone steak and about one-tenth its fat. It is also rich in niacin and has twice the iron of liver. Thus it is one of the most nutritious meats available.

This Jewish recipe for stuffed spleen is one of the least adorned I have encountered.

Stuffed Spleen *(Gefilte milts)* / Jewish

Trim a beef spleen and make a deep, lengthwise incision along one edge. Scrape out most of the pulp of the spleen without cutting the surface. Put this pulp through a food chopper and mix it well with a chopped onion that has been fried in oil until golden, about 2 C bread crumbs, 2 beaten eggs, salt, and pepper. Stuff the spleen with this mixture and sew it shut. Paint with melted butter or oil and bake in a 350°F oven for about 2 hours, basting with hot water.

More often other meats are added to a stew in which spleen constitutes the principal ingredient. These two variants merely indicate the possibilities.

Mixed-organ Stew *(Bruckfleisch)* / Austria

Cut a beef spleen, an inexpensive piece of beef, some beef heart, and calf's sweetbreads or beef pancreas into small slices. Cut a piece of aorta into rings. Fry finely chopped onions in lard until golden. Add finely chopped carrots, celery root, and garlic and cook a little. Pour in a little vinegar and add all the meats except the spleen and sweetbreads or pancreas. Salt and pepper and add a generous amount of red wine and a bouquet garni consisting of thyme, bay leaf, and marjoram. Simmer, covered, for an hour, add the other meats, and continue to simmer until all are tender. Thicken the stew with blood and serve it with dumplings.

Firepot *(Pot-au-feu)* / France

To a heavy kettle containing cold beef, veal, or chicken stock add a beef spleen, a good-sized piece of beef rump or other soup meat, and pieces of marrow bone wrapped individually in muslin. Bring to a boil and skim. Simmer 1 hour and add a stewing hen. Continue to simmer and skim. Add attractively trimmed carrots and turnips, white sections of leek, small onions, and sections of celery. Simmer 3 hours more. To serve, skim the extra fat, unwrap the marrow bones, and add sections of cabbage boiled separately in fatty stock. Other ingredients could include other fowl, fowl giblets, sausages, etc. The beef often is eaten in a separate meal with horseradish sauce and the remainder served with toasted bread, pasta, or rice.

Last, this peculiarly English recipe uses beef spleen as the basis for a rich, dark sauce for other beef dishes.

BEEF GRAVY / ENGLAND

Cut a beef spleen into small pieces. Add an equal amount of chopped fat bacon or trimmed ham fat and some chopped onions. Fry slowly until well browned. Add enough fine oatmeal to take up all the fat and continue to cook until the mixture is browned. Stir in boiling water to make a smooth gravy and simmer with occasional stirring for an hour. Strain, add salt and pepper, chopped parsley, and some prepared English mustard.

STOMACH

WE Americans are given to jargon and euphemisms. Public toilets are "restrooms" and janitors have been replaced almost entirely in some of our cities by "stationary engineers." I like the British for their much more direct use of our language. The journal of the British Society of Gastroenterology is simply *Gut*. No misunderstanding there. Some Americans who will knowingly or unknowingly eat an animal's gut in the form of sausage casings gag at the idea of eating these organs in some other fashion. The enjoyment of chitterlings by many black Americans is the one exception.

The beef stomach is called tripe, and according to the dictionary tripe is something "false or worthless, rubbish." Tripe is also a source of gastronomic bliss to its devotees in many lands. Tripe is actually all four stomachs of cattle, sheep, and other ruminant animals. (As often used in French butchery, the word *tripe* includes too the intestines of pigs, *les boyaux*.)

The four parts of the ruminant stomach are the large rumen, or paunch (*gras-double* or *panse* in French); the reticulum, or honeycomb (*réseau* or *millet* or *cailette*); the omasum, or many-plies or book tripe *(feuillet* or *bonnet*); and the abomasum, or true glandular stomach *(franche mule)*. To add a little more confusion, however, the French sometimes use *gras-double* not only for the rumen but for all of the first three stomachs.

Beef tripe usually is sold already cleaned and parboiled. Its protein content is about one fourth more than T-bone steak but it has only one-twentieth the fat. Those Americans who think they have never eaten tripe should examine closely their favorite brand of canned vegetable-beef soup.

Basic Preparation

Boil already cleaned, parboiled tripe 2 hours in about 4 quarts of water per lb. of meat. Add salt, a stalk of celery, and an onion stuck with some cloves. Use this prepared tripe for the following recipes. (If not available already cleaned, the tripe is slit open, scrubbed well with a stiff brush, thoroughly rinsed, and parboiled for about an hour.)

This first is no doubt the best-known tripe dish and, like many Norman recipes, demands apple brandy or Calvados for authenticity.

TRIPE CAEN STYLE *(Tripe à la mode de Caen)* / FRANCE

In a large earthenware casserole put some pork rind, several onions stuck with a clove each, several carrots, the white parts of leeks, and a BOUQUET GARNI that includes some celery leaves, garlic cloves, and some peppercorns. On these vegetables place prepared honeycomb tripe cut into 2-in. squares and several split and blanched calves' feet. Add a wineglass of Calvados (or dry cider plus some grape brandy) and, if necessary, enough water to barely cover the meat. Salt and sprinkle over all a generous amount of finely chopped suet. Seal the top of the casserole tightly with heavy aluminum foil and put on the lid. Bring to a boil and continue to cook in a 325°F oven for 15 minutes. Then reduce the heat to 300°F and cook overnight. Transfer the cooked meat, including all the meat picked from the bones of the feet, to a smaller casserole. Strain the remainder of the material into a bowl, pressing it through a sieve. Stir in a little tomato purée. Chill this bowl, remove the fat, and pour the remaining sauce over the meat. Reheat in the oven, ladle the tripe into soup plates, and serve with a sprinkling of chopped parsley and chives.

Related Spanish and Italian tripe stews are each as famed locally.

Tripe Madrid Style *(Callos a la madrileña)* / Spain

Into a large heavy kettle place some split, blanched calves' feet and prepared honeycomb tripe. Add a glass or two of white wine. Salt and cover the meat with water. Bring to a boil and simmer for two hours. Add some diced smoked ham and simmer for an hour more. In the meantime sauté some chopped onion and an intact, unpeeled whole *head* of garlic in hot olive oil. When the onion is soft, add chopped peeled tomatoes and *generous* amounts of cayenne and paprika and cook quickly until almost all the liquid has evaporated. Stir this mixture into the tripe kettle, add parboiled and pricked and drained *chorizos* (to get rid of excess fat), and simmer about 30 minutes longer. Remove and slice the sausages, remove the meat from the foot bones, and return these meats to the kettle. Serve as for *tripe à la mode de Caen.*

Milanese Tripe and Beans *(Busecca)* / Italy

Fry some chopped lean bacon in a soup kettle until crisp. Add some butter and sauté until soft some chopped onions, leeks, celery, and parsley, with generous amounts of white turnips cut into a large dice and chopped savoy cabbage. Add some presoaked and drained dried peas or white beans, some chopped peeled tomatoes, and a quantity of parboiled tripe that has been cut into a JULIENNE. Cover the vegetables and meat with water, season the pot with salt and pepper, cover and simmer until the beans are almost done. Add some potatoes cut in large dice and simmer until they are tender. Serve the stew with a generous amount of grated Romano.

Simpler but tasty tripe dishes are represented by these French and Hungarian recipes in each of which tripe and browned onions are complemented by somewhat different accompaniments and seasonings.

Tripe Lyon Style *(Gras-double à la lyonnaise)* / France

Sauté strips of prepared tripe in a generous amount of butter until they begin to brown. ·Add chopped onions, salt, and pepper and continue to cook until both the meat and onions are well browned. Add a little wine vinegar and serve sprinkled with chopped parsley.

Tripe Nice Style *(Tripes niçoises)* / France

Brown chopped onions in olive oil. Add strips of prepared tripe and simmer covered for 2 hours. Add chopped tomatoes, garlic, a BOUQUET

GARNI, salt, and pepper and simmer 4 hours more. To serve, strain the sauce over the tripe and dust with grated cheese.

TRIPE PROVENCE STYLE *(Gras-double à la provençal)* / FRANCE

Sauté chopped onions in oil. When they are browned, add strips of prepared tripe lightly dusted with flour, salt, and pepper and cook for several minutes. Add chopped tomatoes, chopped parsley, and a generous amount of crushed garlic. Simmer for about 20 minutes.

Or, fry chopped onions and BLANCHED salt pork in olive oil until slightly colored. Add 3-in. squares of prepared tripe, a generous amount of white wine, salt, pepper, and a BOUQUET GARNI. Simmer for 1 hour and thicken the sauce with beaten egg yolks. Stir in chopped basil and dust with grated cheese.

TRIPE ROAST *(Pacal pörkölt)* / HUNGARY

Brown chopped onions in lard. Cut parboiled tripe into long, narrow strips and add them and a generous amount of paprika to the onions. Add a wineglass or so of white wine, cover, and simmer 10 minutes.

The paprika in that last dish should remind us too that tripe also featured prominently in the past in some justly famed American regional dishes, such as an authentic Philadelphia pepper pot.

Quite different dishes are the various sausages in which beef tripe serves as the casing for some stuffing or forcemeat.

TRIPE SAUSAGE / ENGLAND

Cut parboiled tripe into 5-in. by 3-in. pieces. Mix pork sausage meat with sautéed chopped onions and spread on the pieces of tripe. Roll and tie or fasten with toothpicks. Roll in cracker crumbs, then in beaten egg, and again in cracker crumbs. Fry in deep fat.

TRIPE ROLL / ENGLAND

Mix soft bread crumbs with seasoned mashed potatoes. Add sautéed chopped onions and green peppers. Spread this mixture on pieces of parboiled honeycomb tripe, roll each firmly, and tie. Dredge the rolls with flour, brush with melted butter, and reflour. Layer bacon strips over the rolls, bake at least an hour at 350°F, and serve with a tomato sauce.

And, as already suggested, tripe may also be prepared as a soup. This is one classic.

TRIPE SOUP (*Flaczki*) / POLAND

Boil a large soup bone in several quarts of water with an onion, celery, a carrot, and some parsley for an hour. Add parboiled tripe cut into strips about 3 in. by 1/2 in. and simmer them until very tender. Thicken with a browned flour-and-butter ROUX, add some marjoram, quite a bit of ground ginger, and salt and pepper to taste; continue to cook for a few minutes. This heavy soup is sometimes garnished with marrow dumplings.

Even the person who initially lacks enthusiasm for any of the above, often because of boiled tripe's slightly slippery texture, will find this very simple preparation surprisingly acceptable.

FRIED TRIPE (*Tripes frites*) / FRANCE

Prepare a light batter (as for CHILIS RELLENOS), cutting in beaten egg whites at the end. Dry the prepared tripe, cut it into squares, dip into the batter, and fry in very hot olive oil. Serve with a hot sauce, such as sauce diable or mustard.

While the reticulum, or honeycomb, is regarded in most countries as the choicest tripe, the essential ingredient of one historically important American dish, the Son-of-a-bitch Stew of cowboy fame, was the milk-filled abomasum, or true glandular stomach, of the calf. This hearty dish's distinctive flavor of renin-curdled milk complemented the stew's other ingredients: the calf's tongue, liver, heart and sweetbreads, onions, chilis, salt, and pepper—surely additional evidence that our eating was once considerably more varied and adventuresome than today.

INTESTINES

THE intestines of animals are used most commonly for sausage casings, and, less often, as is. Butchers and sausage makers classify intestines by their diameter and use the following terms: *Rounds* are the small intestines of cattle, calves, sheep, and hogs; they are used for making fresh pork sausages, frankfurters, *chorizos,* and the like. (*Weasands* are the muscular outer layers of the esophagus; they also are small casings.) *Middles* are the large intestines of cattle and hogs and are used for larger sausages. *Bungs* are the even larger cecum of cattle and the rectum of hogs.

Basic Preparation

Salted casings for sausage preparation are usually purchased as such. They need to be soaked and then rinsed well to free them of salt.

To clean fresh intestines, however, cut them into 4-ft. to 6-ft. lengths and lay each across a smooth flat surface. With the back of a straight-backed knife, start at the center of the piece of intestine and, while exerting pressure on the knife, express the intestinal contents toward each of the cut ends. Casings are then flushed with a stream of water and are ready for use. Alternatively, they may be turned inside out (after expressing the contents) and scrubbed with a brush.

Most of the recipes for sausages that I have included will be found in the pork chapter because pork cuts are used for sausage more than meat cuts of other species. However, virtually any of those recipes could also be prepared using cattle intestines of the proper sizes.

One example of a traditional all-beef sausage is the Yorkshire "banger," which, alas, now often tastes in England like sawdust and oatmeal!

YORKSHIRE SAUSAGE / ENGLAND

Put through a food chopper some lean beef, suet, and bread (4:2:1). Mix in some black pepper and preferred sausage spices. Stuff into rounds and tie off at about 5-in. lengths. To serve, fry the sausages in drippings until crisp and brown and eat them with horseradish sauce.

Much more "daring" is the eating of beef intestines as such. This excellent Peruvian recipe, generically related to their better known and much liked *anticuchos,* is an excellent dish almost certain to be enjoyed by anyone with even a slightly open mind.

BARBECUED INTESTINES (*Choncholis*) / PERU

Marinate overnight pieces of a cow's or sheep's intestines in a mixture of vinegar, much crushed garlic, ground chili pepper, cumin, salt, and pepper. Cut dried chili peppers in half, remove the seeds, and soak them in salted water 24 hours. Mash these drained chilis into a paste. Melt a generous amount of lard and stir in some ground ANATTO. Mix this chili paste, the lard, and a little of the marinade together to make a basting sauce. Brush the pieces of drained intestine with this sauce and grill over charcoal until well browned. The sauce is brushed on several times during the process.

The connoisseur will also wish to try this one.

STEWED INTESTINES *(Panelada)* / BRAZIL

Boil cleaned beef intestines; cut them into small pieces, and mix in salt, black pepper, crushed garlic, chopped onions, and some vegetable oil. BRAISE vigorously for 3 to 4 hours with a minimum of water added from time to time.

MEMBRANES

THE intestines of vertebrate animals are suspended in a thin transparent membrance called the mesentery (or, in French, *fraise*). Lining the abdominal cavity is another transparent membrane called the peritoneal membrane, a large folded extension of which, the omentum, loosely covers the stomach and adjacent viscera. This last, which usually is well-laced with excellent quality fat, is also called the caul (or, in French, *crépinette* or *toilette*).

Beef or calf membranes are most used as wrappers for various forcemeats, which then are grilled or deep-fried. For recipes see the index.

Less often they are also eaten by themselves as a meat. This is one of the few recipes I know.

CALF MESENTERY LYON STYLE *(Fraise de veau lyonnaise)* / FRANCE

Poach some calf mesenteries in a flavorful stock. Dry, cut in slices, and fry them in very hot oil. Add thinly sliced onions, salt, and pepper and cook until the onions are golden. Add some vinegar at the last and serve the *fraise* with chopped parsley.

MAMMARY GLANDS

JUST the mention of *gland* conjures up a variety of negative associations in many people's minds which prejudice them against eating these nutritious organs. The thymus, pancreas, and testicles are the endocrine or hormone-secreting glands of mammals that are large enough to be an item of diet.

Mammary glands are of a different type, however. Anatomically and physiologically they are merely large sweat glands. Those of heifer calves and cows contain muscle tissues as well as the secretory glandular meat. Although it is a meat not commonly encountered in the restaurants of any country, mammary gland is standard peasant fare. As a food, cow's udder resembles pancreas in texture and flavor.

These French recipes, the first for a pot-roasted udder and the next two for stuffed and fried or grilled udder "sausages," are among the few I've encountered in which the glands are prepared other than by simply grilling over charcoal, as in the Argentine *parillada*. Another recipe similar to the first is for a British dish called elder.

POT-ROASTED UDDER *(Tetine pôelage)* / FRANCE

A calf's or cow's udder is skinned, soaked in cold water, BLANCHED, weighted, and cooled quickly in ice water. LARD it with strips of seasoned bacon fat. The udder then may be marinated, if desired, as for a pot roast of beef. In any event, it is browned in butter. Cover the bottom of a kettle with a bed of carrots, onions, and/or turnips also browned in butter. Add the udder and a minimum of stock, wine or the marinade, season as desired, cover the kettle tightly with a heavy lid, and simmer on the stove, basting frequently, until the meat is tender.

CALF UDDER CROQUETTES *(Rissoles de tetines de veau)* / FRANCE

This 18th-century recipe calls for BLANCHING a calf's udder, cutting it into wide strips, folding each around some veal forcemeat, wrapping them in pastry, and deep-frying. As a variation the stuffed udders are skewered, dipped in beaten eggs and bread crumbs, and grilled.

Wouldn't either of these be great house specialities for an enterprising restauranteur in the Grand Tetons National Park? Similar to *rissoles* are

Polish *kromeskis*, for which calf udder has been one traditional wrapper for a minced forcemeat.

MANY persons are not certain what sweetbreads are; some think erroneously that they are the testicles or the pancreas. In gastronomic parlance, however, sweetbreads are the thymus glands of young animals, chiefly of calves and lambs. Besides secreting a hormone, these glands are the source of cells important to the immune process. Their meat somewhat resembles that of both the testes and pancreas, and all three have long been extolled as mind-sharpeners and aphrodisiacs—and have been alternately loved and damned by sufferers from the gout.

In newborn animals the sweetbreads are relatively large, but as animals mature they atrophy. They occur in pairs with the gastronomically most "choice" being the spherical heart gland. I can detect no difference in their taste and enjoy the more elongated throat gland just as well. Sweetbreads' protein content is the same as T-bone steak, but they have one-half the fat.

One of the main sources of confusion about the identity of sweetbreads results from the fact that in the butchering trade both the thymus glands and the much larger and less delicate pancreas of young or old animals are sometimes referred to collectively as sweetbreads. Large pieces—or small, obviously cut, rectangular "sweetbreads"—*are* pancreas. They also are good food, but they should be far cheaper to buy. Both can be prepared by the same recipes, but with pancreas one cannot approach the gastronomic heights achievable with thymus.

Basic Preparation

Sweetbreads are soaked in ice water several hours and the membranes and blood clots carefully removed. Whether they are then BLANCHED depends upon personal preference. Blanching consists of simmering the meat for about 10 minutes in salted water containing a little vinegar or lemon juice, some sliced carrots and onions, and a BOUQUET GARNI. After blanching, they are plunged in ice water to chill and then dried. I think flavor is noticeably lost in the blanching process.

Recipes for veal and lamb sweetbreads are interchangeable.

For persons who have not tried sweetbreads (11.5 percent in one survey of American university students) or think they do not like them (an additional 16.6 percent in this same survey), this dish is an excellent starter.

CALF SWEETBREADS IN CRUST *(Ris de veau en croustade)* / ORIGINAL

Slice prepared sweetbreads and sauté them in butter with some chopped tarragon until they are golden brown. Remove them and sauté sliced mushrooms in the same pan. Add a generous amount of Madeira, some more tarragon, and a little rich beef or veal stock and reduce the liquid by about one-half. Lower the heat, stir in a generous quantity of sour cream, return the sweetbreads to the pan, and simmer them gently. In the meantime, prepare croustades by hollowing some French rolls, buttering them well, and "melba-ing" them under the broiler. Hold them in a warming oven. Over the bottom of the croustades place a warm JULIENNE of crisply cooked green beans that were tossed with butter, cover them with a julienne of lightly sautéed ham and, finally, some of the mushroom sauce, the sweetbreads, and then more of the sauce.

Somewhat easier to prepare and also excellent is this combination of complementary flavors.

STUFFED SWEETBREADS / ENGLAND

Slice sweetbreads into thin halves. Salt and pepper them and sauté in butter and a little beef extract. Spread one half with a mixture of sautéed chopped onions and mushrooms, bread crumbs, and cream (enough to moisten). Cover with the other half of the sweetbread, sprinkle with Parmesan cheese, and broil until the cheese melts and nicely browns.

This next recipe is probably of Mediterranean inspiration but lends itself to American seedless grapes. The proportions of egg white to meat sauce are as in the usual soufflé.

SWEETBREADS VERONIQUE / CALIFORNIA

Cut sweetbreads into 1/2-in. cubes and mix with a supreme sauce. Add white seedless grapes and BLANCHED almonds. Fold in stiffly beaten egg whites and turn the mixture into a buttered casserole. Bake the soufflé in a 350°F oven for 40 minutes.

Sweetbreads are especially delicious simply grilled over charcoal as in an Argentine *parillada*. This is a slightly fancier treatment.

SWEETBREADS MILANESE *(Animelle alla milanese)* / ITALY

Brush prepared sweetbreads with melted butter and roll them in a mixture of bread crumbs and grated Parmesan cheese. Grill over charcoal.

The Italians also combine a variety of ingredients with fried sweetbreads. This very good recipe should suggest many other possibilities for flavor and texture combinations to the versatile cook.

SWEETBREADS WITH ARTICHOKES *(Animelle con carciofi)* / ITALY

Thoroughly trim small artichokes, cut them into eighths, and remove the chokes. Sauté them in olive oil until tender. In another pan brown sweetbreads in butter over a high heat. Mince thin slices of prosciutto and add them to the sweetbreads with a little Marsala, salt, and pepper. Add the artichokes, heat through, and serve.

Sweetbreads may also be coated with a TEMPURA or CHILIS RELLENOS BATTER and deep-fried.

They also make elegant pâtés.

HOT SWEETBREAD PÂTÉ *(Pâté chaud de ris de veau)* / FRANCE

Put lean pork and hard pork fat (1:1) through a food chopper. Mix in beaten eggs, some flour and cream, salt, pepper, and thyme. Blend smooth in an electric blender. Fry a generous quantity of sliced mushrooms lightly in butter and mix half of them into the blended forcemeat. Line an ovenproof dish with a suitable (slightly sweetened) pastry. Add a thick layer of the forcemeat, then a thick layer of fried mushrooms and small pieces of prepared sweetbreads. Add another layer of forcemeat and a pastry lid. Seal the edges, decorate if desired, and brush with egg yolk and water. Bake at 350°F for about an hour.

Or, less often, sweetbreads form the basis for very rich sauces for other foods, as in this unusual recipe.

FROGS' LEGS AND SWEETBREADS *(Cuisses de grenouille et ris de veau)* /
FRANCE

Flour and sauté frogs' legs in butter until brown. Put a generous amount
of butter, thinly sliced mushrooms, some white wine and chicken stock,
salt, and white pepper in a pan and bring to a boil. Add some diced
sweetbreads and simmer for a half hour. Thicken with egg yolks and
cream. Pour the sweetbreads and sauce over the frogs' legs.

PANCREAS

THE pancreas is the rather large, loosely made, lobulated organ that lies in
the mesentery, or supporting membrane of the small intestine. It secretes
pancreatin into the intestine, which helps to digest fat. The pancreas also
contains the "islands" of cells that produce the hormone insulin. It is good
to eat but is considerably less delicate in flavor than sweetbreads. The
protein content of beef pancreas averages slightly less than T-bone steak,
and its fat content about two-thirds.

Belgian cooking makes a unique use of beer, as in this stew prepared
from a variety of tasty innards, pancreas prominent among them.

ORGAN STEW BRUSSELS STYLE *(Choesels à la bruxelloise)* / BELGIUM

Heat 1/2 C of fat from rendered suet in a pan until smoking. Brown in it
a cut-up oxtail and then two pairs of veal sweetbreads. Reduce the heat
and cook gently for about 45 minutes. Add some cut-up breast of veal
and a generous quantity of sliced onions. Cook with occasional stirring
for another half hour. Add a cut-up beef kidney, cook and stir a few
minutes, then add 1–1/2 C of strong beer and a BOUQUET GARNI and
correct the seasoning with pepper and salt and a little nutmeg. Simmer
for 30 minutes, add a beef pancreas cut into pieces, another bottle of
strong beer, and a cup or two of strained stock prepared by boiling some
mushroom trimmings or stems and continue to simmer until the pan-
creas is done. Thicken if desired.

Recipes for beef pancreas are interchangeable with those for the sheep
or pig organ, and most sweetbreads recipes can also be prepared with
pancreas.

Kidneys

To many persons, use of the urogenital system or its products as food poses a special problem, not all of it a Victorian hangover. Yet we *all* eat eggs from animals' ovaries, the very thought of which repulses some other peoples. Kidneys of calves and lambs, and to a lesser extent pigs, are highly regarded and often highly priced delicacies in many countries, yet few Americans eat them. In a student survey at the University of Nebraska, while 45 percent had never tasted kidneys, more students indicated an unwillingness to eat this organ than in the case of any other meat. In fact, the kidneys of almost all mammals and birds are good to eat although those of old animals may taste more of urine than some people prefer—and matter of preference that is, too, because a raw meat dish called *marrara* is eaten in the southern Sudan which actually includes urine and bile as flavoring ingredients. In fact, before we sneer too audibly let us recall that it was a habit of several early European peoples to wash the mouth with urine, a custom said to have persisted in parts of England and Germany into the last century.

The kidneys of different species of animals differ somewhat in their appearance. Those of cattle are deeply lobulated, while sheep and swine kidneys are smooth. Veal kidneys have about the same amount of protein as T-bone steak with about one-ninth the fat. Beef kidneys are slightly higher in fat and lower in protein. The iron and thiamine contents of beef kidneys are higher than those of liver, and they are also excellent sources of biotin, pantothenic acid, riboflavin, and niacin.

Basic Preparation

Kidneys of young animals require only that the ureters and the serous membranes covering the kidneys be removed. If the mode of preparation calls for slicing kidneys, they usually are trimmed of all of their fat. When they are to be cooked whole, a thin layer of fat is left on. The kidneys of old animals are split and presoaked in a number of changes of cold water.

Recipes for veal kidneys may be used for lamb kidneys, and vice versa. Pig kidneys also may be prepared in most of the same ways.

Grilled kidneys are simple to do and excellent. For example, as part of an Argentine *parillada*, halved kidneys are just grilled "as is" over charcoal.

They are also excellent briskly fried in garlic and oil. This Italian recipe was probably originally made with GARUM in place of the anchovies.

KIDNEYS TRIFOLATI *(Rognoni trifolati)* / ITALY

Slice kidneys as thinly as possible. Brown a clove of garlic in olive oil. Add the kidneys, salt, and pepper and brown them over high heat. Add some butter and chopped anchovy fillets and heat through. Garnish with chopped parsley and lemon wedges.

A variant of the same treatment is typical of Provence. Filling the mushroom caps is an extra for which large croutons or rice could just as well substitute.

VEAL KIDNEYS PROVENCE STYLE *(Rognons de veau provençale)* / FRANCE

Split veal kidneys with some adherent fat. Pepper them and sear the cut surfaces in hot olive oil. Turn once and brown the outsides. The interiors should still be pink and moist. Keep the kidneys warm and, in the same pan, sauté in additional oil chopped mushroom stems, crushed garlic and chopped parsley, salt, and pepper. Fill sautéed mushroom caps with this mixture, surround the kidneys with the stuffed mushrooms, reheat all quickly in a hot oven, and serve.

Cream-based sauces are also a natural for kidneys. In this French recipe mustard provides a distinctive flavor, while the German version is slightly sour.

BRAISED VEAL KIDNEYS *(Rognons de veau braisés)* / FRANCE

Salt and pepper intact veal kidneys with a layer of fat attached. Brown them in butter in a casserole. Cover and cook for about 20 minutes in a 350°F oven. Add sautéed sliced mushrooms and cook another 10 minutes. Stir in some heavy cream and French mustard. When mixed well, serve.

BRAISED KIDNEYS *(Geschmorte Nieren)* / GERMANY

Fry some chopped onion in butter until golden. Add thinly sliced calf's kidneys, stir-fry for a few minutes, salt, and stir in a little sour cream. Simmer for about an hour. Stir in a little vinegar and thicken the sauce with a butter-and-flour ROUX.

Kidneys are highly versatile meats and seem as much at home in wine as in cream, or a combination of both, as here.

BRAISED KIDNEYS IN PORT *(Rognons braisés au porto)* / FRANCE

In a shallow pan put sliced veal kidneys, some chopped onions, a piece of lemon peel, a sliced truffle, a bay leaf, salt, and pepper. Cover with port and water (1:1). Cover the pan tightly, bring to a boil, and simmer over very low heat for 1–1/2 hours. Add some sautéed mushrooms and cream, stir, and cook a few minutes longer.

Even without the cream, kidneys can be sautéed in practically any wine to advantage.

SAUTÉED KIDNEYS IN WINE *(Rognons sautés au vin)* / FRANCE

The kidneys are cut into thin slices, salted and peppered, fried quickly in sizzling hot butter, and transferred to a warm plate. Sauté some sliced mushrooms in the same pan and add to the kidneys. DEGLAZE the pan with a wineglass or so of Madeira, sherry, or any red or white wine, add some rich veal stock, cook down by at least half, and thicken the sauce further with a flour-and-butter ROUX (it should be quite thick). Return the kidneys and the mushrooms to the sauce and finish with a little added butter.

For *à la bordelaise* prepare as above but without the mushrooms and with a white Bordeaux wine (and add at the same time some finely chopped shallots). When the kidneys are returned to the sauce, add also some diced, poached, and drained bone marrow. This dish is garnished with chopped parsley.

This is a dish I concocted for our friends Mabel and Reed Nesbit. We enjoyed it as much as they did.

KIDNEYS IN CRUST *(Croustade de rognons Nesbit)* / ORIGINAL

Croustades are prepared by cutting the tops from large hard rolls (in our case San Francisco sourdough) and hollowing them. The cut surfaces are buttered, "melba-ed" in the oven, and then sealed with a mixture of liver pâté and a little mayonnaise. The croustades are filled with kidney slices sautéed *au vin* (as above) and garnished with a slice of the liver pâté and a lightly sautéed mushroom cap.

Most of the previous kidney recipes lend themselves readily to chafing dish cookery at tableside. For those who would impress nonkidney eaters even further with pyrotechnics, these are two good vehicles.

FLAMING KIDNEYS *(Rognons flambés)* / FRANCE

Brown kidney slices quickly in butter, season with salt and pepper, and flame with warm brandy. Remove to a warm plate. In additional butter heat some chopped shallots and button mushrooms. Add a wineglass of port and simmer until well reduced. Add some fresh cream, chopped tarragon, a little Dijon mustard, and a little lemon juice. Stir constantly until smooth. Return kidneys to the pan to reheat. Serve over rice or noodles.

In a Swiss variant for flambéed kidneys, kirsch is substituted for brandy, and for the sauce some Dijon mustard and lemon juice are stirred into the pan drippings.

Kidneys, in fact, are highly versatile meats that feature prominently in most cuisines East and West.

BEEF KIDNEYS AND MUSHROOMS *(Nio sin no ku)* / CHINA

Cut prepared beef kidneys into thin slices. Soak dried mushrooms for 1/2 hour in warm water and finely slice. Stir-fry a little chopped pork fat for 5 minutes. Add some chopped onion and stir-fry until brown. Add the kidneys, mushrooms, and 3 T soy sauce and simmer 1 hour.

They even make an elegant breakfast or supper omelet.

KIDNEY OMELET *(Omelette di rognoni)* / ITALY

Fry a thinly sliced kidney over high heat in a mixture of butter and olive oil. Salt and pepper and remove with a slotted spoon to a warm dish. Prepare a sauce by adding some Marsala or sherry to the pan drippings; scrape and stir with a fork until the wine nearly evaporates. Add a little rich stock and cook briefly. Return the kidneys, heat through, and serve over a plain omelet.

Or, of course, there is that great traditional English pudding.

BEEFSTEAK AND KIDNEY PUDDING / ENGLAND

Cut up some steak and trimmed beef kidneys and shake the meat in a bag with flour and pepper. Remove the meat and knead the peppered flour with finely chopped suet to make a dough. Roll it out. Grease a pudding basin and line it with this dough. Add a mixture of the meat, chopped onions, and chopped mushrooms (and cockles, if desired) and almost fill with lightly salted beef stock. Seal the pudding with a circle of dough, cover it with a floured cloth, and simmer it in a large kettle of water for 3 to 4 hours.

This colorful classic of French cookery deserves a slot in the repertoire of any creative cook. It invariably evokes favorable comments from guests and is also an excellent way to introduce kidneys to the unbeliever.

VEAL KIDNEYS AND VEAL *(Rognonnade de veau)* / FRANCE

Wrap a 1–1/2 lb. loin of veal around a veal kidney with its fat and tie it well. Brown it in a casserole in hot fat and remove. Add chopped onions to the casserole and sprinkle in some flour. Stir to form a lightly colored ROUX. Whisk in some white wine and veal stock until smooth. Salt, pepper, and add a BOUQUET GARNI. Return the meat, cover, and cook over a slow fire until done. Skim the excess fat, stir in a little cream, and slice so that some of the kidney is in each serving.

Finally, as with most other meats, I have included a soup or two based upon kidneys. These are, in fact, merely two national variants on the same sour cream motif.

KIDNEY SOUP *(Nierensuppe)* / GERMANY

Sauté chopped onions in butter until golden. Add a large bay leaf, mace, a little thyme, marjoram, and rosemary. Turn up the heat, add veal kidneys cut into a small dice, and cook quickly until brown. Stir in flour to absorb most of the butter and juices and cook until smooth and lightly browned. Slowly stir in a quart or so of good veal or beef stock, salt, and pepper and simmer for about 30 minutes. Remove the pan from the stove and stir in some egg yolks beaten with sour cream and Madeira. Serve with croutons and chopped parsley as a garnish.

KIDNEY SOUP *(Rassolnik)* / RUSSIA

Fry some thinly sliced onions and chopped celery in butter until golden. Add a generous amount of coarsely chopped spinach (and sorrel leaves if available), some chopped parsley, a finely chopped dill pickle, salt, pepper, and 1–1/2 to 2 qts. of beef stock. Bring to a boil, then simmer for 20 minutes. Add to the soup several calf or lamb kidneys that have been sliced, lightly dusted with flour, and seared on both sides in hot, light brown butter. Thicken the soup a bit with beaten egg yolk, simmer the soup just below the boil for a few minutes, stir in a generous amount of sour cream, and serve.

TESTICLES

"MOUNTAIN oysters" have always been considered a man's dish par excellence, but the belief that they'll make hair grow on a woman's chest is certainly an old wives' tale. I think.

Calves usually are castrated at a big round-up for branding and vaccination, and a *fiesta de huevos,* as the South American gauchos call it, often follows. When I was a veterinary student, the stable hands used to throw dice to see who got the larger, meal-sized "goodies" whenever a horse or mature bull was brought into the clinic for castration.

The testicles of young animals are very good food; they most resemble sweetbreads in texture and flavor. They frequently are simply sliced and sautéed in butter, or they may be served as rich garnishes for other meats.

Recipes for calf, lamb, and pig testicles are interchangeable.

Basic Preparation

Remove the membranous covering (tunic).

GOLDEN CALF TESTICLES *(Cascalopes d'animelles au soleil)* / FRANCE

Calf testicles are cut into 1/2-in. slices. Season them with salt, pepper, and a generous amount of paprika. Dust the slices lightly with flour and fry until golden in a mixture of olive oil and butter. Put them in a warm, shallow casserole and sprinkle with some sieved hard-cooked eggs, finely chopped parsley, chervil and tarragon, and some melted butter. Place in a 350°F oven for 10 minutes and serve.

Blood

A number of people around the world like to drink the warm blood of animals or to eat it as a freshly coagulated pudding. Virtually all nomadic people drink fresh blood, and in the days before Geritol even proper ladies in Victorian England would drop by the slaughterhouse for a monthly tot. I've never really tried it that way, but I did learn many years ago how good blood sausages of various kinds are.

The taste for blood and prejudices against eating it are among the more interesting aspects of this whole food-avoidance business. Blood invariably conjures up visions of Dracula and thoughts of cannibals. The whole spectrum is there. Tibetans usually kill food animals by suffocation just so all the blood will stay in the meat; Jews and Moslems slit the throats of fully conscious animals just so they will bleed out entirely.

Blood is classically a thickening ingredient for sauces or the basis for puddings and sausages. A 1,000-lb. steer yields 30 to 40 lbs.

For all the mammalian blood recipes listed in the index, that of any available species could be substituted.

Blood Pudding (*Blodpudding*) / Norway

To a pint of milk and a pint of water add 5 T sugar, 1/2 t ginger, 1/2 t powdered cloves, and 1 t salt. In this liquid cook 1 C rice and 1/2 C pearl barley until the mixture begins to thicken. Add 2 pts. fresh blood that has been beaten with a wire whisk and 1 T fine oven-dried bread crumbs. Fill greased baking tins, place them in a pan of hot water, and bake for about 2 hours in a 275° to 300°F oven. Slice while warm and serve the pudding with melted butter and powder sugar.

Blood Pudding Cakes / Scotland

In this intermediary between a pudding and a sausage, cow's blood is thickened with fine oatmeal and seasoned to taste. It then is shaped into cakes and fried.

In the Indonesian island of Celebes, or Sulawesi, a similar dish is made by mixing blood with rice and then cooking it.

2

Pork

CHICAGO WAS ONCE proclaimed "hog butcher for the world," and as late as 1917 our domestic and international pork and beef trades were such that both Swift and Armour ranked among the 5 largest corporations in the United States. Pork is now only our second most popular meat, but until 1950 it was number one. Before the advent of refrigerated railway cars, salted (cured) pork was by far the most commonly available meat in America. Then "bringing home the bacon" was truly synonymous with earning a living, and political favors to special-interest groups were met through largesse from the legislative "pork barrel."

Though our pork industry has long boasted that everything is used from the hog but the squeal, some of the pig does not now see its highest culinary or nutritional calling. Huge quantities are overprocessed into expensive junk foods like the supermarket hot dog, a tube of blank gunk that now bears about as much resemblance to its frankfurter antecedent as our soft, never-go-stale bread does to a real loaf.

AVERSION TO EATING PORK

CONTRARY to the virtual absence of prejudice in America against eating the muscle meat of cattle, we find widespread refusal to eat pork among a sizable number of American Jews and Moslems. This is part of an ancient and almost worldwide prejudice whereby pork is irrationally rejected as food by hundreds of millions of Moslems, Orthodox Jews, Ethiopian

Coptic Christians, and such smaller religious groups as the Mandaeans and Zezidi, or Devil worshippers, of Iraq, Iran, and Turkey.

Prohibitions against eating pig meat already existed in Egypt in pharaonic times and were certainly not originated by Moses. Among the Egyptians, the pig was associated with the god Set, who often played an evil role among the gods in the Egyptian pantheon. On the other hand, pigs are known to have been sacred animals among local groups both in Egypt and Babylonia. In fact, in some of the earliest records of pork avoidance it is not clear whether it was because the species was regarded as unclean or as blessed! The earliest recorded attitudes of the Jews about pork are themselves somewhat ambivalent, and the Greeks were not certain whether the Jews too really detested or adored pigs. Whatever, it is clear that various cults in the Middle East and Asia Minor, including the Jews, came to regard the pig as taboo in ancient times and forbade pork eating.

It is interesting that Christianity in general, arising as it did from Judaism, did not share its pork prejudice, while Islam, of similar origins, did. In fact, it was Islam that became the real champion of this prejudice and spread it into many areas of the world, such as Southeast Asia, where pork had long been prized. There is ample evidence that fondness for pork died hard among some of these converted peoples and that surreptitious pork eating survived in some Islamic areas for prolonged periods. Among Moslems today, only a few peoples on the fringes of the Islamic world, as well as a few dissident groups, will eat pork.

ORIGINS OF PORK AVOIDANCE

THERE is also some interesting evidence that swine were already being avoided quite independently by the nomadic Turkic peoples of central Asia before their conversion to Islam; and some Indo-Europeans, such as the Scythians, are believed also to have prohibited pig keeping. On the other hand, these sources suggest that some of these latter peoples were not necessarily prejudiced against use of pork flesh as food if it was available.

Tibetans, who also remain ambivalent about the merits of pig raising, partially base their objections on the carnivorous and scavenging habits of pigs as well as on Buddhist belief that pigs represent individuals guilty of great sin in a previous incarnation. Pig keeping does occur throughout

India, however, but it is regarded as a low-caste occupation. Both the animal and the people who eat its meat are considered unclean by high-caste Hindus, and it is this prejudice which seems to prevail more than that pork eating per se violates the sanctity of life.

It is very doubtful that any of these widely held pork prejudices arose as is stated commonly, through any knowledge of an association of pork eating with specific diseases such as trichinosis. The incubation period between eating infected pork and developing the symptoms of trichinosis is so prolonged it is highly improbable that such a linkage would have suggested itself to the Jews or others. Other possibilities in terms of disease, such as pork tapeworm or salmonellosis, are equally unlikely because similar bases would have existed for rejecting either beef or fowl as food. In the case of the Jews, moreover, at least thirty different kinds of animals besides pigs were proscribed as human food.

The true origins of pork prohibition, therefore, are still highly conjectural, and the alternatives stimulate largely ideological arguments among social scientists of different camps. The explanation which is attractive to many scholars and which I find most plausible is that in some Middle Eastern cultures the transition of the pig from a sacred to a contemptible animal represented a facet of the conflict between settled indigenous peoples of an area who kept pigs and successive groups of invading pastoralists who did not. As we have noted, it has been largely pastoralists who have not kept pigs, probably for no other reason than that pigs are not readily herded or well adapted to grasslands. Pastoralists often prevailed in these early conflicts with settled peoples, and then, as now, their existing beliefs about the incompatibility of pigs and nomadism were probably reinforced by a prejudice *against copying the food customs of their enemies or conquered subjects*—somewhat similar, perhaps, to the "patriotic" ban on German sausages in parts of the United States during World War I. Frederick Simoons has pointed out the common use of derogatory names for ethnic groups associated with particular foods. "Krauts," "limeys," and "frogs" are examples that readily come to mind.

Finally, it is interesting for us to note in considering pork prejudice that pigs are kept about the house as free-roaming pets, both throughout Southeast Asia and in the Pacific Islands. The attitudes of individuals in these areas about the slaughter of pigs for food are mixed and in many ways resemble ours about eating dogs and cats. Beyond these cultural types of prejudices, more generally held pork prejudices in the United States are those against eating organ meats similar to the ones already considered in discussing beef.

Despite such widely held and almost totally irrational avoidances, there is probably no animal for which a greater variety of recipes exist worldwide than for the pig. The art of charcuterie, or pork butchery, is a highly developed one in several cultures, and the infinite range of sausage possibilities alone presents a challenge to even the most creative and versatile cook. In fact, the two acknowledgeably greatest cuisines in the world, the Cantonese and the French, are both heavily pork oriented.

For an American family to fatten a young pig or two requires relatively little in the way of space, facilities, or labor and need not constitute a neighborhood nuisance. Pigs are not inherently dirty, though people sometimes force them to live in filth. Probably in the not too distant future ordinances enacted mostly in the last century in the United States, when there were no controls over numbers of livestock kept in cities, will have to be reexamined to see what animals and how many are environmentally and aesthetically tolerable under conditions of higher food costs and shorter commercial supplies. Such possibilities aside, pigs may also be bought at auction or a whole carcass purchased from the custom butcher for the freezer.

HEALTH RISKS FROM PORK

THE health risks from butchering swine and handling and eating their various parts are associated, as for cattle, chiefly with the muscle meat and the organs of the alimentary tract. The latter risk was mentioned in the introduction to this section. The principal human health problem involving swine in the United States has always been trichinosis. This disease is caused by the barely visible larva of a nematode worm that localizes in the muscles (including the tongue and heart) of pigs and other carnivorous animals, including man. People become infected by eating undercooked pork.

Unfortunately, the United States in this century and the last has had the highest human trichinosis-infection rates in the world, despite the development and use of effective methods for trichinosis control in other countries. In fact, the first director-general of the World Health Organization spoke bluntly to our national trichinosis problem in the same terms we Americans find it so easy to use in describing the disease problems of *other* countries:

There are things that natives do not see that people from outside do see. There is, for instance, the problem in the United States of America of trichinosis, which is regarded with astonishment and horror by many other people in many other countries. It may interest you to know that when travelers come to the United States from European countries their doctors warn them that under no circumstances should they eat pork of any kind because this country in that field is regarded as quite un-civilized by many other countries. This is just a fact. There is no other well-developed country which allows trichinosis among its hogs as this country does, affecting the health literally of millions of people all the time. In no other country would people be allowed to feed raw garbage to their hogs, but there is a sacred cow in this country and its name is business, and this has not been effectively approached, I understand, by the health authorities in this country up to this time. It has been dealt with, and effectively, by every other country which even approaches this country in terms of social and economic development.

Although there are now some requirements for garbage-cooking in the United States, this trichinosis problem still prevents us from safely eating otherwise excellent smoked yet uncooked hams and other pork products, unlike western Europeans. Consider this: in 1964, 482 middle western swine carcasses destined for Portugal were inspected for trichinosis (a routine practice in Europe but long opposed by meat-packers in the United States and therefore not carried out here) under the terms of the export contract. Three of these pigs were found to be infected with *Trichinella*, one of them with 4,361 worms for each *gram* of muscle; that is, an astronomical 1.6 million worms per pound of pork! Considering that each *Trichinella* worm can be seen with the naked eye, that pig was more worms than meat. In fact, its infection level was 4 times that ever detected in any pig before anywhere in the world. American consumers should legiti-mately question just how many infected swine like that one pass unin-spected into our food chain each year, despite long veterinary efforts to require inspection, and are converted into possibly hundreds and thousands of packages of sausage meat. Fortunately, *thorough* cooking kills trichinae, but pork dishes must *never* be tasted during their preparation. In the United States, another danger from eating undercooked pork is toxo-plasmosis.

In considering in this chapter the nutritional value of different parts of the hog, comparison is made with fresh pork ham of the "medium fat class" (all nutritional data refer to percent composition of the raw "edible portion" only). Such hams are protein 15.9 percent, fat 26.6 percent, calcium 0.009 percent, phosphorus 0.178 percent, iron 0.0024 percent, thiamine 0.00077 percent, riboflavin 0.00019 percent and niacin 0.0041 percent.

THE WHOLE CARCASS

A roasted whole pig is deservedly a favored community institution in two areas of the United States—the South and Hawaii—and whole suckling pigs are still enjoyed by some ethnic groups who are not too far removed from their original homelands. On the other hand, many Americans regard the recognizable pig served on a tray with an apple in its mouth and cherries in its eye sockets as psychologically offensive, the carryover of a nearly barbarous custom. These people may object to pork only when it is identifiable as an actual animal. This is surely an irrational form of sublimation. For if this sentimental form of prejudice can be overcome, few examples of holiday or party fare *are* more festive or provide more delicious eating than does a whole pig roast. What a delightful alternative to our ubiquitous holiday turkey.

This regional American recipe was provided by a master Alabama barbecue chef, Jack Wilson. It deserves to become a national institution. It and the second recipe are good starting points for cooking whole pigs because the head is not used and hence the recognition problem is less for the diner.

BARBECUED PIG / SOUTHERN UNITED STATES

Take a dressed 125-lb. hog (minus the head). From the inside partially split the backbone from the shoulders to the pelvis so that the beast can be opened up flat. Place it skin-side up on a large piece of chicken wire. The barbecue pit should contain charcoal or coals from an oak or hickory fire. The grill should be in place and allowed to get hot before the hog on its wire cradle is put on. (The temperature of the grill should be such that it is just possible to hold your hand immediately above it.) This temperature must be maintained during the entire cooking process. After about 8 hours (or when you can feel heat when you place your hand on the upper surface of the hog's hams and shoulders) turn the hog over. This is done most easily by covering it with another piece of chicken wire and carefully inverting the two layers of wire. Care must be taken to prevent the ribs from falling out. Continue to cook for 2 to 3 hours, maintaining the heat as before, but now "mop" the hog thoroughly every 15 to 20 minutes with the following sauce (this process should use all of the sauce): mix 1 gal. cider vinegar, 15 oz. Worcestershire sauce, 15 oz. A-1 sauce, 1 small Lowry's seasoned salt, 4 lemons (juice and grated rinds), a handful of pepper, and two handfuls of salt.

As the hog is cut up for serving, mix the meat with the following serving sauce: Prepare the same quantity of the above basting sauce, but add to it 2 gal. catsup, 1/2 lb. brown sugar, 1 oz. paprika, and several heads of crushed garlic. Bring to a boil and simmer awhile before serving.

Perhaps an even more festive and quite different taste treat is provided by cooking a whole hog in an *imu*, or ground oven, as is done in Hawaii. About it can be created a magnificent backyard luau. (See Elizabeth Sook Wha Ahn Toupin's *Hawaiian Cookbook and Backyard Luau.*)

Kalua PIG, / HAWAII

To prepare your own *imu*, dig a hole 4 ft. to 5 ft. long, 4 ft. wide, and 3 ft. deep. Drive a thick pole into the center of the hole (far enough so that it stands). Place ample kindling around the pole and lots of logs on top of the kindling. The upper surface of the wood should be more or less level. Then on top of the logs place many smooth stones, each about 4 in. to 6 in. in diameter. Round, porous lava stones are preferred, but small cobblestones or others will do. Pull out the center pole and light the kindling by inserting into the hole a torch made of a rag-wrapped stick dipped in kerosene.

Burn the fire for 4 to 5 hours or until the stones are white hot (adding some more wood, if needed). Remove the stones for the cavities of the pig with tongs and level the others out in the bottom of the *imu*. Put a layer of split banana trunks or other small green logs (of a type that will not give an objectionable flavor to the meat) over the stones. The *imu* is now ready to receive the cradled pig.

The skin of a whole, dressed hog is slashed all over with a sharp knife; be careful to cut into the skin but not through it. Coarse salt is rubbed into these slits, and a generous quantity of salt also is sprinkled inside. The pig is placed on its back in a cradle or sling of chicken wire that is first lined with banana or *ti* leaves or with wet corn shucks. Hot *imu* stones are placed within its body cavities. The pig's legs are tied together with wire and the cradled beast is lowered into the previously prepared *imu*.

After the pig is in place it may be surrounded by fowl, fish, yams, bananas, or other suitable foods wrapped in *ti* leaf or corn shuck packages. All of the food then is covered with another piece of chicken wire and a thick layer of banana or *ti* leaves. Moist burlap sacks then envelop the whole, being carefully placed so that the food is well protected from the sand. The sand or dirt is shoveled in and the *imu* is forgotten for about 5 hours.

When it is time to eat, the *imu* is uncovered carefully, layer by layer, and the pig removed by lifting out its chicken-wire cradle. For serving, the meat is torn into portion-sized chunks, or the whole animal is surrounded on the ground by the guests who just reach in.

Young, milk-fed pigs, calves, and lambs are important items of diet for many of the world's peoples, but even real milk-fed veal is rarely eaten in the United States. Suckling pigs are available from most specialty butchers, however, and are so readily prepared in the ordinary kitchen that it is surprising they do not enjoy more general popularity, at least as holiday fare. I suspect that the reason (in addition to an irrational rejection because the meat obviously is the animal) is unfamiliarity and lack of knowledge of how to roast a whole pig. Of the very large variety of recipes worldwide to choose from, I have selected 5 quite different and very good approaches.

The simplest is from Spain; it is a dish frequently encountered there in restaurants as well as in homes.

ROAST SUCKLING PIG (*Cochinillo asado*) / SPAIN

Rub the body cavity of a suckling pig with a generous amount of crushed garlic and put inside a handful or two of chopped parsley, a BOUQUET GARNI, and some chopped onions. Salt and pepper the outside and place the pig in a roasting pan. Cover the bottom of the pan with white wine and water (1:1). Put some pieces of lard on the top of the animal, roast in a 350°F oven for an hour, baste well with olive oil, and continue to baste frequently with oil and the drippings until the pig is crisp and golden brown.

In this German recipe, the pig is stuffed and greater attention is given to preparing it for the diners' admiration.

RHINELAND SUCKLING PIG *(Rheinisches Spanferkel)* / GERMANY

Stuff a salted and peppered suckling pig with the following mixture: the ground liver, heart, and kidneys of the pig; chopped onions, parsley, and thyme previously sautéed in butter; some rolls soaked in milk and squeezed dry; some beaten eggs, nutmeg, and Madeira. Sew up the opening. Tuck the forefeet into slits cut on either side of the neck. Put the pig top-side up on a rack with the hind legs stretched out behind (a block of wood may be tied between the hind legs to keep them straight, and another put between the jaws). Wrap the ears, tail, and snout with foil and brush the pig with a mixture of melted butter and beer. Roast at 350°F, basting frequently with the drippings and more beer and butter until crisp and well browned.

Two other traditional German stuffings are sliced apples mixed with red currants, sugar, and lemon juice or raw sauerkraut with sausages, lean bacon, and juniper berries.

This third recipe is a magnificent Chinese one from the Chou dynasty (1027–256 B.C.). It uses an ancient approach to cooking meat and poultry by encasing it tightly in its own clay "oven," a method that deserves revival.

SUCKLING PIG *(Siu yu jiu)* / China

The pig is stuffed with fresh Chinese dates (for which another fruit might be substituted), then wrapped in straw matting, tied, and the whole encased in clay. The pig then is baked in a ground oven (or ordinary oven at 325°F) for about 5 hours. The clay also bakes in the process and the juices are completely sealed in. To serve, break the clay shell. Traditionally, the cracklings are then removed and ground with rice flour to a gruel consistency. This gruel is mixed with the dates, made into balls, and fried in deep, hot lard. Some of the pork is cut into pieces. These are put in a pot with mixed Chinese herbs and spices and steamed for 3 days (that's authentic but unnecessary). The roast meat then is taken with these two accompaniments. For greater simplicity (and quicker eating!) one might omit the steamed dish altogether.

This is even a fancier way to do a suckling pig. When deboned, the stuffed pig becomes essentially a magnificent sausage that can be displayed, then sliced through for very attractive serving.

STUFFED SUCKLING PIG OCCITANIAN STYLE
(Porcelet étoffe à l'occitane) / FRANCE

Make a midline incision in the pig's abdomen and through it remove
the abdominal and thoracic viscera. Extend the incision to the throat,
cutting down to the sternum, and to the pelvis. Carefully split the
sternum and the pelvis with a strong knife or saw and debone the pig
carefully, dissecting the skin, and as much of the attached muscles as
possible, from the ribs and the pelvic bones. Disjoint the spinal column
near the head and near the beginning of the tail and continue to dissect
out and remove the backbone and rib cage. Disjoint the femurs from
the pelvis and also the humeri from the scapulas. Dissect out and
remove the pelvic bones and the scapulas. Great care must be taken in
this whole process not to nick the pig's skin, which should be intact.
The leg and head bones are left in. Sprinkle the inside of the pig with
brandy, salt, and sausage spices as desired.

The stuffing is prepared as follows: slice the liver and extra pig's or
calf's liver and brown them quickly in hot butter. Prepare similarly the
pig's kidneys and heart and some lamb's or calf's sweetbreads. Coarsely
chop the meats and mix them together. In the same pan fry in butter
chopped onions, shallots, and mushrooms. Add crushed garlic and a
glass of white wine, reduce, and add about 2 C of rich veal, beef, or
chicken stock. To this boiling mixture add some pitted green olives and
allow the mixture to cool. Mix it with sausage meat, desired spices, pork
cracklings, and chopped parsley. Mix in enough beaten eggs to thor-
oughly bind the stuffing and some brandy; stuff the pig full with this
mixture (the amount of sausage meat should be sufficient to do this).
Skewer and sew up the opening, forming the pig to its normal shape. In
the refrigerator marinate the whole pig for 24 hours in a mixture of oil,
brandy, sliced carrots, sliced onions, chopped parsley and thyme,
crushed garlic and bay leaves, and the sausage spices. Baste often.

To cook, place the stuffed pig in a large braising pan on a bed of
drained vegetables from the marinade. Paint the skin of the pig well
with melted lard, cover the pan, and cook on a low flame until the
onions start to brown. Add several glasses of white wine, some brown
gravy, and a BOUQUET GARNI. Roast uncovered in the oven until the skin
is crisp and brown.

Untruss, arrange the pig on a warm serving platter, and garnish with
crépinettes, blood sausages, and the vegetables from the roasting pan.
Pass the strained sauce.

The pig is sliced across so that a slice of pork and the enclosed
stuffing are served in one piece.

Last, this somewhat similar presentation is simmered rather than roasted.

BOILED SUCKLING PIG IN HORSERADISH SAUCE *(Porosenok tushennyi)* / RUSSIA

Bone out a suckling pig (as above) and stuff it not too full with alternating layers of the following: (1) forcemeat of finely chopped veal, bread soaked in milk and squeezed dry, lightly fried chopped onion, nutmeg, salt, pepper, and beaten eggs; (2) thin boiled ham slices; (3) thin boiled tongue slices; and (4) sliced omelets made with chopped parsley. Sew up the pig, wrap it in a clean napkin or other cloth, and tie it into its natural shape. Add the pig bones to a large kettle, place the pig on top, cover with cold water, bring to a boil, and simmer covered for about 1–1/2 to 2 hours (or until a wood skewer easily penetrates the meat). Carefully remove and unwrap the pig, place it on a platter, and allow it to set (about 20 minutes). Slice across the beast and serve the slices with the following sauce: to a warm béchamel sauce add grated horseradish that was sautéed lightly in butter, a little sugar and vinegar (1:1) and salt and bring to a boil. Stir in a generous amount of sour cream.

MUSCLE MEAT

A word is in order on what to look for in pork flesh. In general, good-quality pork has bright-colored, fine-grained flesh without excessive fat. The carcass should be well-rounded, with a smooth, bruise-free skin. Pork is graded U.S. no. 1, 2, or 3, "medium," and "cull."

The diet of swine is reflected both in the flavor of the meat and the characteristics of the fat. Corn-fed hogs have hard, white fat and firm pink flesh, while the fat of forage-fed hogs is usually yellowish and may not completely harden even upon chilling. Peanut-fed pigs, from which Virginia's famous Smithfield hams are made, have liquid or semifluid fat, as well as a very characteristic flavor. Some European swine are fattened upon acorns or other special items of diet in order to give their meat other distinctive flavors.

Traditionally, swine raised in the United States have been of the fatty (or lard) type, while some European pork preferences have tended more to the lean, or bacon-type, hog. However, concern about excess weight and cholesterol intake by Americans is beginning to change this preference. The difference between lard-type and bacon-type pork is particularly noticeable in terms of how much real meat is left after cooking spareribs or bacon.

HEAD

THE meat from the hog's head can be used for making excellent head-cheeses, or more elegant dishes may be prepared as party fare that resemble the original head. For these latter, however, the recognition prejudice must obviously be cast aside.

Wild swine are not uncommon in California, Hawaii, Florida, and the Great Smoky Mountains. Some are feral descendants of once domesticated swine, while in California the true European wild boar also is found plus cross-bred boars and feral swine.

Wild boar's head in the French style is a classic dish, but the head of a domestic hog can be substituted.

BOAR'S HEAD (*Hure de sanglier*) / FRANCE

First dehair the head thoroughly by singeing and scraping. Then carefully skin the head in one piece, being sure not to nick it with the knife. Cut all of the meat from the skull and skin into a 1-in. dice. Cook and skin the tongue and 5 additional pork tongues; dice them, too. Season this head meat, the tongues, and the skin with salt, pepper, preferred sausage spices, thyme, crushed bay leaf, and finely macerated onions and carrots. Rub this mixture into the meat well and allow it to stand overnight in a cool place. Cut the ears from the skin and save them.

Cut boned-out chicken meat into a large dice (there should be about 1–1/2 lbs.) and similarly dice 1–1/2 lbs. of ham, 1 lb. of fatty bacon, and 3/4 lb. of truffles, if available, or mushrooms. Mix all of these ingredients with a generous quantity of BLANCHED pistachio nuts, the boar meat, and the tongue meat. Moisten the mixture with brandy and allow it to stand several hours. Thoroughly mix in about 9 lbs. of good-quality pork sausage meat and 4 beaten eggs.

Soak a large cloth in cold water and wring it out. Spread the boar's head skin on the cloth (outer surface down) and put the stuffing into the middle of the skin. Fold the skin over the stuffing and shape it to resemble the original head. Place it in a large kettle, cover with a stock rich in gelatin made from bones of the boar's head, the chicken

carcasses, and other bones and trimmings. Simmer the boar's head for
4–1/2 hours. Add the ears for the last hour.

Drain the wrapped head and allow it to stand for about a half hour.
Carefully remove and wash the cloth, wring it out, and rewrap, retie,
and reshape the head. Allow the wrapped head to cool in the refrigerator
for at least 12 hours. Untie the head and carefully place it on a bed of
rice on a platter. Skewer the ears in place, insert the tusks, and use
hard-boiled egg whites and slices of mushrooms, or cherries, for the
eyes. Coat the entire head with a layer of dissolved gelatin. Another
layer of golden bread crumbs also is sometimes patted into the almost set
gelatin. Decorate the platter further, if desired, and you have a unique
dish truly fit for a king.

Or, for much less effort and simpler fare, try this interesting Irish
version.

Pig's Face and Cabbage / Ireland

Cut the meat from one side of a pig's head in one piece. Soak it in cold
water overnight and boil it (15 minutes per lb.) with a head of cabbage.
Score the skin and bake the face, skin-side up, in a 350°F oven until the
cracklings are crisp and well browned. The drained cabbage is chopped
and arranged on a platter about the face and served with a sauce made
with the pan drippings.

Bath, England, was once renowned for a similar salted and smoked
dish called Bath Chap.

Pig's head meat, rich in gelatin, can also be the basis for cold, jellied
loaves or headcheeses.

Headcheese *(Sylte)* / Norway

Split a pig's head in two. Soak it in running cold water for 3 days and
then scrub it well. Simmer the head in salted water for about an hour
and then skin it. Return the head to the stock, add a pound each of pork
and veal, and simmer until the head meat falls easily from the bones.
Separate the meat. Line a large bowl with a piece of cotton cloth. Cover
the bottom with pieces of the sliced pork skin. Add layers of the meat
and pork fat and sprinkle each layer with the concentrated gelatin stock,

salt, pepper, powdered allspice, and powdered cloves. Cover with some more of the sliced skin. Gather the cloth tightly and tie the sack snugly. Return the sack to the stock pot and simmer it for another 1/2 hour. Turn off the heat, cover with a disk of wood, and weight it heavily for 24 hours. Remove the sack and immerse it in strong cold brine (1 lb. salt: 2 qts. water) for 5 days. The cloth is removed for slicing, but the *sylte* may be kept in the brine for weeks in a cold place once the cloth is replaced.

And, as for many foods, the French can often come up with the ultimate version.

BOAR'S HEAD WITH PISTACHIOS *(Hure à la pistache)* / FRANCE

Remove the ears, tongue, brain, and excess fat from a pig's head. Soak the head, the tongue, and some extra calve's tongues in brine for 4 days. Wrap the head in a cloth and simmer it in a large kettle of boiling water for about 5 hours. For the last 3 hours add the tongues to the pot. Remove the skin of the head in one piece, if possible, and lay it, inside-up, on a large napkin or piece of muslin. Cut the meat from the head and the skinned tongues into long strips. Arrange parallel layers of meat strips on the skin, alternating pork and tongue meats. Dust them with a mixture of ground white pepper, nutmeg, ginger, and cloves and sprinkle with chopped pistachio nuts. Truffles or other ingredients also may be added as preferred. Repeat this process until all the meat is used. Fold the skin about the meat, tie the napkin about the skin tightly, and return the potted head to the boiling stock in the kettle and simmer for an hour. Remove the meat, carefully undo the cloth, and press the potted head into a brawn mold (a large bowl will do). Weight it and allow the meat to cool and congeal.

The possibilities for pig's head do not begin and end, however, with charcuterie. Here is a hearty, indigenous hog's-head stew from the South that is well designed to stick to one's ribs. It is another Alabama recipe supplied by Jack Wilson.

HOG'S-HEAD STEW / SOUTHERN UNITED STATES

Put in a big kettle a hog's head, 4 lbs. of boned pork, 2 lbs. of stew beef, and a hen. Cover with water and boil until the bones can be easily removed. Return the meat to the pot, add 5 lbs. of onions and 3 gal. of tomatoes, and simmer until the meat falls apart. Add 10 lbs. of diced Idaho potatoes, 3 handfuls of salt, 1 handful of black pepper, 1 bottle of Worcestershire sauce, 1 bottle of A-1 sauce, 1 small Lawry's seasoned salt, and 1 qt. cider vinegar and simmer until the potatoes are done. Add crumbled crackers to thicken if needed.

PIG'S SNOUT

THIS is a very cheap cut of pork that is used primarily for sausages and other charcuterie.

PIG-ORGAN SAUSAGES *(Kiszka z krwią)* / POLAND

Simmer some pigs' snouts, some split pigs' feet, and pieces of pork in salted water containing an onion and some peppercorns. Scald an amount of pork liver approximately equal to the rest of the meat and add this water to the pork stock. Remove the meat from the bones and grind it and the liver in a meat grinder. To the stock pot add 2 chopped onions and 2 lbs. of coarse buckwheat grits (previously washed) for every pound of liver used in the recipe. Cook about 1/2 hour and add the chopped meat, some crushed allspice, and some marjoram and continue cooking until the grits are tender. (Add more water if the mixture becomes too dry.) Salt and pepper to taste. Remove the pot from the heat and cool. Stir in 1 cup of pig's blood per pound of liver used and stuff this mixture into sausage casings. Tie into convenient lengths and simmer the sausages in boiling water for about 20 minutes. Serve cold or hot, the latter by slicing and frying in butter until brown.

Pig snouts are also a principal ingredient of a Brazilian *feijoada*.

PORK AND BEANS *(Feijoada)* / BRAZIL

Wash black beans and allow them to stand in cold water. Cook them until soft. Slowly fry some seasoned pigs' snouts, feet, and ears and Portuguese sausages until nicely browned. Drain the fat. Add the meat to the beans, bring to a boil, and simmer for an hour. Correct the seasoning, skim off any fat, and serve.

TONGUES AND JOWLS

PIG'S tongues may be prepared by the recipes given for beef or lamb tongue. The protein content of pig's tongue is slightly higher, while its fat content is only slightly over one-half that of fresh ham. The jowls, or cheeks, of the pig are a major sausage ingredient and have always been particularly valued also as cheap cuts of pork in the southern United States. This is a fancy version.

PIG JOWLS AND GREENS / UNITED STATES

Fry flattened "cutlets" of pig jowls in foaming butter. Salt, pepper, and dust with flour. Pour over the meat a mixture of onion juice and Worcestershire. Arrange apple slices around the meat and simmer, covered, for about 45 minutes. Add a little water if it tends to dry out. Remove the meat and apple slices to a hot platter and prepare a gravy from the pan drippings, flour, and water. Surround the meat and apples with boiled turnip greens and serve them and the gravy with grits.

EARS

PERHAPS you cannot make a silk purse out of a sow's ear, but you can make some tasty hors d'oeuvres or a supper dish.

Basic Preparation

Clean the ears and soak them in cold water for 4 hours.

PIGS' EARS (Schweinsohren) / GERMANY

Simmer the presoaked ears in clean water for 2 hours and then dry them. Brush with melted butter; season with nutmeg, chopped marjoram, salt, and pepper. Coat with bread crumbs and fry until golden brown in hot lard. Serve with caper sauce.

GRILLED PIGS' EARS (Oreilles de porc grillées) / FRANCE

In this French variation, cut the simmered ears in half lengthwise, dip them in melted butter, then in bread crumbs, and put them in a hot oven until crisply done.

Or for *au diable,* cool the simmered ears, split them lengthwise, brush them with Dijon mustard, dip in melted butter, then bread crumbs, and crisp in the oven as above. Serve with sauce diable.

Pigs' ears are also a traditional garnish for other dishes or make good soups.

PEA SOUP WITH PIGS' EARS *(Erbsensuppe mit Schweinsohren* / GERMANY

Prepare a dried split-pea soup seasoned with marjoram or thyme. Cook some presoaked pigs' ears in the soup until they are tender. Cut them into thin slices and return to the soup.

PIGS' EARS AND SAUERKRAUT *(Schweinsohren und Sauerkraut)* / GERMANY

Simmer presoaked, salted, and peppered ears for 2 hours in sauerkraut containing some caraway seeds, or simmer with cabbage.
    A French variant of this is to cook the ears with presoaked lentils, sautéed onions, chopped carrots, salt, pepper, a clove, and a BOUQUET GARNI, covered with water. Serve as with the *Erbsensuppe.*

MOCK TURTLE SOUP / ENGLAND

Simmer some large presoaked pigs' ears in water overnight with a clove-stuck onion, a bunch of herbs (marjoram, basil, and thyme), and a little vinegar. Allow to cool; skim off the fat and remove and skin the ears. Cut them into thin strips. Strain the stock through muslin and reduce it well over a brisk heat. Season it with mace, white pepper, salt, lemon juice, and a glass of sherry. Add the ear strips and serve hot.

BRAINS

PIGS' brains can be prepared by the recipes given for calf's or lamb's brains. They have two-thirds the protein and about one-third the fat of fresh ham.

Basic Preparation

Soak the brain in ice water for 4 hours and peel off the membranes. Blanch it for 15 to 20 minutes in salted boiling water containing a little lemon juice or vinegar and preferred herbs. Chill in ice water.

PUFF PASTRY CUPS WITH CREAMED BRAINS *(Bouchées à la reine)* / FRANCE

Cook sliced mushrooms in béchamel sauce, add diced, prepared pig's brain (and cooked sweetbreads and chicken, if desired), and then some heavy cream. Stir in a bit of lemon juice and correct the seasoning. Serve in hot VOL-AU-VENT.

For the fully emancipated brain devotee this recipe, like the Colombian one for calf brains, provides the litmus test.

PIG'S BRAINS *(Fai ai o le pua'a)* / SAMOA

A pig's brain is wrapped in banana leaves (or wet corn shucks) and roasted in an *umu,* or ground oven. It is salted after cooking. This is suitable accompaniment for *Kalua* pig or other luau dishes; it can be prepared in an ordinary oven.

SKIN

THE best parts of a pork roast for many are the cracklings, or roasted skin. Pork skin makes up a little over 6 percent of the carcass weight and is inexpensive. These two very flavorful tidbits can be prepared easily as a garnish for other dishes or an excellent hors d'oeuvres.

FRIED PORK SKINS *(Chicharones)* / CUBA

Cut a piece of pork skin into squares or diamonds and deep-fry them at about 370°F until crisp and brown.

This can, of course, also be done in the oven, as in this French recipe.

BAKED PORK SKINS *(Grattons)* / FRANCE

Cut a piece of pigskin with a thick fat layer attached into 3-in. squares. Score the *fat* side of each into small diamonds. Put the skin squares fat-side down into a heavy pan, the bottom of which is covered with melted lard. Bake in a 275°F oven for about 4 hours . Turn the heat up until the cracklings reach golden crisp doneness. Drain and salt.

Cracklings are also ground up (in a blender) and added to this popular Filipino dish as a distinctive flavoring. The enterprising cook could think of other recipes that ground cracklings would similarly enhance.

"LONG RICE" WITH SHRIMP *(Pancit "luglug")* / PHILIPPINES

Fry a whole head of crushed garlic in a little lard. Fry some sliced boiled pork in the same pan. Add cubes of TOFU, some peeled shrimp, and about ½ C of shrimp juice (ground and strained shrimp shells and heads), cover, and boil. Add Chinese celery cut in 1/2-in. pieces, salt, and pepper. In another pan color 1–1/2 C shrimp juice red with ANATTO water. Thicken it with flour or cornstarch and water. Salt and pepper to taste.

Cook presoaked "LONG RICE" in a large amount of water, drain, and arrange it in a flat serving bowl. Cover the "long rice" with the red sauce, then the pork-shrimp mixture, then sprinkle with finely flaked smoked fish *(tinapa)* and powdered, crisp pork cracklings. Garnish with slices of hard-cooked eggs, celery leaves, sliced green onions, and slices of seeded, peeled lemon. Serve with lemon juice and boiled *patis* sauce from *bagoong*.

NECK

PORK necks are particularly inexpensive sausage meat or provide the basis for meat balls like these.

PIG'S-NECK SAUSAGES *(Attereaux)* / FRANCE

Chop equal amounts of pig neck meat and pig liver into bean-sized pieces. Mix with beaten egg, a little vinegar, saltpeter, paprika, salt, and pepper. Form into balls and wrap each in a piece of pig caul. Place in a deep, ovenproof dish and half-cover with a dry white wine. Add garlic, a clove or two, an onion, and a BOUQUET GARNI. Marinate overnight, turning at least once. BRAISE them in the marinade.

They may also be used to prepare a hearty broth.

PIG'S-NECK SOUP *(Orjaleves)* / HUNGARY

Cut up a pig's neck and cover it with water in a large kettle. Boil for an hour, then add sliced onions, kohlrabi, celery root, carrots, a number of

black peppercorns, salt, and some parsley. Simmer until the meat falls
from the bones and disintegrates. Chill and skim off the fat. Strain the
soup, reheat it, and serve with pork liver dumplings.

FEET

PIG'S feet are mostly skin, bones, and cartilage, but largely because of that
their cooked meat is particularly flavorful. Because pickled pig's feet once
graced most bar counters in America, perhaps this most familiar way to
serve this versatile meat should be our point of departure. Pickled pig's feet
have 20 percent more protein than fresh ham and only 3 percent as much
fat. Most European countries have their version; this one is from Den-
mark.

PIG'S-FEET BRAWN *(Sylte svine labber)* / DENMARK

Simmer cleaned pig's feet in salted water until the meat is tender. Put
them in a crock or jar and cover with a boiling marinade of vinegar and
water (2:1) to which were added sugar, some peppercorns, whole cloves,
whole allspice, and salt. Cool and refrigerate for at least a day or two
before serving.

This is quite different, but for those whose adeptness with chopsticks
allows for nibbling from the bones, this sweet-sour dish is certain to please.

PIG'S FEET *(Jiu tiao)* / CHINA

Chop fresh pig's feet into small pieces and boil them until tender.
Drain and retain the broth. Stir-fry some chopped garlic and chopped
fresh ginger in a little oil until slightly browned. Add the pig's feet and
stir-fry 5 minutes more. Add a mixture of 2 T molasses, 3 T vinegar,
and 2 T soy sauce, stir, and sprinkle with 1 t flour. Add a little broth,
stir, and simmer a few minutes.

For another version of sweet-sour pig's feet, this is also worth trying.

PIG'S FEET WITH BANANAS *(Paksiw na pata)* / PHILIPPINES

Clean and cut up several pig's feet and sections of the lower leg. Cover with water. Add vinegar, brown sugar, salt, soy sauce, pepper, a bay leaf, oregano, cloves, and garlic and simmer until the meat is tender. Add 4 fried plantains or firm bananas (cut in pieces) and simmer a few minutes more.

And yet another approach from the Orient produces this inexpensive combination of meat, seafood, and vegetables.

PIG'S FEET WITH *DAIKON* AND *KONBU* *(Tonsoku)* / JAPAN

Boil split and cut-up pig's feet until tender. Reserve the stock, chill it, and remove all the fat. Make a second stock with 3/4 C dried shrimp and water (boil 20 to 30 minutes and strain). Add this to the pork stock. Wash two strips of KONBU cut in half lengthwise. Tie knots in it at 3-in. intervals and cut it into pieces. Soak some dried mushrooms and remove the hard stems. Peel some DAIKON and cut it into quarters. Add the pig's feet, *konbu*, mushrooms, and *daikon* to the stock and cook for 10 minutes. Add a thumb-sized piece of ginger, 4 T SHOYU, 1 t coarse salt, and 2 T sake and cook over low heat for 1 hour, stirring occasionally. Serve with boiled watercress.

As a picnic main course, a barbecue accompaniment, or an unusual hors d'oeuvre, this also is excellent.

ROASTED PIG'S FEET *(Pieds de porc panés)* / FRANCE

Cook pig's feet in salted water containing an onion, a carrot, and a BOUQUET GARNI. Split the feet, brush with butter, roll in breadcrumbs, and grill slowly, or bake until crisp in a hot oven. They may be seasoned first with QUATRE-ÉPICES and served with hot mustard.

A jellied dish that resembles headcheese and could serve as a first course for dinner or as a luncheon dish is *galareta*.

JELLIED PIG'S FEET *(Galareta)* / POLAND

Split some washed pig's feet and cut a few pork shanks into pieces. Cover them with water and bring to a boil. Add some well-browned chopped onions, some chopped celery and chopped parsley, some whole garlic, allspice, and peppercorns and a few bay leaves. Simmer until the meat falls from the bones. Strain and pick out the bones and spices. Return the meat to the stock, add a little vinegar, correct for salt, and pour into a greased loaf pan or other mold. Refrigerate overnight, remove fat from the surface, unmold the jelly, and garnish it with cooked, fancily cut carrots, seeded lemon slices, quartered hard-cooked eggs, and parsley.

In diverse cuisines pig's feet also are stuffed to increase their relatively small amounts of edible tissue. Here are two variations.

STUFFED PIG'S FEET *(Ju tiao)* / CHINA

Put pig's feet with the lower part of the legs attached in cold salted water and bring to a boil. Remove them and carefully cut through the meat to the bone lengthwise on the plantar surfaces and remove the larger bones. Spread the legs and feet open and fill the cavities with long strips of loin pork previously marinated in soy, salt, sugar, and FIVE-SPICE. Bind them shut with string and put into a kettle. Cover with a boiling sauce of water, garlic, ginger, salt, five-spice and star anise. Add a little soy sauce, cover the kettle, and simmer for 4 to 5 hours. Unbind the drained legs and serve on a bed of spinach cooked in a good pork gravy.

STUFFED PIG'S FEET WITH LENTILS *(Zampone con lenticchie)* / ITALY

Prestuffed *zampone* (available from some Italian-American butchers) are pig's feet which have been boned as in the previous recipe and stuffed with a seasoned chopped pork. (In Moderna this is made from acorn-fattened pigs.) But they can readily be prepared at home starting as for *ju tiao* (above). After stuffing, they are boiled for about 1–1/2 to 2 hours and sliced. In the meantime a chopped onion is fried in olive oil until brown and some chopped bacon is added and cooked a bit more; finally some chopped celery, several cups of cooked lentils, and some of the *zampone* stock are added and the mixture cooked about 15 minutes more. The *zampone* is served over the lentils.

Feet are also combined with other cheap organ meats as in this English pig's-feet stew.

PIG'S PETTITOES / ENGLAND

Cut the heart, liver, and 1 lung of a pig into large pieces and boil them with split pig's feet for about 15 minutes. Remove the first 3 meats and chop them finely, allowing the feet to continue simmering until tender. Reduce the stock and prepare a thick sauce from some of it with a flour-and-lard ROUX. Add to this the chopped meats, a slice of lemon, and salt. Stir and cook gently for several minutes. Add a few egg yolks beaten with some nutmeg in a little milk and cook to thicken. Serve in a flat bowl surrounded with toast wedges and the split pig's feet on top.

And this cream of pig's feet and sauerkraut soup interestingly blends sweet-and-sour flavors in a rich stock.

PIG'S FEET AND SAUERKRAUT SOUP *(Kapuśniak)* / POLAND

Cook some cleaned and cut-up pig's feet in a quart of water until tender. Add some well-browned chopped onions, a quart of sauerkraut juice, and 1/4 C sugar. Blend in an electric blender an egg, 1 T flour, and 1 C of cream. Stir this mixture into the soup, bring to the boiling point, correct for salt, and serve with potato dumplings.

Finally, pig's feet are combined with a variety of other traditional meats and ingredients to produce this famous Swiss meal-in-one.

Generically related to an Alsatian *choucroute garnie*, this elaborate *Berner Platte* is prepared in four kettles and is assembled just before serving.

MIXED PLATTER BERN STYLE *(Berner Platte)* / GERMAN SWITZERLAND

In the first kettle sauté some chopped onions in bacon fat until golden. Add washed and drained sauerkraut, some crushed juniper berries, and some dry white wine. Cover the sauerkraut with thick pork chops (preferably smoked) and a good-sized piece or two of Canadian bacon or ham. Simmer covered for 1–1/2 hours, add any type of boiling sausages or a sausage ring, and simmer until they are done.

In the second kettle place some pig's feet or hocks, ears, and tongues. Add some chopped celery, carrots, and onions or leeks, cover the meat with water, season it with salt and pepper, and simmer until tender.

In the third kettle boil small peeled potatoes until tender and drain them.

And, finally, in the fourth kettle cook a generous quantity of green beans until still nicely crisp. Drain, season them, and toss with lots of butter.

Then assemble your creation. Place the drained sauerkraut on one heated platter, the green beans on the other. Artfully top the first with the pork chops, sliced sausages, and ham or Canadian bacon, and the second with the pig's feet, ears, and sliced tongue. Surround the beans with the potatoes and serve the *Platte* with dishes of hot mustard and sour pickles.

KNUCKLES

PIG'S knuckles may be prepared by most of the same recipes as pig's feet, and vice versa. Here is another.

FRIED PIG'S KNUCKLES *(Kirántott sertéscsülök)* / HUNGARY

Cover some cleaned pig's knuckles with water and boil for 10 minutes. Remove, cool, and skin. Return the knuckles to the stock, add salt, and simmer until the meat begins to fall from the bones. Dip pieces of the meat in beaten egg, coat them with bread crumbs, and fry them in lard until golden brown.

TAILS

PIGTAILS are perhaps not so gastronomically renowned as oxtails, but they do have their partisans and are another inexpensive source of high-quality protein.

PIGTAILS *(Queues de porc)* / FRANCE

Scald pigtails and immerse them in brine for 2 to 3 days. Put them into a kettle with clove-stuck onions, sliced leeks and carrots, peppercorns, a BOUQUET GARNI, and water to cover. Simmer for 2 hours. Cut into pieces and serve the tails on mashed potatoes with chopped parsley. Reduce some of the stock for a sauce.

Pigtails also may be cooked by any of the recipes for pig ears, or whenever bits and pieces of pork are required.

HEART

SO much for the pig's extremities. Let us now consider its more controversial internal organs. Prejudices against eating hearts or other organ meats of swine and others of our most common domestic animals range from mere avoidance to outright abhorrence. It is commonplace for Americans irrationally to reject all of these valuable items of diet out of hand without ever having tried most of them. Though reasons of flavor or texture are frequently given for these prejudices, their origin is almost invariably a feeling of disgust at the prospect of eating things like "guts" or "glands." The fact that organs of markedly differing tastes and textures often are lumped together in the imaginations of these avoiders is proof of this collective aversion. It is not uncommon, for example, to find people who believe that two such diverse meats as liver and tongue have the same "objectionable" taste.

Pork heart has a slightly higher protein content than fresh ham with only one-seventh its fat. It is also one-fourth richer in thiamine than pork liver.

The following recipe is an excellent initiation to what we Americans have come euphemistically to call "variety meats." It is served simply with rice.

PORK HEART WITH ORANGE SAUCE *(Cour de porc à l'orange)* / FRANCE

Brown some pig hearts, chopped onions, and a strip or two of lean bacon in butter and olive oil. Transfer the meat and onions to a casserole and, in the pan in which they were browned, prepare a browned butter-and-flour ROUX. Whisk in some stock and red wine to make a smooth sauce. Add crushed garlic, salt, pepper, and some bitter marmalade. Cook a bit and pour this sauce into the casserole. Simmer the hearts for about 1–1/2 hours or until tender.

Cut the hearts into thin slices and put into a shallow ovenproof dish. Reduce the sauce a bit, correct the seasoning, and add to it some orange juice, grated orange peel, and orange liqueur. Coat the heart slices with the sauce and return to the oven to warm. Sprinkle with chopped parsley and pass the rest of the sauce.

Equally good with plain rice is this Chinese recipe for stir-fried pig's heart and scallions.

STIR-FRIED HEART *(Nan chow sin)* / CHINA

Trim a pork or beef heart and cut into a 1/8-in. JULIENNE. Marinate it and some sections of scallions in a mixture of cornstarch in cold water, a little soy sauce, some sherry, sugar, salt, and minced ginger. Drain the meat and vegetables and stir-fry them in medium-hot oil. (If *pork* heart is used, it should be *thoroughly* cooked through.)

Filipinos prepare a number of rich stews combining heart with various other organ meats.

PORK-ORGAN PEPPERPOT *(Binagis)* / PHILIPPINES

Boil good-sized pieces of a pig's heart, pork meat, pork liver, and a pig's kidney until tender in a large kettle of water, Slice each. Sauté ample crushed garlic and sliced onions in oil. Add the pork meat and fry. Add the heart and kidney. Season with salt and add 3/4 C̆ vinegar. Bring to a boil and add the liver and some strips of sweet red pepper and hot red pepper.

And, as with many of the meats discussed here, quite original soups can also be prepared.

PORK HEART SOUP *(Zuppa di cuore di maiale)* / ITALY

Cut two pigs' hearts into small pieces and brown them and a little chopped bacon in lard in a soup kettle over a high flame. Add salt, pepper, a wineglass of dry red wine, rosemary, a crumbled bay leaf, a little tomato paste, and a little water. Simmer for about 15 minutes, add about a quart or so of water, cover, and simmer for about 1–1/4 hours more. The soup is served over toasted bread.

LUNGS

PIG'S lungs, like those of other species, are very cheap. Their protein content equals that of ham, but they contain virtually no fat and can be imaginatively prepared, as in this other Filipino mixed-organ stew with tomatoes.

STEWED PIG ORGANS *(Bopiz)* / PHILIPPINES

Boil pieces of pig's lungs until tender. Trim out the pieces of cartilage and chop with about half the quantity of raw pork liver and a pig's heart. Fry garlic and sliced onions in oil; then add a dozen quartered tomatoes. Add the meats and 1/2 C water (more or less) and cook until tender. Season with salt and pepper.

Somewhat similar is this other peasant stew from France, though this one incorporates wine plus different seasonings.

GARNISHED PIG'S HEART *(Ferchuse)* / FRANCE

Melt a pound of chopped pork fat in a heavy kettle. Turn the heat up very high and add the lungs, heart, and liver of a pig (all cut into about 1-in. cubes) and salt, pepper, and other spices, if desired. Brown the meat quickly and sprinkle it with about 3 heaping tablespoonfuls of flour. Stir until the flour is golden brown. Add enough red wine and stock (3:1) to just cover the meat. Bring to a quick boil, stir well, turn the heat down, add chopped shallots or onions, a number of cloves of crushed garlic, and a BOUQUET GARNI. Simmer for about an hour or until the heart is tender.

Lungs are referred to as lights in the southeastern United States, where simple but hearty meat meals like this are traditional.

PORK LIGHTS AND LIVER STEW / UNITED STATES

Parboil a pig's lungs for 20 minutes and cut them up. Place the pieces of lungs and a cut-up pork liver in a kettle and cover with water. Add chopped onions, chopped red peppers, and salt. Simmer until almost done, add pieces of potatoes and carrots and cook until tender. Thicken if necessary.

With somewhat more imagination, pig's lungs can also provide the meat filling for some very tasty stuffed dumplings.

PIG'S-LUNG DUMPLINGS FOR SOUP *(Malac tüdö galuska levesbe)* /
HUNGARY

Boil pieces of pig's lungs until tender and put through the fine blade of a
food chopper. Fry finely chopped onions in lard; add the chopped
lungs, some chopped parsley, salt, pepper, and marjoram and fry a bit
longer. Remove from heat and stir in some bread crumbs lightly
browned in lard. Use this mixture to fill raviolis made from regular pasta
dough. Cook in soup and serve.

Or they can be the basis for an unusual oriental soup course.

PIG'S-LUNG SOUP *(Jiu feh tan)* / CHINA

Simmer a pig's lung cut into slices in a generous amount of boiling
stock in a covered pot for 4 hours. Add shredded Chinese cabbage, some
grated ginger, sliced water chestnuts, and bamboo shoots and simmer 5
minutes more. Stir in salt and pepper to taste, a little sugar, and a little
soy sauce and simmer another 5 minutes. Almonds and lotus roots also
are added sometimes.

LIVER

PIG'S liver contains more connective tissue than calf's or lamb's liver and is
somewhat less delicate in flavor. Nevertheless, it is deserving of far more
common use than it sees in this country for no other reason than its
cheapness. Pork liver has even higher protein content than beef liver and
one-fourth more than fresh ham. It is also much richer in iron than beef
liver and is an excellent source of the B vitamins. It provides very good
barbecue fare simply grilled or baked.

SKEWERED AND GRILLED PORK LIVER
(Spiedini di fegato di maiale grigliati) / ITALY

Cubes of liver are wrapped in a piece of pig or lamb omentum and
skewered alternately with bay leaves and cubes of bread. These are
brushed with bacon fat and grilled over charcoal.

Or pork liver prepared and skewered as above also may be placed in
a greased baking dish, seasoned with salt and pepper, sprinkled with
olive oil, and baked in a 375°F oven about 10 minutes on a side. The
meat is sauced with some white wine mixed with the pan juices.

Or, grilled Tuscan style, the liver cubes are coated with a mixture of fine bread crumbs, crushed garlic, and fennel seeds. They are seasoned with salt and pepper, wrapped in pieces of pig's omentum, skewered, painted with pork fat, and grilled.

Similarly gentle treatments are afforded pig's liver by the Chinese, as in this stir-fried dish of liver and vegetables.

PIG'S LIVER WITH SPINACH *(Po tsai tsu kan)* / CHINA

Cut partly frozen pig's liver into a JULIENNE and BLANCH it about a minute. Coat the drained liver with the following sauce: thoroughly mix some soy sauce, sherry, and cornstarch (2:1:1) and stir in a little sugar and some minced ginger. In a WOK briefly stir-fry some 1-in. sections of scallions and some sectioned garlic cloves. Add the liver and stir-fry until it starts to brown. Add some presoaked dry mushrooms which have been cut into a fine JULIENNE. Continue to stir-fry about 2 minutes. Add a generous quantity of small, tender, stemmed spinach leaves and stir-fry until barely wilted.

More commonly, however, pig liver is marinated first in vinegar or subjected to other more robust treatment, as in these Polish and Filipino versions of liver and onions.

FRIED LIVER *(Wątroba)* / POLAND

Pour a cup of boiling vinegar over sliced pork liver and let it stand for a few minutes. Drain, season with salt and pepper, and coat with bread crumbs. Fry sliced onions in butter until golden, remove them, and fry the liver slices in the same pan. Serve the liver on a bed of onions, with or without a pork gravy. Beef liver may be prepared the same way.

BRAISED PORK LIVER *(Kilawin)* / PHILIPPINES

Soak sliced pork liver in vinegar, salt, and pepper. Sauté 6 cloves of crushed garlic in lard until light brown. Add some sliced onions and fry until golden. Add the liver. Press the liver to express the blood. Add some sliced pork and cook 5 minutes, continuing to press the meat with a spoon. Salt and pepper. Add vinegar and water (1:1) to cover and simmer 15 minutes or until tender and the sauce is thickened. Thicken further with cornstarch if necessary.

Perhaps the most common use of pig's liver is to prepare pâtés or sausages. This Italian *crostini*, for example, uses different seasonings than in the recipe already given for beef liver *crostini*.

Liver Paste *(Crostini)* / Italy

Mix chopped pork liver, some chopped anchovy fillets, chopped preserved peppers, and chopped garlic and fry in a little olive oil. Add marjoram, salt, and pepper and cook further until brown. Add a little water and cook 5 minutes more. Spread on bread triangles fried in butter.

Most European cuisines have their own variations on pork liver pâté. These are two others as examples.

Liver Loaf *(Leberkäse)* / Germany

In an electric blender thoroughly blend pieces of pig's liver and fat bacon (3:1) and some onion. Knead into this mixture some rolls previously soaked in milk and squeezed dry, some marjoram, salt, and pepper. Line a greased baking tin with short pie pastry into which some grated cheese has been incorporated. Fill the tin with the liver paste and cover with the cheese pastry and seal. Bake in a 350°F oven for about an hour and serve with a caper sauce.

Liver Pâté *(Lever postei)* / Norway

Soak sliced pork liver in some ACIDULATED cold WATER. Grind the drained liver with a little fresh pork, some onion, and some anchovy fillets several times through the finest blade of a food chopper. Mix in well a little milk, some beaten eggs, and enough cracker meal to form a soft, moist paste. Season with salt, pepper, and ground cloves. Fill loaf pans that have been well greased and lined with thin slices of fresh pork. Place in a pan of warm water and bake in a 350°F oven for about 1–3/4 hours. Unmold the loaf and serve it cold.

Such pâtés are served in Scandinavia in a variety of artful fashions. This traditional open-faced sandwich has always been a favorite of mine, partially because of its name.

Vet's Night Snack *(Dyrelägens natmad)* / Denmark

On a buttered slice of rye bread, place a layer of a Scandinavian liver pâté. Top it with a thin slice of salted meat *(fenalår* would do well) and then some finely chopped onions.

Similar preparations may be formed into croquettes and fried for serving as an hors d'oeuvre. These two recipes from Italy and Malaysia are very different.

Liver Balls *(Polpette di fegato)* / Italy

Mix chopped pork liver and chopped salt pork (in proportions of about 3:1) with some bread (previously soaked in water and squeezed), a little chopped parsley, some grated Parmesan, salt, and pepper. Bind with egg yolk (about 2 per lb. of meat), shape into balls, dip in beaten egg, roll in bread crumbs, and fry in butter until golden brown.

Pig Liver Balls / Malaysia

Mix 1 t powdered coriander, 1 T vinegar, 5 mashed onions, the squeezings from 1 C water mixed with tamarind (or orange or grapefruit) pulp, 1 t sugar, and 1 t salt. Marinate in this mixture for 1 hour a pig liver cut into slices and pricked with a fork. Then boil the liver in this marinade until the liquid is almost evaporated. Put this liver and about one-half as much lean pork through the fine blade of a food chopper. Add 1/2 t of ground star anise, 1/2 t of ground cinnamon, 1 t ground pepper, 2 beaten eggs, and some cornstarch and mix well. Roll into walnut-sized balls and fry in oil over a slow fire until thoroughly cooked through.

Simpler yet are these Welsh faggots that are baked and served for supper in their own gravy.

Faggots / Wales

Through the finest blade of a food chopper put a pig's liver, some suet, and several onions. Season with salt, pepper, and sage. Mix with enough bread crumbs to form easily into small dumplings. Bake these in a 350°F oven for 30 minutes and serve with a thin gravy prepared from the seasoned pan drippings and water.

In addition to frying, liver balls may also be simmered and served in soups or as the central ingredient of a boiled dinner.

LIVER DUMPLINGS (*Leberknödel*) / GERMANY

Knead together ground pig's liver, some rolls soaked in water and squeezed dry, some chopped onion, marjoram, salt, pepper, and beaten eggs (about 3 per lb. of liver). Form into small dumplings and add to boiling salted water containing an onion stuck with a clove and a bay leaf. Bring to a boil and simmer until the dumplings float to the surface. Serve with boiled cabbage and potatoes.

Liverwursts, or liver sausages, are also easily prepared at home if one has a sausage-stuffing attachment for the food chopper.

CHRISTMAS LIVER SAUSAGE (*Jul leverkorv*) / SWEDEN

Grind pork liver, fat pork (2:1), and some chopped onions several times through the fine blade of a food chopper. Salt and pepper and stir in a little sugar. Stuff sausage casings, tie off at 4-in. to 6-in. intervals, and simmer in salted water for 30 minutes. To serve, fry the sausages in butter.

SPLEEN

THE protein content of pig's spleen is slightly higher than that of fresh ham, while its fat content is about one-seventh. This hearty English country dish features baked pig's spleen plus most of its other innards.

PIG'S FRY / ENGLAND

Cut a pig's spleen, liver, kidneys, heart, brain, and a piece of its belly into small pieces. Dust them thoroughly with well-seasoned flour and put in a shallow baking dish. Add water almost to cover and some bacon fat. Bake in a 350°F oven for about an hour. Thicken the sauce, if necessary, with cornstarch and cold water and serve it with mashed potatoes, greens, and onions cooked with sage.

Still simpler is a Samoan mélange to accompany a whole pig or other luau fare.

ROASTED PIG ORGANS *(Totoga)* / SAMOA

The spleen, heart, kidneys, lungs, and coagulated blood of a pig are cut into small pieces, mixed, salted, and wrapped together in banana leaves or soaked corn husks. They then are covered with breadfruit leaves or wet burlap and baked in the ground oven.

STOMACH

WHILE tripe is a more widely known meat than pig's stomach, many interesting recipes for the latter are found in diverse cuisines. For one thing, pig's stomach is naturally made for stuffing, and it is not surprising that many peoples eat it that way. It has slightly higher protein content than fresh ham and about one-third its fat.

Basic Preparation

Pig's stomach must first be cleaned and BLANCHED. Cut the stomach open and wash it thoroughly in cold water. Dry with paper towels. Sprinkle flour onto its inner surface and thoroughly rub it in to remove the mucous membrane. Repeat this if necessary and scrape off any remaining mucus with a knife. Thoroughly wash the stomach again and then give it a final washing in ACIDULATED WATER. Place the cleaned meat in cold water in a large, heavy kettle and rapidly bring it to a boil. Discard this water and repeat the boiling process. The stomach then is ready to prepare.

Pig haggis was eaten by the Romans. They stuffed pigs' stomachs with a mixture of chopped pork and pigs' brains, eggs, and pine nuts seasoned with lovage, asafoetida, anise seed, ginger, rue, GARUM, and oil. The stuffed stomach then was rolled in brine-soaked bran and roasted. Romans also stuffed pig's stomach with ham, liver, fish roe, eggs, and fruit, all mixed into a paste. Here are some further possibilities for a really conversational main course.

PIG HAGGIS / IRELAND

Stuff a well-cleaned pig's stomach with a mixture of mashed potatoes, chopped onions, sage, salt, and pepper. Sew it up, drape it with fatty bacon, and roast at 350°F for at least 2 to 3 hours with frequent basting. Serve this haggis with applesauce and a pork gravy.

YRCHINS / ENGLAND

Stuff the cleaned stomachs of small pigs with a well-seasoned pork sausage meat, sew them up, drape with bacon, and roast them as above with frequent basting. Insert almond slivers all over the stomachs (so that they each look like a hedgehog or sea urchin), carefully ladle over all a thick batter of egg, flour, and pig blood, and return the stomachs to the oven to brown well. Sprinkle these "urchins" with chopped parsley and serve.

ROASTED HOG'S MAW / PENNSYLVANIA DUTCH

Make a 3-in. incision in the stomach where the esophagus joins, turn it inside out, and clean it as above. Stuff the stomach loosely with a mixture of seasoned sausage meat, bread, diced potatoes, chopped parsley, salt, and pepper. Sew it shut. Roast it for 2 to 3 hours.

STUFFED PIG'S STOMACH *(Töltött malac gyomor)* / HUNGARY

In a large kettle containing salted water boil for at least 2 hours a pig's head, some pork skin, several pounds of fat pig's cheek or other fat pork, an extra pig's tongue or two, and a couple of pig's knuckles. Remove the meat from the bones and cut it into 1-in. cubes. Put the skin through a food chopper and mix it with the meat. Add about a pint of pig's blood and enough fat from the surface of the cooking stock to make a moist and soft mixture. Season with salt, black pepper, paprika, and a generous amount of crushed garlic. Stuff this mixture into one or more cleaned pigs' stomachs, sew up the openings, and then simmer the stomach just *below* the boiling point for about 2–1/2 hours. Drain the stomach, prick it in several places, place a lightly weighted board on top of it, and allow it to cool. Instead of simmering, the stuffed stomach also may be smoked.

The Chinese also use pig's stomach as a meat and not merely a container. These three recipes are for slow simmering in a soy-based sauce, as a stir-fried dish with abalones and vegetables, and as the basis for a special soup garnished with quail eggs.

STEWED PIG'S STOMACH *(Hon tsao tsu tu)* / CHINA

Place 2 prepared pigs' stomachs in a heavy kettle. Just cover with boiling water. Add 2 T dark soy sauce, 1 T light soy sauce, 1 T sherry, a green onion, and 2 to 3 thin slices of ginger. Bring to a boil, cover the kettle, and simmer for 3 hours or until the meat is tender. Add a little sugar for the last 20 minutes of cooking. Cool the meat enough to handle, cut it into strips 1/2 in. by about 2–1/2 in. and serve it in the cooking stock.

PIG'S STOMACH AND ABALONE *(Tsu tu pao pi)* / CHINA

Cover a large, unopened can of abalone or a large fresh abalone with water and simmer it for 4 hours. Remove, cool, and save the liquid. Slice the abalone diagonally. Slice some water chestnuts. Soak a number of dried mushrooms and discard the hard stems. Combine 3 T Chinese oyster sauce with all but 1/4 C abalone liquid. Add abalone, water chestnuts, and 2 C sliced bamboo shoots. Cut a pig's stomach into strips 1/2 in. by 1–1/4 in. In a WOK momentarily stir-fry some chopped garlic and chopped ginger in oil. Add the stomach and stir-fry quickly. Add a mixture of 1 T soy, 2 t sherry, 2 t salt, and 2 t sugar and stir-fry 1 minute more. Add 2–1/2 C water and 1/4 C abalone liquid and simmer 5 minutes. Remove all to a deep pot and simmer 1 hour more. Add the mushrooms and simmer 30 minutes. Finally, add the abalone mixture and simmer several minutes more.

This soup is specially valued in China to stimulate the flow of a mother's milk.

PIG'S-STOMACH SOUP *(Tsu tu tan)* / CHINA

Place a prepared pig's stomach in a kettle of rich chicken stock. Add a few slices of ginger, half an onion, a piece of uncooked Chinese or Virginia ham, 1 T sherry, and 1 T light soy sauce. Cover and simmer for about 2 hours. Add some diced bamboo shoots and salt and simmer another hour or until tender. Add shelled, hard-boiled quail eggs during the last 30 minutes. Cut the meat into strips 2–1/2 in. by 1/2 in. and return it to the soup. Serve the soup with side dishes of light soy sauce for dipping the strips of meat.

INTESTINES

THE ancient use of the intestines of pigs, as well as of cattle and sheep, for casings to preserve a great variety of seasoned forcemeats is still their principal culinary use today. A whole book this size could easily be written on the great variety of regional sausages. It is impossible to do justice here to these possibilities, but assuredly the art of sausage making should be revived in many more American homes. It provides possibilities for imaginative uses of all kinds of meat scraps as well as for practically all organ meats and thus, like wine or cheese making, it is a particularly creative aspect of gastronomy.

The different classes of sausage casings are described in the chapter on beef (pages 56-57). Pork intestines have about 2/3 the protein of ham and a little less fat.

Basic Preparation

See page 57.

Some representative sausage recipes are given here. For additional sausages made from meats other than pork, see the index.

PORK SAUSAGE MEAT

Chop a mixture of lean and fat pork in desired proportions and mix it with salt and spices. Meats often used include head meat, cheeks, lips, snouts, damaged tongues, esophagus, diaphragm, stomach, and intestines. The binding qualities of most of these meats vary. This will determine the maximum proportions of different ingredients possible for certain types of sausages. For example, beef in general binds better than does pork. Nonmeat binders, such as raw egg, sometimes are added too. The chopping may be done coarsely with a knife, through food chopper blades varying in fineness, or in an electric blender that grinds the meat to a paste, depending on the type and consistency of sausage desired. Because of the danger of trichinosis, *never taste raw pork sausage meat during its preparation.*

A little cold water may be incorporated in the sausage meat; other commonly added ingredients include brandy, chopped truffles, crushed garlic, chopped lean beef, chopped fresh bacon, pimentos, and wine and saltpeter (to make the color pink and prevent botulism spores from germinating).

Common sausage spices include pepper, savory, coriander, thyme, bay leaf, cumin, marjoram, sage, cinnamon, chives, and juniper berries, alone or in combinations.

The sausage meat is stuffed into the rounds or middles of pigs, lambs, or cattle, depending on the diameter desired, and are twisted or tied off in different lengths. Pork sausages are sold fresh or poached, although some types first are dried in the air or in a low-temperature oven or are lightly smoked. See Sleight and Hull (1977) for smoking suggestions.

These are the usual fresh sausage links in the United States. Their protein content raw is about two-thirds that of fresh ham, and they usually have about twice the fat.

Pork Sausage Links *(Saucisses chipolatas)* / France

A pork sausage meat is stuffed into narrow rounds and twisted or tied off in 2-in. lengths.

This next is one of my favorite sausages.

Garlic Sausage *(Kielbasa)* / Poland

Coarsely chop pork and veal (3:1), add a little water, salt, pepper, whole mustard seeds, and crushed garlic (1 whole *head* per 2 lbs. of meat). Mix well, stuff prepared middles, tie off at about 6-in. lengths, and smoke. (They also can be covered with water in a baking dish and baked in a 350°F oven until the water has evaporated.) These very good sausages resemble German knockwurst, and their protein and fat contents are about the same as fresh ham.

Pork Sausage *(Kiszka)* / Poland

Coarsely chop pork, cover it with water, and boil until tender. Add marjoram, salt, and pepper. Add this meat stock to washed buckwheat grits (2 lbs. per 3 lbs. of meat) and simmer for a half hour or so. Mix the meat and buckwheat and stuff into prepared middles. Tie them off at about 4-in. lengths. Cook before serving.

Pork Sausage *(Chorizos)* / Spain

Blend together in small amounts in an electric blender a ground pig's liver and a fresh pork fillet, with an equal quantity of pork fat. (Alternatively, chop the meats coarsely, as is done usually in Mexico.) Add and blend in salt, cumin, coriander, sweet red peppers, a little cayenne, a few juniper berries, and a little tomato purée. Stuff into prepared pork rounds, tie off, rub with olive oil, and cold-smoke for 6 to 7 days. Juniper berries may be added occasionally to the ashes.

ROAST SAUSAGE *(Bratwurst)* / GERMANY

Finely grind veal and pork loin (1:2) several times through the finest blade of a food chopper. Add water (1 C per 3 lbs. of meat), salt, pepper, nutmeg, and mace. Stuff pork rounds and tie off. Cover with hot water, bring to a boil, remove from the fire, and let stand for 5 minutes. Drain, dip in milk, and grill over low heat until well browned and *thoroughly* cooked through.

WHITE PORK SAUSAGE *(Boudin blanc de porc)* / FRANCE

Put lean pork and fresh pork fat (4:7) through the fine blade of a food chopper and then blend to a smooth paste in an electric blender. Blend in butter (about 1/2 as much as the lean pork) or a mixture of butter and goose fat, eggs (4 per lb. of lean pork), cream (1 C per lb. of lean pork), and some chopped onions that have been fried in butter until soft. Add salt (about 5 t per lb. of lean pork), white pepper, and very little spice mixture. Stuff pig middles or rounds and poach them as for blood puddings.

TOULOUSE SAUSAGE *(Saucisse de Toulouse)* / FRANCE

Coarsely chop lean pork and hard pork fat (3:1). Mix in salt, white pepper, a little sugar, and a little saltpeter. Allow to stand in a cool place overnight. Stuff into rounds. These sausages may be poached or brushed with butter and grilled. They are traditional in the *cassoulets* of Toulouse.

HOMEMADE PIG INTESTINE SAUSAGE *(Andouilles de ménage)* / FRANCE

Cut the cleaned large intestines of a pig into thin strips. Add pieces of bacon (2 parts intestine to 1 of bacon). Belly pork may be substituted for all or part of the bacon and well-cleaned pig's stomach or calf's mesenteries for some or all of the intestines. Simmer the meat with a BOUQUET GARNI and an onion in salted water for 2 hours. Drain, and cut the meat into small pieces. Add some white wine, coarsely chopped and sautéed mushrooms, onions, and parsley, salt, pepper, and other seasonings as preferred. Other optional ingredients include egg yolks or a little much-reduced stock.

Stuff the cleaned middles of a pig with this mixture, tie it off at intervals of 4 in. to 8 in. Prick the sausages in several places and immerse them in rapidly boiling salted water containing a BOUQUET GARNI, some cloves of garlic, and some sliced carrots and onions. Cover the kettle and simmer gently for 2 hours. Allow the sausages to cool in the stock until easily handled, drain them, and leave them pressed under a weighted board in a cool place until cold. They are served slashed, painted with melted butter, and grilled, or they may be fried in butter.

HARD TRIPE SAUSAGE *(Andouilles de troyes)* / FRANCE

Soak a calf's mesentery and the udder of a young beef in cold water and then BLANCH them for about 30 minutes in boiling water. Dry them and cut into small pieces. Sauté a generous quantity of chopped mushrooms in butter with some chopped shallots and chopped parsley. Add pepper, salt, nutmeg, and a glass of white wine. Remove from the heat and thicken with 5 egg yolks. Stir in the meat and stuff the mixture into the colon or rectum of a pig. Tie off both ends and poach the sausage for about 45 minutes in stock and white wine (1:1). Allow to cool in the pot.

The four recipes that follow are for well-known regional dishes in which sausages figure prominently. A few others may be found in the index.

GARNISHED SAUERKRAUT PLATTER *(Choucroute garni)* / FRANCE

Line a heavy kettle with some strips of smoked bacon. Add well-drained fresh sauerkraut and mix into it salt, pepper, several onions (each stuck with a clove), some pieces of carrot, a large BOUQUET GARNI, a generous quantity of juniper berries tied in cheesecloth, and some lard or goose fat. Cover with some more bacon strips. Pieces of various meats, such as smoked pork, ham, or goose, and corned beef, also may be put in with the sauerkraut. Fill to cover with chicken stock or a mixture of chicken stock and a light white wine. Bring to the boil and then place the kettle in the oven to simmer for about 4 hours. Near the end of the cooking period add a good assortment of different sausages, cover the kettle, and cook further until the sausages are done. Discard the vegetables, bacon strips, and seasonings, drain the sauerkraut well, and arrange it on a large platter. Garnish the plate with the sliced meats and the sausages and serve the *choucroute* with boiled potatoes.

GAME STEW (*Bigos*) / POLAND

Fry some cut-up bacon. Add chopped onions and pieces of pork, veal, beef, lamb, venison, and bear (or any other game). Fry over high heat until the meat is lightly browned. Add vegetable stock to cover, a couple of glasses of wine, and some mushrooms and simmer until the meat is tender. Add some *kielbasa* cut into pieces and sauerkraut that has been cooked with some chopped tart apples. Season with salt and pepper and simmer for about 15 minutes. Arrange the ingredients attractively on a platter.

SAUSAGE STEW (*Ragoût chipolata*) / FRANCE

Combine BRAISED chestnuts, small glazed white onions, sautéed button mushrooms, and cooked *chipolata* sausages with a rich brown gravy flavored with Madeira. Serve this ragout with the roast from which the gravy was prepared.

LENTIL STEW WITH SAUSAGES (*Guisado de lentejas con chorizos*) / SPAIN

Cook some lentils by covering them with salted water, bringing to a boil, and simmering them until just tender. Drain them. Fry chopped onions in olive oil until well browned. Add some chopped peeled tomatoes, crushed garlic, and *chorizos* cut into pieces. Cook over a low heat until the sausages and tomatoes are cooked. Stir in the lentils and some strips of pimento, salt to taste, heat thoroughly, and serve.

Pig intestines, or chitterlings, may also be served as a meat rather than only as a container for other meats.

A well-known English dumpling, Down Derry, is probably a good starting point for someone who suspects he is not going to like chitterlings.

DOWN DERRY / ENGLAND

Season fairly dry mashed potatoes with salt, pepper, and fried chopped onions. Boil sections of cleaned pig small intestines with desired seasonings until tender. Cut them into 1-in. pieces and fry them in bacon drippings. Shape 1–1/2-in. dumplings from the potato mixture, incorporating a piece of the cooked chitterling in the center of each. Roll the dumplings well in grated cheese and bake them in a 350°F oven until golden.

Both of the next two recipes are also very good; the second is an excellent ingredient for a *choucroute garni* or a mixed grill. With a suitable dip sauce, it also makes a cheap and novel hors d'oeuvre.

PIG INTESTINES LYON STYLE *(Andouillettes à la lyonnaise)* / FRANCE

Open the small intestines of a pig, wash them thoroughly, and cut into pieces. Fry in lard or butter. When they are nearly done, add some sautéed chopped onions and finish cooking. Finally stir in a little vinegar and some chopped parsley.

GRILLED PIG INTESTINES WITH SAUERKRAUT *(Andouillettes à la strasbourgeoise)* / FRANCE

Sections of prepared intestine cut as above are grilled slowly over charcoal and served on a bed of BRAISED sauerkraut.

Classic chitlings from the southern United States resemble the French recipe from Lyon but, particularly in the Gulf Coast states, are prepared in more piquant versions, such as this one.

CHITLINGS / UNITED STATES

Marinate pieces of pig's small intestines overnight in vinegar and chopped onions. Drain and put in a kettle with a little marinade, bay leaves, garlic, and tabasco. Cover and simmer about 2 hours. Add chopped onions and salt and cook a few minutes more.

In 1978 Salley, S.C., drew 20,000 devotees to its thirteenth annual chitling festival, the "Chitlin Strut."

Tagalog, Spanish, and Chinese influences characterize Filipino cooking generally. Most purely Tagalog are several tasty and hearty mixed-organ stews. *Dinuguan* is a particularly popular stew in which intestines are usually an ingredient, the thickening is with blood, and peppers are the prominent seasoning.

PIG'S ORGANS IN BLOOD SAUCE *(Dinuguan)* / PHILIPPINES

Cut various pig's organs (e.g., intestines, liver, heart, pancreas, stomach) and fatty pork into small pieces. (The liver is a must.) Cook them in a minimum of salted water and vinegar (2:1) until tender. Sauté an ample amount of crushed garlic and sliced onion in oil, add it to the organ mixture, and cook 5 minutes. Add little by little about half as much coagulated pig's blood (cut into small pieces) as there is meat, while stirring the mixture constantly. Add about twice as much water as blood, salt to taste, and continue cooking for a few minutes. (The blood and water could be blended first in an electric blender.) Add some hot peppers just before serving.

A more subtly seasoned combination of pig intestines and other meats is this popular cold weather Chinese stew.

PORK INTESTINES WITH FISH CAKE AND LIVER *(Tsu tsa so, ue pi, kan)* / CHINA

Mix 2–1/2 C rice with 1 T oil and 3/4 T salt. Add this rice mixture and some pork bones to 6 qts. boiling water and simmer 30 minutes. Remove the bones. Marinate 1 lb. sliced pork liver 15 minutes in a mixture of 1 T cornstarch, 1 T sugar, 1 T crushed ginger, 1 T crushed garlic, and 2 T soy sauce. Simmer the liver for 3 minutes in 3 C boiling water and remove. Take 1 lb. of cleaned pig intestines, sprinkle with 2 T salt, and let stand 15 minutes. Trim off excess fat and wash the intestines again. Run several cloves of garlic through the intestines twice. Rinse. Simmer the intestines in 5 C boiling water 8 minutes and wash a third time. Add the intestines and 1 lb. chopped pork to the rice mixture and simmer 50 minutes. Drop in 1 lb. fish cake by tablespoon-fuls and simmer 5 minutes. Remove intestines, cut into 1/2-in. lengths, and return to the gruel. Add the liver and simmer 1 minute.

MEMBRANES

THE transparent serous membranes that line the abdominal cavity and envelop and suspend its various organs are used principally like intestines, as wrappers for various forcemeats which then are usually fried or baked. They are excellent for such purposes because they are well laced with fat. The high-quality fat of itself is much valued for fine pastry making.

FLEAD PASTRY / ENGLAND

This choice pastry fat is stripped from a pig's omentum and cut and beaten well into some flour, seasoned with salt, and made into a dough with cold water. It is rolled out and used for very flaky piecrusts and the like.

Two variants on membrane sausages suggest the great variety of dishes any imaginative cook could devise using these useful wrappers.

PORK-STUFFED OMENTUM *(Crépinettes de porc)* / FRANCE

Pig's omentum is soaked in cold water and cut into squares or rectangles. Any pork sausage meat is placed on each piece and rolled (by first folding over the side flaps) into a cigar shape. *Crépinettes* are usually broiled or baked after painting with melted butter, or they may be fried. Ingredients commonly added to a basic pork sausage meat include BLANCHED pistachios or roughly chopped chestnuts.

Gayettes are *crépinettes* shaped like spherical dumplings. The English name is faggots. This is one good recipe.

PORK SAUSAGE WITH SPINACH *(Gayettes aux épinards)* / FRANCE

Cook washed and well-drained spinach and beet greens with no additional water until they are just done. Chop them with a few fresh sorrel leaves (or a little lemon juice). Stir in some flour and a pork sausage meat (which may contain up to 1/3 pork liver, spleen, and lungs) and some brandy. Wrap balls of this mixture in squares of omentum and place them side by side in a greased baking dish. Pour a little melted lard over them and bake for about 45 minutes at 350° F. Eat hot or cold.

Similar dishes are Polish *kromeskis*, in which the wrappers are omentum, bacon, or calf's udder.

MAMMARY GLANDS

THE sow's mammary glands are usually incorporated in sausage meats. This is the only recipe I have found for preparing them as such.

STUFFED SOW'S UDDERS / ANCIENT ROME

Remove mammary glands and associated skin in one piece. Prepare a stuffing of salted sea urchin gonads, ground caraway seeds, and pepper. Fold the meat in two and sew the edges. Roast it in the oven until the skin is crisp and serve with HALEC and hot mustard. This dish alone could *make* a culinary reputation for anyone.

SWEETBREADS

PIG'S sweetbreads see less use than those of calves or lambs. These two English recipes are among the very few I have found, but pig's thymus gland could be prepared by any of the calf or lamb recipes. For their preliminary preparation, see page 60.

Pancreas can substitute for sweetbreads in these recipes.

PIG'S HARSLET / ENGLAND

Mix chopped pig's sweetbreads, pig's liver, lean and fat pork, chopped onions, salt, pepper, and sage. Wrap them in a square of pig's omentum and sew up the "sausage." Roast over coals or in the oven and serve sliced with a sauce of reduced port wine and mustard.

PANCREAS

PIG'S pancreas may be prepared by any recipe for beef or lamb pancreas. Its protein content is slightly less and its fat content one-fourth less than for fresh ham.

PORK PANCREAS AND SWEETBREADS / ENGLAND

Put a thin slice of ham, some finely chopped celery, and a BOUQUET GARNI in an earthenware pot and fry them in butter. With the drained fat make a lightly cooked flour ROUX and stir in some cream, salt, and pepper to make a thick sauce. Place sliced, BLANCHED pig's sweetbreads and pancreas on top of the fried ham and celery. Pour in the sauce and simmer until the meats are tender. Serve in the pot with slices of dry toast.

KIDNEYS

PORK kidneys are smooth skinned like those from sheep and may be prepared by all recipes for these same organs from cattle or sheep. They have slightly higher protein content than fresh ham and about 14 percent of its fat. They are also excellent sources of B vitamins.

Basic Preparation

Kidneys from young animals are trimmed of the ureters and fat and the membranes peeled off. Those of older pigs are split, the fat and other white tissues trimmed out, and the halves soaked in several changes of ice water.

This is an excellent recipe for kidney novices. It is good over pasta.

BRAISED PORK KIDNEYS (*Brasato di rognoni di maiale*) / ITALY

Fry some thinly sliced pork kidneys in olive oil over high heat for 3 minutes. Put the kidneys in a strainer and let them drip.

In another pan brown some chopped onion in olive oil until golden. Add the kidneys and cook over high heat 1 minute. Add a wineglass of white wine or Marsala, a little tomato paste, salt, and pepper and cook about 3 minutes. Remove from the heat, add chopped parsley, and serve.

A sweet-and-sour sauce substitutes for the tomatoes and wine sauce in this equally flavorful German recipe.

SOUR KIDNEYS (*Saure Nieren*) / GERMANY

Fry chopped onions in lard until golden. Add thinly sliced pig's kidneys and stir-fry for 2 minutes. Transfer the kidneys to a warm platter and stir some flour into the lard and drippings to form a ROUX. Stir in a little vinegar and enough meat stock to make a creamy sauce. Add salt and the same amount of sugar as vinegar. Pour this sauce over the kidneys and serve.

In these two Chinese recipes kidneys are combined with complementary vegetables. The second is a particularly festive dish.

PIG'S KIDNEYS AND SNOW PEAS *(Wen to jao hwa)* / CHINA

Split, trim, and slice some pig's kidneys. Parboil them for 10 minutes, cool them quickly, and drain. In a WOK quickly stir-fry a few ginger slices in peanut oil. Stir in some salt and add the kidneys. Stir and add some quartered water chestnuts and 1-in. sections of scallions. Stir-fry about 2 minutes. Add a little of a mixture of soy sauce, whiskey, and sugar. Raise the heat, cover, and cook about a minute. Add a generous quantity of snow peas, stir, cover, and cook about a minute more. Quickly thicken with a little cornstarch-and-water paste.

PORK KIDNEY FLOWERS *(Jao hwa)* / CHINA

Cut 2 pork kidneys in half lengthwise and remove the connective tissue. Score the outside of each half into 1/8-in. squares. Cut the kidneys into 1-in. squares and soak them in several changes of cold water for 2 to 3 hours. Marinate them in a little Chinese wine for 5 to 10 minutes and then stir-fry in lard, but do not brown. Add 1 C water, some soy sauce, salt, sugar, a thinly sliced cucumber, some shredded water chestnuts, and chopped onions. Cook a minute or so and thicken with cornstarch in cold water.

This very hearty garlicked German supper dish of pig's kidneys with sausages goes well with noodles or with cabbage or sauerkraut and boiled potatoes.

SAUTÉED KIDNEYS *(Geroestete Nieren)* / AUSTRIA

Cook some diced lean bacon in butter. Add finely chopped onions and crushed garlic and fry until soft. Add sliced pig's kidneys, salt, pepper, and paprika and stir-fry for a few minutes. Add sliced frankfurters or knockwurst and sliced mushrooms. Cook a few minutes more and serve.

Finally, for some colorful before-the-guests pyrotechnics this unusual and good-tasting dish is highly recommended.

PORK KIDNEYS LIÈGE STYLE *(Rognons de porc à la liègeoise)* / FRANCE

Sauté whole pig's kidneys in butter in a shallow casserole. Add more butter, salt, pepper, and garlic. Put the casserole uncovered into a 350°F oven and cook about 25 minutes. Add a little stock, 2 to 3 crushed juniper berries per kidney, and cook 5 minutes more. Then add some warm gin. Ignite the dish and serve.

UTERUS

I have included this next recipe for the cook who has successfully subjugated most of the family's food prejudices and is interested in having his or her culinary reputation recognized.

UTERUS SAUSAGE *(Vulvulae botelli)* / ANCIENT ROME

Stuff the uterus of a pig with a mixture of cumin, pepper, leeks, GARUM, pounded pork meat, and pine nuts. Cook the sausage in water and oil with some *garum,* dill, and leeks added.

TESTICLES

PIG'S testicles are an excellent food that resemble sweetbreads in texture and taste. They can be prepared by recipes listed in the index for testicles of other species.

Basic Preparation

Peel off the membranous tunics that cover the organ.

The first recipe was given to me by a southern specialist on mountain oysters.

MOUNTAIN OYSTERS / UNITED STATES

Pig's testicles are split and parboiled about 10 minutes. They then are salted, peppered, coated with Aunt Jemima's pancake mix, and fried in lard until golden.

Pig testes can also be substituted for sweetbreads, as in this luncheon dish.

PORK TESTICLES IN CREAM *(Animelles de porc à la crème)* / FRANCE

Soak skinned pig's testicles in cold salted water for several hours. Slice and fry them in butter until golden brown. Add cream and some butter to a hot béchamel sauce and then add the fried testes. Cook in the top of a double boiler for 10 minutes. Serve in VOL-AU-VENT shells.

BLOOD

THE blood of animals has been used in many cuisines to thicken stews and soups from time immemorial. Pig's blood is also the principal ingredient of some renowned sausages. Blood sausages usually contain slightly less protein and slightly more fat than fresh ham, and 5 to 10 pounds of blood can be collected from a mature 225-lb. hog. These first two are some of the best.

PORK BLOOD SAUSAGE (Boudin noir de porc) / FRANCE

Mix cubes of pork fat and chopped onions, both of which have been very lightly fried, with pig's blood (2 cups per lb. of fat) and a little cream. Season with salt, pepper, and other spices as preferred. Loosely fill cleaned pig's intestines with this mixture. Tie off the sausages at convenient lengths and poach them in salted water at a temperature of 190° F for 20 minutes. If they rise to the surface, prick them to allow the air to escape. Drain, cover with a damp cloth, and cool. To serve, the sausages are lightly slashed, painted with butter, and grilled at some distance from the coals.

This version of another classic is the home recipe of a ranch manager I met in Azul, Argentina.

BLOOD SAUSAGE BASQUE STYLE (Morcilla a la vasca) / ARGENTINE BASQUE

Collect the blood of a hog, add some salt, and stir it vigorously to defibrinate. Boil until very tender the cleaned pig's head, kidneys, diaphragm, and other organs not to be used otherwise. Put this meat through a food chopper. Add salt, pepper, crushed garlic, cumin seed, nutmeg, a little cinnamon, oregano, and chopped parsley. Stir in chopped green onions sautéed in oil and the defibrinated blood. Mix throughly and stuff cleaned pig or cow intestines. Tie off at about 1-ft. intervals and cook the sausages in a large volume of water kept below the boiling point. Store the morcilla in a cool place. These are traditionally served grilled as part of a *parillada*. Argentine blood sausages are also commonly seasoned with anise.

More unusual blood sausages are these from Norway that combine fruits with the blood.

BLOOD SAUSAGE *(Blodpølse)* / NORWAY

Strain the blood of a pig through a cloth. Mix into it some finely chopped pork fat, some parboiled rice, seedless raisins, salt, pepper, allspice, ginger, a generous amount of sugar, and enough flour to make a thin paste. Fill cloth casings about 3/4 full. Simmer the sausages for 1/2 hour. They are served sliced and fried in butter.

Or, alternatively, mix together per 1 qt. of pig's or cow's blood, 3/4 lb. diced lard, 3/4 lb. diced pork, 10 diced tart apples, 2 C sugar, 1 t soda, 1-1/2 t salt, and 1/4 t pepper. Loosely fill 4-in.-diameter cloth casings in lengths of about 1 ft. Boil for 2 hours and, to serve, slice and fry in butter.

SCRAPS

MY last pork recipes are for two dishes other than sausages that can use the trimmings from a pig carcass. The former is regionally popular in the United States and is deserving of wider use. The latter is for a hearty central European meat soup.

PAWNHASS, OR SCRAPPLE / PENNSYLVANIA DUTCH

Cook pork scraps in water and put them through the fine blade of a food chopper. Return the meat to some of the broth (1:2) and continue to cook. Stir in, for each 20 lbs. of cooked meat, 2 lbs. buckwheat or rye flour, 1 lb. oatmeal, 7 lbs. finely ground untoasted cornmeal, 2 oz. black pepper, 10 oz. salt, 1/4 oz. mace, 1/4 oz. nutmeg, and 1/4 oz. sage or thyme. Cook the scrapple until it is thick enough to "pile up." Scrapple contains something over one-half the protein and about half the fat of fresh ham.

PIG-SCRAPS SOUP *(Malac aprólék leves)* / HUNGARY

Sauté chopped onions in lard until golden, add a generous amount of paprika, the cut-up trimmings from a suckling pig (feet, tail, diaphragm, liver, etc.), salt, pepper, and a bay leaf. Cover and continue to cook with occasional stirring until the meat is about half done. Add water sufficient for the quantity of soup desired and the amount of ingredients present. Thicken it slightly with a browned flour-and-lard ROUX and simmer until the meat is very tender. Add a few squeezes of lemon juice, correct the seasoning, remove from the stove, stir in a pint of sour cream, and serve.

3

Lamb & Mutton

L AMB AND MUTTON are among the most accepted and enjoyed meats worldwide. They are, in fact, conspicuously absent from Frederick Simoons's *Eat Not This Flesh*. For only in rice-raising parts of Asia are there human populations of any size that do not keep and eat sheep at all. Since these paddy areas are topographically unsuitable for sheep raising, the absence of sheep eating from the six southern provinces of China and nearby areas is probably nothing more than a case of the historic unavailability of the species. That mutton and lamb recipes are prominent in north Chinese cuisine and that Malaysian Moslems also relish sheep meat support this conclusion. Moreover, the Japanese government's campaign to popularize lamb and mutton, begun on their northern island of Hokkaido in the last century and accelerated after the post–World War II growth in trade with New Zealand and Australia, has met with some success.

AMERICAN AVERSION TO LAMB

ODDLY, therefore, it is only among a fairly large and growing segment of the American population that there is strong evidence for a real lamb and mutton aversion. This American prejudice against sheep meat has become more marked with each generation's further removal from its countries of origin, and in partial consequence the American sheep industry has been slowly dying. From 29 million sheep in 1960, we have less than 18 million today, and our annual per capita lamb consumption in 1977 was a mere

1.7 pounds. In the southeastern United States, especially, sheep raising has virtually ceased, and for the last 20 years obtaining a leg of lamb in most southern supermarkets has usually involved an advance order of at least a week. Even 40 years ago a survey of American western and middle western university students showed that they too disliked lamb over 5 times as commonly as they disliked beef.

This countrywide trend has potentially serious implications for our future because sheep, like goats, are animals that can produce high-quality protein on noncompetitive feed regimens, utilizing land areas that have no alternative food-producing use. Furthermore, with unnecessary legal restrictions removed and little effort, a sheep or two could be kept by many American families living in small towns and suburbs. Raising even one lamb each year could result in considerable food savings for many American families. For those interested, there are a number of good books available on sheep husbandry, and detailed butchering instructions for sheep are provided by Romans and Ziegler (1977). Like beef and pork, lamb is substantially cheaper purchased either on the hoof or as the entire carcass.

Most of the great increase in beef consumption in the United States, in fact, has been at the expense of lamb, and, rather amazingly, Americans ate more *imported* hamburger in 1977 than they did lamb and veal combined. This growing avoidance of lamb is in part due to lamb's post–World War II price vis-à-vis beef, pork, and poultry, a result of the cheap feed-grain era that began then and has only recently shown signs of ending. While it is doubtful that this noncompetitive price disadvantage will be perpetuated, more and more Americans in the meantime become less and less familiar with lamb and stronger in their belief they do not like it. Perhaps our lamb prejudice is psychologically deeper than that, however, as Moore has suggested in noting that Americans consider beef a more "masculine" meat than lamb, a belief at least partially borne out by the folklore involving cattlemen versus sheepmen in our wild west. If that is so, it is high time we put our macho attitudes aside. For not only should sheep become increasingly important to us as meat producers, but we should recognize that another of their food-producing potentials is completely unknown in the United States, namely, that sheep are very good milk producers. In fact, many excellent milking breeds of sheep are raised in other countries that could profitably be much more widely introduced. At present most Americans' only acquaintance with sheep milk has been in the form of a real Roquefort cheese imported from France. This is too bad because sheep milk contains 1.7 times the protein, 2.1 times the butter fat, and 1.7 times the calcium as milk from the Holstein cow.

Taste as Our Aversion Criterion

Taste, however, is the reason given most frequently by Americans to explain why they don't eat lamb. And this taste prejudice becomes virtually absolute in the case of meat from adult sheep. Even the word *mutton* has long been almost total anathema to all but a few American housewives, yet so-called mutton taste is highly valued throughout most of the world and probably has been the most-enjoyed meat taste, for example, in my own family. On the other hand, how many American housewives would ever acknowledge serving mutton? Surely nothing labeled mutton is any longer for sale in our supermarkets. We Americans do, however, eat some of the world's oldest "lamb," and, unlike that of most other countries, all sheep meat sold in the United States invariably passes for lamb.

These trends in our taste for lamb and mutton demand reversal before this valuable food resource ceases to be available for our future. This is an appropriate place, therefore, to consider briefly what we mean when we say we do not like the *taste* of lamb (or any other food). First of all, many people will claim not to like the taste of something they have never tried. Children do this frequently, and that form of childish self-deceit persists too commonly among the present generation of American adults. Taste prejudices against certain foods also result from *inadequately explored* sensations associated with eating them. With only 1.7 pounds of lamb eaten per year in any form by the *average* American, little wonder many children do not grow up to appreciate its flavor. That many of our food prejudices merely represent sensations inadequately explored is obvious from our common usage of expressions like "acquired taste" or "cultivated taste." Our sense of taste, therefore, *is* modifiable and educable. If most Americans have made the effort to acquire a taste for beer or coffee, as examples, how much better to do it for lamb and mutton.

What is identified as taste, on the other hand, is physiologically more complicated than that. For taste itself simply involves detection of different combinations of the four sensations of sweet, bitter, salt, and sour by special nerve endings on the tongue. Individuals' abilities to detect the *intensities* of mixtures of these sensations in foods vary markedly. But when we say we like or do not like the taste of lamb, we usually imply a more complex combination of responses. Most persons recognize, for example, that what they regard as taste also includes an important component of "smell." That is apparent whenever we experience a clogged nose during a cold. Unlike the four tastes, over 60,000 distinct smells have been identified for different chemical substances, many of them present in foods, and almost all of these substances are detectable by what we think is simply our sense of taste. And, besides this very important smell component, taste may also reflect other sense responses involved in eating, like pain and touch. Our sensitivities to and perceptions of these also vary widely.

That is perhaps enough to say about the purely sensual explanations for such a very important American food prejudice as that against eating sheep meat. Let us get on, then, with losing it.

THE WHOLE CARCASS AND MUSCLE MEAT

HUSBANDMEN call an animal a lamb as long as it has not developed its permanent teeth. During the period when its permanent teeth are erupting, a sheep is, more strictly speaking, a hogget, and after 12 months of age it is mutton. Lamb should have light pink to bright red, firm, fine-grained flesh with well-distributed white fat. *Agneau de lait* (or *agneau de paulillac*, as it is sometimes called) is exclusively milk-fed lamb with white, tender meat comparable to European veal. It is not often available in the United States. Mutton is darker in color than lamb, often with a brownish to purplish tinge. It has more flavor and much more fat than lamb. As for most meat from adult animals, mutton should be hung in a cool place for at least 3 or 4 days before cooking.

For purposes of comparing the nutritional qualities of some of the even less eaten parts of sheep than their muscle meat, a leg of lamb graded U.S. Good (raw "edible portion" only) is made up of 18.1 percent protein, 14.6 percent fat, and contains 10 mgm calcium, 165 mgm phosphorus, 1.5 mgm iron, 0.16 mgm thiamine, 0.12 mgm riboflavin, and 5.2 mgm niacin per 100 grams of meat. A further point to note is that, in contrast to beef and particularly pork, no worm parasites are transmissible to man from eating undercooked lamb or mutton. Toxoplasmosis may, however, be contracted in that way.

Since American prejudices against cooking a sheep whole extend beyond the relatively minor prejudices associated with animal recognition (considered in the chapters on beef and pork) and relate also to perceived qualities of the meat itself, I shall begin this chapter with a few recipes for lamb or mutton which are less familiar than the roast leg or chop and which, in my experience, have been universally liked by Americans who have tried them.

MONGOLIAN BARBECUE *(Mon ko kao zo)* / TAIWAN

Mutton (or venison, beef, or horsemeat) is cut into paper-thin slices. This is facilitated by partially freezing the meat. The diner then takes a bowl and mixes in it *any* combination he wishes of slivered scallions, chopped Chinese parsley, crushed garlic, rice wine, sugar water, soy sauce, hot pepper sauce, sesame oil, shrimp oil, vinegar, and ginger juice. Thin slices of the meat are marinated briefly in the chosen mixture, then rapidly cooked by tossing with long chopsticks on a *very* hot griddle. The meat is then eaten with plain Peking buns. In restaurants in Taiwan the griddle used is a large perforated WOK inverted over a brisk hardwood fire built in a circular barbecue pit.

A simpler Japanese variant of the Mongolian barbecue is usually prepared (using mostly lamb or mutton slices) on a special heavy cast-iron domed griddle called a *jingisukan-nabe*. This is put over a charcoal hibachi or gas burner. I brought ours back with me from Japan, but they are now available in many oriental stores. Any griddle will do, however.

MONGOLIAN MUTTON BARBECUE *(Jingisukan)* / JAPAN

A piece of mutton fat is put on the griddle to melt and grease it and the thin slices of mutton or lamb then are quick-fried by each diner to the desired crispness. Thinly sliced onions also are cooked the same way, and the cooked meat and onions are dipped into a thick sauce of soy with much grated ginger. This dish is eaten most commonly on the northern Japanese island of Hokkaido.

The Korean name for a similar dish is *bul-gogi*. For it the lamb is marinated first in a mixture of soy sauce, brown sugar, sesame oil, roasted and ground sesame seeds, AJINOMOTO, and chopped green onions, and then it is fried on the hot griddle.

This next is another great lamb dish that could throw a scare into McDonalds or at least repeat the U.S. pizza craze that began in the late 1950s.

BARBECUED LAMB *(Shawarma)* / ARABIC COUNTRIES
(Döner kebab) / TURKEY

Bone out a whole sheep, keeping the pieces of the meat as big as possible. Slice the pieces *thinly* so as to get the largest number of slices of maximum diameter. Separate all of the available fat and slice it similarly. There should be about one-tenth as much sliced fat as meat. (In the Middle East fat-tailed sheep are raised and so this is easy. If insufficient mutton fat is available, you will have to supplement it with beef fat.) Marinate the meat and fat slices in a cool place for several days in the following mixture: 1–1/2 qts. of wine vinegar, the juice of at least 2–1/2 lbs. of lemons, 3 or 4 finely chopped onions, 6 to 8 cloves of crushed garlic, and a few teaspoonfuls of coarsely ground black pepper.

Skewer all of the meat on a *vertical* skewer by starting with the smallest slices and gradually working up to the largest. Skewer a thin layer of fat between every several layers of meat. Put the loaded skewer in place before a full-length vertical charcoal, gas, or electric grill or open fire, with the small end of the cone on the bottom. Rotate very slowly by motor or occasionally by hand. With a very sharp knife cut off paper-thin slices of the crisply roasted outer surface of the *shawarma*. Eat by rolling the meat up inside a half-loaf of Arabic bread with a sprig of mint and a thin slice or two of ripe tomatoes; or eat it with other Arabic food as a main course. Delicioso!

This traditional mutton ham is still very popular in Norway although its original purpose, as a means to preserve mutton, is no longer so critical. Fenalår has an excellent flavor.

MUTTON HAM *(Fenalår)* / NORWAY

For a 6- to 8-lb. leg of mutton, work a mixture of coarse salt, saltpeter, and sugar (1 handful: 1 T:2 T) thoroughly into the meat. Hang the leg over a pan and over the next 4 days "baste" the meat with the drippings. Dry the meat well and then smoke it lightly. Hang it in a dry, well-ventilated place for 7 to 8 months.

During the process the meat will shrink considerably. If the outer layer of fat becomes rancid, that will need to be discarded, but the meat itself can be eaten.

Finally, variants on this lamb "hamburger" are to be found from Poland to Malaysia. It is equally good as a main course or for a picnic.

MEAT BALLS *(Kefta)* / ARABIC COUNTRIES

Knead together ground mutton (or kid or lamb), finely chopped mint, parsley, and green onions. Form on skewers into long "sausages" and grill them over charcoal. Serve with yoghurt or *cacık* (yoghurt plus chopped cucumbers, crushed garlic, and mint or dill) as a sauce.

THE WHOLE CARCASS

A whole roast lamb is also easily done and provides an exciting and colorful main course *cum* exhibition for a summer gathering. Around the Mediterranean the lamb is usually simply spitted on a stout iron rod and occasionally rotated by hand as it roasts over a bed of charcoal embers. But an even more colorful way to roast a lamb is before an open bonfire, as is done in Argentina. Either way, the results are so good and the processes so colorful that animal-recognition prejudices should be minimal.

LAMB ROAST *(Asado)* / ARGENTINA

An eviscerated lamb or kid (with the kidneys left in) is spread-eagled on a wrought-iron cross. To do this, the sharpened main support rod of the cross is threaded the length of the carcass along the backbone from the tail to the neck. The feet are removed and the carcass is suspended from the arms of the cross by its Achilles tendons. The rib cage is opened flat by making one or more cuts through the ribs on either side of the backbone. Stiff wire coat hangers are used as spreaders. The meat of the hams and shoulders also is split open to the bones and secured flat with stiff wire skewers. The cross bearing the flattened carcass is driven into the ground before a hot wood fire. When the inside is done, the cross is turned around with the outside surface facing the fire. All one needs to complete the meal is some good bread and a red *vin ordinaire*.

A fancier dish that can be prepared in an ordinary oven is a stuffed whole suckling lamb.

STUFFED SUCKLING LAMB *(Agneau de pauillac farci)* / FRANCE

Sauté chopped onions in butter until golden. Add the chopped liver and kidneys of the suckling lamb, chopped parsley, beaten eggs, brandy, salt, and pepper and mix well. Rub the body cavity of a suckling lamb with olive oil, thyme, salt, and pepper. Fill it with the above stuffing mixture, cover the stuffing with omental fat, and sew the animal up. Insert slivers of garlic all over the lamb and rub it well with oil. Put it breast-up in a pan on a bed of peeled and sliced potatoes in a 450°F oven. After 3/4 hour, reduce the heat to 350°F and roast for about 3/4 hour more.

HEAD

ALL pastoral peoples also have traditional ways to use the head of an adult sheep or a lamb. Most supermarkets in Mexican and Basque areas of California usually have whole lamb's heads available, and any butcher can obtain them. Prejudices against cooking or eating dishes like these will include the same animal-recognition ones that apply to boar's head. This is also, of course, what can make such dishes specially interesting, even festive. Here are four different ways of doing it, two from Scandinavia, one from the Middle East, and one from North Africa. The first provides hearty finger food specially good for a barbecue or a different cocktail party. It is from the still almost medieval Baltic Sea island of Gotland, where I had a pleasant work-visit in 1972.

LAMB'S HEAD (*Lammskallar*) / SWEDEN

Scrub and scrape the wool from a lamb's head and then split the head longitudinally. Brush and clean the teeth, nasal passages, mouth, and tongue and simmer the head in water for 2 hours. Skin the halves, remove the brains, and trim out the salivary glands and connective tissues. Salt and pepper the halves and coat them well with bread crumbs. Grill the head halves over charcoal or bake them in an oven. The brains may also be crumbed and grilled separately and then replaced. With the fingers, eat the meat, tongue, and eyes dipped in a sweetened sauce of hot mustard. If served as a main course, the usual accompaniment is turnips and potatoes mashed together.

This recipe is quite different but is suitable for similar occasions.

ROAST LAMB'S HEAD (*Süt kuzusu başı*) / TURKEY

Boil two skinned lambs' heads with a carrot, a turnip, an onion, garlic, peppercorns, thyme, bay leaves, and salt for 30 minutes. Scrub the heads, dry them, and rub well with butter. Wrap the heads in the omentum of a sheep and then in grease-proof paper. Wrap again in plain brown paper and finally in wet paper towels or newspaper. (Aluminum foil could substitute for the outer paper wrappers.) Bake in a 350°F oven for 1–1/2 hours. Remove the two outer layers of paper and return the package to the oven for 1/2 hour. Serve the heads in the grease-proof paper.

These two other sheep's-head recipes call for boiling or steaming the head to recover all of the meat that is difficult to remove otherwise. Another dish from Iran similar to this first one is simmered all night and then eaten for breakfast.

BOILED LAMB'S HEAD *(Bouzellouf)* / NORTH AFRICA

Take a sheep's head and a couple of sheep's feet. Sear them over an open flame to dehair, wash them thoroughly with a brush, and season well with salt, cayenne, and cumin. Then boil or steam them until the meat comes from the bones.

This next recipe probably represented originally a way to preserve meat.

LAMB'S HEAD *(Smala-hovud)* / NORWAY

Drive a stake into the nostrils of a lamb's head and, holding it by this handle, burn off the wool over an open fire. Scrape the skin with a knife. Repeat the singeing and scraping until no wool remains and the skin is nicely browned. Split the head in two lengthwise (and reserve the brain for some other dish). Remove the turbinate bones in the nose and soak the head overnight in cold water. Pack it in dry rock salt for 24 hours or *longer*. To serve, put the halves in a tightly covered kettle with sufficient water and cook until the meat falls off. *Smala-hovud* is eaten in western Norway.

TONGUE

LAMB'S tongue is probably the most delicate and tasty tongue meat readily available. Its protein and fat contents are only slightly less than those of a leg of lamb. Tongue recipes given for other species are all equally suitable for sheep's tongue.

See page 19 for preliminary steps in preparing either of these two Turkish specialties.

POACHED EGGS, TONGUE, AND YOGHURT *(Çılbır)* / TURKEY

On each round of warm toast put a slice of cooked lamb tongue and then a trimmed fried egg. Serve covered with beaten yoghurt, a spoonful of melted butter in which some paprika has been blended, and some chopped pickled dill.

TONGUE WITH TOMATO SAUCE *(Salçalı dil)* / TURKEY

Fry chopped shallots in butter until golden. Stir in some flour and cook to form a soft ROUX. Whisk in milk and cream (1:1) and cook to form a thick, smooth sauce. Add some beaten yoghurt, a little tomato purée, a little white wine, salt, and pepper. Stir the sauce for about a half hour over hot water in a double boiler and pour it over a number of boiled and skinned lamb tongues arranged in a shallow casserole. Run this under the broiler for a few minutes to brown the surface and serve.

BRAINS

NUTRITIONALLY, lamb brains have about two-thirds the protein and one-half the fat of a leg of lamb. Prejudices against eating brains have primarily to do with the *idea* of eating this organ that controls the mind, senses, and body. This prejudice is particularly reinforced by the appearance of the intact brain. Secondary sources of prejudice are brains' consistency and, lastly, their taste. The best initial approach to their appreciation, therefore, is usually in some fairly disguised form, several of which are included in the beef chapter. All recipes given for brains of different animal species may readily be interchanged.

Basic Preparation

Soak lambs' brains in ice water for several hours and remove the covering membranes. BLANCH for 15 minutes in boiling salted water containing a little lemon juice or vinegar, a BOUQUET GARNI, sliced onions, and carrots. Plunge into ice water. Some cooks prefer not to blanch brains if they are to be subjected to further cooking.

This is a very tasty "beginner's dish" for persons unadjusted to the sight of unmasked brains.

FRIED BRAINS *(Beyin tavası)* / TURKEY

Roll slices of poached lamb brains in flour, beaten egg, and crumbled *feta*-type cheese. Deep-fry them in very hot oil. Drain and serve with lemon wedges.

In this next one, the anatomy of the brain is obvious, but the flavor combinations are ones most diners will already have experienced and enjoyed with other more familiar meats.

LAMB BRAINS NEAPOLITAN STYLE

(Cervello di agnello alla napoletana) / ITALY

Put some olive oil in an earthenware casserole. Add halved, parboiled lambs' brains, turn them over to coat with oil, add salt and pepper, some capers, crushed garlic, chopped pitted ripe olives, and bread crumbs. Bake in a 400°F oven for 10 to 15 minutes.

Mexican food is reaching an expanding audience in the United States, though we have access to relatively little variety in samplings from this magnificent and original cuisine. This recipe should be enjoyed by many, therefore, as an interesting variant on a common theme. Tell your non-brain-eaters simply that you are serving them tacos. Let them discover the difference.

BRAIN TACOS *(Tacos de sesos)* / MEXICO

BLANCH some lambs' brains but, in addition to the vinegar or lemon juice, add to the salted water some garlic, a bay leaf, and a sprig of parsley. Cut these prepared brains into small cubes. Fry some chopped onions in butter until golden, add a chopped peeled tomato, cook a little longer, and add the brains and some chopped green chilis. Cook until the liquid has practically evaporated. Soften some corn tortillas by heating them, fill them with the brain mixture, and roll them up and fry with the seam-side underneath until as crisp as desired. Garnish the tacos with shredded lettuce and sliced radishes.

This well-seasoned North African dish of braised brains is very good served over rice or COUSCOUS as a one-dish meal.

BRAIN CASSEROLE *(Mokh)* / ALGERIA

A parboiled sheep's brain is cut into small pieces (the tongue sometimes is used too). The pieces of meat are mixed in a casserole with cumin, cayenne, garlic, and wild parsley. Some oil and a little water are added and the mixture is braised for about 3/4 of an hour.

Prejudice against the idea of brains must assuredly be overcome for this one: there is no disguising the origin of this attractive dish with its fine combination of flavors.

SHEEP'S BRAINS *(Bhoona bheja)* / PAKISTAN

Fry chopped onions lightly in GHEE or oil. Add crushed garlic and a generous amount of finely chopped or grated ginger and cook for several minutes. Place a whole sheep brain in the pan, salt it, and fry it on all sides until done and evenly browned. Serve the brain with its sauce and sprinkle with fresh chopped Chinese parsley (coriander).

This equally good recipe for the brain connoisseur is even simpler to prepare. It goes very well with most other Middle Eastern foods.

BROILED BRAINS *(Enképhali tis skáras)* / GREECE

Marinate lambs' brains in olive oil and lemon juice, skewer them, and grill over charcoal. Serve as is or with a sauce of beaten eggs, salt, and lemon juice (with or without some chicken stock) simmered and stirred until thickened.

Last, there is this Turkish brain salad that is also eaten commonly in the Arabic world. There, it or spinal cord similarly prepared is almost a must for a *mezze*, or a huge feast of mixed hors d' oeuvres.

BRAIN SALAD *(Beyin salatası)* / TURKEY

Cut poached lambs' brains into pieces and top them with a dressing of olive oil, lemon juice, and chopped parsley.

FEET

THIS classic Turkish use for sheep's feet can also be prepared from head meat. Without the meat it is called *cacık*. Either can be served cold as an accompaniment of rice or other meats or diluted as refreshing cold soups.

SHEEP'S FEET WITH YOGHURT *(Yoğurtlu paça)* / TURKEY

Simmer a number of well-cleaned sheep's feet in salted water to cover, to which lemon rinds, garlic, and a little olive oil have been added. When the meat falls from the bones and the gelatin goes completely into solution (overnight), separate the meat and cool it in a serving dish. Mix with it a generous amount of beaten yoghurt mixed with some of the cooled, degreased, and strained sheep's-foot stock and more crushed garlic. Serve with chopped cucumbers seasoned with salt, lemon juice, and chopped mint leaves.

For a warm version, prepare the meat as above and cut it into strips. Fry slices of white bread in oil and cover the bottom of a shallow serving pan with them. Add just a little stock and cover these moist croutons with strips of meat. Reheat and cover with a sauce prepared by cooking yoghurt and stock (2:1), a number of cloves of garlic, paprika, and butter. Add additional butter and paprika and serve.

The name of this one is so unmistakably English that it is hard to imagine it without an accompanying pint of bitter. With or without, it is very good.

BATTERED TROTTERS / ENGLAND

Clean some sheep's feet and simmer them in salted water with some onions, carrots, celery, and a few peppercorns until the meat comes loose from the bones. Remove the meat, dip pieces of it into a batter, and fry in deep fat. The strained stock is reduced until somewhat thickened and served as the sauce.

TAIL

LAMBS are docked when young, and their tails have provided most pastoral peoples with a special seasonal item of diet. This first recipe is for one of the many meat pies for which English cooking is especially known. There are very few ingredients, it seems, the English are *not* willing to put in a gravy and cover with a crust.

LAMB'S-TAIL PIE / ENGLAND

Scald the docked tails, remove the wool, and cut them into joints. Simmer them with pieces of parsnip and turnip, a little barley, and water to cover. When the meat is tender, turn the mixture into a deep casserole, add some chopped hard-cooked eggs and green peas, and season to taste. Cover the pie with a crust and bake.

There is nothing peasanty about this next recipe, however. It is a fine example of the excellent and original, but much neglected, North African Arabic cuisine. Lamb shanks and other cuts sometimes receive similar treatment, and I recommend them highly.

LAMBS' TAILS AND HONEY (*Kharouf bel asal*) / MOROCCO

Scald and remove the wool from a batch of lambs' tails. Brown them well in oil and then simmer them in a seasoned stock. When tender, coat the tails well with warm honey, sprinkle them generously with chopped pistachio nuts or toasted almonds, and serve.

A stock I like to use for this dish contains the DEGLAZED material from the frying pan, a generous BOUQUET GARNI, whole garlic cloves, cinnamon, honey, and some sweet vermouth.

Moore, in noting the American "antipathy for . . . viscera of animals" and the fact that they "are generally looked on as inedible, and arouse faint undertones of disgust," attributes this general aversion partially to a "feminine" quality of such meats compared to muscle meats and "in part . . . the immigrant turning his back on the hardships of another continent." Generally, she concludes, Americans regard visceral meats as "exotic, effete and liked by people of questionable vigor and action." Perhaps this is the mythological basis for their absence from our supermarkets and our tables. What makes American prejudices against eating organ meats doubly unfortunate is their low cost and high nutritional value. Almost all organ meats have vitamin contents higher than those of muscle meat, and for vitamins A and C organ meats are our only important meat sources.

HEART AND LUNGS

SHEEP'S heart and lungs may be prepared by all recipes for the equivalent beef organs. Sheep's heart has slightly less protein and about two-thirds the fat (while the lungs have more protein and only about one-fifth the fat) of a leg of lamb. The recipe below is one of many that combine various organ meats with contrasting accompaniments.

LAMB ORGANS WITH ARTICHOKES *(Coratella di agnello con carciofi)* / ITALY

Salt and pepper some artichoke hearts cut into eighths and fry them in lard until tender. In another pan fry thinly sliced lungs of a lamb and some chopped onions in lard for about 15 minutes. Salt and pepper them and add a wineglass of red wine. Add a thinly sliced lamb's heart and cook a few minutes. Add a sliced lamb's liver and cook briefly so it is still pink on the inside. Add another glass of wine and the artichokes and heat through. Stir in some chopped parsley and a little lemon juice and garnish the plate with lemon wedges.

LIVER

THE protein, vitamin A, thiamine, riboflavin, niacin, and iron contents of lamb livers exceed even those of pork and beef livers. They are thus one of the most nutritious foods available to man. Though recipes for beef, pork, and lamb liver could be interchanged by the American cook with little problem, regional prejudices or species availability would make an authentic version of the first recipe prepared with pig's liver, for example, highly improbable. What is particularly interesting to see in recipes like this is what "new" seasonings that combine with liver the Asian cuisines can introduce into the cosmopolitan cook's repertoire.

LAMB'S LIVER WITH GARLIC *(Mi'laaq mashwi bi toum)* / ARABIC

Rub cubes of lamb liver with a paste made of crushed garlic and salt. Marinate them in a mixture of the remainder of this paste, some olive oil, salt, pepper, and finely chopped mint. Skewer and broil over charcoal. Sprinkle with lemon juice.

One distinctive feature of much of Arabic, Turkish, and related cuisines is their propensity for dishes served tepid or cold. In fact, many dishes in these cuisines are *best* left over a day so that the flavors have a chance to marry. Such cold, cooked dishes are especially characteristic of "universal hospitality" cultures where the wife must constantly be prepared for unexpected guests. For those who have not tried liver cold, this dish, which is typically served with a spread of mixed hors d'oeuvres, is one place to begin.

FRIED LIVER (*Ciğer kebabı*) / TURKEY

Beat a lamb's liver with a mallet or the flat side of a cleaver and then cut it into 3/4-in. cubes. Season with salt and cayenne pepper, roll in flour, and deep-fry in very hot oil. Allow to cool, cover with sliced green onion and chopped parsley, and serve.

Arabic influences are also very prominent in this recipe, as in much of Spanish cooking. One tends to forget sometimes that for 700 years large parts of Spain were Arabic and Moslem, while only 500 years have elapsed since the end of Moslem rule.

LAMB'S-LIVER STEW (*Chanfaina*) / SPAIN

Boil a lamb's liver in salted water; then cut it into a large dice and reserve some of the stock. Fry 2 chopped onions in olive oil, adding some chopped pimentos, parsley, and mint when the onions are almost golden. Season with cumin, cinnamon, salt, and pepper. Add the liver and cook over a high heat for several minutes. Add a few tablespoonfuls of the stock and cook a few minutes more. Thicken with some bread crumbs blended smoothly with a little water. *Chanfaina* also may be prepared with pork liver.

This is an "oriental" variant of liver and onions quite different from the fairly familiar Venetian or Lyonnaise themes, but one that is equally good.

LIVER AND ONIONS (*Tok yev sokh*) / ARMENIA

Slice several large onions into rings and sauté them in butter until golden. Add lamb's liver cut into cubes and fry until it is browned. Stir in a little flour and several spoonfuls of tomato paste. Then stir in enough water to cover. Add salt, pepper, cayenne, oregano, and basil, bring to a boil, and simmer until the sauce becomes very thick. Serve with a garnish of chopped raw onions and chopped parsley.

And for the following two treatments of lamb's liver such unaccustomed accompaniments as coconut and curry spices make for unusual and tasty dishes.

Lamb's Liver with Coconut Cream *(Kaleji)* / India

Fry chopped onions in GHEE or oil until golden, add crushed garlic, chopped chilis, chili powder, and GARAM MASALA. Stir well and add lamb's liver cut into cubes, quartered tomatoes, and some cooked peas. Salt and simmer, covered, for about 10 minutes. Add a generous amount of coconut cream and simmer, covered, until the liver is tender.

Lamb's Liver with Spices *(Eeli palya)* / India

Fry chopped onions, crushed garlic, grated coconut, Bengal gram, chili powder, pepper, cinnamon, and salt in hot peanut oil. Add a lamb's liver cut into small pieces and some butter and continue to cook for several minutes. Add water barely to cover and cook just until it completely evaporates. This dish is traditionally eaten by nonvegetarians in Mysore State after a marriage.

Iceland has been a country with few resources other than its hot springs, fisheries, sheep flocks, and hard-working people. This quite different liver sausage exemplifies their combinations of a very narrow range of traditionally available foodstuffs. Until recently sheep were only slaughtered in Iceland in the autumn, and most of their meat was then smoked for preservation throughout the year.

Liver Sausage *(Lifrapylsa)* / Iceland

Blend together in an electric blender pieces of lamb's liver and lamb fat (2:1). Mix or blend in 1 C milk per lb. of liver and a mixture (almost as much as the combined amount of liver and fat) of rye flour, whole wheat flour, and oatmeal. Salt. Fill sausage casings loosely, tie off at intervals, and simmer in salted water for 3 to 4 hours. Serve hot or cold.

A variation incorporates lamb kidneys as part of the meat and increases the amount of fat used.

Spleen

This is the only recipe for lamb's spleen I have found. Nutritionally, this meat contains more protein and only one-fourth the fat of a leg of lamb.

Fried Lamb's Pluck / England

This dish uses not only the spleen but also the lamb's liver, heart, lungs, and pancreas. The spleen and lungs first are parboiled 10 minutes in salted water and all the organs are sliced. They are seasoned with salt and pepper, dredged in flour, and fried in butter. Remove the meat, add a little flour to the butter in the pan, and cook the ROUX until lightly browned. Add a wineglass of sherry or Madeira, a little stock, and a few drops of Harvey's or a similar spice sauce. Pour this sauce over the fried pluck. Pig's spleen, heart, and lungs may be prepared by the same recipe.

Stomach

Like cattle, goats, and other ruminants, sheep have four stomachs: the reticulum; the rumen, or largest stomach; the omasum; and the true glandular stomach, or abomasum. Like the pig's stomach, the sheep's rumen is stuffed and served whole in a number of cultures. From a nutritional standpoint, lamb tripe has over 3/4 the protein content of a leg of lamb and a little over 1/3 its fat.

Basic Preparation

The washed paunch (rumen) of a sheep is soaked for several hours in salted water then turned inside out and washed again. Turn it right-side out and it's ready.

Fit to be piped in on Burns' nicht is this classic dish of Scotland, the only country in which sheep's stomach or oatmeal enjoys such national prominence.

Haggis / Scotland

The liver, kidneys, heart, and lungs of the sheep are covered with water and boiled for 2–1/2 hours. Half of the liver is coarsely chopped and the remainder plus the lungs and heart are put through the fine blades of a food chopper. These meats are mixed together with 1–1/2 C medium oatmeal, 1 lb. of finely chopped beef suet, 2 finely chopped onions, 1 t each of pepper, grated nutmeg, coriander, ginger, and mace, 2 T salt, juice of 1 lemon, and 3–1/2 pts. of stock. Plums, currants, or other fruits sometimes are added too. Fill the paunch, leaving sufficient space for the oatmeal to swell, sew up the opening, place the haggis in boiling water, and simmer for 1–1/2 hours, pricking it occasionally. It is served on a stiff napkin. Traditional accompaniments of haggis are lots of whiskey and turnips in either order.

Not to be outdone by that gem of Scottish cookery, the English make their own claim too, albeit a less-famous one.

Afromchemoyle / England

Stuff a cleaned sheep's rumen with a mixture of bread crumbs, finely diced sheep fat, pepper, salt, and saffron. Sew it up and steam or boil.

In an even more interesting-sounding dish from Corsica, a lamb's rumen is stuffed with a mixture of spinach, beets, herbs, and the animal's blood, but I have been unable to learn how it is cooked. My guess is that it is roasted.

In common with haggis, North African *osbane* also combines turnips with stomach (whatever the anthropologists may make of that). Prejudice aside, haggis is a dish I could personally do without were it not for the whiskey, but these tripe sausages are another matter.

Tripe Sausage (*Osbane*) / Algeria

Cut a cleaned sheep's stomach into pieces about 5 in. by 2–1/2 in. Fold and sew the side edges of each piece together, leaving the ends open so as to form square "sacks." Stuff these sacks with a mixture of what is left of the cleaned stomachs, intestines, liver, lungs, pancreas, and spleen of the sheep (all put through the fine blade of a food chopper), a little rice, salt, cayenne, and black pepper. Add some cut-up turnips or squash, sew the packages shut, and simmer the *osbane* in salted water over a very low heat for about 1 hour. *Osbane* also may be prepared by stuffing these ingredients into sheep intestines and tying them off at intervals.

North African influence is also clearly detectable in this generically similar dish from across the Mediterranean.

LAMB'S FEET AND TRIPE SAUSAGE *(Pieds et paquets)* / FRANCE

Cut 3-in. squares of prepared lamb tripe and make a slit in one corner of each. Put a spoonful of the following stuffing on each square: a mixture of finely chopped lamb intestines, finely chopped lean bacon, chopped parsley, crushed garlic, nutmeg, salt, and pepper. Fold the corners over the stuffing and secure the package by pulling three of them through the slit in the fourth. Lightly brown some chopped onion and chopped salt pork in a heat-proof dish. Add some sliced carrots, an onion studded with a clove or two, some whole garlic cloves, chopped tomatoes, nutmeg, salt, and pepper. Cook and stir this mixture a few minutes. Place lamb's feet on top of these vegetables and then the tripe packages on top of them. Partially cover with white wine and stock (1:1), bring to a boil for a few minutes, cover, reduce the heat, and simmer on the stove or in the oven for about 8 hours. The liquid is replaced if necessary.

Sheep tripe is also *an* ingredient of many soups, but in this one it occupies the place of honor.

TRIPE SOUP *(İşkembe çorbası)* / TURKEY

Cut prepared lamb's tripe into 2-in. squares. Add ample water, a lemon's rind, and several cloves of garlic. Simmer for 2 hours, cool, and skim the fat. Cut the tripe into 1/2-in. pieces and return it to the stock. Reboil and remove the lemon rind. Add paprika, a cup of red wine vinegar and a little stock to the skimmed fat, boil it, and add it to the hot soup.

INTESTINES

WHILE intestines of sheep are as commonly used as those of cattle and swine for sausage casings (as in the *Bockwurst* recipe below), sausage stuffings made from the organs or muscle meat of sheep are more difficult to come by. The only reason for this appears to be regional customs— which suggests that the creative horizons for the home or retail sausage maker have really not been at all approached. The two recipes here for an

English mutton sausage and Italian *turcinelli* are merely examples of sheep-sausage possibilities. For prior cleaning of the intestines, see page 57.

Mutton Sausage / England

Stuff sheep's small intestines with a mixture of chopped lean mutton, mutton fat, bread crumbs (2:1:1) and some chopped boiled bacon or ham, seasoned as desired. Tie off, fry in mutton fat, and serve with mint sauce.

Lamb Sausages *(Turcinelli)* / Italy

Finely chop the liver, cleaned stomachs, and heart of a lamb. Season the mixture with salt, pepper, and oregano and stuff it into cleaned lamb middles. Tie the gut off at intervals such that each *turcinello* is about the size of a small orange. Thread the string of sausages onto a spit and grill them over charcoal for 35 to 40 minutes.

Bockwurst is a classic German white sausage usually made with the small intestines of sheep. They typically contain about 11 percent protein and 24 percent fat.

White Sausage *(Bockwurst)* / Germany

Finely grind veal, lean pork, and suet (4:3:2) several times. Mix in heavy cream (1 qt. to 9 lbs. meat), chopped chives, chopped onion, salt, pepper, mace, and nutmeg. Stuff sheep rounds and tie off in 5-in. lengths. Cover with hot water, bring to a boil, and simmer 15 minutes.

Sheep intestines are also eaten as such in various cultures. This Malaysian recipe combines Middle Eastern Arabic influences (the Moslem use of sheep meat) with traditional south Asian ingredients like coconut and tamarind.

Sheep Intestines with Coconut *(Keraub perut)* / Malaysia

Boil the cleaned intestines of a sheep and cut them into small pieces. Fry grated coconut and pound it with fresh chili peppers (or use an electric blender). Add tamarind (or substitute grapefruit) juice and salt. Stir into this mixture the cooked intestines and sliced raw onions and serve with rice.

Both the small and large intestines are standard ingredients, too, in a famed Argentine *parillada*, or mixed grill. It and the similarly traditional *asado* together make use of the whole sheep.

MIXED GRILL (*Parillada*) / ARGENTINA

In this traditional mixed grill of the Argentine pampas, various visceral organs and cuts of meat, usually of lamb, mutton, or beef, are grilled over charcoal. Commonly included are slices of udder, *chinchulines* (sections of braided small intestine), *tripa gorda* (pieces of large intestine), sliced or halved kidneys, blood sausages, pieces of pancreas and sweetbreads, and sections of ribs or other meat. With a bottle of wine, a green salad, and some bread, a gland-rich *parillada* makes a terrific meal.

SWEETBREADS

THE protein content of lamb sweetbreads is slightly less, and the fat content about three-fourths less, than those of a leg of lamb. Although particular recipes for lamb, calf, or pig thymus may originate from different cultures, the American cook can substitute one for the other without hesitation and produce results similar to the traditional.

Basic Preparation

Soak sweetbreads in ice water several hours and peel off the membranes. Whether then to BLANCH them is a choice for the cook. To blanch, simmer for about 10 minutes in salted water containing a little lemon juice or vinegar, a BOUQUET GARNI, and some sliced onions and carrots. Plunge the blanched glands into ice water and dry them well.

This first recipe, for a very rich, creamed sweetbreads-and-mushroom stew, obviously does not require that the organs be blanched first.

RAGOUT SOUP *(Raguléves)* / HUNGARY

Put one pair of lamb or calf sweetbreads, the giblets from 2 chickens, several whole carrots, and a stalk or two of celery in a saucepan. Add salt and some peppercorns, cover the ingredients with water, and simmer until the meat is tender. Discard the vegetables, chop the meats, and return them to the liquid. Sauté some chopped mushrooms in butter and stir in flour to make a ROUX. Add some of the meat stock, stir, and cook until smooth. Thicken the stew with this sauce, simmering and stirring for several minutes. Beat some egg yolks, stir in a cup or so of cream, and distribute this into bowls. Ladle in the stew.

Sweetbreads are such a deliciously delicate yet rich meat of themselves, however, that many people prefer them prepared like calf's or lamb's liver, in the simplest possible fashion. This Spanish specialty, and particularly the even simpler Arabic grill that follows it, allow for fullest enjoyment of the sweetbread's innate goodness.

BAKED SWEETBREADS *(Mollejas al horno)* / SPAIN

Slice prepared sweetbreads and coat them with a paste made of olive oil, much crushed garlic, chopped parsley, and pieces of bread. Place in a greased shallow casserole and bake in a 450°F oven until golden brown.

MIXED GRILL *(Douara fi el fhem)* / ARABIC COUNTRIES

Alternate pieces of lamb's sweetbreads and liver and whole kidneys on skewers. Brush with olive oil and grill over charcoal.

PANCREAS

SHEEP pancreas has the same protein content as a leg of lamb and a little over a third of its fat. It is also one of many organ meats used for sausage fillings or for hearty stews or casseroles, as in this North African dish, which is served over COUSCOUS or rice.

MIXED-ORGAN CASSEROLE *(Douara bekbouka)* / MOROCCO

Cut the pancreas, lungs, liver, spleen, cleaned stomachs, and cleaned intestines of a lamb into small pieces. In a casserole mix some olive oil, chopped onions, and crushed garlic. Cook until golden and add paprika, black pepper, cumin, and some water. Cook for a few minutes, add the meats, and continue to cook until they are tender.

Somewhat similar uses for virtually any available odds and ends of sheep or other organs and muscle meats are eaten all over the world and provide much of the nutritional backbone to peasant diets. Some such dishes, as scrapple or this Swedish *pölsa*, are intended to be stored and used as needed to supplement other seasonally available meats.

SCRAPPLE *(Pölsa)* / SWEDEN

Cut into pieces the pancreas and *any* other of the visceral organs and odd bits of meat (bones left in) of a lamb, calf, or pig and put them in a kettle. Cover with cold water, boil, and skim. After a while add barley (about one-fourth the total weight of meat) and some bay leaves and simmer for several hours. Pick out the meat, discard the bones, and pass the meat through the coarse blade of a food chopper. Allow the barley and stock to cool, skim the fat, and return the meat. Add chopped onions browned in fat, a little marjoram, and some molasses and simmer for about a half hour. The *pölsa* can be kept frozen and a piece chopped off as needed. Patties of it are fried and eaten with boiled potatoes, loganberry sauce, and pickled beets.

KIDNEYS

THE kidneys of lambs and calves are regarded in much of Europe as such delicacies that the butcher often sells them at a higher price than the best beefsteak or veal. The fact that they are so underrated in the United States is largely ignorance of what is being missed and the irrational custom of lumping all organ meats into one rejected category of foods. Lamb kidneys contain slightly less protein and only one-fifth the fat of a leg of lamb. They are richer in thiamine than lamb's liver and are also excellent sources of the other B vitamins.

Like pig kidneys, sheep kidneys have a smooth, nonlobulated surface. For preliminary steps in their preparation, see page 64. This first recipe for lamb kidneys is a good one to introduce kidneys to persons who *think* they do not like them.

LAMB KIDNEYS WITH HORSERADISH AND CREAM (*Rognons d'agneau au raifort*) / FRANCE

Sauté chopped onions in butter until golden. Add 1/2 C veal or chicken stock and simmer. In another pan quickly sauté in hot butter sliced lamb kidneys previously seasoned with salt and paprika. Transfer them to a plate and cook sliced mushrooms in the kidney juices and butter. Remove the onion pan from the heat and stir in a generous quantity of heavy cream, some chopped parsley, and a little white wine vinegar. Add the kidneys and mushrooms, stir well, and reheat without boiling. Immediately before serving blend in freshly grated horseradish to taste.

Many different accompaniments for grilled kidneys are traditional from country to country. Several French writers on foods acknowledge only two cuisines as the equal of France's overall in their variety, subtlety, and artistry—the Cantonese and the Turkish. It is unfortunate, therefore, that the Turkish gastronomic tradition is still so poorly known in the United States. Turkey's restaurants are one of the many reasons traveling in that country is such a treat.

Oddly, the recent American discovery of, and infatuation with, yoghurt is still almost completely limited to snacks or dessert uses of this versatile food. The recipe below is an excellent one to introduce yoghurt's remarkable range of other uses in cooking (see also chapter 21).

GRILLED KIDNEYS WITH YOGHURT (*Böbrek ısgarası yoğurtlu*) / TURKEY

Split sheep kidneys, brush them with melted butter, and grill them over charcoal. Put them in a serving dish, season with salt, pepper, and lemon juice, cover with yoghurt, and sprinkle with chopped chives or green onions.

GRILLED KIDNEYS / MEDITERRANEAN COUNTRIES

In another, more Western, Mediterranean variation, marinate 1-in. cubes of kidney and bacon squares in a mixture of red wine, oil, grated onion, salt, coarsely ground pepper, dry mustard, and a dash of cayenne. Alternately skewer the kidneys and bacon and grill over charcoal, basting with some of the marinade.

Still another way is to marinate lamb kidneys and 2-in. cubes of lamb in olive oil with thyme, finely chopped onion, salt, and pepper. Alternate them on skewers and grill over charcoal. Sprinkle with lemon juice before serving them with small grilled tomatoes and well-grilled green peppers.

Skewered Kidneys *(Rognon en brochettes)* / France

In a French version of grilled sheep kidneys they are cut into uniform pieces, salted and peppered, and skewered alternately with lightly fried squares of bacon. Brush them with melted butter and grill over charcoal, or coat first with bread crumbs and then grill. Either way, serve with an appropriate compound butter or any sauce for grilled meats.

The last lamb kidney recipe I will include is for a rather unusual but very good Russian soup. The interestingly flavored cucumbers that provide much of this soup's distinctive flavor could also be used by the imaginative cook in other dishes.

Kidney and Cucumber Soup *(Sup iz pochek i ogurtsov)* / Russia

Cut trimmed lamb or veal kidneys in half and simmer them in water for about an hour, skimming as required. Cut into a JULIENNE parsnip, celery, and onion and sauté in butter in a soup kettle. Add diced potatoes, a bay leaf, the strained kidney stock, and sliced peeled cucumbers (which have been presoaked for several days in the refrigerator in brine containing oak or cherry leaves, sprigs of dill, grated horseradish, red pepper, crushed garlic, and a little tarragon), Simmer for about 15 minutes. Add some of the cucumber brine to taste and a generous amount of chopped sorrel or lettuce. Add the thinly sliced kidneys. Garnish the plate with chopped dill and a dab of sour cream.

TESTICLES

TESTICLES and tails of lambs provide seasonally abundant meats in many countries, and it is not surprising that they are highly valued by rural peoples. Many stories and jokes extol the supposed aphrodiasic or macho properties of testicles as an item of diet, and for such reasons they are traditionally reserved exclusively for men in some countries. As with most organ meats, recipes for testicles are interchangeable among species.

Lamb Testicles *(Bagg testiklar)* / Sweden

In this Gotlandic recipe, the covering membranes are removed from some lamb testicles, which then are split, seasoned with salt, pepper, and crushed garlic, coated with bread crumbs, and fried in butter until golden brown.

BLOOD

BLOOD, including sheep's blood, is commonly used as the main ingredient in blood puddings and blood sausages or as a thickening ingredient for other foods. An adult sheep yields 3 to 5 pounds.

Civets, like the one below, are stews thickened with blood (see the index for others). This recipe concludes those for the three mammals Americans already prefer most as items of diet—cattle, swine, and sheep. It was intentionally saved for last and was contributed by Ghana's director of veterinary services, Dr. Sidney Quartey. Enjoyment of this nutritious and flavorful stew native to that part of the world from which about 12 percent of us originate could be regarded as a test for our true emancipation from irrational prejudices against eating the full range of meats from these three animal species that are so readily available to us.

MEAT STEW *(Ntsin)* / GHANA

Collect the blood of a sheep or goat in a bowl and stir it vigorously with some added salt to prevent clotting. Cut some of the liver, lungs, kidneys, heart, brains, tripe, intestines, pancreas, and any other organs you wish into small pieces, wash them well, and put them in a large kettle. Add enough water to cover the meats and cook over a brisk fire. Chop some onions and add them and a number of whole tomatoes and hot peppers to the pot. Boil the *ntsin* until these vegetables are just soft. Remove the cooked tomatoes and peppers, grind them to a paste, and return them to the pot. Simmer the dish until the meats all are very tender. Pass the blood through a sieve and stir it into the *ntsin* until the sauce becomes well thickened. Serve this flavorful and nutritious stew over boiled rice, with yams as the traditional accompaniment.

Having gone this far, I will now introduce some meats less well known to Americans, hoping that they will enrich the diet and broaden the mind.

4

Meat of Goats & Wild

Ruminants

O UR ALMOST UNIVERSAL American prejudice against the idea of eating mutton is paralleled by our virtually complete avoidance of goat meat. Fewer than 100,000 goats are slaughtered under federal veterinary inspection in the whole United States annually (as compared to over 30 million cattle), and even this small amount of meat is not all consumed by people. It is strange that the delicious meat of kids, at least as good as lamb in taste and much enjoyed in so many countries, is assumed to be inedible by all but a few Americans. The exception is Texans, who perversely like kid yet for some strange reason disdain lamb!

Goat-meat prejudices appear to be largely based on the belief that this animal and its meat have an objectionable smell, that this produces an unpleasant-tasting meat, and that, in addition, goat meat is very tough. The fact is, few Americans have ever tried it. In my experience, those of us who have been exposed to it in travel or work abroad generally like it. During the years I was a veterinary student, my wife and I served goat meat to many friends, who had assumed they would not like it, only to be very pleasantly surprised.

Unlike the case with sheep milk, goat milk does have a still small but growing clientele in the United States, particularly among people allergic to cow's milk. The potential for increasing our goat production both for meat and milk purposes is great, and goats, like sheep, can be raised easily as single animals or in small flocks by families with relatively little proper-ty. City and county ordinances first adopted in the last century to prevent the keeping of then excessive numbers of livestock in urban and suburban areas need now to be realistically reconsidered in terms of man's future food needs. The future must surely permit suburban and small town families who wish to, to keep at least one self-propelled lawn mower *cum* food source, and it is encouraging to note that a few suburban com-munities, San Bruno, Calif., notable among them, have recently allowed "mini farms."

There are no special health precautions necessary in preparing or eating goat meat in the United States.

THE WHOLE CARCASS

COMMENTS on whole sheep apply equally to goats, and recipes in the two sections are interchangeable. These particular recipes traditionally use kid; they are excellent for large parties.

STUFFED KID *(Kharuf mahshi)* / SAUDI ARABIA

Rub a skinned and eviscerated kid inside and out with a mixture of chopped onions, chopped coriander leaves or parsley, chopped fresh (or ground, candied) ginger, ample salt, and coarsely ground pepper. Stuff the kid with a mixture of cooked rice, chopped mixed nuts (pistachios and almonds and whole pine nuts), and sultana raisins or seedless grapes (proportions of about 8:5:3) plus the residue of the rubbing mixture. Sew up the opening, paint the kid with melted butter, and roast on a spit over charcoal (or in a 275° to 300°F oven) until the meat is well browned and tender. Traditionally the kid is placed on a mound of pilaf (the stuffing) in the center of a large round copper or brass tray placed on the floor. The guests sit around it and dig in.

Equally festive is the party built around the *pachamanca.*

ROAST KID *(Cabrito en pachamanca)* / PERU

The *pachamanca,* or ground oven, is prepared as indicated for an *imu* (page 77). Line a chicken-wire sling well with banana leaves (or wet corn husks). A whole kid (or lamb or suckling pig) is rubbed well inside and out with a paste made of lots of crushed garlic, powdered cumin, salt, pepper, and lard. Place the animal on the sling and cover it with banana leaves or husks. Lower the sling onto the hot stones. Other traditional foods to place with the kid on the sling include pieces of horsemeat jerky, skinned guinea pigs and rabbits washed with vinegar, stuffed or unstuffed chickens, ears of corn, white potatoes, and sweet potatoes. These are each sprinkled with salt and wrapped separately in banana leaves. Other customary inclusions are a covered pot of salted pigs' feet and some wrapped goat's-milk cheeses. Banana leaves are placed all around the food and hot stones are arranged around them and also over the top. Burlap may be arranged over all to keep out the dirt, which in any event is then shoveled back into the hole and mounded up over the oven. After 3 hours or so the food is done and the *pachamanca* is opened.

A sauce to serve with the meat is prepared as follows: soak seeded fresh chili peppers in saltwater overnight. Drain them well and blend them in an electric blender with lots of crushed garlic and salt. This sauce is made in large quantities. Sliced onions and chili pepper strips pickled in vinegar are another traditional accompaniment of the *cabrito*, as of course are lots of flowers, singing, and other fun.

MUSCLE MEAT

SINCE this is the first food-animal species we will discuss that is, in itself, unfamiliar to most Americans as an item of diet, some regional recipes for ordinary cuts of goat muscle meat are given as *examples* of ways they can be prepared. However, kid meat also lends itself to all recipes for lamb. Kid chops, leg or shoulder, or crown roasts, rack of kid, saddle of kid, baron of kid, kid meat balls (see *kefta*) and kebabs of various kinds of kid are all as good as those prepared from lamb. Most ordinary cookbooks cover this subject sufficiently well, so repetition of these commonplace recipes is unnecessary here.

Goat meat's protein content approximates that of sheep meat. However, the fat content is less.

The following recipe for a kid roast is an especially good way to prepare a leg, saddle, or rack of kid.

BAKED KID (*Cabrito delicioso*) / PERU

Mix together chopped parsley, garlic, and mint with salt, pepper, and lard. Spread this thickly over a piece of kid and bake in a 350°F oven, basting often with the juices of the meat.

Kid is also BRAISED with different mixtures of seasonings in most Mediterranean and Middle Eastern cuisines.

BRAISED LEG OF KID *(Brasato di coscia di capretto)* / ITALY

Brown a leg of kid in a mixture of butter and olive oil. Remove the leg and brown in the same pot some sliced carrots, sliced onions, chopped celery, and chopped parsley. Return the meat, salt and pepper it, add 1 C dry white wine and 1 C stock, cover the pot, and cook on low heat for about 2 hours, turning the meat occasionally. Remove the leg and strain the sauce. Return the sauce to the pot and finish it with 1 T butter and a little water, cooking and stirring until the sauce is well blended.

This more highly seasoned braised kid dish is served in a rich cream sauce.

KID LOCARNO STYLE *(Capretto alla locarnese)* / ITALIAN SWITZERLAND

Thoroughly brown a seasoned, good-sized cut of kid in hot butter. Reduce the heat and add to the pan some crushed juniper berries, chopped mint, chopped sage, ground nutmeg, and ground cinnamon. Stir and cook for a few minutes. Add a cup of so of white wine, cover the pot, and simmer the meat until tender. Remove the meat. Add a cup or more of heavy cream and a little rum to the strained sauce, bring to a boil and reduce it until the sauce is thick and creamy. Return the kid to the sauce, reheat, and serve.

While kid is also used commonly as the basis for regional stews, meat of adult goats is almost always subjected to stewing because of its relative toughness. This should not discourage the cook, because in stews this flavorful meat is tender indeed.

GOAT STEW *(Caldereta)* / PHILIPPINES

Lighly brown crushed garlic in oil. Add sliced onions and tomatoes and fry until soft. Add cut-up goat meat, salt, pepper, and paprika and partially cook. Transfer to a casserole, cover the meat with some meat stock, and continue cooking until tender. Add quartered potatoes and cook until almost done. Prepare a mixture of ground beef liver, bread crumbs, a little vinegar, sugar, and a generous amount of stock. Blend it in an electric blender or force it through a sieve and add it to the goat meat and vegetables. Add at the same time sliced pimentos, some green peas, and some chopped ham. Cook until the potatoes and peas are done.

The Iberian origins of a portion of Filipino cuisine are evident in the generic similarity of this Portuguese goat stew.

KID CASSEROLE (*Cacarola de cabrito à regional*) / PORTUGAL

Fry chopped onions, crushed garlic, bay leaves, and chopped peeled tomatoes in olive oil in a casserole. Add to the casserole roasted kid meat cut into cubes, a JULIENNE of carrots, potatoes cut into small balls, peas, and chopped mushrooms. Mix well. Moisten with a little stock, simmer on a low fire for 10 minutes, and then place in a 400°F oven for 20 minutes or until the potatoes are done. Sprinkle with parsley.

Particularly good curries are also made from goat meat. We serve this first recipe often in our house with a pilaf and assortment of sambals.

GOAT CURRY (*Kari kambing*) / INDONESIA

Trim all fat from several pounds of goat meat and cut it into 1-in. cubes. In a kettle sauté in about 1/2 C oil until golden 4 to 5 cloves of crushed garlic and 4 chopped onions. Add a crumbled bay leaf, 1 t cinnamon, and 5 to 6 cloves. Cover and simmer for a few minutes. Add the goat meat and cook uncovered over moderate heat until most of the water in the meat has evaporated and the liquid thickens slightly. Stir in some salt, about 2 T prepared curry powder, 1 t paprika, 1 t ground pepper, 1 t ground cumin, 1 t ground coriander, several peeled and chopped tomatoes, and enough water to just cover the meat. Cover the kettle and simmer until the meat is very tender.

CURRIED GOAT / JAMAICA

For a somewhat simpler, drier curry, rub cubed goat meat with salt and pepper and let it stand for an hour. Repeat the rubbing with a mixture of prepared curry powder, crushed red peppers, and chopped green onions. Cook the meat *without water* in a heavy pot, stirring frequently, until it is tender.

Cured hams have been prepared in many cultures as means for preserving other meats than pork. Similar to the Norwegian *fenalår*, or mutton ham, considered in the last chapter, is this English goat ham.

GOAT HAM / ENGLAND

Rub a leg of goat with saltpeter and hang for a day in a cool, dry place. Pickle it in saturated brine for 8 days and follow this by smoking for 3 weeks. It is cooked as one would a cured pork ham.

VISCERAL ORGANS

IN all recipes given for using the visceral organs of sheep and lambs, the same organs of the goat may be substituted. This single recipe provides a further example of the common practice in North Africa of preparing tastefully seasoned dishes of various mixtures of organ meats.

STEWED KID MEAT AND ORGANS *(Tagine bel kharouf)* / MOROCCO

Marinate good-sized pieces of kid in lemon juice, olive oil, bay leaves, rosemary, peppercorns, and cloves in the refrigerator for 24 hours. Dry the meat and brown it in oil with onions and garlic. Put the kid in an earthenware vessel and add the chopped liver, heart, kidneys, lung, and pancreas and appropriate vegetables. Cover with the marinade, cover the vessel, and cook the kid in a medium oven until the meat may be easily separated from the bones. Serve the meats with fried lamb or kid meat balls (see *kefta*) covered with a sauce prepared from the strained and thickened marinade. The accompaniment is rice or COUSCOUS.

WILD RUMINANTS

WILD cervids and bovids were once extremely numerous in the United States and provided the dietary mainstay of the Indians and early colonists. Some species like the bison were slaughtered almost to extinction for "sport" with often only their tongues, or less, being salvaged for food. This was assuredly one of the most disgraceful facets of the American Westward Movement. With this waste also came a cultivated avoidance of game by the large part of our population that began to regard venison or bison not as the excellent and valuable foods they are but as strong-tasting vermin which only the poor or rustic would enjoy eating. We still suffer the legacy of this now common unfamiliarity and disdain many Americans feel for game. For example, in contrast to Europe, one rarely encounters venison or other game in our markets and uncommonly in our restaurants.

Though meat of the following cervid species is now taken by sportsmen in considerable quantities in the United States and even sold commercially in some local areas, the wives of many hunters will not cook it and their families will not eat it. Perhaps the biggest job, in fact, of many American hunters is giving their meat away, finding someone who will eat it. One suspects, with reason, that much of the U.S. bag of deer and other species each year suffers long deterioration in the freezer and final discard or ends up in the dog's bowl. This is unfortunate from the food, and sometimes also from the conservation, standpoint.

Generally speaking, wild ruminants can be prepared by most recipes for beef or mutton, and I have arbitrarily chosen not to lengthen this book unduly by adding the recipes for many regional European venison specialities.

Although venison is frequently treated heavy-handedly in its preparation to disguise its "gamy" taste, with proper butchering it is very similar to beef and can be prepared in the same manner. Butchering instructions can be found in Romans and Ziegler's *The Meat We Eat*. The taste of the meat is also influenced by the particular animal's diet and the stage of its sexual cycle. More specifically, the meat of the American elk *(Cervus canadensis)* is darker than beef but similar in taste. That of the whitetail deer *(Odocoileus virginianus)* is most commonly available and is excellent. The western mule deer *(O. hemionus)* has slightly drier meat. Vension in general is about 21 percent protein and 4 percent fat.

Among American bovids, the bison *(Bison bison)* population has made sufficient comeback that its meat is commercially available in certain areas, and some restaurants even have begun to specialize in its preparation. Our other bovid species are ecologically threatened.

The most common forms in which American Indians ate these game meats were as dried meat, or jerky, or in a form called pemmican made from jerky. There are perhaps as many "authentic" recipes for pemmican as there are for *bouillabaisse*. All agree that you start with jerky (originally made from deer, bison, bear, or other game).

MINCEMEAT *(Pemmican)* / AMERICAN INDIAN

Jerky is finely shredded by pounding. This is mixed with rendered animal fat. Most recipes agree on a proportion of dry meat to liquid fat of from 1:1 to 2:1. No salt is added. Oftentimes dried berries, other fruits, or spices are mixed in. Pemmican thus was the forerunner of American mincemeats. Pemmican is either packed in animal-skin bags or cleaned sausage casings and is eaten either raw or cooked.

The viscera of wild cervids and bovids may all be prepared as for their domestic counterparts. The name of one such dish that persists in our vocabulary is humble pie, an English pie prepared from the deer's innards and traditionally given to the servants.

5

Horsemeat

I F ASKED TO EXPLAIN their personal aversions to eating horsemeat, a few Americans might say something about the taste of the meat not comparing favorably with beef. Many others would mention the "nobility" of the horse and therefore its unsuitability for food. Perhaps a few people would relate their horsemeat prejudice to the lingering effects of prohibitions by the Catholic Church that were intended to break the horsemeat-eating habits originally associated with horse worship by the ancestors of many of us. Our horsemeat prejudices deserve to be specially examined, therefore, for like those of Hindus against beef and Jews and Moslems against pork, they have progressed from taboos to avoidance to abhorrence, with present-day rationalization largely in terms of taste, odor, or whatever. No one likes to appear to be irrationally prejudiced, so in this chapter we really begin to tred upon our American vulnerability.

In striking contrast to our customs, horse is by far the preferred meat in Mongolia and other parts of Central Asia. Mare's milk is another staple food of this whole area. The Chinese and Japanese also enjoy horsemeat as much as any other meat, and it is now available and fairly frequently eaten throughout much of Europe.

In pre-Christian times, horsemeat eating in northern Europe figured prominently in Teutonic religious ceremonies, particularly those associated with the worship of the god Odin. So much so, in fact, that in A.D. 732 Pope Gregory III began a concerted effort to stop this pagan practice, and it has been said that the Icelandic people specifically were reluctant to embrace Christianity for some time largely over the issue of their giving up horsemeat. In Sweden these many years later, horsemeat still outsells lamb and mutton combined.

The Angles of England were among those peoples who regarded the horse as too holy an animal to eat routinely, reserving it for communion meals, and some believe that this prohibition has carried over into the strong prejudices in England today against eating horsemeat. It has, of course, been reinforced since by the general value of the animal for draft, transport, and military use, and these values are confusedly mixed with the religious (just as they have been in many countries also for cattle). The one area of England where horsemeat is at all commonly eaten today is Yorkshire. There it is called "kicker," and "kicker-eater" persists in the rest of England as a derogatory term for Yorkshireman.

The domestication of the ox gave man for the first time a source of power greater than his own and thus was the key to the meaningful development of agriculture and an important key to civilization. The horse similarly became the key to overland trade, far-flung empires, and powerful armies in providing man with speedier land transportation and communication than his own legs could provide. Waves of less civilized horsemen than the cattle-culture peoples they conquered spread out of central Eurasia from the second millennium B.C. onward and brought with them, like the legendary centaur enemies of the Greeks, a completely changed world.

More Americans are descended from these horse-culture peoples than from all others, so the rather similar origins of our own horsemeat avoidance and the Hindus' beef avoidance should interest us since we find it so easy to condemn the latter and so easy to excuse the former. For among our Indo-European forebears, many legends bespeak the prime religious importance of the horse, not only as a manifestation of Odin worship but as the Gaul's horse goddess Epona, who was but a form of the Celtic people's mother goddess. Among Teutons, Slavs, and Iranians the sun traversed the heavens in a horse-drawn chariot. The Zoroastrian scriptures, the *Zend-Avesta*, speak of the "undying, shining, swift-horsed Sun," and Iranians prayed "Hail to Ahura Mazda . . . hail to the sun, the swift-horsed!" Their goddess Drvâspa's name meant literally "she who keeps horses in health." In fact, a mixture of bull and horse worship occurred among many Indo-European peoples, and not uncommonly gods like the Iranian Tistrya, the leader of the stars against the planets, could appear as horse, bull, or man.

The Food Potential of Horsemeat

Horsemeat is called *chevaline* in France and often, like pork, is sold in separate butcher shops. From time to time there have been strong movements to increase the use of horsemeat in French cuisine, for it can be prepared essentially as one would beef. In 1865 a large *banquet hippophagique*, sponsored by a dean of veterinary medicine, was held in the Grand Hotel in Paris to help popularize the practice, and similar banquets were held periodically both in France and in England from 1868 on. Local demand now exceeds supply, and Argentina alone exports about 140 million pounds of horsemeat to Europe each year, most of it for human consumption. Mule and donkey meat also are highly prized in some countries, particularly the meat of donkey foals, which is made into pâtés. Horse foals are also eaten in parts of Spain.

It is probable that a considerable taste for horsemeat is but superficially latent in many Americans. In any event, during the beef shortage in 1973 and because of high beef prices since, quite a bit of newspaper publicity has been given to butcher shops doing a land-office business in horsemeat in places as widely separated as Connecticut and Washington. One butcher reported daily sales of around 4,500 pounds of stew meat as well as horsemeat salami, hot dogs, and other products, and at least one chain of horsemeat butcher shops now exists in the northeastern United States. In 1972 the U.S. federal veterinary services passed the meat of 68,000 horses as suitable for human consumption.

What the Purple Stamp on Meat Means

This is a good point, therefore, to mention briefly just what government inspection of horsemeat and of our other meats means. Two kinds of purple stamps appear on meat carcasses: One indicates the *grade* of the carcass, that is, its conformation or quality; the other—more important— stamp, the wholesomeness of the meat. It is necessary for these stamps to be distinguished by those purchasing meats.

The concepts of meat "quality" are seldom considered by the American consumer except with respect to beef. Beef is advertised as U.S. Prime, U.S. Choice, and U.S. Good, and it is also wholesaled and retailed in the lower grades of "standard," "commercial," "utility," and "canner and cutter." In addition, many retailers market meat that is *not* federally graded and for which they often invent their own advertising grades, such as "corn-fed supreme," "royal pen-fed," or the like.

What do these grades mean to the purchaser of meat? For the most part, nonfederal grades mean nothing. In the federal beef-carcass grades, prime is the highest grade, followed by choice, and then good. These grades largely reflect the amount of *fat* in the carcass. For example, a prime beef carcass usually is more than 30 percent fat, a choice carcass is 22 percent or more fat, and so on. Therefore, the cook and consumer should be clear what fat content in beef means. Fat contributes flavor, and well-marbled beef (beef with well-distributed fat) usually tastes best. The energy quality—or calories—of fat is about twice that of protein. However, it is because of the protein, not the fat in animal foods, that they are a unique and scarce dietary food source for man. Moreover, high consumption of fats in general leads to obesity, and saturated animal fats and cholesterol are associated, like cigarette smoking, with increased risk of coronary heart disease. Therefore, in selecting meat for the table, one needs to understand something of the relationships of meat "quality," not only to taste but also to cost and to one's family's health.

Pork production in the United States has represented a more extreme situation with respect to the fat content of the meat produced. When our family first ate leaner pork in Europe—and also in Lebanon—we were amazed at how much better it tastes there than in the United States. Fat content in sheep meat, as in beef, is also directly related to flavor although American consumer preference for lamb seems to be for meat with less "sheep flavor" and therefore less fat.

Also with respect to fat in meat, the less there is, the drier and tougher the meat tends to become on cooking and, therefore, the shorter the cooking period recommended. This relationship is most clearly evident when one compares the lower fat contents and shorter cooking times required for game versus those for the fatter domestic counterparts. For this reason, we have always felt in our family that the eating quality of an American pork roast is considerably improved by long cooking at 225° to 250°F.

The other more important stamp on meat means that the animal has been examined for health status before slaughter by a veterinarian and that the slaughtering operation and processing and hygienic maintenance of the plant are under veterinary supervision. The inspection of each carcass and its parts for disease is generally done by a trained lay meat inspector, who holds any questionable carcasses for the veterinarian to examine. Depending on the nature of the lesions detected, the entire carcass or specific parts of it may be condemned. In questionable or unusual instances, the carcasses may be retained in a separate cold room while pathological, microbiological, or toxicological tests are carried out in the laboratory. The thoroughness of this consumer-protection process is limited in some instances by inadequate legislation, as for trichinosis control (see page 74) or for certain important infections such as salmonellosis or toxoplasmosis, which often present no visible lesions in infected animals. Routine microbiological sampling techniques for detecting most of these inapparent infections exist and should be employed, but Congress has thus far failed to enact the necessary legislation, and the meat industry has not indicated much interest in undertaking such consumer-protection efforts voluntarily.

The overall fields of food hygiene and consumer protection can be said to have begun in 1868, when the govenment of Prussia passed a law to require that all nonfarm slaughtering be confined to public slaughterhouses, where it could be carried out under veterinary supervision. Compulsory meat inspection in the United States began in a few of our large cities in the 1870s as a result of a critical health problem. For example, an 1868 report by the New York Cattle Commission noted that it had become "apparent to the Metropolitan Board of Health, in New York City, that the alarming increase of obstinate and fatal diarrhea in the Metropolitan District was caused by the use of diseased meats." As a result, New York City appointed its first veterinary public health officer in 1873, and by 1890 that city's health department had at least 11 staff veterinarians to combat this urgent disease problem. U.S. federal veterinary efforts in this field began in 1890, but it was not until 1906, as an aftermath of Upton Sinclair's *The Jungle,* that the meat industry's opposition to controls could be overcome sufficiently for the first workable legislation for consumer protection and veterinary inspection to be passed by Congress.

Some horsemeat, like beef, pork, and lamb, is slaughtered under federal inspection in the United States, and no special health risks are involved in its consumption. However, one often has to buy horsemeat frozen because the demand is not great, and that now limits somewhat the cuts available and the uses to which they can be put. Neither my wife nor I had knowingly eaten horsemeat until the first few years of our marriage. Once we did, we made great use of it and have enjoyed many a good cheap meal on that account.

MUSCLE MEAT

WHILE the foal or grown horse is sometimes roasted whole in certain cuisines of Central Asia, I have never encountered a specific recipe. The Siberian Yakut wedding feast, however, is built around a boiled horsehead garlanded with horsemeat sausages.

Retail cuts of horsemeat are similar to those for beef. The meat, as such, is leaner, slightly sweeter in taste, and usually slightly tougher than comparable cuts of beef. It contains about 22 percent protein, compared to the 14.7 percent of T-bone steak (and about one-tenth the fat of the latter). It may, however, be substituted for beef in practically any familiar recipe.

Two introductory recipes acceptable on a taste basis to everyone are these for a moist meatloaf that my wife and I have prepared often, particularly during my veterinary student years, and for bolognese spaghetti sauce, as commonly made from horsemeat as from beef.

VETERINARY STUDENTS' MEATLOAF / ORIGINAL

Mix together ground horsemeat and ground pork (3:1) with bread soaked in milk (2 slices per lb. of meat), some finely chopped onions and chopped celery, beaten egg (1 per 2 lbs. of meat), salt, pepper, dry mustard, crushed garlic, and a little Worcestershire sauce. Form into a loaf and bake at 350°F. After the first half hour, pour off the fat and ladle over the loaf a mixture of canned tomato sauce and water (2:1) and some crushed garlic. Sprinkle with grated Parmesan cheese and bake until done.

SPAGHETTI SAUCE BOLOGNESE *(Salsa alla bolognese)* / ITALY

Mix ground horsemeat and ground pork in proportions of about 3:1. Brown the meat in a little olive oil. Add chopped onions, and when they are golden and soft, add crushed garlic and sauté a little longer. Stir in chopped peeled fresh or canned tomatoes, tomato paste, and water as required. Simmer about a half an hour, then add some chopped fresh basil and oregano, a teaspoonful or so of sugar, salt, and pepper, and about a cup of red wine. Continue to simmer, covered, for at least several hours, replacing some of the water if the sauce becomes too thick. About a half hour before serving, stir in about a cup of grated Romano cheese and continue to stir until the cheese is melted. Taste for seasoning and serve over pasta cooked *al dente.*

Many Swiss also prefer horsemeat for its leanness to beef for their classic meat fondue. It is a good way to first try horsemeat undisguised.

DEEP-FRIED HORSEMEAT *(Fondue bourguignonne)* / SWITZERLAND

Cut lean horsemeat in 1-in. cubes. Each guest skewers an individual cube and deep-fries it in a pot of hot oil placed in the center of the table. Serve with bowls of assorted meat sauces, including aïoli sauce.

Another excellent horsemeat recipe is as *teriyaki*.

GRILLED HORSEMEAT *(Sakura nabe)* / JAPAN

Cut horsemeat into thin strips and thread them on soaked bamboo skewers. Marinate the meat in a mixture of SHOYU, grated fresh ginger, crushed garlic, and sugar and broil them on a hibachi over charcoal. Beef, chicken, pork, and whale meat can be prepared this same way.

Another less familiar but equally delicious Japanese dish also prepared with horsemeat as well as beef or chicken is *shabu-shabu*. It is excellent for informal entertaining.

MONGOLIAN FIREPOT *(Shabu-shabu)* / JAPAN

Start a charcoal fire in a *shabu-shabu* (also called *mizu-taki-nabe* or, in Chinese, *hwo-gwo*). These firepots in traditional brass or copper (or aluminum) are now available in most oriental stores. Fill the moat with a boiling meat stock and bring the stock again to a boil (any pan and charcoal hibachi could substitute but not as colorfully). Add to the pot sliced mushrooms, sliced bamboo shoots, spinach leaves, edible chrysanthemum leaves, blocks of TOFU, and thinly sliced pieces of horsemeat (about 2 in. by 4 in. and loosely rolled). Cook until done. Diners pick out items they wish with chopsticks and transfer them to their own bowls, which contain an appropriate sauce.

Mingeiya Restaurant in San Francisco has its own secret and delectable sauce recipe for beef *shabu-shabu* which, after many attempts, I have come close to duplicating.

Blend in an electric blender 2 eggs, 2 T Japanese vinegar, and 1/2 C peanut oil, all at room temperature. *Slowly* add 1–1/2 C oil until the consistency of a thin mayonnaise is achieved. Blend in a generous amount of crushed garlic and freshly ground black pepper. Then stir in 2/3 C sour cream, 4 T MIRIN or sherry, 5 to 6 T SHOYU, a drop or two of sesame oil, and some previously blended chutney and A-1 sauce.

At the end of the *shabu-shabu* dinner a delicious soup is prepared in each person's bowl with 1 part of this sauce leftover in the bowl, 2 parts stock from the pot, and a little *shoyu*.

Spanish *charqui* is a variant of Arabic *basterma* (Arabic for our familiar word *pastrami*) and similar dried meats prepared by the Incas and other American Indians.

HORSEMEAT JERKY / NORTH AND SOUTH AMERICA

Hang long, thin strips of horsemeat well apart in the hot sun or in a well-ventilated *dry* place until they become black, tough, and thoroughly dry. This will take several days.

Some cooks soak the horsemeat in brine (concentrated seawater is sometimes used) prior to drying. Others coat the meat first with crushed black pepper, thyme, marjoram, or oregano. Jerky can be given a smoky taste if cured downwind from a fire.

If conditions are humid or insufficiently warm, the drying process may be sufficiently delayed to *introduce a risk of botulism*. The highly lethal toxin produced by the botulism bacillus is destroyed by *thorough* cooking.

Horsemeat jerky is the basis for several classical Peruvian recipes with their origins from Inca times. Obviously they were made originally from llama, guinea pig, or some other native meat.

Ollucos WITH JERKY *(Olluquitos con charqui)* / PERU

In place of *ollucos*, which are not available in the United States, peel some sweet potatoes (or white potatoes or Jerusalem artichokes), cut them into pieces, and put them in a pan of water. Roast an equal weight of horse jerky in the oven until brown and then shred it. Pound a small portion of the shredded horsemeat to a paste in a mortar. Fry some finely chopped onions and a generous amount of crushed garlic in lard until golden. Stir in some ground fresh yellow chili peppers (previously seeded and soaked in salted water for an hour), chopped marjoram, salt, and pepper. Add all the horsemeat and mix well to coat the meat with the sauce. Then add the potatoes (or Jerusalem artichokes) and a little broth and cook over a slow heat until the potatoes are done. Add more water if needed during the cooking. Serve over rice.

PIQUANT STEW *(Picante tacneño)* / PERU

Remove the seeds from dried chili peppers (in Peru a large quantity is used) and soak them in salted water overnight. Roast a pound or two of horsemeat jerky in the oven until just brown and then boil it until tender. In another pot boil an equal weight of cleaned cow's or sheep's omasum and abomasum (tripe) and some parsley until the meat is tender, and in a third pot boil one or two well-cleaned cow's feet and some celery until the meat comes loose from the bones. Skim the stocks as required. Now remove the meats and chop them finely. Strain and pool the three stocks and reserve them.

Boil and mash (without adding liquid) enough potatoes to equal the total weight of the meat. Finely chop a number of onions and cook them and the soaked chilis in a cup or two of water until it completely evaporates and the vegetables just begin to burn. Immediately add a cup or so of oil and stir to prevent the vegetables from sticking. Cook for several minutes and carefully drain off most of the oil and reserve it. Return the pot to the stove, reheat it, and add the meat and mashed potatoes. Stir in some of the reduced stock and continue to cook and stir to form a very thick smooth mixture. Stir in some of the oil before serving and garnish the dish with chopped hard-boiled eggs.

Donkey meat, particularly that of foals under two years of age, is more flavorful than horsemeat and is highly valued in several cuisines. It is especially used for making pâtés.

VISCERAL ORGANS

THE visceral organs of the horse are eaten in Central Asia, but I have been unable to secure recipes. However, the *Larousse Gastronomique* cites one historic tale that at Sedan, King Wilhelm of Prussia served *cervelle de âne à la diplomate* to Napoleon III. Diplomate sauce for fish contains truffles, lobster butter, and cream, but just how Napoleon's donkey brains were prepared is anyone's guess.

6

Dog & Cat Meat

I F OMISSION were the better part of valor, I would probably forget about this chapter altogether. I can already see the "letters to the editor." But such an omission in discussing America's food prejudices in a food-short world would be like writing about India's food prejudices and passing over the "holy cow." Here is where our American vulnerability on the world food scene really shows—where reason stops and our emotions tend to take over completely.

While one could visualize no possibility for ever meaningfully increasing the American protein food supply by *raising* dogs or cats expressly for human food, we should become concerned for the future about what happens to the over 13 million unwanted and unneeded dogs and cats *now* being humanely destroyed in city pounds and shelters in this country yearly (and for the reasons this problem exists). Some 3,500 puppies and kittens are born every hour in the United States, and the surplus among them represents at least 120 million pounds per year of potentially edible meat now being totally wasted. And even the disposal of this huge number of dog and cat carcasses poses an immense ecological and financial problem to the governments of many of our cities, some of them cities where some people *now* cannot afford to eat much meat! So what about dogs and cats as human food? What is their meat like and who eats it?

Dogmeat Eating Worldwide

Dogs have been eaten by man through all his history. Hippocrates, for one, much praised dogmeat as a source of strength, and, to the Romans, suckling puppy was a dish considered fit for the gods. The Celtic ancestors of many of us relished dogmeat, too, and (to the surprise of many readers, we can be sure) dogmeat eating still survives in parts of Europe today, and not just during periods of war-induced famine. It has been a traditional European belief, for example, that dogmeat is a preventive of tuberculosis.

Of course, the Chinese, too, have for centuries raised special breeds of dogs, such as the black-tongued chow, expressly for food, and in that country dogmeat is also regarded as being a disease preventive, in their case, a preventive of heat prostration in very hot weather. It also is enjoyed today by many other peoples throughout Southeast Asia, the Pacific islands, and parts of Africa.

In the Americas, the Mexican hairless dog was the principal food species of the Aztecs, and it was recorded at the time of the Spanish conquest that a single market near Mexico City sold over 400 fattened dogs per week as food. Still closer to home, dog eating was widespread among the Indians of the eastern United States, the Central Plains, and California. In fact, in some tribes it persists to this day, although the practice is rarely admitted. This reluctance to divulge came home to me in a letter from a friend who was trying to help provide North American Indian recipes for this book: "I just called a Sac-Fox friend from Iowa," he wrote, "to find out how they cook their dogs for ceremonial eating. He was completely put off, saying that outsiders weren't supposed to know that they still ate dogs—although several times he had spoken to me of the terrible conflict he experienced as a child of raising an affectionate puppy which was dear to him, and the pride of having *his* dog eaten for the ceremony. He was completely unwilling to tell me how their dogs are cooked—but then he said he hoped that I could find out how *other* people cooked theirs and let hin know!"

It may come as something of a surprise, too, that dogmeat also is eaten today in parts of Hawaii and American Samoa, although almost everyone there also officially denies it. When we went to live in Hawaii after the war, we learned that not only was dog traditionally relished by the Hawaiians and other Polynesians, who prized it above both pork and chicken, but that it is still being eaten by some Hawaiians and Filipino-Americans. One Filipino insisted that "it's better to eat surplus dogs than allow them to become a menace." Which certainly makes sense.

In fact, the Hawaiians were at a complete loss to explain the really inexplicable attitudes about dogs and pigs of the early British and American explorers and exploiters who visisted their islands. The Hawaiians raised both species and kept them both as pets, Hawaiian women even suckling their young—and they also ate both species. Why these strangers should consider the dog as *only* suitable to be a pet and the pig as *only* suitable for food completely escaped and baffled them—as, of course, it should any rational man.

Those Englishmen and Americans who did venture to try dog and recorded their reactions for posterity generally liked it, as their writings suggest. For instance, dogmeat was eaten and enjoyed by Captain Cook, and, referring to a roasted leg of dog, another English visitor to New Zealand in 1777 wrote that it "tasted so exactly like mutton, that it was absolutely indistinguishable." A later voyager to Hawaii described dogmeat as "bearing a close resemblance to lamb, and . . . consequently a dish that few who have tasted would despise."

In Hong Kong and Taiwan, dogmeat today often goes by the euphemistic name "fragrant meat." Not long ago the international press carried a story from Hong Kong about some European tourists who were traveling around the world with their dog and went to dine at a highly recommended restaurant. They encountered a formidable language barrier but persisted in ordering a resplendent dinner and, amidst much confusion and gesturing, also conveyed, so they thought, the additional idea that their poodle was hungry, too, and was there not something in the kitchen he might eat. As the dog was led off by the waiter, they commenced to embark on their delicious, many-coursed dinner. Its culmination was a triumphant processional from the kitchen. The silver tray with domed lid was ceremoniously unveiled for the meal's pièce de résistance only to reveal—you guessed it—their dear poodle. The article stated that they cut short their world cruise precipitously and flew directly home. Which is, of course, a very sad story, if true, but also clearly a case of conflicting values and tastes. On mainland China there are said to be relatively few dogs anymore after a deliberate campaign to eliminate them as pests and wasters of food. Most of these surplus dogs were disposed of in people's stomachs.

EXPORTING OUR PREJUDICES

ONE other serious problem in our failure to appraise objectively the irrationality of our own food prejudices while condemning those of others has been the export of our prejudices elsewhere, to the disadvantage of others. As pointed out by Schultz, "Outsiders who hope to improve conditions in underdeveloped areas, sometimes . . . introduce *new* food avoidances to the communities they came to help. [If the outsiders] show repugnance toward consuming goats, . . . rats, . . . crows, insects, intestines, and blood, then the people they are educating may likewise give up those . . . foods and lose valuable proteins." British and American abhorrence of dogmeat eating, for example, has been so forcefully and insensitively conveyed to other peoples who traditionally obtained badly needed protein from such sources, that the practice is being hidden or has even become illegal, as now on Taiwan. What a disservice to mankind to promote one's own irrational hang-ups, particularly concerning so important a matter as food.

HUMANE CONSIDERATIONS

NOR does the commonly voiced "humane" issue do other than beg the question. In 1959 Lt. A. P. O'Meara, a graduate of West Point, was convicted and fined $200 in Peoria, Ill., for "cruelty to an animal." He had killed a stray dog by a quick blow to the head and barbecued it as a demonstration of the edibility of dogmeat. How ridiculous a basis for a legal decision. I have long been a staunch advocate of humaneness in all relations of people to animals (and other people). And I have personally been as fond of dogs as any person. In the food use of animals, humaneness means the husbanding of animals in ways that are healthful and do not induce undue fear, stress, or pain. And these elements of fear and pain should be especially guarded against in the *way* animals are killed. Some commonplace practices in meat production are notoriously inhumane. Kosher killing of cattle and sheep, for example, by slitting the throat of a fully conscious animal should be prohibited as a barbarous holdover from less enlightened times. It has no more to do with the essentials of religion than the long-abandoned bloody sacrifices of animals at the altar that are similarly described as necessary religious ritual in the Old Testament.

As for the dangers involved in eating dogmeat, the possibility of trichinosis requires that dogmeat be thoroughly cooked. The handling of the dog's intestines also demands very special precautions (see pages 9-10) in areas like the western United States in which a small tapeworm of the dog *(Echinococcus granulosus)* passes eggs in the dog's stool that cause hydatid disease in man, infection with a parasite that grows in the human liver or other organs like a tumor.

THE WHOLE CARCASS

WHOLE roast dog is traditional in Hawaii and Samoa while dogs are also grilled whole in Hawaii, the Philippines, and Indonesia. In Indonesia, Korea, and parts of Africa, the whole singed and eviscerated dog often is rotated on a spit before the open fire. My own first personal knowledge that dog is eaten today was acquired when, as a boy, I used to lie on the floor and pour over many photograph albums belonging to a dentist cousin of mine who had spent long periods during the 1930s in the former Netherlands East Indies and elsewhere in the Far East. There were a number of photos in his collection of dogs being spit-roasted, grilled, and oven baked by appreciative Indonesians.

I have found no publications on the nutritional value of dogmeat, but it probably differs little from lean pork.

ROAST DOG *(Imu-baked 'ilio)* / HAWAII AND SAMOA

The most common of traditional methods for cooking whole dog in Hawaii was in the ground oven, or *imu*. As with pigs, the Hawaiians traditionally killed dogs by strangulation or by holding their nostrils shut, in order to conserve the blood. The hair is then removed by singeing and rubbing with hot stones (native Hawaiian dogs were of a short-haired terrier type). The head, entrails, and genitalia are then removed; the cooking procedure resembles that given for *Kalua* pig. Dog also is prepared in the *imu* by wrapping pieces of the meat in *ti* leaves. The Samoan *umu* also employs hot stones but is constructed on the surface, more like a New England clambake.

BROILED PUPPY / HAWAII

The delicate puppy meat usually is prepared by flattening out the entire eviscerated animal and broiling it over hot coals. It also may be spitted on sticks. The traditional Hawaiian accompaniment for dog cooked in any way is sweet potatoes.

BOILED STUFFED DOG / BURMA

The Chins of Burma stuff dogs with a sweet gelatinous rice and boil them whole.

MUSCLE MEAT

DOG hams in China are much renowned. A European visitor to China, in describing his experience of this delicacy, remarked that "one taste led to another, and resulted in a verdict for reason; for in summing up, after a hearty meal, I pronounced the dog ham to be delicious in flavour, well smoked, tender and juicy." In fact, in China pork and dog hams often are cured together because it is considered that without a dog ham or two present in the cure, the pork product does not have its characteristic goodness either. Similarly interesting is the fact that rendered dog fat is used in cooking some special Chinese dishes, also to obtain the desired flavor.

DOG HAM (La tsan) / CHINA

Two slightly different processes are employed in China for dog ham, both usually carried out in early spring when the weather is not extreme and the wind brisk. In the first process (Yuennam), the leg of the dog is trimmed and rubbed thoroughly with rock salt using about 2–1/2 lbs. of salt for a hundred pounds of meat. The leg then is squeezed to express all the blood possible. Next, the hams are packed tightly in layers in a wooden tub. On the 5th and 10th days, they are removed, rubbed again with a similar quantity of salt and repacked with the other side up. They are allowed to cure like this for 15 to 20 days. Then the hams are hung in a well-ventilated and shaded place for 6 months.

For Kimwah ham, on the other hand, rock salt is heated in a pan and about 5 lbs. of hot salt is rubbed into 100 lbs. of dog thighs. The hams are packed in a wooden tub and the top weighted with a heavy stone. They are turned every 5 days and, after 1 month, are removed, coated with sesame seeds, and hung to dry for 4 to 5 months in a shaded, well-ventilated place.

A popular belief is that dogmeat, cat meat, and rat meat have been eaten in Europe as an extreme measure *only* during periods of war-induced famine. I hate to put an end to that fantasy. Many persons would be very surprised to learn that smoked dog ham *(Hundeschinken)* is prepared in normal times not only in China but also in parts of Switzerland and in other European Alpine countries. In fact, the only two cases of human trichinosis diagnosed in Switzerland in recent years resulted from the patients eating their dogmeat too rarely cooked!

Foxes are eaten too in Switzerland, especially in a popular hunters' dish called *Fuchspfeffer* (pepper fox). In western Switzerland hunters also eat fresh fox meat in the field grilled over a fire on skewers as the Hawaiians and Indonesians also do with dogmeat.

This is another traditional Swiss recipe for dried and salted raw dogmeat. It is prepared in a similar fashion to Swiss *Bindenfleisch,* or dried beef, which also is called *viande de Grisson.*

DRIED DOGMEAT *(Gedörrtes Hundefleisch)* / SWITZERLAND

Hang a dressed dog carcass for 8 to 10 days at about 36°F and then debone it, retaining as large pieces as possible. Pack these in oak barrels in the following salt mixture for 7 days at 45° to 50°F: for each 20 lbs. of meat, use 7 oz. salt, 1/6 oz. saltpeter, 1/3 oz. sugar, 1/3 oz. cracked black peppercorns, and 1/2 bay leaf. Repack the pieces after two days, putting those pieces which were on the bottom on the top. Liquid will be drawn from the meat. After 7 days, add some red wine containing crushed garlic to the brine that has formed and leave for several more days. After this curing, wash the meat in warmish water, but don't soak it. Run a piece of binding cord through the end of each piece of meat and press it between two boards in an open press (that is, with free air circulation between the pieces) in a drying room at a room temperature of 50°-55°F and 72 to 75 percent humidity for 5 to 6 weeks. After this pressing process, hang the pieces of meat freely in the same drying room for another 1–1/2 to 4–1/2 months (depending on their size).

Traditionally, dried dogmeat is served as paper-thin slices.

Many readers will be further surprised to learn that laws requiring veterinary postmortem examination of dogs for human consumption are currently on the books in several other European countries. That for Belgium, for example, was passed in 1885 and required that, besides veterinary inspection, dogmeat, like horsemeat and pork, be sold in separate butcher stalls.

Another dried dogmeat preparation is for jerky.

SMOKED DOG *(Tapan aso)* / PHILIPPINES

The meat is cut in thin strips, sun dried for several days, and then smoked in the flue over a hardwood fire. It then is eaten as is or cooked like any jerky. According to an unnamed United Nations friend, among the international set in Manila smoked dog is a "tremendous hit at cocktail parties."

In addition to roasting unadorned dog over charcoal, some traditional Indonesian recipes are as elaborate as this *saté*.

COCONUT-CREAM–MARINATED DOG ON SKEWERS *(Saté bumbu dendeng)* / INDONESIA

Cut dogmeat into pieces and marinate them in a mixture of coconut cream with a little soy sauce, pounded garlic and onions, ground coriander, ground cumin, salt, and pepper. Skewer, broil over charcoal, and serve with a pickled hot pepper sauce.

To me, this next recipe sounds rather unappetizing, but I feel the same way about simply *boiled* pork or lamb.

BOILED DOG / HAWAII

Put convenient-sized pieces of dogmeat in a cooking calabash with water and boil them by adding hot stones. Presumably those who would appreciate such simple fare now could prepare it more conveniently on the stove in a pot!

Dogmeat also is eaten just plain boiled in Africa and Korea.

With any imagination at all, cooks can devise additional, more appetizing possibilities for boiling dogmeat. In Vietnam, dog chops are simmered with white wine, and ground dogmeat is made into traditional sausages that are often boiled. The following also sounds very good. It is a Filipino method of BRAISING dogmeat that is also applied to pork and chicken.

Dogmeat Stew (*Adobo aso*) / Philippines

Cut dogmeat and chicken into pieces. Add crushed garlic, bay leaf, and black pepper. Barely cover with water and vinegar (1:1) and simmer until tender. Increase the heat, evaporate the liquid, add oil, and brown the meat pieces. Serve the *adobo* with a sauce made by DEGLAZING the pot with water and salting to taste.

In Chinese tradition, dogmeat is especially associated with heat and is eaten most during the dog days *(fu-t'ien)*, July 19 to August 18, to ward off heat prostration. In fact, a special dogmeat-eating ceremony called *a-chee* used to be held in China.

Red-cooked Dog (*Hon tsao go zo*) / China

Cut the meat of a puppy into bite-sized pieces and sauté in a WOK in oil, ginger, and garlic until brown. Add soy sauce, sugar, fermented bean curd, dried bean curd, and water. Simmer until tender. At the end stir in a little rice wine and serve with lettuce.

Probably most Chinese recipes for pork are also applied to dogmeat, as this recipe obtained for me in China by Man Tat Yan would suggest.

Stir-fried Dog (*Nan tsao go zo*) / China

Eviscerate and clean a puppy. Remove the hair by singeing in a rice-straw fire; continue this heat treatment until the skin is golden brown. Cut the meat into cubes and dry-fry them in a WOK. Add oil, ginger, garlic, and dried, salted black beans to another *wok* and stir-fry for 10 minutes. Add the meat, soy sauce, green onions, and deep-fried bean curd. Stir momentarily.

VISCERAL ORGANS

DOG'S brain and blood also were eaten by the Hawaiians in the past and their entrails by the Tahitians. No doubt contemporary Samoan recipes for pig's blood and organs also apply to the preparation of dog. Dakota Indians enjoyed dog liver raw.

That exhausts my repertoire of dog recipes. What about cat?

CAT MEAT

CAT also is eaten today, and enjoyed, in many parts of the world. According to the American outdoorsman Bradford Angier, our native American wildcats, the lynx and the cougar, taste very much like the white meat of chicken, have no gamy overtones, and are the preferred meats of some North American Indians. Angier himself has prepared them fricasseed, thickening the stock, and then adding some vermouth, cream, and lemon juice for a sophisticated nonindigenous touch.

Domestic cat, on the other hand, tastes more like rabbit than chicken and has often been sold as rabbit in Europe. No doubt more people have eaten cat than would admit it, and the fact that they cannot taste the difference seems reason enough to enjoy it for what it is, an abundant and often wasted meat.

I have found no data on the nutritional value of cat meat.

MUSCLE MEAT

This recipe comes from the part of Spain that produced the gauchos and most of the great conquistador leaders. A Spanish acquaintance from Alcantara says that it is preferred there to a similar rabbit stew.

ESTREMADURAN CAT STEW (*Caldo de gato estremadura*) / SPAIN

Cut a dressed cat into serving-sized portions, salt them, and brown each well in olive oil. Add to the pan some white wine, bay leaves, and thyme. Cover and simmer for about 30 minutes. Add shelled peas, shelled fava beans, sliced carrots, sliced turnips, diced potatoes, and chopped onions. Add water barely to cover and simmer until the vegetables are done.

A very differently flavored cat stew is also much enjoyed standard fare in Ghana. Its other ingredients show how great was the South American–West African culinary exchange during the days of the barbarous slave trade.

STEWED CAT (*Agyinamoa forɔw*) / GHANA

The cat is skinned, dressed, and cut into large pieces. These are fried until well browned in a mixture of peanut oil and butter. Add to the pan some water, tomato sauce or purée, salt, and chopped hot red peppers. Simmer the cat until it is tender and serve it with rice.

While the Chinese prefer puppy meat over adult dog, the meat of mature cats is most commonly eaten there.

STEAMED CAT AND CHICKEN *(Chin tsen mao zo, ti zo)* / CHINA

Cut the meat of a mature cat and a chicken into cubes and steam them until tender with water chestnuts, pieces of fresh sugar cane, fresh ginger root, and preferred herbs.

Cat meat is also stir-fried and sautéed by the same Chinese recipes as dog. It is eaten too in China as smoked meat.

Last, this dish, sometimes called "three snakes" or "five snakes," is considered a great Chinese delicacy.

DRAGON, PHOENIX, AND TIGER SOUP *(Lung fung foo)* / CHINA

Boil fillets of snake and ginger root for about 1 minute and drain. Line the bottom of a pan with pork skins and cook them in a small amount of water until they are gelatinized. In another pot prepare a broth from the meat of an old cat and a chicken. Remove the meat and add to the broth mushrooms, bamboo shoots, abalone, cloud ear fungus, scallops, and dried tangerine peel and cook about 15 minutes. Add the snake meat, pork skins, and shredded cooked chicken and boil for 10 to 15 minutes longer. Other ingredients sometimes used include ham, lean pork, and fish's stomach. Finally, add lemon leaves and chrysanthemum leaves and serve the soup with rice wine.

In a much simpler version, pieces of snake and cat are steamed for 3 to 4 hours with some ginger root. Only the broth is eaten after seasoning it with salt.

Other Organs

The eyes of cats were described as being offered in Cantonese food shops in the last century, but I have not discovered how they were prepared.

7

Rabbit & Hare

I N THIS CHAPTER and the next three we shall be considering the food value of small animals that can be raised practically in any backyard, garage, or basement—plus a few of their wild relatives. Rabbits, which have been domesticated since Roman times, offer particularly attractive possibilities for increased production of animal protein and an augmented family supply of cheap, nutritious meat. Domestic rabbit meat contains 50 percent more protein than T-bone steak with only a little over one-fifth its fat. It is almost as rich in niacin as beef liver and as tasty and acceptable as chicken. Wild rabbits and hares are similar in nutritional value but even leaner.

Because a small number of rabbits can be fattened on lawn trimmings, home garden produce and trimmings, and vegetable discards from markets plus a little concentrate supplementation, they should be much more commonly eaten by Americans than they are. Practical husbandry and feeding directions for those who want them may be found in Giammattei's *Raising Small Meat Animals.*

American prejudices against eating domestic rabbit fall into two main categories. The first is the recognition problem complicated by the emotional feeling that "bunnies" are pets given at Easter and, therefore, are not food animals. The second basis for our prejudice is the problem of relative unfamiliarity posed by the virtual absence of domestic rabbit meat from American supermarkets and our growing belief that unfamiliar foods are probably not good. In fact, one survey of U.S. university students indicated that 8.4 percent had never eaten rabbit, and 9.4 percent of those who had would not eat it again.

Not only are domestic rabbits not seen in American markets, but wild rabbits and hares are almost never sold in our markets or offered in our restaurants. In contrast, hunters' quarry in Europe commonly enter the restaurant trade and are frequently offered in city as well as village markets. One suspects, moreover, that many of the small game animals killed by hunters in this country each year never reach any table.

These marketing and use practices all contribute to a growing unfamiliarity with game on the part of potential consumers and with it prejudices many Americans share for any meat with a suspected gamy flavor. This prejudice is unfortunate because four species of wild cottontail rabbits (*Sylvilagus* spp.) occur abundantly throughout the United States and could potentially furnish more meat than any other species of North American game. Even Coney Island, N.Y., takes it name from its own once abundant cottontail population. Cottontail meat is light in color and fine in texture and is very much enjoyed by those willing to give it a fair trial. The European rabbit *Oryctolagus cuniculus*, which is also the domesticated food rabbit of the United States, is found wild only on the San Juan Islands of the state of Washington. Its meat, too, is light in color and very good.

Hares are also abundant game species in the United States, though most Americans are confused as to just what hares are, chiefly because we are accustomed to calling some of them jackrabbits. Biologically, the chief differences between hares and rabbits are that hares are born with hair and open eyes and can hop about immediately, while rabbits are naked, blind, and helpless at birth. The most common American hares are the varying hare *(Lepus americanus)* and the jackrabbit *(Lepus* spp.). The latter is the larger (with a record size of 13 lbs.) and the more widely distributed. Hare meat contains little fat and is, therefore, fairly dry. Younger animals are the most tender, while LARDING or BARDING adult carcasses improves their taste and tenderness considerably.

Basic Preparation

References to butchering instructions have been given for several of the meat-producing species considered so far, but the ease with which a family can raise its own rabbits (and the abundance of wild rabbits and hares) recommends that some butchering details be included here.

Live rabbits should be lifted by grasping the skin behind the neck with one hand and supporting the rump of the animal with the other. They should never be lifted by their ears. Killing is by stunning; that is, by striking a sharp blow with a hammer or other suitable object to the poll of the head. The rabbit is then suspended by a hook or nail between the Achilles tendon and bone of one of the hock joints, and the head is quickly severed at the atlas joint with a sharp knife. Alternatively, the vertebrae of the neck may be quickly and completely dislocated; this renders the animal immediately unconscious and severs major blood vessels in the neck. The animal is then hung as above and the blood accumulates beneath the skin in the neck region. For more detailed directions for the dislocation operation see page 218.

To skin the rabbit or hare, suspend it as indicated. Remove the tail and distal portions of the three free legs at the hock or knee joints. Cut incisions in the skin of the rear legs from the hock to the base of the tail. Peel these leg skins down to the tail, free the anus by circling the surrounding skin with the knife, and peel the body skin like a glove down over the entire carcass and remove it.

To dress the carcass, make a long, median incision through the belly muscles from the pelvis to the sternum. Split the pelvis and the sternum with the knife or poultry shearers and spread the body cavities open. Carefully peel out the urinary bladder intact and then the intestines, stomach, and liver all in one piece. Separate the liver. Remove the heart and lungs together and separate. Remove the kidneys. Wash the carcass thoroughly under running cold water and drain. Chill it for 24 hours at the lowest refrigerator setting above freezing.

In the case of wild rabbits and hares (and of other wild mammalian species in the United States), lethargic, ill-appearing, or abnormally behaving specimens should not be taken. Such animals may have tularemia, Rocky Mountain spotted fever, or other infections transmissible to man. In any event, when handling the animal and when butchering it and handling the fresh meat, rubber gloves should be worn and the animals' ectoparasites (ticks and fleas particularly) should be avoided. Most of these latter desert the animal soon after its death and may bite man.

Rabbits and hares are commonly cooked whole.

The Whole Carcass

This first recipe is like that for lamb *asado,* and it is a dish we sometimes prepare in our farmhouse in Spain before the kitchen fire.

Roast Rabbit *(Conejo asado)* / Spain

Oven and flatten the rib cage by breaking the ribs. Rub the carcass inside and out with white wine. Insert a metal stake in and out along the spine and spread-eagle the rabbit, using pieces of unpainted wire coathangers inserted through the two front and two hind legs and across the rib cage. Brush it thoroughly with aïoli sauce to which some prepared hot mustard has been added. Stick the stake in the ground in front of an open fire. Rotate the rabbit several times, brushing it frequently with the sauce. Throw some rosemary or bay branches on the fire occasionally, if they are available. Serve the rabbit with more of the sauce.

Conejo asado, of course, can also be prepared over charcoal or even in the regular oven, but not so colorfully.

Very different seasoning ingredients are used in this traditional English recipe for a roast hare.

Roasted Hare with Beer / England

Dust a dressed hare with black pepper, a little ground cloves, and some fine oatmeal. Fry it in butter until brown, put it in a pan, dot with pieces of butter, and roast at a low heat, basting frequently with beer. Drain the hare, flour it lightly , put it in another pan, baste with melted bacon fat, and return to a hotter oven to brown more. Prepare a gravy from the drippings from the first pan. Serve with red currant jelly and buttered brown bread.

This simpler French recipe is for roast hare served in a rich sour cream sauce.

Roast Hare *(Lièvre rôti)* / France

A seasoned hare is BARDED with fat and roasted in a 450°F oven. When it is almost done, add several cups of sour cream to the pan. The sauce is strained before serving.

Hares and rabbits may also be marinated to advantage before roasting. The secret of the following recipe is the deliciously tart sauce, and plenty of it. This is our family's traditional version of *Hasenpfeffer,* which differs in its marinade from others often encountered.

PEPPER RABBIT *(Hasenpfeffer)* / GERMANY

Put the hare or rabbit in a crock and cover it completely with sliced onions and a marinade of cider vinegar (diluted 1:1 with water—pure vinegar is a little strong for *Hasenpfeffer)* that has been brought to a boil with several bay leaves and some peppercorns. Keep the marinated hare or rabbit in the refrigerator for about 2 days, turning it occasionally. Then dry the carcass well and lightly dredge it in seasoned flour. Fry it in hot butter or lard until it is well browned on all sides. Put the meat in an open casserole, add half of the marinade, and roast it at 350°F with occasional turning until the meat is very tender.

In the meantime reduce the other half of the marinade by about half. Transfer the *Hasenpfeffer* to a warm serving platter. The pooled pan juices and reduced marinade then are thickened with a ROUX of flour lightly browned in butter in the pan in which the rabbit has been fried. Stir into the sauce some sour cream, correct for salt, strain some of the sauce over the rabbit, and pass the remainder in a sauce boat.

Hasenpfeffer, like *Sauerbraten* (see also, for example, Hungarian oxtails), is traditionally served with potato dumplings, *Kartoffelklösse.* Here is our family's particularly good recipe: rice a number of boiled and peeled potatoes. With your hands thoroughly mix in some egg yolks. Knead into this potato mixture fine cracker meal, adding more and more until the mixture is dry enough that it doesn't stick to the hands (it will take more cracker meal than you think). Fry some small bread croutons in butter. Place several of these in the center of a piece of potato dough and form it with the hands into a snowball-sized dumpling. Shortly before one is ready to serve the *Hasenpfeffer,* carefully drop the *Kartoffelklösse* one at a time into a large kettle of rapidly boiling salted water. Remove them with a slotted spoon as soon as they rise to the surface. The *Kartoffelklösse* are garnished with more croutons and should be eaten with generous amounts of the sour sauce. As leftovers they are good, if not better, sliced and fried in butter until golden brown.

Somewhat similar recipes may be found throughout central Europe.

The following from Hungary is particularly good, not so tart as *Hasenpfef-fer* but slightly sweet. Unlike many of the other capitals of Eastern Europe, and particularly Moscow, which is now a gastronomic desert, Budapest has managed to preserve many of its good restaurants and much of its noteworthy cuisine.

MARINATED RABBIT *(Bepácolt nyúl)* / HUNGARY

Cover a dressed hare or rabbit with the following marinade: in lightly salted water (with a bit of tarragon vinegar), boil for about 2 hours some sliced onions, carrots, parsnips or turnips, bay leaves, and a few peppercorns. Cool. Marinate the rabbit in the refrigerator for 2 days, turning it occasionally. Dry the rabbit and LARD it with some bacon strips. In a roasting pan sauté the thoroughly drained marinated vegetables in some lard, add the rabbit, and roast in a 350°F oven until about half done. Remove the roast, sprinkle the vegetables with flour, brown them with continual stirring over moderate heat, and stir in a generous wineglass of dry white wine and then about twice as much sour cream and some of the marinade. Simmer, add 1 T prepared hot mustard, a teaspoonful or so of sugar, and a little more tarragon vinegar. Blend these ingredients in an electric blender or simmer them for about 20 minutes and press through a fine sieve. Add the juice and a little grated rind of a lemon, return the rabbit to this sauce, and simmer it until tender.

In many cuisines whole rabbit or hare is also stuffed and then roasted. This English dish is served with currant jelly and interestingly incorporates cider in the stuffing. In both of these ingredients it betrays a distant Norman connection. The French recipe that follows it makes good use of the rabbit's liver in addition to its muscle meat.

STUFFED HARE / ENGLAND

Dress a hare, stuff it with a mixture of brown bread crumbs, suet, chopped onion, mixed herbs, nutmeg, pepper, salt, and anchovy paste, all moistened with cider, and sew it up. Roast, basting often with red currant jelly and butter. Thicken the drippings for a sauce.

STUFFED RABBIT *(Lapereau farci)* / FRANCE

Stuff a young rabbit with the following mixture: the chopped rabbit liver, an equal amount of chopped lean ham, and a little chopped,

BLANCHED salt pork, salt, pepper, and thyme. Sew shut and place in a roasting pan. Surround with small carrots, chopped onions, and a BOUQUET GARNI. Cover the rabbit with bacon slices and roast at 325°F for 1 to 1–1/2 hours, basting occasionally. Remove the rabbit and carrots from the pan, discard the *bouquet garni*, pour a cup of white wine in the pan, and blend the wine and pan drippings well over a low heat. Serve the rabbit surrounded by the carrots and pass the sauce.

MUSCLE MEAT

PIECES of rabbit or hare may also be prepared by several of the previous recipes and by these as well. The first two are for festive saddle of hare, one with a sauce of sweet cream and the rabbit's liver, the other sauced with sour cream and juniper berries. A third, generically similar dish incorporates the famous regional mustard of Dijon.

TOASTED HARE WITH MILK GRAVY / ENGLAND

Stuff a saddle of hare with a bread stuffing (as for poultry) and sew it up. Bake it for 1–1/2 hours in a 400°F oven, basting frequently with a pint or so of milk placed in the dripping pan. The milk and drippings are seasoned and thickened with the sieved liver of the hare and a butter-and-flour ROUX. Sweet cream is added and this sauce is served over the hare.

SADDLE OF HARE IN CREAM *(Hasenrücken in Sahne)* / GERMANY

Salt a saddle of hare and wrap it in bacon. Brown it well in olive oil. Add a generous quantity of sliced onions, a sliced carrot, sliced celery and leek, salt, pepper, and a few juniper berries. Roast until done and remove the meat. Heat the drippings and vegetables on the top of the stove and add some meat stock. Simmer the sauce, strain it, and thicken with cornstarch and water. Add sour cream, lower the heat, and then add the juice of a lemon and some white wine. Serve the hare with this sauce.

RABBIT DIJON STYLE *(Lapin à la dijonnaise)* / FRANCE

Brush pieces of rabbit well with Dijon mustard and bake them for about 1 hour or until tender in a 400°F oven. Salt and pepper. Serve the rabbit with a sauce made by adding cream, salt, and pepper to the pan juices.

Rabbit, like chicken, lends itself particularly well to broiling or grilling, and variations in barbecue marinades and sauces are legion. Generally speaking, any recipe for broiler or fryer chickens could be applied with advantage to rabbit. From my boyhood in Virginia, I remember rabbit prepared by the usual fried chicken recipes and served with a cream gravy.

BROILED RABBIT / MEDITERRANEAN COUNTRIES

Cut a rabbit into pieces, marinate them in olive oil, lemon juice, and rosemary leaves, and skewer and grill over charcoal.

In this Austrian recipe the boned, marinated hare meat is seared by broiling, then slowly sautéed. The traditional European accompaniment of red currants is readily replaced by cranberries in the United States.

BONED BROILED HARE (*Hasenrücken ausgelöst*) / AUSTRIA

Bone out a hare and cut the flesh into strips. Flatten them slightly with the side of a cleaver, pepper them, and marinate in a little lemon juice and olive oil. Quickly sear the pieces of hare under a broiler or over charcoal. Then put them in a pan with melted butter and cook slowly, basting with the juices. Serve with baked cored apples filled with red currants and the pan drippings.

A classical French treatment for sautéed rabbit depends upon addition of chasseur sauce.

FRIED RABBIT IN CHASSEUR SAUCE (*Lapereau sauté chasseur*) / FRANCE

Cut a young rabbit in pieces and fry it gently in a mixture of butter and olive oil. Add chasseur sauce, cover, and simmer until tender.

These next five very different European variations of sautéed or stewed rabbit each use regionally popular seasonings. In the first three wine is also added and, in the fourth, either milk or beer. All five well illustrate the culinary versatility of rabbit meat and suggest the virtually endless possibilities for its preparation.

SADDLE OF HARE WITH HORSERADISH *(Hasenrücken mit Meerrettich)* / GERMANY

LARD a saddle of hare, salt it, and cook for 30 minutes in a covered pan with a minimum of water. Add a glass of port wine, some nutmeg and cinnamon, and simmer, covered, until the hare is tender. Reduce the sauce a bit, stir in some red currant jelly and grated horseradish. Serve this sauce over the hare.

JUGGED HARE *(Tippehas)* / GERMANY

Bone a hare and arrange in successive layers large pieces of the meat, black bread crumbs, sliced bacon, and sliced onions in a casserole. Season each layer with salt and nutmeg. Tuck in some chopped garlic, a bay leaf, and some juniper berries. Cover with a mixture of meat stock and red wine (1:2), cover the casserole, and cook in a slow oven until the hare is tender.

BAKED RABBIT *(Zając pieczony)* / POLAND

Dredge a quartered rabbit in flour and brown the pieces in butter. Add to the same pan some chopped onions, chopped mushrooms, and garlic and cook until soft. Add some chopped thyme, a few bay leaves, some meat stock, and some white wine or wine with a little vinegar. Cover and bake in a 350°F oven (or simmer on the stove) until the rabbit is tender. Salt and pepper to taste.

FRIED HARE *(Hare stekt i en panne)* / NORWAY

Marinate a young hare in milk or beer in a cool place for 12 hours. LARD the animal. Thread a skewer through the vertebral canal to prevent the back from curling. Salt and pepper. Heat butter until brown in a heavy pan and thoroughly brown the hare. Lightly brown some chopped onions and sliced carrots in the same pan. Cover the hare with boiling game stock, cover, and simmer for 1–1/2 to 2 hours. Remove the meat and skim and strain the stock. Thicken the latter with a butter-and-flour ROUX and add cream; finish with more butter. Ladle this sauce over the cut-up hare and serve it with currant jelly.

STEWED RABBIT *(Nyúlpörkölt)* / HUNGARY

Brown a generous amount of chopped onions in lard. Stir in half of a small can of tomato paste and *much* paprika. Add a disjointed rabbit, cover, and cook over a low heat until tender, turning the rabbit frequently, adding a little water if required.

The language of the coastal area of Spain where we have our farm-house is Valenciano, a dialect of Catalan. It is an area famous for its regional cuisine; perhaps its most famous dish is a great *paella*, which is made more often with rabbit than with chicken.

RICE WITH RABBIT AND SHELLFISH *(Paella a la valenciana)* / SPAIN

A *paella* is a Spanish version of an Arabic pilaf. In Spain we prepare it outside over an open fire, but our method of preparation in the United States differs somewhat because a big *paella* pan will not fit well enough on top of our stove to cook things properly. The overall result either way is very good.

Make a paste of olive oil, much crushed garlic, lemon juice, salt, and pepper and rub it into pieces of rabbit. Brown them in oil in a heavy kettle. Remove the rabbit. Add a little more oil to the kettle, lightly sauté chopped onions and sliced mushrooms in it, and then add to them the amount of rice required. Stir and cook the rice a few minutes. Add some saffron and a volume of chicken and/or seafood stock equal to that of the dry rice. Bring to a boil. Cover the kettle tightly and simmer over very low heat until the liquid has completely evaporated and little steam appears when the lid is jiggled. During the last hour or so of cooking, place the rabbit on the rice to steam and finish cooking.

Spread this pilaf on an oiled *paella* pan (a large, round pan with about 2-in. sides and handles). Arrange on it in an attractive pattern the pieces of rabbit, as well as shrimp and squid, which have been fried in crushed garlic and oil, sections of fried *chorizo*, and any or all of the following: steamed mussels, clams, or other molluscs, a boiled spiny lobster, or other freshly cooked crustaceans or shellfish. Decorate the *paella* with strips of pimento and crisply cooked JULIENNED green beans. Place the pan on top of the stove to thoroughly heat through and serve.

Some European rabbit casseroles add other distinctive ingredients. The common Spanish culinary use of almonds reflects, again, the profound Arabic influence on Spanish cuisine.

RABBIT WITH ALMONDS *(Conejo con almendras)* / SPAIN

Brown pieces of rabbit in olive oil in a casserole. Add a generous amount of chopped tomato, a head or more of crushed garlic, some chopped onion, a clove or two, a bit of cinnamon, and a wineglass of brandy.

Simmer for about 20 minutes and add the following mixture: in an electric blender blend until smooth some toasted almonds, the raw rabbit liver, and a little water. Salt the casserole, cover the rabbit with boiling water, and cook until the rabbit is tender. Before serving, pass the sauce through a sieve and thicken it further with a mixture of oil and flour.

In a similar recipe, the amount of garlic is substantially reduced and a bay leaf is substituted for the cloves and cinnamon. Some parsley is blended with the above liver sauce and less water is added to the casserole. A handful of pine nuts is thrown in about 10 minutes before serving and a number of stewed prunes right at the end. This sauce is not strained or thickened. Our family likes both.

Other parts of the world further west add to the cook's repertoire of possibilities for sautéing rabbit or hare or preparing interesting casseroles. This Spanish recipe, for example, obviously saw its origins in Mexico. The cuisine of Spain is, in fact, a unique amalgam of Arabic, American, and European influences. The seeming incongruity of chocolate and meat in this and other Spanish dishes of Aztec inspiration does not suggest the excellent results obtained. Chocolate rabbit should encourage further experimentation with chocolate by any resourceful meat cook.

CHOCOLATE RABBIT (*Conejo en chocolate*) / SPAIN

Cut a rabbit into pieces and put them into a deep casserole. Add some olive oil, red wine, sliced onion, crushed garlic, grated baker's chocolate, salt, pepper, and a BOUQUET GARNI. Cover and simmer until the rabbit is tender.

Yoghurt and eggplant are other exceedingly valuable ingredients in meat cooking whose uses have been little explored in the West. These two very flavorful Indian and Turkish recipes exemplify their potentials in the American kitchen.

RABBIT IN YOGHURT (*Khar gosh korma*) / INDIA

Marinate salted pieces of a rabbit overnight in the refrigerator in cooking yoghurt. Add a generous quantity of quartered onions sautéed in GHEE, 1 t cumin, 1 t ground coriander, ground chilis to taste, several ground cloves and cardamon seeds, a generous amount of grated fresh ginger, and much crushed garlic. Add a little water and simmer, covered, until the rabbit is very tender.

RABBIT AND EGGPLANT *(Tavşan güveç patlıcanlı)* / TURKEY

Dust pieces of rabbit in seasoned flour and brown them in oil. Remove the rabbit and in the same pan fry sliced onion and peeled, sliced eggplant until golden. Put the rabbit on the vegetables. Add some chicken or rabbit stock, a little tomato purée, chopped parsley, and several garlic cloves. Cover and simmer until the rabbit is tender. Add a glass of red wine and some ripe olives. Thicken the sauce.

Finally, this classical English country recipe shows what can be done with the old, tough rabbit or superannuated hare. One area in which English cooking surely excels is in the expressiveness of their recipes' names. Who could improve upon "mumbled"?

MUMBLED RABBIT / ENGLAND

Put some whole onions and a bunch of parsley in the body cavity of a dressed old rabbit and simmer it in lightly salted water until the meat falls from the bones. Chop up the meat, onions, and parsley and return to the strained, reduced, and thickened stock. Add mushrooms, peas, salt, pepper, some sour apple pieces, and cider. Serve on toast.

Rabbit meat is also the basis for some locally renowened pâtés. Like all pâtés, these two recipes indicate ways to preserve meat usable for preparing very flavorful hors d'oeuvres.

RABBIT PÂTÉ *(Pâté de lapin)* / FRANCE

Put boned rabbit meat, fat pork belly, lean ham and onions (5:4:1:2) through the fine blade of a food chopper. Mix well with a generous amount of crushed garlic, chopped thyme, salt, and pepper. Pour over enough rosé wine and some brandy to moisten well. Marinate at least 4 hours and drain the meat mixture. Make a creamy batter from some of the marinade, flour, and eggs, and mix this into the meat. Pack into ovenproof dishes well lined with strips of pork fat. Cover with more fat strips and seal well with a flour and water paste. Bake in pans of hot water in a 340°F oven for about 3 hours. Cool thoroughly with the seal in place.

POTTED HARE / WALES

Make a paste of the following by first putting through the fine blade of a food chopper and then an electric blender: 3 lbs. hare meat, 1 lb. pork fat, some pepper, salt, nutmeg, marjoram, thyme, and parsley. Pack this paste into earthenware pots (higher at the edge than the middle). Seal them tightly with pastry dough and bake in a moderate oven for 2 hours. Remove the crust and cover the meat with about an inch of clarified butter or lard. The covered pots may be kept for 3 to 4 months in a cool place. Serve on bread.

Sausages in infinite variety can also be prepared from practically all meats. This *boudin*, for example, incorporates the rabbit's liver and blood as binders for the forcemeat.

RABBIT SAUSAGES *(Boudin de lapin)* / FRANCE

Prepare a thick *panada* by boiling bread crumbs in milk. Allow it to cool. Beat into the *panada* a mixture of rabbit meat, hard pork fat, and lean pork (2:1:1) that were well blended in an electric blender with some eggs. Fry some finely chopped onions and shallots in butter until they are wilted, mix in the minced rabbit liver and a little rabbit blood, and cook gently for a few minutes. Add this onion-blood mixture to the meat-*panada*, season with salt, white pepper, black pepper, nutmeg, cloves, cinnamon, chopped parsley, chives, and tarragon and knead well with the hands. Stuff into rounds and poach.

This rich soup with that much used English soup ingredient, barley, also incorporates the liver and blood of the hare for its thickening. Like the "mumble" recipe, it is a good way to realize a hearty meal from a tough beast.

HARE SOUP / ENGLAND

Cut up an old hare into small pieces and put them in an earthenware casserole. Add mace, salt, onions, a red (salted) herring (previously soaked for 8 hours), some mushrooms, a glass or so of red wine, and 3 qts. water. Cook in a 450°F oven for 3 to 4 hours. Strain the soup and add to it some cooked barley and a quarter pound of butter. Thicken the soup with the hare's liver (scalded and pressed through a fine sieve) or with hare blood. Reheat without boiling.

This and the next are both medieval classics from opposite sides of the channel.

JUGGED HARE / ENGLAND

Brown seasoned and floured pieces of hare in butter and place them in an earthenware crock. Add sliced onions and carrots, a BOUQUET GARNI, and a pound of red currant jelly. Cover the crock tightly and place it in a pan of boiling water in a 350°F oven and cook for 3–1/2 hours. Thicken the sauce with the sieved hare's liver or cornstarch and cold water and serve.

JUGGED HARE (Civet de lièvre) / FRANCE

Originally a civet was a game or poultry dish thickened with the animal's blood, and this version is prepared that way.

Draw and skin a young hare and save the blood and liver. Cut the body into several pieces, season them with salt, pepper, thyme, and a crushed bay leaf, put them in a bowl, and slice some onions over the meat. Pour over this a little oil and brandy (2:1), turn the pieces of meat once to coat well, and then several times more during a 3 to 4 hour period.

Parboil some squares of lean bacon and then brown them in a generous quantity of butter. Remove them from the pan and reserve. Add to the same pan and brown some quartered onions. Thoroughly dredge the pieces of hare in flour and fry them in the pan with the onions until they, too, are well browned. Add red wine to cover, a BOUQUET GARNI, and a clove of garlic. Cover the pan and simmer for about 1 hour. Remove the pieces of meat, add the marinade to the cooking pan, then strain this combined marinade and cooking stock and reserve it.

Put the hare in a casserole, add the fried bacon and a number of small onions and small mushrooms that were lightly browned in butter. Pour the strained cooking stock over the hare. Cover the casserole and put in a 350°F oven for 45 minutes. When the meat is done, add a mixture of the finely chopped hare liver, the blood, and about a half cup of cream; stir and simmer a few minutes until the sauce thickens. Correct the seasoning and serve garnished with large, heart-shaped croutons.

Again, in this dish from Provence we have in the use of anchovies with meat another holdover from the liberal Roman use of GARUM, or fermented fish sauce, as a basic seasoning.

HARE FILLETS PROVENCE STYLE *(Filets de lièvre à la provençale)* / FRANCE

LARD fillets of hare with rinsed anchovy fillets. Sprinkle with salt, pepper, and crushed garlic, wrap in bacon, and cook in a covered pan with a little olive oil for about 45 minutes, basting occasionally. Remove the meat and prepare a sauce by blending into the pan juices some tomato paste, white wine, and bouillon thickened with hare's blood or egg yolk.

VISCERAL ORGANS

SEVERAL of the previous recipes have incorporated rabbit's liver or blood or both, chiefly as thickeners. The other organs of the rabbit and hare are edible, too, just like those of the pig or lamb, but it has been more difficult to locate recipes. Rabbit kidneys have been especially prized and may be prepared by most other kidney recipes.

Most typically, rabbit viscera are added to rabbit and other meats to provide the basis of hearty stews, like this Gypsy dish of the fields.

RABBIT STEW / GYPSY

The meat is cut from the bones of a parboiled rabbit into 1-in. pieces. A buttered bowl lined with suet pastry is filled with the rabbit, some pieces of boiled bacon or lean ham, the rabbit's liver, heart, and kidneys, some small birds (if available), some chopped onions, mushrooms, basil, marjoram, thyme, salt, and pepper. Fill the pastry-lined bowl with stock, seal on a pastry lid, cover the top with a cloth, and tie it down securely. Place the bowl in a pan of water and boil it for 3 hours.

The following is the only recipe I have found, however, for use of these other parts of the rabbit by themselves.

HARE GIBLETS *(Hasenklein)* / GERMANY

BLANCH the cleaned stomach, head, heart, and lungs of a hare. Marinate them in the refrigerator for 3 days in some red wine containing a sliced onion, salt, and pepper. Cut the meats into pieces and fry them with some chopped fat bacon. Sprinkle with flour and stir and cook until the flour is browned. Stir in the heated marinade and some rich beef stock and simmer until the sauce is thick and smooth and the meats begin to fall apart.

Unborn rabbit fetuses were a delicacy in Europe in Roman times and later. In fact, so that they could be eaten by priests and monks during Lent, the Catholic Church once ruled them nonmeat.

8

Rodent &

Other Mammalian Meat

A S FAR AS this book is concerned, chapter 6 on dog and cat meat will probably most challenge our cultural prejudices concerning perceived "kinship" relations of animals to man and point to the irrationality of all such beliefs as determinants of what constitutes food. If so, this chapter on rodents and chapter 20 will probably share honors in indicating how whole groups of animals also come to be classified in our minds as repugnant, even nauseating, and through such prejudices be eliminated completely from our potential repertoire of foods.

On the other hand, some rodents probably have a potential for greater utilization as food on a world scale equal to that for rabbits and second only, perhaps, to that from further production of small ruminants. In taking into account this widely held disdain for, and even fear of, rodents among Americans, it should probably prove salutary to consider just what rodents *are* in order to note at the outset that there are certain commonly occurring rodents against which American feelings are less than polar.

SQUIRRELS

SQUIRRELS are as much rodents as are mice and rats, but they often are fed and otherwise encouraged by many urbanites in the same fashion as are some birds. In addition, squirrels are one rodent that is not completely foreign to American cuisine. Necessity or economics or choice could well stimulate our further experience of squirrels as food and, in the process, open our minds to the culinary possibilities of other rodents. Moreover, because squirrels, like many other rodents, can be and sometimes are serious pests capable of destroying immense quantities of human and animal foodstuffs, it is often necessary to limit their populations. Why not, then, "kill two social birds with one stone" and eat them down to reasonable numbers?

Sky-high prices being asked for beef in the United Kingdom have recently encouraged British families to rediscover some good old English country recipes for kinds of fish they had not eaten since "the war," for tripe and hearts and spleen, *and* for squirrels and some of their other edible pests. The following appeared in a February 1973 issue of the *Cambridge News*:

Now did you know that people are seriously considering the grey squirrel as an alternative to the Sunday roast beef? The idea of consigning it to the casserole comes from the Kent Branch of the Country Landowner's Association who met in Maidstone recently to discuss the possible ravages of the grey squirrel in Tree Planting Year. Mr. J. H. Walker told the meeting, "I would much prefer grey squirrel to chicken. If you look at the business with a completely detached air and get over any unfounded objections, you will find grey squirrel is much nicer."

. . . Grey squirrel is not unknown to British chefs and there is even the story of a well-known professor of veterinary science who lunched at a London restaurant. When the headwaiter asked if he had enjoyed the chicken, the professor replied that the squirrel was very good. In answer to the waiter's protests, he picked up a small piece of bone, "You'll not find a bone like that in any animal other than a squirrel," he said.

Pursuing the idea of the squirrel as a gastronomic delicacy, I asked Pembroke chef, Stan Crown. "I have cooked rats and snakes and all sorts of things when I was in the jungle," he said, "and they could be tasty. As for squirrel, flavour it up well with wine, sauté it first, then braise it with onions and turnips. Serve it with a nut sauce, say chopped walnuts—as squirrels are so fond of nuts."

How delightfully English that last touch!

Though also numerous enough to be pests in some parts of the United States, squirrels are even less appreciated here for their culinary virtues than are our hares and rabbits. How, then, can we use this good meat as food?

Before we begin with them and other small mammals, we should note that from the health standpoint the ticks of American rodents and other game may transmit Rocky Mountain spotted fever and tularemia. The fleas of prairie dogs, ground squirrels, and other rodent species may also be hosts for plague in the western third of the United States. Raccoons are a reservoir of rabies in the southeastern United States, and another infection that may involve American game is Q fever. Lethargic animals or abnormally behaving animals should not be handled or eaten; rubber gloves should be worn when skinning and dressing game, and all meat should be well cooked.

Basic Preparation

Squirrels and most other rodents are skinned and dressed in the same manner as rabbits and hares.

For cooking this type of rodent we can, in fact, resort almost completely for illustrative purposes to traditional *American* recipes not as commonly eaten now as in years past. For squirrel is an almost essential ingredient for authentic versions of native American dishes like Brunswick stew and burgoo. I still have very vivid memories from my Virginia boyhood of Brunswick stew, although more often than not my mother or the mothers of my friends made it with chicken rather than the original squirrel, rabbit, and turkey. Because it is almost certain to be enjoyed by even the most inveterate rodent hater, let us begin our rodent eating with this southern American classic.

BRUNSWICK STEW / UNITED STATES

Quarter several squirrels, season them, and dredge in flour. Brown the pieces in lard and then sauté some sliced onions in the same pan. Add quartered peeled tomatoes, a sprig of thyme, and water to cover. Cover the pan and simmer the squirrel about an hour. Add okra cut into pieces, corn cut from the cob, shelled lima beans, coarsely chopped pimentos, chopped parsley, and a little Worcestershire sauce. Cover and continue to simmer until the vegetables are done. Correct the seasoning and thicken, if required, with some pieces of blended lard and flour.

Burgoo is an Appalachian relative of Brunswick stew. It also illustrates the latent versatility of an emancipated American cuisine.

BURGOO / UNITED STATES

Put into a large kettle squirrels, rabbits, pigeons, wild ducks and/or stewing chickens, and a beef shank cut into large pieces. Cover with salted water, bring to a boil, cover the kettle, and simmer until the meats are tender. Remove the meats, debone them and cut into eating-size pieces, and return them to the pot. Bring to a boil again, add almost any vegetables cut into large pieces (potatoes, turnips, onions, snap beans, butter beans, okra, sweet and hot peppers, and sweet corn are all traditional), and season with more salt if required, black pepper, and rosemary.

A simpler squirrel stew, this English version also shows some mixed influences from across the Channel.

STEWED SQUIRREL / ENGLAND

Hang skinned squirrels overnight in a cool place and then marinate them for 24 hours in red wine containing garlic, chopped onions, chopped carrots, and salt. Cut up the squirrels, dry the pieces, flour them, and brown in butter in a pan. Cover with the marinade, cover the pan, and simmer the squirrel for 2 hours. Add some orange juice, thicken the sauce, and serve.

If they are first LARDED or BARDED with salt pork or fat, squirrels can also be prepared by virtually all braising, stewing, and casserole recipes for rabbit or chicken.

This final recipe for squirrel is from one of the more interesting regional cuisines of the United States, a fierce blend of Acadian French, Spanish, black, Indian, and other influences in Louisiana.

CAJUN SQUIRREL RAVIOLI / UNITED STATES

Debone several squirrels and pass the meat through the fine blade of a meat grinder. Sauté it in bacon fat and garlic. Add chopped cooked spinach or watercress, salt, and pepper and use the mixture as a filling for raviolis.

Native kangaroo rats or jerboas may also be prepared by recipes for squirrel or rabbit.

OPOSSUMS AND RACCOONS

WHILE opossums *(Didelphis marsupialis)* and raccoons *(Procyon lotor)* are not rodents, they are still eaten in the American South and are lumped together with rodents in many people's minds. The fact that we do have American recipes for them is sufficient reason to consider them here. Moreover, the meat of both of these species is similarly prepared, and both have long had their champions in the rural South. The opossum feeds mostly on wild berries, and its meat has an agreeable flavor. Opossum has over twice the protein of T-bone steak and less than one-third the fat. Raccoon has about the same protein content as opossum but slightly more fat.

Basic Preparation

Opossums and raccoons should be skinned as soon after killing as possible, care being taken to remove intact the glands inside the front legs and on the back. Excess fat is also trimmed off. Aging for several days is a matter of preference. Presoaking (and parboiling) are usually desirable for all but the youngest animals.

THE WHOLE CARCASS

OPOSSUMS (and raccoons) are often roasted whole. Both of these recipes are traditional.

POSSUMS AND 'TATERS / UNITED STATES

Rub some young or presoaked and parboiled adult opossums with a mixture of salt and black and cayenne pepper. Dredge them in flour and brown in a minimum of oil. Transfer to a roasting pan and add some water. Roast in a hot oven for about an hour. Add peeled sweet potato halves and more water if needed and cook, covered, until the potatoes are almost done. Sprinkle the meat and potatoes with brown sugar, lemon juice, and melted butter and return to the oven uncovered until the surface is well browned.

A variation on the above for either opossum or raccoon calls for seasoning the carcass with sage and pepper before roasting, cooking the sweet potatoes separately, and omitting the brown sugar and lemon juice.

Either species may also be stuffed before roasting whole in this somewhat similar recipe.

Ozark Stuffed Opossum / United States

Parboil a cleaned opossum and then rub it well inside and out with salt and pepper. Stuff it with a mixture of dry bread crumbs, chopped chestnuts, and applesauce and sew or skewer the opening. Put the animal in a baking dish, cover it with slices of sweet potatoes, and add some boiling water and about 1/2 C lemon juice to the pan. Dab the opossum with a generous amount of butter. Baste frequently during the baking.

Barbecued Opossum or Raccoon / United States

Opossums and raccoons are excellent simply split and broiled over charcoal. They may also be marinated in and basted with a barbecue sauce suitable for pork.

Muscle Meat

Baked Opossum or Raccoon / United States

The animal is first cut into pieces and steamed in a colander or pressure cooker. The meat then is covered in the baking dish with a dressing made of dry bread, some of the liquor from the pressure cooker, beaten eggs, and a generous amount of sage, ground cloves, and salt and baked.

Young opossums or raccoons can also be prepared by most recipes for rabbits or fryer chickens. They are also the basic ingredients of stews eaten in the rural South, including the famous *calalou* of the Gulf states.

FRIED 'COON STEW / UNITED STATES

Cut young raccoons into small pieces with a cleaver and soak them in cold salted water for several hours. Dry them and trim off all fat. Salt, pepper, and dredge in flour. Brown in lard until the meat falls from the bones. Pick out the bones. Add quartered potatoes, rice, chopped onions, sliced carrots, sliced green peppers, sliced okra, and quartered tomatoes and cook for 30 minutes or until the potatoes are tender.

CALALOU / UNITED STATES

Heat peanut oil in a heavy soup kettle and brown in it opossums, raccoons, pigeons, chickens, ducks, rabbits, and pork and/or kid cut into bite-sized pieces. Add shrimp tails, cut-up spiny lobsters, crayfish, and/or other crustaceans and sauté a bit longer. Cover with water and add salt, cayenne, rosemary, chopped parsley, marjoram, peanuts, and chopped orange peel. Cover the kettle and simmer until the meats are very tender. Add cut-up okra, onions, eggplant, and 2-in. sections of corn *on* the cob and simmer until these vegetables are done. Calalou should be the consistency of a thick stew and often is served with rice.

Porcupines *(Evethizon dorsatum)* are another small American mammal that is eaten, particularly in some of the northern parts of New England. Its liver is considered a regional delicacy, but I have not run across specific recipes for the animal or its liver. Writers simply state that it is eaten stewed or curried. Col. William Byrd II of colonial Virginia also praised "the surprisingly sweet flavor of polecat meat." Four different representatives of these members of the weasel family inhabit the United States. They serve as reservoirs of rabies in the western part of the country and should probably be avoided there for that reason if not for others.

GROUNDHOGS AND PRAIRIE DOGS

RETURNING to other American rodents, then, the woodchuck, or groundhog *(Marmota monax)*, was said to have been one of the most important items of diet among several North American Indian tribes, being far more plentiful and easier to obtain than deer. On the other hand, some Algonquin tribes that regularly enjoyed muskrat and beaver shunned the groundhog completely. It is eaten today in the hill areas of north Georgia.

The prairie dog, *Cynonys*, is still commonly eaten by Indians and has a slightly "earthy" taste. It, like the groundhog, is abundant, occurring in large "towns" in the Southwest. In fact, at the turn of the century one prairie dog town on the plains of Texas extended 100 miles in one direction, 250 miles in the other and contained an estimated 400 million prairie dogs!

For these species all recipes for squirrel and rabbit can be adapted with quite similar results.

Let us now turn to the one domesticated rodent now available in the United States that has great unexploited food-producing potential for our own and other populations throughout the world, the guinea pig *(Cavia cobaya)*

GUINEA PIG

MANY of us have at least heard about eating squirrels and some of the other small mammals considered so far in this chapter. I confess to not knowing that guinea pigs were also eaten until I first traveled in South America. I was then amazed to discover that, in fact, these animals now provide perhaps 50 percent of all the animal protein eaten in Peru! What is more, they are very easily raised almost entirely on vegetable and fruit scraps and lawn clippings and require minimal housing. On the west coast of South America wild, olive-colored guinea pigs are still eaten, but most families, even in the cities, keep at least one cage of domestic guinea pigs in the backyard. Commonplace is the removal of about two kitchen floor tiles to make a pen right in the kitchen floor to hold two guinea pigs and dispose of kitchen vegetable trimmings.

Guinea pigs have been a major food animal in this hemisphere from time immemorial, and Columbus discovered that even the Arawak Indians of the Caribbean raised them for the table. They are, in fact, delicious, and these two traditional Peruvian recipes I obtained from Dr. Elva Lopez-Nieto of the veterinary school of San Marcos University in Lima are merely indicators of the animal's food potential. One young mature guinea pig provides more than enough meat for an adult; it could be prepared to advantage by virtually any recipe for chicken or rabbit.

Basic Preparation

Kill the guinea pigs quickly by disarticulating their neck vertebrae as one would a chicken—that is, the hind feet are securely grasped in the left hand and the head in the right, with the right thumb on the vertebra at the base of the skull. A quick pressure down with the thumb while at the same time pulling up abruptly on the legs with the left hand disconnects the neck bones and severs the spinal cord. The animals are then scalded in boiling water, as for a chicken or pig, and plucked clean. They are *not* skinned.

A ventral midline incision is made from the lower jaw to the pelvis. The animal is eviscerated and then split open and flattened out by cutting through the lower jaw and the pelvic bones. The pigs are then washed and dried.

GUINEA PIG CREOLE STYLE *(Cuyes a la criolla)* / PERU

Soak plucked and cleaned guinea pigs in salted water for 2 hours, dry them thoroughly, and let them stand in the air for an hour. Cut them into quarters, salt them, and fry in very hot oil until brown. Reduce the heat and continue to cook until done. They are even better grilled over charcoal.

Some of my students at the University of California built a party one evening around this excellent Inca-inspired guinea pig dish from Peru. It combines all three traditional Andean ingredients—chilis, peanuts, and potatoes—and every student liked it.

GUINEA PIG AREQUIPA STYLE *(Cuyes a la arequipeña)* / PERU

Prepare as above (basic preparation) and then heat through in the following sauce. Fry finely chopped onions and a generous amount of crushed garlic in oil until golden. Add fresh yellow chili peppers (previously seeded, soaked in saltwater, and ground into a paste), black pepper, and salt. Cook a bit and add quite a bit of ground toasted peanuts (or peanut butter), several boiled potatoes, and a couple of potatoes mashed with a fork.

One other animal of the guinea pig family, the agouti *(Dasyprocta aguti)*, occurs wild in the Gulf Coast region of the United States. It can also be prepared by the above recipes or by those given for suckling pig.

If *you* will also try these recipes, I say *bravo* for coming this delicious distance with me in shedding your old dining prejudices against rodents. Now let us give your newfound convictions a real test.

RATS AND MICE

BROWN rats and roof rats were eaten openly on a large scale in Paris when the city was under seige during the Franco-Prussian War. Observers likened their taste to both partridges and pork. And, according to the *Larousse Gastronomique*, rats still are eaten in some parts of France. In fact, this recipe appears in that famous tome.

GRILLED RAT BORDEAUX STYLE *(Entrecôte à la bordelaise)* / FRANCE

Alcoholic rats inhabiting wine cellars are skinned and eviscerated, brushed with a thick sauce of olive oil and crushed shallots, and grilled over a fire of broken wine barrels.

What won't the French do next?

In West Africa, however, rats are a major item of diet. The giant rat (*Cricetomys*), the cane rat (*Thryonomys*), the common house mouse, and other species of rats and mice all are eaten. According to a United Nations Food and Agricultural Organization report, they now comprise over 50 percent of the locally produced meat eaten in some parts of Ghana. Between December 1968 and June 1970, 258,206 pounds of cane-rat meat alone were sold in *one* market in Accra! This is a local recipe that shows the South American influence on West African cuisine.

STEWED CANE RAT / GHANA

Skin and eviscerate the rat and split it lengthwise. Fry until brown in a mixture of butter and peanut oil. Cover with water, add tomatoes or tomato purée, hot red peppers, and salt. Simmer the rat until tender and serve with rice.

Rural Thais, particularly in Pathum Thani province, also relish rice rats and eat them, especially when pork and chicken prices are seasonally high. In one day an organized rat hunt netted 20,000 specimens. Roasted or fried, they sell locally for 35 cents to $1 per pound and are said to "taste like rabbits and are better than chicken."

In the United States we have several equivalents of the West African cane rat and the Thai rice rat. These are the rice rat (*Oryzomys* sp.) of the Southeast, the cotton rat of the South (*Sigmodon hispidus*, which has been domesticated for the laboratory), and widely distributed wood rats of the genus *Neotoma*. All can also be prepared by recipes for rabbit or fryer chickens.

Because of the importance of rodent meat in the dietary of such countries as Peru and Ghana and their potential as food species, this is probably a good point to consider briefly something about protein deficiency disease itself, since its discovery also occurred in Ghana.

Protein-deficiency Disease

Protein-deficiency disease is one of the great killers and stunters of infants worldwide. It was first described as a clinical entity in Ghana less than fifty years ago by the British woman physician Cicely Williams, with whom it was my privilege later to work in the School of Public Health of the American University of Beirut. She described a disease that was already recognized by the Ghanaians and called by them *kwashiorkor*, a word in the Ga language meaning, literally, "the disease of an infant displaced from its mother's breast by a newborn brother or sister." It is now known medically by that name worldwide.

Its symptoms, as Cicely Williams first noted them, usually develop when a mother stops breast-feeding her baby and the child must make an immediate transition to an adult diet. That type of diet simply may be "ungumable" for an infant or grossly deficient in balanced protein or both. From her observations among the children of Ghana of the consequences of such an abrupt diet change, Dr. Williams wrote her now famous clinical reports in the early 1930s.

The protein-deprived child, if its intake of calories is adequate, more often than not *looks* fine at first glance. In fact, the child might even be rather plump. This is misleading, however, for if you press his skin with your fingers, you see that the subcutaneous tissues are mushy and water-logged and the imprint of your touch remains. Later the skin becomes scaly and, in black children, it becomes blotched and develops areas of depigmentation. The child's hair may lose its color too, and curly hair will tend to straighten. Or the hair may fall out altogether. These are some of the outward signs of kwashiorkor that we now recognize all too familiarly worldwide.

If this protein-deficiency disease in children is complicated by insufficient calories, as it often is, then an even more disturbing clinical picture is seen. It is called "marasmic kwashiorkor." For here gross body wastage also occurs and death for the child is even more rapid. These poor infants are sometimes referred to medically as "spiders," for that is how emaciated they usually look.

In the years that have passed since Cicely Williams's original work on kwashiorkor, we have learned a great deal more about other, less visible, signs of this terrible malady. For example, we now know how it permanently affects a child's physical development and, even worse, how protein deficiency may produce a variety of psychic disturbances that, even if the child survives, can irreversibly retard mental development. Furthermore, even a subclinical case of kwashiorkor predisposes a child to infections. And if a marginally nourished child contracts dysentery or measles or some other infection, this illness itself may precipitate a full-blown, acute episode of kwashiorkor. A truly vicious cycle is at work. Unless some animal protein (or a mixture of plant proteins supplemented with certain essential amino acids) is fed these children, they almost surely die. And even those children who can be saved may already have been so affected physically or mentally that they will be at a relative disadvantage for the remainder of their lives.

Perhaps the courage to try eating such "exotic" food animals as the rice or wood rat, as people do in Ghana to help prevent kwashiorkor, will come from knowledge that not only in the French but also in the other greatest of cuisines, the Chinese, rats are an item of diet.

In Canton they usually are eviscerated, heavily salted, and then sundried in the open air. They are purchased this way in the market and the dry meat is prepared by most methods of traditional Chinese cookery. For those in need, please note, too, that in China rat meat is considered to have hair-restorative properties!

MUSKRAT

RAT is not completely absent now from the North American dietary. The ubiquitously distributed muskrat (*Ondatra zibethicus*) is eaten in Canada, French Louisiana, and elsewhere. Here are recipes to prove it.

Basic Preparation

Skin muskrats as one would a rabbit (page 181) and carefully remove the glands inside the legs. Eviscerate the animal.

BAKED MUSKRAT / CANADA

Rub the rats inside and out with salt and pepper. Fill with a stuffing of choice and sew the cavities shut. Cover the rats with strips of bacon or thinly sliced salt pork and bake them in a 400°F oven until browned. Reduce the heat to 325°F and continue baking until the meat is tender, basting frequently with the drippings.

CAJUN MUSKRAT / UNITED STATES

Simmer prepared muskrats in salted water containing onions, garlic, and a BOUQUET GARNI until the meat falls from the bones. Reduce the stock, add French mustard, pepper sauce, and sherry and thicken it with egg yolks. Return the meat to this rich sauce and correct the seasoning.

Young muskrats also may be fried or grilled as in the recipes for guinea pig. Older animals should be soaked in cold, salted water overnight and then parboiled first. Muskrat may be prepared, too, by any recipe given for wild rabbit or hare.

Muskrat represents a considerable untapped food source, even near our cities. An Associated Press item in 1978 indicated, for example, that over 200 professional muskrat trappers earn their livings within 10 miles of New York City, where they take over 24,000 animals a year. In all of New Jersey about 400,000 muskrats are harvested annually, their pelts bringing an average of $8.75 each—while their carcasses are discarded. This tremendous meat waste occurs despite the statement of one trapper that their meat tastes "like beef, better than rabbit."

Various mice have also been eaten for millennia. The Romans domesticated the dormouse *(Glis glis)*, a European rodent resembling the chipmunks, or ground squirrels, of North America. The ancient veterinary author Marcus Terentius Varro said that Romans built runs for dormice under nut trees. They also kept mice in the kitchen in special earthenware jars and fattened them on acorns, chestnuts, and other nuts.

Stuffed Dormice / Ancient Rome

Prepare a stuffing of dormouse meat or pork, pepper, pine nuts, broth, asafoetida, and some GARUM. Stuff the mice and sew them up. Bake them in the oven on a tile.

While living in England in 1972, I read that one enterprising person had revived the Roman practice of raising the dormouse for food and was hoping that modern Englishmen would again relish this meat as much as the Romans once did.

Field mice of many species also are eaten in several cultures, often prepared simply as in this Mexican recipe.

Roasted Field Mice (*Raton de campo asado*) / Mexico

Skin and eviscerate field mice. Skewer them and roast over an open fire or coals. These are probably great as hors d'oeuvres with margaritas or "salty dogs."

Farley Mowat also gives this innovative arctic explorer's recipe for *souris à la crème*.

Mice in Cream (*Souris à la crème*) / Arctic

Skin, gut, and wash some fat mice without removing their heads. Cover them in a pot with ethyl alcohol and marinate 2 hours. Cut a piece of salt pork or sowbelly into small dice and cook it slowly to extract the fat. Drain the mice, dredge them thoroughly in a mixture of flour, pepper, and salt, and fry slowly in the rendered fat for about 5 minutes. Add a cup of alcohol and 6 to 8 cloves, cover, and simmer for 15 minutes. Prepare a cream sauce, transfer the sautéed mice to it, and warm them in it for about 10 minutes before serving.

Sounds like a gourmet's survival meal to me.

BATS

This is the only recipe I have been able to discover for eating these flying rodents, although they are prized in China and elsewhere in the Orient. Too bad, because bats occur in the millions and are probably terrific to eat many ways. Bats behaving abnormally or flying in daylight should be avoided. They can serve as reservoirs of rabies.

BAKED BAT *(Pe'a)* / SAMOA

Flame fruit bats to remove the hair, or skin them. Eviscerate and cut the bats into small pieces. Bake them in the ground oven, or *umu*, over hot rocks or fry them with salt, pepper, and onions.

OTHER MAMMALS

FINALLY, a word or two about a few other nonruminant mammals that are found wild in North America. The European wild hog *(Sus scrofa)* has been introduced and established in the Great Smoky Mountains of North Carolina and the coastal range of California. It interbreeds with feral domestic swine that are more widely distributed (e.g., Florida, the Ozarks, Hawaii). A native pig is the smaller collared pecary *(Tayassu tajacu)*, which occurs north of the Mexican border. The meat of the latter is quite dry, but if BARDED with fat it may be deliciously prepared by any recipe for suckling pig.

The nine-banded armadillo *(Dasypus novemcinctus)* is an agricultural pest in Texas and adjacent states and is eaten there by some. Armadillo is eaten much more commonly in Central and South America.

BAKED ARMADILLO / UNITED STATES

Stuff a dressed armadillo with a mixture of chopped potatoes, cabbage, carrots, apple slices, garlic, butter, salt, pepper, and oregano. Bake at 350°F, basting liberally with melted butter and drippings every 20 to 30 minutes. It is served in the shell.

And last but not least, the bears that were once very numerous in North America were a major item of diet for Indians and European settlers alike. Moreover, bear fat was their most commonly used cooking fat. It and maple syrup are both ingredients for authentic Boston baked beans. Bear meat was also one of the most common original ingredients of mince pies. Today trichinosis is contracted in the United States by eating undercooked bear meat. As most of our bear species are now geographically localized and protected, their practical present or future use as a significant food source is nil. I end this chapter, however, with a traditional Chinese bear meat delicacy to stress again the great versatility and thrift of this imaginative cuisine. While Elizabeth David's condemnation is perhaps a bit exaggerated, this recipe for bear's paw suggests the disturbing core of truth in her belief that "in Chinese cooking everything that can be eaten is eaten, and in American cooking everything that can be thrown away is thrown away."

BEAR'S PAW *(Shon tsan)* / CHINA

Pack the washed paw of a bear in clay and bake it in an oven. Allow it to cool, crack the clay, and remove it. This will also remove the hair. Simmer the paw in frequently changed water until its gamy smell disappears. When the paw meat is very soft, continue to simmer in a minimum of water with shredded lean ham, shredded chicken, and sherry until a thick sauce results. Slice the paw and serve it in this sauce.

Are you now about ready to move on to fowl?

Part Two

FOWL

FOWL

A bird in the hand is worth two in the bush.

WHY WOULD a small wild bird "in the hand" be worth any-
thing at all? Purely and simply because it is very good to eat. Our
ancestors who composed—and understood—that proverb enjoyed nothing
more than a good blackbird pie or some crunchy sparrows roasted over an
open fire—and they still are being enjoyed in many countries.

Many Americans, however, would absolutely refuse to eat a starling or
a sparrow for some of the irrational reasons we shall consider later.
Pigeons, which contribute importantly and inexpensively to the animal-
protein supply of diverse peoples, are also similarly overlooked as a source
of food in this country, and even such popular fowl in America as chickens
and turkeys are not eaten to their fullest advantage. Add to these losses the
fact that valuable and tasty domestic species like geese and guinea hens are
rarely seen in our better restaurants, much less on the American table.
Overall, we have a situation with birds in our dietary where we have an
even narrower range of preferences and food options than for red meat.

Thickly coated and almost tastelessly uniform junk-food chicken,
deep-fried to its lowest common culinary denominator, is fast becoming
the new standard for an American "dining out" experience. And the
unnecessarily expensive plastic-wrapped package of chicken breasts or
drumsticks has almost completely substituted for the possibilities remem-
bered from childhood of a whole bird (with feet for the stock pot) and

maybe even a few free egg yolks. One wonders, in fact, what proportion of urban American families today would starve before figuring out how to cope with a live chicken with its feathers and "insides." When, also, is the last time you saw a real roasting chicken in the supermarket?

9

Chickens, Turkeys, Ducks, & Geese

I N OUR CONSIDERATION of the effects of ignorance and prejudice upon use of mammalian meats, we began to explore this "unmentionable cuisine" with the more familiar species, so let us do the same with fowl. Chicken is now the third most popular meat in America, following beef and pork, and since 1910 our annual per capita consumption has increased 179 percent while that for all meats together has remained quite constant. How different the situation today, when chicken is one of our cheapest meats, from those seemingly far-out promises of President Hoover in the early '30s to create an America so prosperous as to put a "car in every garage and a chicken in every pot"!

Despite the Great Depression, the development of the American poultry industry beginning then has been no less than phenomenal. In fact, it began a generally unheralded "feathered revolution" worldwide almost as consequential to the nutrition of many peoples as the highly touted "green revolution" of more recent years. Consider that in 1930 the average 9-week-old chicken weighed 1.66 lbs. and had to be fed 13.2 lbs. of feed to produce 1 pound of gain; today's chickens that same age weigh an average of 2.64 lbs. and can be produced at an expenditure of only 2 lbs. of feed, or slightly more, per pound of gain!

These remarkable developments in genetics and nutrition became possible only after a number of epidemic infections of poultry were brought under effective control in the United States, thus permitting chickens to be raised in very large numbers at a considerable economy of scale. With that, the raising of chickens expressly for meat, instead of chicken meat being chiefly a by-product of egg production, became possible for the first time. The implications for American nutrition and that of peoples in many other countries have been profound. Many urban families, in particular, for whom chicken or any other meat had been an expensive luxury, suddenly found available an affordable source of animal protein.

These changes in poultry husbandry have also resulted in the greater and greater concentration of poultry production and marketing at all levels in the hands of a few large industrial concerns. The small-family-farm chicken producer has largely been forced out of business in the process or into the role of contractual "employee" to these very large firms.

The overall consequences of these changes aside, what we have almost forgotten along the way is the fact that a small flock of fowl can be maintained at relatively little cost by many families today just as in the past. Supplementation of commercial feeds by kitchen scraps and garden wastes and surpluses (or allowing chickens to scavenge) could provide another way for many of us to cut food costs, dispose of some otherwise useless waste materials, and have better and more interesting food to boot. As in the case with the potential for cheaper red meat provided by rabbits and guinea pigs, American families with small yards can easily raise some fowl. For them, Giammattei's book *Raising Small Meat Animals* provides a practical guide.

In China, in fact, a tremendous duck population is maintained by an ingenious system of scavenging and waste utilization, and many European farmers and even nonfarm families with little property maintain a small duck or goose flock. At little cost, they are rewarded by some festive fare now virtually unknown to Americans.

POULTRY AVOIDANCE

DUCKS are commonly regarded as Eastertime pets rather than as food in America, and this reason for not eating duck was given by the 5 percent of American university students surveyed who say they avoid duck meat. However, the prejudices we have against eating our more commonplace fowl—chickens and turkeys—have almost entirely to do with their edible innards. Of university students surveyed, only 0.7 percent indicated a dislike for chicken meat and only 0.4 percent for turkey.

It would probably surprise many of us, therefore, to learn that prejudice against eating chicken meat is not unknown elsewhere in the world. This prejudice occurs, for example, among certain groups in Ceylon and Tibet, as well as in the Arabian peninsula. High caste Hindus also tend to avoid chicken meat. Mongols do not eat it either, nor do the Tuareg of North Africa and many tribes of the sub-Sahara. In fact, eating chicken for a member of the African Walamo tribe is a reason to be put to death.

In some other areas, a chicken-eating taboo applies only to women. In parts of rural Vietnam, for instance, pregnant women do not eat chicken meat because they believe it is poisonous, and among certain Philippine tribes it is thought that if a woman with a newborn child eats chicken she will die. Some other Filipinos believe that women must not eat chickens that "lay here and there in different places" or they will become unfaithful to their husbands. In fact, among the Kafa of Ethiopia, women who disobey a similar taboo are made slaves. Only men eat chicken meat among the aboriginal Kamar people of India and in the Marquesas Islands of Polynesia.

The origins of most of these chicken prejudices are not well understood. In India, for example, the same degree of prejudice is not associated with eating ducks, geese, and wild birds as there is with eating chicken. In some places the reason, as with many mammals, probably is originally religious because either the chicken, or at least the cock, was considered sacred or its entrails and bones were used for divining purposes. Among the Azande tribe of the Sudan, for example, chickens as oracles are too valuable to be eaten though they are raised in large numbers for these religious purposes. Evidence exists that cockfighting also had religious origins, and this bloody custom still persists enthusiastically (and unexplainedly) among some Buddhist and Hindu groups who generally abhor cruelty to animals or the taking of life. Thus poultry keeping in some areas is done for religious or fighting purposes rather than as a source of food. Similar attitudes also may have existed in years past in parts of Europe. In his *Eat Not This Flesh*, Simoons cites a statement by Julius Caesar that the Britons considered it wrong to eat chickens but kept them for "pastime and pleasure."

Other reasons given for chicken prejudices by those who observe them include the belief that the chicken as a scavenger is a dirty animal, like the vulture. This view is common in India. The Japanese, on the other hand, frequently keep chickens as pets and, on that account, may be reluctant to eat their own animals. They have no particular qualms about eating other chickens received as gifts or purchased for food.

What we shall consider here, however, are only the edible parts of common fowl species we rarely eat. Most readily available to us is the broiler chicken.

POULTRY TYPES AND QUALITY

A fryer or broiler is a young chicken usually under 12 weeks of age. When dressed it should be well fleshed and have soft, pliable, smooth-textured skin without feathers, blemishes, bruises, or freezer burn. Its breastbone cartilage should be flexible and the meat resilient to the touch. A Cornish game hen is a younger broiler, often 5 to 7 weeks of age and with at least partial Cornish breed ancestry. The older the chicken, the coarser the skin and less flexible the breastbone cartilage, and the darker and tougher the meat.

Live grades for chickens are U.S. Grade A (or No. 1), U.S. Grade B (or No. 2), and U.S. Grade C (or No. 3). Animals below these grades are "rejects." Live grading is based on health and vigor, feathering, conformation, fleshing, fat covering, and defects. Dressed birds are marked either U.S. Grade A, B, or C.

Basic Preparation

Kill chickens and other birds of comparable size quickly and without mess by disarticulating the first vertebrae of the neck. Immobilize the bird's legs firmly with the left hand (by inserting the index finger between its legs and then pressing your hand against the right side of your body). Hold the bird's head firmly with the right hand, placing the tip of the thumb at the neck joint between the head and the first vertebra. Simultaneously, in one smooth motion flex the head sharply over the bird's back while pressing down hard with the thumb and drawing tightly on the legs to quickly separate the first neck joint (stop pressing when you feel bones separate so as not to pull off the head). This action immediately renders the bird unconscious, then severs the spinal cord and major blood vessels. The blood collects beneath the neck skin. Fowl can, of course, also be killed by deftly chopping off the head.

Plucking the feathers of chickens and other fowl is easier when they are scalded first by dipping the bird for one-half to three-quarters of a minute in about 130°F water. To dress a bird, cut off the head, the neck, the wing tips, and the feet. From the head end separate the skin in front of the breast and with the fingers loosen the food-filled crop, esophagus, and trachea from their membranous attachments. Next open the abdomen with a midline incision from the vent (ano-genital opening) to the middle cartilage of the breast. Place the hand into the body cavity through this incision and loosen the attachments of all the visceral organs of the abdomen and thorax with the fingers. Carefully withdraw all of these viscera. The light pink lungs and the dark red kidneys may have to be removed separately by peeling them out with the fingertips. Wash the carcass well with cold water inside and out and dry it with paper towels. Chill promptly in a refrigerator at a cold setting for about 12 hours.

Is this effort monetarily worthwhile? It certainly is, as is the cutting up of a dressed fowl oneself. The California price in the autumn of 1978 for a whole fryer chicken was 7 cents to 10 cents less *per pound* than for the same fryer cut up.

Since there is essentially no prejudice in the United States against preparing the whole carcasses or eating the muscle meat of chickens and turkeys, I have limited consideration of these species here to food uses for their viscera and other odd parts that are too commonly discarded by the American cook. Though some Americans avoid domestic duck because it is too "greasy" and might reject goose, were it more available, for the same reasons, recipes for whole duck are at least readily available. Stronger prejudices exist, of course, against eating wild ducks or geese, particularly because of the "muddy" or fishy taste of some types.

We shall consider first, therefore, the use for food of common fowls' heads.

HEAD

THE heads of poultry are commonly discarded by Americans or fed to the dogs. Avoidance would principally be on grounds of recognition and merely the idea of eating them. They are edible, however, and I have come increasingly to believe that the signs of great cuisines are their abilities to lovingly and artistically create good eating with such very ordinary ingredients.

Basic Preparation

Scald the heads, carefully remove all the feathers, clean the mouth, trim the neck, remove blood clots, and cut off the beak. Poultry heads are used most commonly in stews or soups or in the stock pot. There is no reason why the organs of the several species are not essentially interchangeable in these three recipes.

This first is a Languedoc recipe for a south-of-France stew of turkey heads and other odd parts and viscera.

FOWL STEW (*Alicuit* or *Alicot*) / FRANCE

Cut some bacon into small squares, BLANCH them, and brown lightly in butter. Remove the bacon and in the same pan fry a dozen tiny onions until golden. Remove them and add the initially prepared heads, feet, wing tips, gizzards, and hearts from two turkeys or geese. Salt and brown the pieces well over high heat. Add crushed garlic and sprinkle the meat with flour, stir, and allow it to lightly brown. Add a glass of white wine and reduce. Cover the meat with turkey or chicken stock, add a BOUQUET GARNI, the bacon and onions, and some small carrots. Bring to a boil and then reduce heat to a very low simmer for about 45 minutes. Add the livers about 10 minutes before serving. Arrange these turkey or goose pieces in a shallow dish, garnish attractively with the carrots, onions, and other garniture and pour the sauce over all.

This Hungarian goose stew is similar except for the vegetable accompaniments and seasoning.

GOOSE GIBLETS FRICASSEE (*Becsinált libaaprólék*) / HUNGARY

Cover the prepared head, neck, wings, and giblets of a goose with salted water and simmer, covered. After about 10 minutes remove the liver and continue to simmer the rest for another 50 minutes. Add some chopped tomatoes, chopped celery, chopped onion, chopped parsley, and some peppercorns and simmer until the vegetables and meat are done. Blend some flour and water and a little lemon juice in an electric blender. Blend in a cup or so of the hot stock and then stir into the stew. Serve over rice.

This more liquid version is for a hearty cream of vegetable and fowl bits soup.

Fowl Giblets Soup *(Geflügelkleinsuppe)* / Germany

Put into a soup kettle the following prepared parts of a turkey, goose, or large chicken: the head, the neck cut into several pieces, the gizzard, the skinned and declawed feet, the wings cut into two, and the heart. Add a few whole onions, leeks, and carrots, some peppercorns, and plenty of salted water. Cook for 1–1/2 hours, skimming as necessary. Remove the meats and boil a number of potatoes in the soup until they are very soft. Thicken the soup with some blended butter and flour and then press it through a sieve or blend it in an electric blender. Stir in a little chopped parsley, add some cream, and pour this hot soup over the giblets and pieces in a soup tureen.

COCKS' COMBS

Cocks' combs are a traditional garnish used principally by French cooks.

Basic Preparation

Cut off the combs, pick them all over with a needle, and while holding them in flowing cold water squeeze them to force out the blood. Cover with cold water in a pan and then heat the water rapidly until the skin of the combs can be rubbed loose with a cloth sprinkled with salt. Remove the skin completely, soak the combs again in cold water until they are white, and then put them into boiling salted water to which a green onion and a parsley sprig have been added. Boil for about half an hour and drain.

Cocks' Combs *(Crêtes de coq en attereaux)* / France

Wipe dry some prepared cocks' combs. Marinate in olive oil, lemon juice, and finely chopped parsley. Drain and skewer in threes on small decorative skewers. Dip in beaten egg, sprinkle with fine bread crumbs, and fry until golden in clarified butter. Use to decorate appropriate entrees.

NECK

THE chief uses of the fowl's neck are to include it as a part in recipes for sautéed chicken pieces or to add it to the stock pot. Another interesting use for their skins is as sausage casing. Necks can be obtained cheaply at poultry-processing plants or can be accumulated in a plastic sack in the freezer for all such uses.

STUFFED TURKEY NECK *(Cou de dinde farci)* / FRANCE

Any sausage meat is stuffed into a turkey's-neck skin which then is sewn or tied off at the ends. It may be roasted with the turkey (in which case there should be plenty of drippings in the pan) or poached for 40 minutes. It is then cooled in the stock and sliced to serve.

STUFFED GOOSE NECK *(Töltött libanyak)* / HUNGARY

Mix equal amounts of ground goose meat, veal, and beef, some crushed garlic, some bread soaked in milk and squeezed, and some finely chopped onions. Make a thin butter-and-flour ROUX and stir in a little goose or chicken stock until smooth. Add the meat mixture, a little lemon juice, pepper, and salt; mix well and cook on a low heat until the liquid has evaporated and the meat is done. Cool and stir in some beaten eggs. Fill the whole intact skin of the goose's neck loosely with this mixture and sew up or tie off the ends. Brown the stuffed neck well in butter and then simmer for about 30 minutes in stock to which a sliced carrot, a sprig of parsley, peppercorns, and a bay leaf have been added. Slice the neck on a diagonal in 1/2-in. slices.

WINGS

WINGS of fowl are left attached in recipes for the whole carcass, or the separated wings are treated as any other piece of the bird. Commonly, however, the last wing tip joint is cut off before roasting or grilling fowl because it usually burns or dries out before the other parts of the fowl are done. These can be frozen and saved for this frugal but tasty supper or put in the stock pot.

TURKEY WINGS NICE STYLE *(Ailerons de dindonneau à la niçoise)* /
FRANCE

Fry seasoned turkey wing tips in a mixture of hot olive oil and butter
until they are nicely browned. Remove them and in the same pan sauté
some chopped onions, add some chopped peeled tomatoes and a little
crushed garlic, and cook for a bit. Return the wing tips to the pan, add a
BOUQUET GARNI and a glass or so of dry white wine, and cover to simmer
for about 20 minutes. Correct the seasoning, add some button mush-
rooms and ripe olives, and simmer for about 10 minutes or so. Add
chopped tarragon before serving.

FEET

THE feet of fowl are the one part I miss most in American supermarket
presentations of these animals. When you buy fowl in Europe, you know
you will get these choice candidates for the stock pot as well as the head and
innards. Poultry feet are excellent stock ingredients because they are
especially rich in gelatin. If they are to be used for other dishes as a meat,
they should first be scalded, the outer layer of skin peeled off, and the nails
clipped.

This single recipe is for a cheap, peasant's main dish that contains some
valuable animal protein.

GOOSE LEGS IN STEWED CABBAGE *(Gänseschenkel in Schmorkohl)* /
GERMANY

Rub some goose legs with salt and brown them in goose fat. Add some
finely chopped onions and water to cover and simmer until tender,
adding a shredded cabbage about an hour before the legs are done. Add
some vinegar and sugar (2:1). Strip the meat from the legs and serve it
mixed with the cabbage.

BONES

PICKED-OVER fowl bones provide the makings of stocks for stews, soups, or
sauces. The cheapest thing is to use the carcasses and bones of already
cooked fowl, but the stock produced is quite inferior for some purposes,

especially sauces. The classic French white sauces are all made from chicken stock or from veal or fish.

CHICKEN OR OTHER FOWL STOCK

To make first-class stock for sauces, use an old hen or buy cheap chicken backs and feet or use the wing tips, necks, and odd bits from chickens being used for something else. Put them in a soup kettle, cover with water, add salt and peppercorns, and bring to a boil. Simmer for about an hour, skimming the scum from the surface. When it ceases to form, add some celery leaves, parsley, pieces of carrot, and an onion or two or some leeks. Garlic or herbs can be added, too, if desired. Simmer for several hours longer, correct the seasoning, and strain. Finally, filter or clarify. The fat can be removed after the stock has cooled. If you use an old hen, there will be enough fat to keep.

The recipes for velouté and white chaud-froid sauces were considered in chapter 1. They can be made from chicken stock.

Béchamel Sauce

This is a sauce traditionally made (and so used in this book) by stirring heavy cream into an appropriate velouté sauce. If a simple béchamel sauce is indicated, it is merely boiling milk thickened with a butter-and-flour ROUX.

Mornay Sauce

This sauce is a thick béchamel in which grated Parmesan or Gruyère cheese is melted.

Supreme Sauce

This is a traditional béchamel sauce based on chicken stock, with more heavy cream added, and finished by removing it from the stove and stirring in some butter.

LIVER

THIS is one unasked-for liver even the most liver-hating American household frequently receives. One suspects, however, that the liver and other giblets in the little plastic sack inside the supermarket chicken are simply discarded by many American cooks, fed to the dog or cat, or, at best, boiled up with the neck as stock. Too bad, because chicken livers are choice food that has slightly higher protein content and a little more than half the fat content of chicken meat.

The same prejudices against eating any liver generally apply to fowl livers, namely, the very idea of eating the innards of an animal or the "different" taste. Yet here, in a sense, is some "free" food that can be wrapped in a small piece of aluminum foil and dropped into a plastic sack for fowl livers that is kept in the freezer. When enough accumulate, you have the good makings of one of the following dishes.

Recipes for fowl livers are generally interchangeable among species, though if other livers are substituted for goose liver, add some butter to compensate for their lesser fat content.

Basic Preparation

Carefully trim out the gall bladder without breaking it.

These first five recipes for fowl livers are all for excellent hors d'oeuvres. *Hi siu tong gon*, in particular, is guaranteed to be enjoyed by even the person who is convinced he does not like liver (or mesentery, for that matter).

DEEP-FRIED CHICKEN LIVERS WITH CRAB (*Hi siu tong gon*) / CHINA

Press a chicken liver on a board with the palm of the hand and carefully split it with a knife into 2 thin slices. Repeat for as many livers as desired. Soak the livers in soy sauce and sherry. Cut pieces of fatty pig mesentery or omentum into pieces 3 in. by 6 in. Put a drained slice of liver on a rectangle of mesentery, then several pieces of crab meat, a piece of crab roe, and top with another slice of liver. Roll up the mesentery into a small package by first folding in the sides. Deep-fry these packages for 10 minutes. (Egg-roll wrappers, available in Chinese groceries, could be used in place of the pig mesentery.)

After your guests have exclaimed over that one, bring these two on and get even more "ohs and ahs."

FRIED CHICKEN LIVER BALLS *(Beignets de foies de poulets)* / FRANCE

Chop chicken livers finely and brown them in hot butter. Add some chopped sautéed mushrooms and stir into this mixture some thick béchamel sauce. Allow to cool, roll pieces into walnut-sized balls, dip them in a thin batter, and deep-fry.

GRILLED CHICKEN LIVERS *(Rumaki)* / JAPAN

Chicken livers are wrapped about water chestnuts with a piece of bacon around both. Skewer and marinate in a mixture of SHOYU, sherry, crushed garlic, and grated ginger. Grill over charcoal on the hibachi until the bacon is crisp.

For livers *teriyaki*, simply omit the water chestnuts and bacon.

At that point you can pass some *crostini*, and if your friends have finally begun to make the liver connection or have become too demanding for your recipes, you can tell them they are partaking of the very newest and most "in" thing—a liver and wine tasting.

LIVER PÂTÉ *(Crostini)* / ITALY

Brown some chopped celery, carrots, and parsley very lightly in olive oil. Chopped chicken livers are added, as is the blood squeezed from a piece of beef spleen, and some chopped tomatoes (1:1:1). This mixture is cooked for 5 minutes. Then blend it in an electric blender with boiled onions, some anchovy fillets, and capers. Salt to taste. Pack the paste into a serving dish and heat it in a pan of boiling water for 30 minutes. Spread on French bread or crackers. If another thickener is used in place of the blood, blend in a beef bouillon cube or so.

With everyone fully into the spirit of the event, bring on next this unusual sweet and spicy taste treat.

DEEP-FRIED SIMMERED CHICKEN LIVERS *(Tsa paw ti kan)* / CHINA

Simmer some chicken livers for about 15 minutes in water containing soy sauce (4:1), some brown sugar, and some cinnamon. Drain, dredge the livers in flour, and deep-fry them until golden brown. Drain again and serve sprinkled with finely chopped scallions and almonds.

Now you are ready to get down to the real thing and complete everyone's emancipation from at least one prejudice.

FRIED GOOSE LIVER IN MILK *(Tejbesült libamáj)* / HUNGARY

Soak a goose liver and a piece of goose fat in milk to cover overnight. Cover the pan and boil until the milk has evaporated, then brown the liver in the goose fat, being careful to avoid burning it. Cool, slice, and dust with paprika. Yes, this *is* eaten in Hungary as an hors d'oeuvre.

These next two recipes could accomplish the same emancipating goal with absolutely delectable main courses or luncheon dishes.

VEAL BIRDS HUNTER STYLE *(Saltimbocca di vitello alla cacciatora)* / ITALY

Sauté chicken livers in butter until done. Chop the livers with some prosciutto, several sprigs of parsley, and a little sage. Salt and pepper. Spread the prepared liver mixture on thinly sliced veal cutlets. Roll each one up and tie it (or fasten it with toothpicks). Brown these rolls well in butter. Sprinkle with flour, add 1 C Marsala or sherry, and cook until the wine nearly evaporates. Place the rolls on slices of toasted bread. Make a sauce with the pan drippings and about 2 T of stock.

CHICKEN LIVER FLAN *(Flan de foies de volaille chavette)* / FRANCE

Cut about a pound of chicken livers into thick slices, salt and pepper them, and fry in hot butter. Remove the livers and sauté some sliced mushrooms in the same pan. Add the mushrooms to the liver slices, and in the pan in which they were both fried cook down about a cup of

Madeira and then add about 1–1/2 to 2 C thin béchamel sauce and 1 C of cream. Return the livers and mushrooms to this sauce and continue to cook until the sauce is quite thick. Put this mixture as the bottom layer in an almost baked flan crust or in tart shells, cover them with soft scrambled eggs to which some grated Parmesan cheese and butter have been added, sprinkle them with more cheese and melted butter, and brown the flan in a very hot oven.

These next two recipes are for other one-dish meals based upon bird livers.

EGGS AND CHICKEN-LIVER CASSEROLE *(Cassuola di fegatini di pollo con uova)* / ITALY

Brown finely chopped chicken livers in butter, add some Marsala or sherry and some water, and cook about 10 minutes. Break eggs (1 per chicken liver used) in a shallow buttered casserole and dot with butter. Salt and pepper. Bake in 400°F oven for 10 minutes. Cover the eggs with the cooked livers, garnish with some cooked asparagus tips, and bake 5 minutes longer.

STEWED CHICKEN LIVERS *(Wątróbki z kur)* / POLAND

Soak chicken livers in milk for about 6 hours. Brown some butter and stir in an equal volume of flour to make a ROUX. Add enough chicken broth to make a smooth sauce. Pour in some Madeira and cook a little more. Drain the livers and lightly flour them. Add them to the cooking sauce along with sliced onions and some dry mushrooms cut into pieces. Cover and simmer for 15 minutes. Salt to taste and serve.

This variation on a liverwurst from Sweden is for another sausage that uses the neck skins of geese or other fowl as its interesting casings. Goose liver is quite rich in fat, averaging 10 percent (and 16.5 percent protein). Pâté de foie gras from force-fed geese has, on the other hand, 43.8 percent fat and 11.4 percent protein.

GOOSE LIVER SAUSAGE *(Gåsleverkorv)* / SWEDEN

Put through the fine blade of a food chopper equal amounts of goose and calf's liver. Sprinkle the liver with a little flour and mix it with a little cooked rice, some finely chopped onions, and some seedless raisins, season it with salt, pepper, and a bit of marjoram. Moisten the mixture with some molasses, some beaten eggs, and enough milk to make a soft paste. Sew up one end of the neck skins from several geese, stuff them about 2/3 full with the mixture, sew the open ends, and simmer the sausages in water for about an hour. Slice and serve. This sausage may be prepared in sausage casings, if preferred.

In this, the pâté is stuffed into apples instead and served with roast goose or roast pork.

BAKED APPLE WITH GOOSE LIVER *(Äpfel mit Gänseleber)* / GERMANY

Stuff apples with a mixture of finely chopped goose liver and pork sausage. Place in a shallow buttered casserole, add a glass of wine, cover, and bake until done.

This is one of many simple Chinese combinations of livers with vegetables and seasonings that are either simmered or stir-fried.

CHICKEN LIVERS IN OYSTER SAUCE *(How yo ti kan)* / CHINA

Cut chicken livers into 1/2-in. slices (this is facilitated by first BLANCHING them momentarily in boiling water). Boil a cup of chicken stock in a WOK and add 2 T Chinese oyster sauce, 2 T light soy sauce, 1 t sugar, and a little salt. Add the livers and several minced scallions and simmer covered for a few minutes. Thicken with some cornstarch and cold water and garnish with smoked ham cut into very fine JULIENNE.

And last, two Italian recipes for fowl livers with ham or artichokes.

CHICKEN LIVERS WITH SAGE *(Fegatini di pollo alla salvia)* / ITALY

Cook chopped chicken livers, chopped prosciutto, some chopped sage leaves, salt, and pepper in butter for about 15 minutes. Remove the livers and finish the sauce by adding some Marsala and butter and cooking a few minutes more. Serve the livers and sauce over bread triangles fried in butter.

CHICKEN LIVERS WITH ARTICHOKES *(Fegatini di pollo con carciofi)* /
ITALY

Trim some artichokes well, cut each into eighths, and remove the
chokes. Toss with lemon juice, drain, and cook until well browned in 3
T olive oil. Salt and pepper. In another pan cook chicken livers in
butter for about 5 minutes. Add them to the artichokes along with some
chopped prosciutto and cook 2 minutes. Add chopped parsley and the
juice of half a lemon, mix well, and serve.

STOMACH

BIRDS have two stomachs, a glandular and a muscular. This latter, or
gizzard, grinds up hard seeds with grit so that they then can be digested in
the glandular organ. The thick wall of the gizzard is all dark meat muscle.
It is often used in recipes with birds' hearts and/or livers. Gizzards and
hearts can be individually wrapped in foil and accumulated in separate
sacks in the freezer.

Beyond the idea of eating stomach, there should be no taste prejudice
against eating gizzards. Like mammalian tongue, they are just plain ordi-
nary meat. As there is no waste, they can make for very cheap meals.
Chicken gizzards contain 20.1 percent protein and 2.7 percent fat.

Basic Preparation

Slice into the gizzard along its greater curvature, cutting through its thick,
white, fibrous inner lining. Carefully peel out this lining without spilling
its feed and grit contents. Trim off excess fat and wash the gizzards.

Again, we will start with a tasty, inexpensive hors d'oeuvre.

DEEP-FRIED CHICKEN GIZZARDS *(Tsa ti tsun)* / CHINA

Well-trimmed gizzards are cut in halves or thirds and their surfaces
scored several places with a knife. They are marinated in soy sauce,
sugar, and sherry, drained, dipped in cornstarch, and deep-fried. They
again are drained and seasoned with black pepper. Ginger and/or
crushed garlic also may be added to the marinade.

This is an equally good introduction to all the giblets.

CHICKEN GIBLETS *(Tori-motsu)* / JAPAN

Trim some chicken gizzards and hearts. Cover them with a mixture of water and SHOYU (2:1). Stir in some sugar (same volume as that for the *shoyu*), a lot of grated ginger, and several garlic cloves. Bring to a boil and then simmer for 2 to 3 hours or until the giblets are tender. If too much of the sauce evaporates or the giblets become too salty, add water. For the chicken livers, simmer liver halves in a mixture of water and *shoyu* (3:2) with a little sake, sugar, and grated ginger added. Add some scallions and continue cooking very briefly. Drain and serve all the giblets hot or cold with boiled rice and a SHOYU-WASABI dipping sauce.

This stir-fried gizzard recipe, however, is for a dinner course.

STIR-FRIED CHICKEN GIZZARDS *(Sen tsao ti tsun)* / CHINA

Trimmed chicken gizzards are cut into 3 or 4 pieces. A sliced onion and a few slices of ginger are stir-fried briefly in hot peanut oil in a WOK. The gizzards are added and stir-fried for a few minutes. Then add a little soy sauce, sherry, sliced water chestnuts, sliced bamboo shoots, and some water. Simmer, covered, until the bamboo shoots are crisply tender. Correct for salt and, if desired, thicken with some cornstarch and cold water. Some diced TOFU may be substituted for one or both of the vegetables.

Last, an inexpensive but good soup that also uses all three organs.

CHICKEN GIBLET AND GREEN PEA SOUP *(Ti tsa tin to tan)* / CHINA

Prepare a rich chicken-and-pork stock. Bring to a boil and add chopped chicken gizzards, hearts, and shelled green peas. Cook until nearly done. Add chopped chicken livers, 1 T or so of soy sauce, and salt and pepper to taste. Boil a minute longer and serve.

INTESTINES

I have encountered only a few recipes for bird's intestines; one is given below, and a second in chapter 11, on small birds. If you choose not to eat them yourself but feed them to the dog, bird intestines are far cheaper obtained this way, from the bird itself, than purchased as "chicken parts" in canned dog foods. Your dog would probably also appreciate the difference.

Basic Preparation

Draw sections of the intestines between a cutting board and the straight back of a knife to express their contents. Slit open with a small scissors and wash under running water. Dry between paper towels. *Note the cautions in the introduction to the meat section*, pages 9–10.

This is for another rich, mixed-organ stew made from the chicken, for which the adaptive Filipino cuisine has several versions.

CHICKEN ORGANS IN BLOOD SAUCE *(Dinuguan manok)* / PHILIPPINES

Fry a good quantity of crushed garlic and sliced onions in oil. Add chopped tomatoes, chopped raw chicken meat and internal organs (e.g., slitted and washed intestines, liver, heart, gizzard, and kidneys), and cook 10 minutes. Add vinegar, salt, pepper, a laurel or bay leaf, and a pinch of oregano. Stir in chicken blood diluted with water (1:1). If the blood has coagulated, blend it and the water in an electric blender or press through a sieve. Cook a bit longer to thicken and serve with rice and hot pickled peppers.

TESTICLES

MY neighbor and colleague Rosie Rosenwald is probably the world's leading authority on turkey testicles. And on that account, and others, cocktails at his house generally are a mixture of surprise and delight (delight in watching initiates' faces as they try to figure out what they are eating). These meats are available frozen from turkey packers and on order through many local butchers.

TURKEY TESTES A LA ROSENWALD / UNITED STATES

Partially thaw frozen turkey testicles and express the organ from its membranes by squeezing it as one would peel a Concord grape. Coat the glands with well-seasoned bread crumbs and deep-fry them individually in 325° to 350°F oil until golden brown. Rosie serves them with margaritas.

Turkey "fries," which are the size of jumbo olives, also may be prepared by any recipe for sweetbreads. They are particularly good sautéed in brown butter.

Or if you feel very experimental and in a nostalgic mood, use this as one course for a reconstructed Roman orgy. It could use turkey testicles as readily.

SMALL BITS STEW *(Minute apicianum)* / ANCIENT ROME

Cook together in a mixture of olive oil, wine, and GARUM, capon testicles, some small fish, tiny meat balls, suckling pig sweetbreads, leeks, and mint. Add pepper, coriander, a little honey, and more wine. Thicken with pieces of flour and oil.

BLOOD

BLOOD is a classic thickener for civets, or blood stews, and for soups. However, this first recipe is for a richly sauced chicken dish festively finished at the table.

CHICKEN IN BLOOD SAUCE *(Poulet au sang)* / FRANCE

Kill a chicken and collect its blood. Mix 2 to 3 T red wine with the blood. Cut up the plucked and drawn bird and fry the pieces in butter. Remove the chicken and cook lightly in the same pan a dozen small white onions and a number of similarly sized squares of bacon. Add a dozen button mushrooms and remove all from the pan when they are done.

Add a little flour to the pan, mix well, and cook slightly. Stir in 2 C red wine and a little liquid from a beef-and-vegetable soup or stew. Cook this sauce a bit, correct the seasoning, and then strain it. Return the chicken and garnishes to the pan, add a BOUQUET GARNI and the strained sauce, and simmer, covered, for about 45 minutes. Before you are ready to serve, stir in the chicken blood and wine to thicken the stock. Add some warm brandy and ignite. Serve in a bowl and garnish with heart-shaped croutons.

This very unusual Chinese soup recipe combines three different coagulated proteins as its solid phase—blood, eggs, and soy bean. The result is as good as it is colorful.

CHICKEN BLOOD SOUP *(Ti sheh tan)* / CHINA

Cut a block of TOFU into thin strips 1-in. long. Fry a well-beaten egg in oil as a very thin omelet. Prepare a second omelet and cut both into thin strips. Boil 3 C water, add 1 C chicken blood, and simmer 1 minute. Remove the coagulated blood and cut it into thin, 1-in. strips. Reboil water, add the *tofu* and coagulated blood, and simmer for 10 minutes. Add the eggs, 1 t vinegar, 1 t soy sauce, and a pinch of pepper.

Whether this last recipe for common fowl is rightly a stew or a soup is all in the eyes of the beholder. Like many eastern European dishes, it combines fruits, meats, and milk in very satisfying ways.

DUCK SOUP *(Czarnina)* / POLAND

Kill a duck or goose and catch its blood in a bowl containing about 1/2 C vinegar. Stir to prevent the blood from coagulating. (Pig's blood also may be used.) Put some pork spareribs in a pan, add the wing tips, necks, and giblets (and, if desired, the plucked and cleaned head and the feet) of the fowl. Cover the meat with water, boil, and skim. Tie a stalk of celery, some parsley, a small onion, a few allspice, peppercorns, and cloves in cheesecloth or muslin and add to the soup and simmer for about 2 hours. Remove the spice sack and add some dried prunes, dried apples or pears, and some cherries or grapes and simmer for about 1/2 hour. In an electric blender, blend about 2 T flour, 1/2 C of the blood, and 3 T of the soup stock. Stir this into the soup. Add a little sugar and a cup of cream and bring to the boiling point. Serve with potato dumplings or with noodles.

10

Pigeons

IN THIS CHAPTER and the next I want to discuss the merits of our beginning to eat our bird pests. We have such birds in great abundance in the United States, and particularly costly losses each year are attributable to three introduced pest species alone—the starling, the English sparrow, and the urban pigeon.

These pigeons especially could be a valuable free food resource for many of us if we did what Europeans and Asians and others do: build a pigeon roost or loft in our yard or on our garage or on the roof of our apartment buildings so that the pigeons will nest there rather than under the eaves or in ventilators and grillworks. Though not domesticated, these wild pigeons are so domiciliated (dependent on man and his surroundings) that they by far prefer housing made for them than scouting out nest harborages on their own. By having them nest in accessible roosts and lofts, we can harvest their squabs for free food and keep their numbers under control in the process.

Not only is urban pigeon control as now practiced in the United States a costly affair, spawning companies with names like "Bye Bye Birdie," but uncontrolled pigeon breeding in building ventilator ducts and similar sites can result in human cases of a psittacosislike infection for which they sometimes serve as a reservoir.

Of course, pigeons can also be seriously raised by breeding domestic squabber stock, and this is another excellent way for a family to raise cheap meat of very good quality, though certainly not free meat. Persons interested in starting a small-scale squab-production unit should consult a good introductory book like Giammattei's *Raising Small Meat Animals*.

As squabs—that is, immature, 25- to 30-day-old pigeons about to leave the nest—pigeon meat has always constituted a choice food for kings—or luxury restaurants. It is dark and rich and responds wonderfully to the most delicate culinary care. Mature pigeons are also edible, but their flesh lacks the unique flavor of squabs and requires somewhat more robust treatment in the kitchen.

A whole cookbook could easily be written about cooking pigeons. To maintain balance, however, and still indicate a considerable range of possibilities for low-cost or no-cost meals, I have selected enough different kinds of pigeon recipes from a number of cuisines to suggest what most Americans are now missing.

We were once, of course, probably the most pigeon-eating country of all. In fact, for the table, and, I am afraid, for "sport" or purely as an outlet for our aggressions we decimated and made extinct an estimated 9 billion passenger pigeons. The largest recorded flock of these birds that once "darkened the sky" of America was 240 miles long and a mile wide and contained an estimated 2,230,000 pigeons. An American hunter in 1770 who fired one shot from his blunderbuss into one such flock is said to have downed 125 pigeons.

Most of us enjoy seeing city pigeons strutting about our streets and parks, if we do not personally suffer the consequences of their markedly excess numbers. Pigeon-eating prejudices are prominent, therefore, among elderly people and others who make a routine of feeding them from park benches yet are ignorant of their pest roles. Others reject all "game" without trial or simply shun the untried and unfamiliar. A little experience with squabs on the plate and a little information about the need to keep them in check could result in some delicious, cheap, food rewards for many of us. The protein content of squab meat is slightly less than that of chicken, but it contains almost 3 times as much fat. In addition to the recipes given here, many others for Cornish game hens, chicken broilers, quail, and the like are also suitable for or adaptable to pigeon.

Basic Preparation

For instructions on killing and dressing pigeons, see page 218.

The first recipes given are for squab, while those at the end of the chapter are suitable for adult pigeons as well as for squab.

We begin with an easy-to-prepare dish equally at home on a picnic or as the main course of a meal.

BROILED SQUAB *(Waka dori no yaki tori)* / JAPAN

Simmer for a few minutes a mixture of sake, MIRIN, SHOYU (3:3:1), sugar, salt, and pepper and then cool. Pour this marinade over halved squabs and keep them in the refrigerator overnight, turning occasionally. Skewer the squabs and broil them over charcoal, basting with the marinade.

The skin of squabs browns beautifully on frying and, in these recipes, the fried bird's fine flavor is allowed simply to speak for itself or is subtly accented by a little ginger, anise, and other touches of the Orient.

FRIED SQUABS *(Gerbratene junge Tauben)* / GERMANY

Dip quartered, seasoned squabs in beaten egg and roll them in bread crumbs. Fry them in butter.

FRIED SQUABS *(Su tsa nen kuh)* / CHINA

Quarter medium-sized squabs and marinate them in a mixture of soy sauce, sherry, a little salt, some sugar, a little FIVE-SPICE, grated ginger root, and some sliced onions. Dry the pieces and fry them in hot oil until brown.

Or frying may be merely the first step to make more attractive the birds in an elegantly flavored casserole.

PIGEON IN ORANGE PEEL SAUCE *(Jiu pi kuh)* / CHINA

Marinate some squabs in a mixture of soy sauce, sherry, ginger, sugar, salt, and pepper and then deep-fry them until golden. Drain and place them in a deep casserole. Add some grated, presoaked dried orange peel, some dried Chinese dates, and chicken stock to cover. Simmer the pigeons for 50 minutes and serve.

This squab casserole recipe from Charleston, S.C., clearly betrays the French origins of that city's traditional cuisine.

Squab Carolina / United States

Place a stalk of celery and a few slices of carrot into the body cavity of each squab. Fry the birds until well browned in a mixture of butter and olive oil. Add sliced onions to the pan and fry until golden. Add dry white wine, sherry, dry vermouth, and stock (4:1:1:2), sliced ripe olives, salt, pepper, and some oregano. Cover and simmer until the birds are tender. Garnish with chopped parsley and sauce with the pan drippings.

Stuffed squabs may also be baked to advantage *en casserole* with various garnishes.

Pigeons with Chestnuts (*Duiven met kastanjes*) / Belgium

Rub some squabs with salt and pepper and stuff them with a mixture of the chopped giblets, bread crumbs, butter, chopped parsley, thyme, salt, and pepper. Brown the birds in butter and transfer them and the pan juices to a casserole. Add some red wine and chicken stock, cover, and cook in a 350°F oven. After 1/2 hour add shelled chestnuts and continue to cook until the pigeons are tender. Surround the pigeons on a platter with the chestnuts and serve with a sauce prepared from the pan stock thickened with a butter-and-flour ROUX to which some cream is added at the end.

Boned-out squabs can provide the bases for very delicate dishes, such as this famed regional Chinese use for Hong Kong's pigeon pests.

Hong Kong Pigeon (*Shang kan kuh*) / China

Shred the meat of some squabs and chop several chicken and pigeon livers. Mix all of these with a beaten egg yolk, salt, and pepper and stir-fry quickly in oil. Reduce the heat and after a few minutes add sliced, presoaked dried mushrooms, sliced bamboo shoots, chopped water chestnuts, chopped green peppers, pieces of green onion, and a few slices of ginger. STEW over medium heat for 10 minutes and add a little AJINOMOTO, light soy sauce, sugar, salt, pepper, and a few drops of sesame oil. Simmer a minute or so and serve the mixture in crisp lettuce shells on a bed of freshly fried noodles.

Finally, squab combines with another ingredient raised in the United States almost exclusively for export to the Orient for an unusual soup. We should begin keeping some of our ginseng at home.

Squab and Ginseng Root Soup *(Jo kuh ton sen kan)* / China

To a boiling fowl stock add some quartered squabs and some sherry and simmer, covered, for about 15 minutes. Add about 1/2 C ginseng root (for soup) cut into slices, a little sliced ginger, and a bit of soy sauce. Cover and simmer until the squabs are tender; correct the salt and serve.

Mature pigeons often lack sufficient fat, and their meat is tougher and less delicately flavored. They are almost always BARDED with salt pork or other fat and roasted with frequent basting, slowly simmered in casseroles, or made into pâtés or pies. They make excellent eating by any of those routes, and squabs, of course, could also be cooked by any of these recipes too.

Roasted Pigeon *(Gebackene Tauben)* / Germany

Pigeons are stuffed with pilaf, chopped bacon, or grapes, painted with melted butter, salted, and baked, basting often with the drippings and white wine or brandy. Some cooks will also BARD the birds with salt pork strips before roasting.

In this more unusual recipe, the stuffing introduces fat and moist ingredients *beneath* the birds' skins as an ingenious way to combat the natural tendency to dryness of the mature pigeon's meat.

Stuffed Pigeons *(Töltött galamb)* / Hungary

With the handle of a knife or other blunt instrument, separate the skin of the breast, back, and legs from some pigeons. Stuff the space between the skin and muscles with the following mixture: finely chopped fried bacon, chopped hard-boiled eggs, raw egg yolks blended with soft butter, bread soaked in milk and squeezed, chopped parsley, salt, and pepper. Season the cavities of the birds with black pepper and marjoram. Truss the legs, paint the birds with lard or bacon fat, and roast them in a 400°F oven, basting frequently with the lard and the drippings. Allow to stand for a bit after removing from the oven, split each bird in two, and arrange them attractively on a bed of rice.

The negative qualities of the meat of older pigeons are readily overcome by slow simmering in some stock, as in this simple recipe that originated in the American South, where it is also used to prepare doves.

STEWED PIGEON / UNITED STATES

Brown the birds in lard or oil, remove them, and sauté some chopped onions in the same pan. Return the pigeons, salt and pepper them, and add some chopped parsley. Add a cup of tomato juice or chicken stock, cover the pan tightly, and simmer the birds until done.

Garlic plus a little wine can considerably upgrade such a pigeon stew to the gastronomic equivalent of a *coq au vin*.

PIGEONS IN RED WINE *(Pichones en salsa de vino tinto)* / SPAIN

BARD some pigeons with strips of bacon and brown them well in olive oil. Add a generous amount of sliced onions and carrots, and when the onions are golden add several cloves of crushed garlic. Cook a minute, add chopped pigeon giblets, salt, and pepper and a few glasses of dry red wine. Cover and simmer until the birds are tender.

Pigeons are first stuffed for this generically similar dish that combines a typically English treatment of game with a slight trans-Channel touch.

JUGGED PIGEONS / ENGLAND

Stuff four pigeons with the following mixture: their finely chopped boiled livers, bread crumbs, 2 hard-cooked egg yolks, chopped parsley, chopped suet, melted butter, salt, pepper, nutmeg, and grated lemon rind, all bound with a beaten egg. Salt and pepper the birds and put them in an earthenware crock. Add chopped celery, cloves, mace, and a BOUQUET GARNI. Cover the pigeons with white wine, cover the crock tightly, and cook it for 3 hours in a pan of boiling water. Strain the stock and thicken it with a butter-and-flour ROUX. Garnish the pigeons with lemon wedges and serve them with the sauce.

Marinating pigeons first in wine or, more unusually, in citrus juices, as in this Spanish recipe, then slowly simmering them, much enhances both the flavor and texture of even the toughest and driest birds.

PIGEONS AND PEAS *(Pichones con guisantes)* / SPAIN

Salt and pepper some pigeons and marinate them overnight in equal parts of orange juice, lemon juice, and olive oil. Drain the birds and brown them well in oil. Add the marinade, a bay leaf, some marjoram, and some dry white wine. Cover and simmer until tender. Correct the seasoning, add cooked peas, heat through, and serve.

Besides such typically Spanish accompaniments as peas, lentils, or beans, pigeons also respond beautifully to such Slavic additives as fruit and sour cream.

PIGEONS IN CREAM SAUCE *(Potrawka z gołębi)* / POLAND

Fry quartered pigeons in butter until brown. Remove them and fry several sliced onions until golden in the same pan. Add a generous amount of chicken stock, some sliced, peeled apples, some sliced mushrooms, and a little lemon juice. Bring to a boil and add a wineglass of Madeira. Thicken this sauce with a browned flour-and-butter ROUX. Stir in a generous quantity of sour cream, add the pigeons, and simmer until they are tender.

Or try stuffing and baking pigeons in a traditional English country squire's pie complete with beefsteak.

COMPOTE OF PIGEONS / ENGLAND

Stuff six pigeons with a forcemeat containing mushrooms. Wrap them in strips of bacon and place in the bottom of a large pan. Add the necks,

giblets, some ham, mace, thyme, parsley, bay leaves, onions, a gener-
ous amount of sherry, and chicken or pigeon stock to cover. Simmer for
1 hour and carefully remove the pigeons. Place them side by side on a
thin layer of beefsteak in a buttered casserole lined with piecrust. Cover
the pigeons with strips of bacon and bake at 350°F for 1–1/2 hours.
When done, add 6 yolks of hard-cooked eggs and fill the casserole with a
thick velouté sauce prepared from the defatted and strained pigeon stock
with some mushroom slices added.

For a "downstairs" transition fit for a Wimpole Street "upstairs," some
touches of elegance substitute for the beefsteak of the countryman's more
robust creation.

Pigeon Pupton / England

Line a buttered casserole with a seasoned forcemeat. Cover the bottom
with a layer of bacon and then as many dressed pigeons as will fit. On
these arrange slices of sweetbreads, asparagus tips, some mushrooms, 2
cocks' combs, a cooked ox palate cut into small pieces, and the yolks of
several hard-cooked eggs. Fill the spaces and cover the top with another
layer of the forcemeat. Bake in a moderate oven and serve with a gravy
prepared separately from pigeon trimmings and giblets.

Finally, two versions of a Frenchman's pigeon pie.

Pigeon Pâté with Mushrooms
(Pâté chaud de pigeon aux champignons) / France

Line a straight-edged pie plate or flan mold with dough and then with a
veal paste. For making the paste, blend in an electric blender some
chopped lean veal and suet (2:1). Blend in one at a time 4 eggs per lb. of
veal, salt, and pepper. Finally blend in some pieces of ice (about 3/4
the weight of the veal) until the paste is very smooth. Cover the bottom
of the coated pie plate with mushroom slices (and, if available, truffles)
lightly sautéed in butter. Arrange on this bed two pigeons each cut into
quarters and browned in butter. Dot the birds with pieces of butter,
cover the pie with a round of dough, prick it with a fork, and make a
small round opening for a funnel. Bake in a 350°F oven for about 1

hour. Just before serving add with a funnel some hot chicken béchamel sauce flavored with Madeira.

In a variation from Languedoc, the pie is prepared similarly, but in place of the mushroom slices the pigeons are surrounded with slices of salsify that have been boiled and then fried in butter, some BLANCHED and pitted ripe olives, slices of chicken or pigeon livers sautéed in butter, some chopped, blanched, and fried lean bacon, and small button mushrooms. Substitute a rich veal gravy for the béchamel sauce at the end.

In fact, the possibilities for adding and subtracting ingredients to complement a pigeon stew are almost as varied as a cook's imagination. Recipes like this one considerably expand European-based horizons.

PIGEON PULAO / INDIA

Cut several pigeons into pieces and simmer them until tender in water to cover and a gauze or other cloth bag containing the following seasonings: 1 t coriander seed, 1 t fennel seed, a number of chopped garlic cloves, a piece of fresh ginger, and a coarsely chopped onion. In another pan, fry some chopped onion in GHEE and add pigeons and strained stock, 2–1/2 C of cooking yoghurt, 1 t cumin, 1–1/2 t sugar, several whole cloves and cardoman seeds, some BLANCHED almonds and pistachios, grated coconut, saffron, salt, and a pound of uncooked rice. Add water to cover all by about 1 inch, cover tightly, bring to a boil and then simmer gently until little steam appears when the lid is jiggled and the rice is sufficiently dry and done.

And this Chinese recipe for boned-out pigeon meat combines it with "long rice" noodles.

MINCED PIGEONS (*Hung tsai kuh zon*) / CHINA

Remove the meat from the bones of several pigeons and chop it finely. In a WOK fry some "LONG RICE" in hot oil, drain, and arrange it on a platter. In a small amount of hot oil, stir-fry some chopped water chestnuts, some chopped onions, chopped celery, chopped mushrooms, and chopped bamboo shoots for about 1 minute. Add 3 T soy sauce 1/4 C chicken stock, 1 T sugar, 1/2 t salt, and 2 T sherry and simmer

1 minute. Add 2 T oil and thicken with a mixture of cornstarch and cold water. Add the pigeon, stir for 1 minute, and pour it all over the "long rice."

Boned pigeon meat is also used for classic pâtés in several cultures.

PIGEON PÂTÉ *(Curamalan)* / ARGENTINA

Cook until tender some pigeons in chicken or pigeon stock to which were added some sautéed onions, red wine, salt, and pepper. Remove the meat from the bones and, with lemon juice and a little of the stock, blend it in an electric blender to a smooth paste. Stir in some beaten eggs and bread crumbs, pack in a buttered mold, and bake in a moderate oven until well set. Unmold the pigeon, surround it with a pilaf, and serve with a sauce prepared from the strained stock thickened with egg yolks and cream.

This last recipe for a pigeon stuffing for roast turkey is from the sixteenth century and was gleaned from *Réalités*. It also features an unusual sauce. We have not tried it yet but plan to.

ROAST TURKEY WITH RASPBERRY SAUCE *(Dinde aux framboises)* / FRANCE

A 4- to 5-lb. turkey is prepared for roasting and stuffed with the following mixture: the chopped raw meat (including giblets) of 2 pigeons, a little over 1 lb. of chopped veal, 7 oz. lard, some capers, 8 chopped cloves, 4 egg yolks, salt, and pepper. Season the bird and roast. This dish then is sauced with some thinly sliced mushrooms sautéed in butter, to which are added some turkey stock and a BOUQUET GARNI and then simmered for 30 minutes. This is thickened with a flour-and-butter ROUX; 1 T wine vinegar and 1 t lemon juice are added and the sauce simmered further for about 15 minutes. At serving time the *bouquet garni* is removed and the sauce finished by throwing in a handful of fresh raspberries.

Well! And all that just to use a couple of pigeons.

11

Small Birds

STARLINGS *(Sturnus vulgaris)* and English sparrows *(Passer domesticus)* are among the most costly pest bird species. These animals, introduced into North America from Europe, take a multimillion dollar toll each year in food and feed grains and other crops. Beyond that, the mass roosting of starlings in parks and other populated sites has been responsible for epidemics of a sometimes serious infection, histoplasmosis, whose fungal agent multiplies in soil contaminated by starling feces.

All American starlings are descendants of two batches of 60 and 40 birds released in New York's Central Park in 1890 and 1891 by Eugene Schieffelin (he also introduced sparrows). Here at the University of California we now have one of several research programs directed solely to development of methods to combat their depredations (the bird first arrived here only in 1940 and now outnumbers all other California birds but the English sparrow).

Eating such pest birds would be an excellent way to help keep their numbers in check and reap some nutritious free meat, providing variety to our dietaries at the same time—sort of killing two birds with one stone. Europeans have eaten starlings and sparrows from at least Roman times, and I have collected a number of recipes from other parts of the world too.

The prejudices that exist against eating small birds in America seem to stem in part from the same confusion as confronts other proposals for their control. That is, a distinction is not made in some people's minds between birds that are costly and dangerous pests and many species of songbirds and others, whose insect-controlling, pollinating, entertaining, and other functions considerably exceed or at least balance the damage they do. This issue is complicated, too, by the terrible examples of Italy and some other Mediterranean countries where "sportsmen" seem bent on the destruction of all birds and indiscriminately kill valued as well as pest species.

Lesser prejudices against eating small birds arise from ignorance that they are edible and from knowledge that very little birds, like sparrows, may be cooked and eaten whole—bones, viscera, and all—just as most of us do sardines, oysters, and some other marine animals. Finally, some few people who fully appreciate their pest roles may avoid them as food along with other similarly detested "vermin."

That small birds were once fairly commonplace fare in America, however, is indicated by comments recorded by foreigners of our eating habits. Thus Thomas Grattan, British consul in Boston around 1840, wrote that "excellent beef, mutton, veal and lamb are to be had in all the large cities of the United States. But the national taste certainly runs on pork, salt-fish, tough poultry, and little birds of all descriptions."

THE WHOLE CARCASS

THE only real problem, I find, with preparing small birds is the effort involved. A few hints should reduce it substantially.

Basic Preparation

If the birds have been shot, they should be eviscerated promptly. The glands at the base of the tail contain unpleasant-tasting material, so they also should be removed. For many tastes, the flavor of most birds will improve if they are hung in a very cool place for several days. I have found, too, that (depending on the species) dry plucking may be easier than scalding or plucking under a stream of hot water, so some experimentation is in order.

Time can be saved in plucking by first cutting off the head and the last joint of each wing, or even the whole wing which, on small birds, has very little meat anyway. After plucking, cut off the feet and make an incision with scissors through the belly wall from the sternum to the vent. Stick your index finger through this hole, hook the gizzard and withdraw it and the attached intestines and ceca through the hole. The liver, heart, lungs, and kidneys can be left in. Wash out the body cavity.

Sparrows are so small that you may prefer to skin them rather than to spend all the time required for plucking. This is fine, but the meat will have a tendency to be drier unless the birds are to be marinated first or cooked in a stock. In general, remember that wild birds are almost fat-free and, on that account, need to be quickly cooked or even LARDED or BARDED beforehand. From one of the following recipes you will have from a starling-sized bird about two bites of flavorful meat on each side of the breast and another couple of bites from the legs.

We have often eaten small birds broiled this way in the Middle East or as *tapas*, Spanish hors d'oeuvres.

GRILLED SMALL BIRDS (*'Assafeer*) / ARAB COUNTRIES

Rub prepared starlings or other small birds with salt and pepper. Skewer them and broil over charcoal. They may also be rubbed with lemon juice and fried in butter. In the Middle East and elsewhere, the smallest broiled birds usually are not drawn and are eaten bones and all.

The Japanese broiling process is slightly more involved but the result is worth it.

BROILED SPARROWS (*Suzume yaki*) / JAPAN

Broil birds slightly over charcoal; dip in a sauce of equal parts of SHOYU, sake, and MIRIN; return to the broiler. Repeat this alternate dipping and broiling several times. Split the bird open but keep in one piece, sprinkle with fresh-ground pepper, and serve.

In addition to broiling, small birds may also be sautéed or deep-fried.

SMALL BIRDS SAUTÉED IN BUTTER (*Ortolans sautés au beurre*) / FRANCE

Open birds along the backbone and remove the backbone and viscera. Flatten each bird out. Salt and pepper and fry each quickly on both sides in hot butter. Place each bird on a large round crouton and sauce them with a rich game-bird gravy to which some cognac has been added.

DEEP-FRIED SMALL BIRDS *(Tsa huang chu)* / CHINA

In China and Japan small rice birds are defeathered but not eviscerated before being marinated in soy sauce and deep-fried.

They may be roasted, too, but because they lack fat, care must be taken to avoid drying out the meat.

ROASTED BIRDS *(Manulele)* / SAMOA

Small birds are wrapped in *ti* leaves (or moist corn husks) and baked with other foods in the ground oven, or *umu*. They thus make good luau food to accompany a *kalua* pig.

An alternative way to keep the birds from drying out during roasting is to moisten them first with a sauce or fat and then put the birds for roasting in a covered casserole. These are very different dishes that use that approach.

SMALL BIRDS IN MISO *(Ko tori no miso zuke)* / JAPAN

Eviscerated birds are dipped in MISO, placed in earthenware bowls, and roasted in the *kamado* (Japanese smoke oven) or other oven. They are basted several times with *miso*.

STARLINGS LIÈGE STYLE *(Etourneaux à la liègeoise)* / FRANCE

Place a piece of butter blended with some juniper berries in each prepared starling. Brown the birds in melted butter in an earthenware casserole. Brush with additional juniper butter. Cover the casserole and bake in a moderate oven. The last few minutes, cover each bird with a large crouton fried in butter and sprinkled with gin.

There are many other similar French recipes, some of which call for boning the birds completely, which is not an easy thing to do. This next is the fanciest recipe for small birds I have included, although one encounters mention of other taste-tempting dishes like the classic *bisk* of an earlier day that contained not only small birds but sweetbreads, cocks' combs, and similar delicacies. This, however, will have to suffice for the devoted small-bird gastronome.

STARLINGS IN CRUST *(Etourneaux en croûte à l'ardennaise)* / FRANCE

Remove the backbones from some prepared starlings. Rub them with a mixture of salt, white pepper, and mixed spices. Stuff with a bread stuffing containing the birds' livers, some mashed juniper berries, and, if available, some liver pâté and truffles. Wrap each bird in a piece of pig's omentum. Pack tightly in a shallow baking dish on a bed of the backbones, chopped onions, and chopped carrots, all browned in butter. Paint the birds with a lot of melted butter and BRAISE in a hot oven for about 10 minutes. Unwrap the birds and place them in a large bread croustade that has been buttered, "melba-ed" in the oven, and sealed with a paste made by blending in an electric blender some fried chicken livers, mushrooms, and egg yolks. Bake in a moderate oven for a few minutes and at the last minute pour in a sauce made by reducing a cup of sherry added to the braising pan, straining, and adding a cup of demiglace or other rich brown sauce. Garnish with some pieces of truffles lightly sautéed in butter.

As in a recipe already given for suckling pig, a "casserole-oven" can be created by the cook about the bird itself, thus preserving all its juices and saving plucking labor. The result is also very colorful.

BIRDS IN CLAY *(Dich' v gorshkakh)* / RUSSIA

Draw small unplucked birds, put some butter and salt in the cavities, and coat them individually with wet clay. Place them in the hot ashes of a fire or in the oven and bake the clay. To eat, crack the clay and remove it and the attached feathers. If desired, these birds also may be preseasoned with various herbs.

The French usually LARD or BARD small birds before roasting. In such recipes as this, where the birds are exposed directly to the oven's heat, an overcooked bird can become very tough.

Roasted Small Birds (*Oiseau rôti*) / France

Birds are wrapped in thin pieces of bacon, skewered, and roasted in a very hot oven for 12 minutes. Serve on croutons. We have found that the meat of starlings prepared in this way is *just* cooked in 12 minutes at 500°F. The skin is not browned, however, and they could be roasted a little longer to suit individual tastes.

Roasted birds also lend themselves to festive displays, as in this typical Italian main dish of "blackbirds" in a *polenta* pie.

Small Birds with Polenta (*Polenta con uccelletti*) / Italy

Pour a 1–1/2-in. layer of *polenta* with cheese into a buttered, heat-proof dish and sprinkle with grated Parmesan cheese. Half-roast starlings or other small birds in the oven (see above, or fry them quickly in butter) and press them individually into the surface of the *polenta*. Brush them with melted butter and complete the baking. Add some dry white wine to the drippings from the pan in which the birds were originally roasted and sprinkle this sauce over the dish or use some reduced game stock flavored with Marsala.

Small birds also may be partly roasted or fried and finished on a bed of pilaf.

The problem of small birds' lack of fat may also be overcome readily in their preparation by cooking them in a sauce. This is another very attractive Italian presentation.

Small Birds in Casserole (*Cassuola di uccelletti*) / Italy

Salt and pepper small birds and brown them quickly in hot olive oil. Add them to a casserole in which a sauce made of chopped anchovy fillets, chopped ripe olives, crushed garlic, tomato paste, and a little chicken stock and vinegar has been simmering. Cover and simmer for another half hour. Serve the birds in soup plates on large croutons of

Italian or French bread fried in olive oil and garlic and pass the sauce separately.

A similar Turkish method of preparation combines other flavors.

STARLING STEW WITH OLIVES *(Karatavuk yahnisi)* / TURKEY

Fry some chopped turnips and carrots. Add a little stock and a glass of red wine. Place some starlings or other small birds in the pan. Add a thin purée of boiled potatoes mashed with beaten egg, dry mustard, and some stock and a little beer. Cover with stock and cook for about 30 minutes, adding some ripe olives near the end.

Finally, here are two recipes for very simple bird soups that should stimulate the cook to experiment with others.

BIRD SOUP *(Kuş çorbası)* / TURKEY

Dredge cleaned small birds inside and out with flour and allow them to stand for about an hour. Wash off the flour and put the birds in a pan. Add ample water, simmer until tender, and remove the birds. Fry chopped onions until golden, add the strained stock and some presoaked lentils, and cook until the lentils are done. Salt and pepper. Return the birds to the soup, cook a few minutes more, and serve.

BIRD SOUP *(Sua manu felelei)* / SAMOA

Boil birds with onions, salt, pepper, and rice. Thicken the stock if desired.

VISCERAL ORGANS

As mentioned, charcoal-broiled or deep-fried sparrows or other very small birds are sometimes cooked whole without eviscerating. This is the only recipe I have found, however, that specifically calls for a small bird's internal organs. I am sure there are others, but this unusual pâté, which must have some mythological or other special significance, is at least a starter.

SNIPE PÂTÉ CANAPÉS *(Schnepfenbroetchen)* / GERMANY

Pass snipes' intestines, some goose liver, mushrooms, parsley, a sardine fillet, some white bread, and a shallot or piece of leek through a food chopper. Salt and pepper and mix the ingredients well. Lightly sauté this mixture in butter and blend it well in an electric blender with some raw egg yolk. Spread this paste heavily on croutons previously fried in butter. Sprinkle with grated Parmesan cheese, lemon juice, and melted butter. These sandwiches are thoroughly heated through in a 350°F oven.

12

Reptiles

THIS CHAPTER on recipes for reptile meat has been put here because reptiles and birds are related zoologically. In fact, a recent theory has it that dinosaurs were warm-blooded and more birds than reptiles. Anyway, with this chapter I will finish our consideration of land vertebrates as underutilized sources of human food.

The suggestion of reptiles as food will cause many Americans to think first of canned rattlesnake meat, which for a number of years has been available in gourmet food shops and is regarded by far-out eaters or profligate spenders largely as a gastronomic curiosity in the same category as chocolate-covered ants. Our tendency is to forget, sometimes, that turtles are also reptiles and that in the past they enjoyed considerable popularity as food in the United States. Some, in fact, like the diamondback terrapin, were once hunted nearly to extinction. Some of the great sea turtles are still threatened ecologically because they and their eggs are being ruthlessly plundered. California, alone among our states, now prohibits either the sale or importation of sea turtle meat for this reason. The total estimated world consumption of turtles (plus frogs) in 1963 was 90,000 tons.

Turtle soup is still fairly commonly seen on the *cartes* of many of our French-style restaurants, but it would be very rare indeed to find an American restaurant that now prepares it from scratch. This need not be the case, because in much of the United States turtles and terrapins have always been numerous, and even the diamondback terrapin of our East Coast made a great comeback once the pressure on it was reduced.

Moreover, in some of the West Indies, Malaysia, and perhaps elsewhere, turtle hatcheries have now been established, too, in which the eggs can be protected and the animals returned to the sea, with the controlled harvest of a reasonable number possible.

Since turtle and terrapin meat were quite familiar and were enjoyed by previous generations of Americans, let us begin our renewed reptile eating with them before turning to lizards and snakes.

TURTLE AND TERRAPIN

SOME U.S. turtles, such as the common musk turtle and yellow mud turtle (called the "stink pot"), have odoriferous glands that make them unsuitable for food. Of good food species, the largest nonmarine turtle of the United States is the alligator snapping turtle *(Macroclemys temminckii)* of the Southeast that weighs as much as 200 lbs. Occurring throughout the eastern half of the country is our principal food species, the common snapping turtle *(Chelydra serpentina)*. It reaches 50 lbs. Specially good eating, too, are the ornate box turtle *(Terrapene ornata)*, the map and false map turtles *(Graptemys geographica* and *G. pseudogeographic)*, the painted turtle *(Chrysemys picta)*, the several sliders, the smooth soft-shelled and spiny soft-shelled turtles *(Amyda mutica* and *A. ferox)*, and others. The Carolina box turtle *(T. carolina)* of the eastern United States commonly feeds on mushrooms that do not harm the turtle but are poisonous to man. Thus, it may be dangerous to eat.

Prejudices against eating turtle meat range from regarding these animals as lethargic and loathsome, or dangerous (as in the case of snapping turtles), or cold and slimy, or otherwise as nonmeat. Their armored appearance and known survival as relatives of dinosaurs project them so far back into our evolutionary memory that we conjure up associations of primordial ooze more than culinary delight. Finally, recipes one finds in some cookbooks are apt to put off all but the most intrepid and athletic cook. Escoffier, for instance, starts out his turtle soup recipe this way: "For soup, take a turtle weighing from 120 to 180 lbs. and let is be fleshy and full of life." "Take a 180-lb. turtle!" has, in fact, become one of our family exclamations for the absurd or assinine.

Virtually all sea turtles, fresh or brackish water terrapins, and land tortoises are edible, and preparing them need not be a more formidable chore than killing and dressing a live chicken or turkey.

Diamondback terrapin's protein content is 18.6 percent (with 3.5 percent fat); for green turtles they are 19.8 and 0.5 percent, respectively.

Basic Preparation

Scrub the animal thoroughly. Decapitate it with a sharp cleaver and cut off its toes. Unless otherwise indicated, further handling then may be facilitated by putting the turtle on its back on a wooden surface and nailing it to the surface with a large nail through the center of the ventral shell. Cut the skin about the base of each leg, the neck, and the tail and peel it off. This is more easily done if two persons work together, one on the right front leg and the other on the left rear leg. The legs, neck, and tail then are removed by disarticulating with a sharp knife while twisting them free. The ventral shell is cut free, and it and the nail are removed and the turtle gutted. The gall bladder should be carefully removed intact. The rest of the meat is detached with a knife and cleaver and the watery fat trimmed off and discarded. The meat then is rinsed well and dried with paper towels.

The first recipe is for roasting the whole turtle as a luau dish.

Baked Turtle (*Laumei*) / Samoa

Eviscerated turtles are placed in the ground oven, or *umu*, with other meats, seafoods, and vegetables and baked whole.

These reptilian meats are also very good barbecued over charcoal. I had the following and similar delicacies once years ago on a 24-hour Qantas layover on the beautiful Indian Ocean island of Mauritius.

Skewered Turtle Meat / Mauritius

Marinate 1-in. cubes of turtle meat in lemon juice, salt, crushed garlic, and a little oil. Alternate on skewers with pieces of turtle liver and grill over charcoal. Serve with boiled turtle eggs, a hot chutney sauce, and rice.

The next two recipes for sautéed and deep-fried turtle meat are from a privately published cookbook I saw in Hawaii that had been written by a British civil servant on one of the Pacific islands.

SAUTÉED TURTLE / BRITISH COLONIAL

Cut turtle meat in 1–1/2-in. squares, salt and pepper them, and fry the squares in butter until brown. Add sliced onions, green peppers, mushrooms, crushed garlic, and some fresh tomatoes peeled and chopped. Moisten with stock and cook until tender. Garnish with chopped parsley and serve with rice.

DEEP-FRIED TURTLE / BRITISH COLONIAL

Cut turtle meat in thin slices, dip in beaten egg mixed with a little water, salt, and pepper. Then dip in bread crumbs and deep-fry in hot oil. Serve with melted butter and garnish with lemon and parsley. Turtle slices may also be prepared *à la meunière*.

Next is the classical American terrapin stew that almost made our diamondback terrapin extinct. This animal now occurs again in considerable numbers and this great recipe needs to be served.

PHILADELPHIA TERRAPIN / UNITED STATES

Parboil for 10 minutes in a large amount of salted water several large diamondback or Juniata terrapins that have been decapitated but are still intact otherwise. Remove the loosened skin and dry the animals with paper towels. Refill the pot with clean, salted water and continue to boil the terrapins until their shells crack and the legs are tender. Drain and cool. Remove the flat ventral shell and separate the meat into pieces; keep the eggs and liver (after removing the gall bladder intact). Put the pieces of liver and meat in the top of a double boiler. Make a ROUX of flour and butter and add cream to make a thick sauce. Blend this sauce into the yolks of about a half-dozen hard-cooked chicken eggs. Pour the complete sauce over the meat and add the terrapin eggs. Season the mixture with salt, cayenne, and paprika. Heat through and add some sherry before serving.

OZARK TERRAPIN / UNITED STATES

In this variation from the Ozarks, the meat and liver from the terrapins are cut up and mixed with the blood collected when the animals are decapitated. These are sprinkled with flour and simmered in a little water for about 10 minutes. Add salt, cayenne pepper, black pepper, mace, some brandy, and a cup of sherry. Simmer until the meat is tender; add heavy cream and a generous amount of butter. Add the peeled terrapin eggs or the yolks of hard-boiled chicken eggs and thicken further, if required, with a butter-and-flour ROUX.

Calipash, whose origins are disputed and probably mixed, can be a very festive reptilian main course, particularly if it is served in its own shell. This colorful treatment could, of course, be given to other turtle recipes as well.

CALIPASH / UNITED STATES

In a soup kettle sauté chopped onions and garlic in butter until golden. Add turtle or terrapin meat cut into small cubes and lightly brown. Cover with salted water and allspice, mace, cloves, basil, tabasco, and a small hot pepper. Simmer until the meat is tender. Thicken the stew well with a browned butter-and-flour ROUX. Stir in a little lemon juice and some sherry. Ladle it into the cleaned and boiled shells of one or more turtles. Add boiled turtle eggs for a garnish, cover the stew in the shell with a sheet of pastry dough, brush it with milk or butter, make a few holes for the steam to escape, and bake in a 350°F oven until the crust is done.

This is another stew contribution from that British Pacific island cookbook. The sauce and general treatment could advantageously follow the first recipe I gave for goat meat curry, with the addition of the coconut cream.

TURTLE CURRY / BRITISH COLONIAL

Boil turtle meat in salted water until tender. Dice and add to a curry sauce made with coconut cream.

Fiji is now the home of not only its indigenous Melanesian-Polynesian people but of an equal number of Indians descended from indentured plantation labor and a handful of people of European and other extractions. This recipe shows influences of the two largest population groups.

TURTLE CASSEROLE / FIJI

Dredge cubes of turtle meat in flour. Salt. Mix them with sliced onions in a casserole. Cover with sliced tomatoes. Prepare a sauce from coconut cream, a little lemon juice, salt, and some chopped chilis and pour over the meat and vegetables in the casserole. Cover the dish and steam or bake in a slow oven for 2 hours, adding water if necessary.

For a very Mediterranean–Middle Eastern version of the same, try this Maltese ragout. Malta is the home of a polyglot cuisine reflecting the checkered history of the island and especially its Arab past.

TURTLE RAGOUT / MALTA

Fry chopped onions in olive oil in a deep casserole until golden. Add a bay leaf, chopped mint, a cup of tomato juice, salt, and pepper and simmer for several minutes. Then add some halved seedless grapes, pine nuts, chopped apples, and capers and simmer for about a half hour. Add lightly floured cubes of turtle meat and some red wine. Cover the casserole and simmer the stew until the meat is tender. Serve over large croutons fried in olive oil.

Many of us have at least tried turtle in a restaurant in the form of canned *potage à la tortue*. These two soups are both pleasant alternatives to that much played theme.

TURTLE SOUP (*Sopa de tortuga*) / MEXICO

Cut turtle meat into small cubes and brown them lightly in olive oil. Add chopped onions, carrots, and celery and cook them until soft. Stir in crushed garlic, several bay leaves, a sprig each of basil and thyme, and a hot red pepper and cook a bit longer. Add a quart or so of water, salt, and a glass of dry red wine and simmer the soup until the meat is tender. Garnish with boiled turtle eggs or slices of hard-cooked birds' eggs and thin slices of lime.

TURTLE SOUP (*Kwe zo tan*) / CHINA

Cut the turtle meat into pieces and put in a pan. Add water, some rice wine or sherry, some chicken wings and feet, a few dried mushrooms, some *jeou chii tzyy* berries, and dried "dragon's-eye" fruit. Simmer for at least 3 to 4 hours and add a little soy sauce, a little more wine, and salt to taste.

LIZARDS

CONSIDERING the past importance of reptiles of the turtle family in the history of American cuisine, more of us should probably not be adverse to trying them. If we can go that far, only a step further in stretching the palate could convince us that lizards are merely turtles *without* shells. In the Southwest we are favored with some large lizards that would make our experimenting more than worthwhile. The major food species in the United States is the pygmy iguana, *Dipso-saurus dorsalis dorsalis*. Its total length is about one foot and its meat is commonly eaten in Mexico. Iguana tastes rather like chicken.

Some of the same prejudices probably apply to eating lizards as to turtles, with the antediluvian dinosaur association even more pronounced.

Once these are overcome, lizard may simply be skinned and eviscerated, then roasted or barbecued over charcoal.

Alligators and crocodiles are also good eating and are important protein sources in some parts of Africa. At Victoria Falls, Rhodesia, for example, one hotel dining room regularly offers crocodile thermidor and another serves a crocktail cocktail, whatever that might be.

SNAKE

BY the same process of evolutionary palate widening that we applied so briefly to lizards, snakes merely become turtles without shells or external legs. Realistically, however, snake-eating avoidances are far stronger than for other reptiles. For one thing, snakes as a group are commonly feared, though only a small minority are dangerously venemous or are powerful constrictors. Distasteful to many is the fact they slither, sometimes very rapidly, and because of their flexible spines can writhe and turn and entwine when they are caught. Some people think they look slippery or slimy, but they are not. Others find their protruding tongues especially repulsive, and some are simply hung up on Adam and Original Sin! Collectively, these are very strong prejudices.

Yet in the Far East snake meat is a delicacy much enjoyed—even highly poisonous snakes are eaten. A friend of mine with the United Nations sent me these directions, for example, for preparing a stew from poisonous kraits in Laos: "the snake is removed from its cage by hand—a process which requires skill and some care! It is stunned or the head is cut off. The carcass then is skinned and eviscerated, cut up into 1- to 2-in. pieces and boiled with some green vegetables. About 6 inches at the tail end are discarded. I have an idea that rice wine is probably added." All very simple.

The Chinese, in particular, are highly inventive and adaptive in their cooking, and many Americans have developed sufficient confidence in their culinary virtuosity and judgment to try a Chinese dish with the ingredients unknown. What makes China's cuisine so extensive is, of course, Chinese inventiveness and willingness to experiment with ingredients and palates. Take the matter of rattlesnakes and bourbon. In 1971 I was introduced to a Chinese café owner in a little town in western Montana who also ran a thriving export business in rattlesnakes. Actually his product was a preparation of rattlesnakes drowned in bourbon, marinated (aged?) for 4 to 5 years, filtered through a piece of bread, and then shipped to San Francisco's Chinatown, where it is in great demand as a remedy for rheumatism! I had the chance to inspect his wares, but unfortunately none of the elixir on hand was yet aged sufficiently to uncork and sample.

This gentleman also extolled the culinary value of snake meat and reminisced and waxed eloquent about dishes he had transplanted from China to Montana with interesting modifications. This is one:

MARINATED SNAKE COOKED WITH RICE *(Tsuh zo fan)* / CHINA ADAPTED TO AMERICA

The snake is skinned, gutted, and cut into pieces of a size manageable with chopsticks. These are marinated in a mixture of soy sauce, garlic, ginger, and bourbon whiskey. The snake meat is placed over partially cooked rice and the cooking continued until the meat and rice are done.

He also prepared snake by stir-frying the shredded meat or making meat balls with any appropriate vegetables or treating it as red-simmered meat.

But leave it to the English to reduce a recipe to its "essentials." This is about as simple as they come.

COOKED SNAKE / ENGLAND

Cut off the head and tail from a snake. Skin and draw it and simmer whole in seasoned water containing some vinegar.

More appetizing by far is a simple Japanese recipe for grilled snake, quite similar to that used for eel, which would make equally good picnic fare or a conversation-promoting hors d'oeuvre.

GRILLED SNAKE MEAT *(Hebi ryori)* / JAPAN

Boil snake heads and backbones in fish stock and discard them, reserving the stock. Add MIRIN and SHOYU. Marinate 3-in. strips of snake meat in this sauce, thread each on a bamboo skewer, and grill over charcoal until brown, painting frequently with some of the marinade.

"HEDGE EELS" *(Anguille des haies)* / FRANCE

For similar artistry, grass snakes are also prepared in France by most French recipes given for eel.

Finally, an elegant snake soup using a recipe obtained for me from China by Man Tat Yan.

SNAKE SOUP *(Shuh zo tan)* / CHINA

Cut a skinned and cleaned snake into 4-in. to 5-in. pieces. Slash each piece with several diagonal cuts. Dry each well and coat lightly with cornstarch. Brown scallion sections and slices of ginger lightly in hot oil and remove them. Brown the snake pieces quickly in the same pan in very hot oil. Return the scallions and ginger, add a delicate chicken or fish stock, bring to a boil, and simmer, covered, for 10 minutes. Add a little sherry and vinegar, some chopped Chinese parsley, and a drop or two of sesame oil. Cover again and simmer a few minutes more.

My Chinese Montanan friend also recommended highly another classical Chinese snake and cat meat soup, but would only dissolve in giggles when I said I would like the recipe. He insisted I did not *really* want to know, then that he was sure people did not eat it "these days," and, finally, that he could not recall the recipe. Of course it *is* still eaten, and Man Tat Yan obtained that recipe too (it is included in the chapter on cat meat; see page 177).

Part Three

FISH

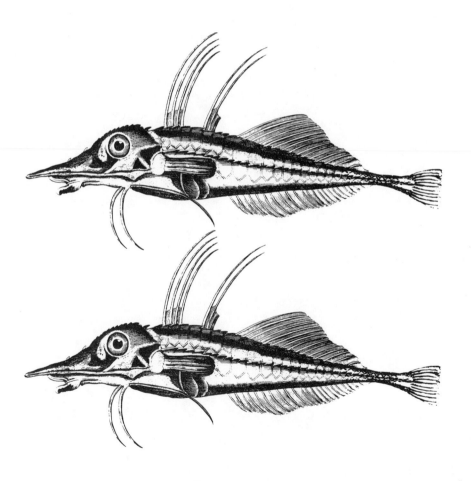

F I S H

A fish out of water stinks.

AND SO in our quest for adequate, high-quality protein for our future diet and the further education of our taste buds, we shall move unceremoniously from the land into the sea. Much has been made in the popular literature in recent years of the sea's vast "untapped potential" for feeding man. The fact is that most popular species of commercially caught and marketed marine fish are already being fished to their limits—or beyond—and there appears to be relatively little potential for them. Competition on major fishing banks is already intense, particularly between countries like Japan and Norway, which have depended almost solely for some time upon the sea's resources to prevent protein malnutrition among their peoples, and other aggressive fishing nations like the Soviet Union. The once immense, overworked sardine fishery of Peru and Ecuador practically disappeared because of such intense pressures, and disagreements over legal fishing rights recently brought Iceland and Great Britain to the point of war.

Should fish be written off, then, in considering our total food resources of the future? Not at all, for there are in the sea a variety of species of what we in this country commonly call "trash fish," but are edible indeed. In fact, a number of fish we Americans have avoided eating until now are ingredients in classic dishes of other countries. Not fishing for them or converting some of them into animal feeds and fertilizers as we do now may not be wise actions for the future. Other underutilized food resources are some of our freshwater fisheries, particularly if we are successful in cleaning up more of our badly polluted rivers and lakes. Unfortunately, however, experience with, and therefore fondness for, freshwater fish has declined markedly in comparatively recent times in the United States. In England, too, usage and enjoyment of freshwater fish decreased as saltwater fish became at least temporarily more available. To Englishmen and Americans, now accustomed more than formerly to sea fish, freshwater fish are increasingly described as having an "earthy" taste, and the consumption of once prized species is now becoming confined almost completely to "poor folk." This trend has not been as true for continental Europe. There, freshwater fish like carp, lampreys, and eels are much prized. Though almost entirely shunned in America, all three occur in abundance here and are ours for the taking.

Lastly, freshwater fish farming and mariculture both provide possibilities for increased fish production, the former now, the latter for the future.

FISH PREJUDICES

ONE university student survey showed that fish were rejected by an astonishing 22.6 percent of young Americans. For particular species, rejection ranged from a high of 30.08 percent for anchovies down to salmon (canned?), which only 3 percent rejected. Handling and preparing a *whole* fish, even one already gutted and scaled, now exceeds the interest in seafood of most American cooks, and a significant portion of the present generation has never even seen a real fish market with boxes and boxes of whole fish on ice. Most Americans would probably not know where to begin, in fact, with an intact fish with scales and guts *in situ* on a hungry day.

These American fish prejudices, to the extent they have been studied, seem to center upon the smell of fish and, for oily species, also upon their taste. Fish heads and tails intact create an additional problem of animal recognition sufficiently large that even to buy a fish with these valuable parts in place is now almost impossible in many of our towns and cities. Lastly, Americans reject some very tasty fish simply because their bones make eating them just too much trouble. These are all kinds of prejudices that we can be carefully educated out of.

It might surprise us, therefore, that the fish avoidances of some people are more deeply rooted than many of ours. For example, in this country strong fish avoidances on the part of the Navajo, Zuni, and Apache tribes of the Southwest relate to beliefs about the sacredness of water and therefore of water creatures. Similar prejudices are also evident in other parts of the world, especially in India and parts of Africa. Besides pressures in India to avoid taking animal life at all, special populations of fish are regarded as sacred and therefore are particularly shunned. Beyond that, fishing among Hindus is considered a low caste occupation and fish generally, as well as fishermen, are regarded as unclean.

Similarly, in areas of Africa fish are likened to snakes, which by some peoples are thought divine and by others, filthy and smelly, in both cases inedible. These prejudices are unusually common among nomadic peoples, and cattle keeping and fishing in Africa are seldom found to go hand in hand. Both the Masai and Turkana of East Africa, for example, find the very idea of eating fish abhorrent. Simoons has also cited evidence in his *Eat Not This Flesh* for similar attitudes among nomadic peoples of or originating from central Asia. Other beliefs are more specific. In Malaysia, for instance, fish are not fed to children in the belief (perhaps with some justification if they are undercooked) that they will "cause" worms.

One possibility for the origin of some such fish avoidances would seem to be the ease with which fish spoil in warm climates and the associated odors which some peoples at least consider noxious. In Baghdad I have observed that fish are only sold alive, there being little, if any, market for those already dead. Thus all of the little restaurants along the Tigris which serve Baghdad's famous *masgoof* keep these big fish alive in pens in the water. It is of interest in this regard that in the Middle Ages the city fathers of Basel in Switzerland had already passed a law which required old fish to be labeled as inferior food and sold only to strangers. In Switzerland today, one almost invariably finds live tanks still for trout and some other species, not only in fish markets, but also in supermarkets and in restaurants.

A few years ago the U.S. Food and Drug Administration branded as unfit for human consumption and labeled "filthy" nutritious meal made from whole fish, because it contained the viscera of the fish. No health problem was involved, merely one of misguided aesthetics. Of course, we do eat clams, oysters, and other animals with *their* viscera intact, and sometimes, as with oysters, we eat them *alive.* This is the kind of regulatory stupidity the future can ill afford.

FISH QUALITY AND SAFETY

WHAT, then, need we know about fish quality and safety? Some Americans are hesitant to buy a whole fish because they do not know what to look for. Fresh fish have bright, well-rounded eyes with jet black pupils and transparent corneas. Their body surfaces are iridescently shiny and are covered with a uniformly thin, and nearly transparent, layer of slime. Gills are bright and slime-free. The odor is clean and does not even begin to suggest decomposition.

As fish age and begin to spoil, their eyes become sunken and shrunken, the pupils cloudy, and the corneas opaque. The body surfaces lose their brightness and sheen, and the slime layer becomes irregularly thickened and finally yellowish and brown. The gills first take on a bleached-out appearance, then become greyish brown, and are finally covered with a thick slime layer. The flesh becomes soft and finally mushy and an odor of decomposition is clearly evident.

Because of serious worm parasites they may carry, freshwater or brackish water fish should *never* be eaten raw. Many freshly caught and sanitarily handled saltwater fish have until recently been considered safe to eat raw, but where gutting is not done promptly, cases of *Anisakis* worm infection have been reported from several countries from eating raw herring or other raw fish. Safety recommends, therefore, that all fish either be cooked or otherwise adequately treated before eating.

13

Amphibians

B EFORE WE MOVE on to fish per se we will consider first the eating
possibilities for those related animals "neither fish nor fowl,"
the amphibians. It has always seemed strange to me that frogs are much
more widely appreciated items of diet in many countries than are their
cousins, salamanders—or, for that matter, snakes or lizards. It makes little
rhyme or reason, really.

Gigging for frogs was a favorite pastime of ours during my under-
graduate years in college, and nothing tasted better than some freshly fried
frogs' legs and a bottle of beer late after a successful night's catch. We
merely skinned the legs, dusted them with flour, salt, and pepper and fried
them chicken-style. While almost any kind of frog is edible just as long as it
is large enough to make the effort worthwhile, only large bullfrogs are
eaten to any extent at all in the United States. The one exception is that
legs of smaller frogs (like turtle meat) are authentic ingredients for a
Louisiana gumbo, that great American "bouillabaisse" thickened with okra
and powdered sassafras leaves.

Prejudices against eating frogs or salamanders as food center upon their
cold and slippery feel, their unappealing swampy or algal-grown habitats,
and the expectation that they will smell and taste fishy. In my experience,
these expectations are never realized, and the individual who puts
squeamishness aside sufficiently for just one bite of frog meat or is tricked
into eating frog meat even once finds that it is, in fact, like a more
delicately flavored and textured chicken than he has ever eaten.

Frogs are numerous throughout the United States. The largest species, those most valuable for food, include the bullfrog *(Rana catesbeiana)*, which is up to 8 inches from snout to vent and ranges over the eastern half of the country; *R. areolata*, the gopher frog, of the Midwest (up to 4–1/2 inches); the green frog *(R. clamitans)* of the East, Midwest, and South, which is up to 4 inches long; and the pickerel frog *(R. palustris)* of similar range, whose body is as long as 3 inches. Other species are edible, but require greater effort.

The protein content of frogs' legs is greater than that of T-bone steak and they have scarcely any fat.

Basic Preparation

Frogs are killed by quickly severing the spinal cord between the head and first neck vertebra with a sharp knife. After skinning, the frogs are cut across the body just ahead of the pelvis (except for the first recipe). The feet are then cut off and thrown away with the rest of the body. The joined pairs of legs are soaked in several changes of ice water for 4 to 6 hours (which swells the meat). Finally, they are thoroughly dried between paper towels.

THE WHOLE CARCASS

SURPRISINGLY, I have discovered only one recipe for cooking whole frogs, but although such treatment risks recognition prejudice, the possibilities for interesting dishes seem endless. Many frogs'-legs recipes could be adapted easily, using appropriate accompaniments for stuffings. Certainly this would be an excellent approach to using small frogs and ending up with a sure conversation piece.

In the Philippines, a really interesting dish of sweet-and-sour whole stuffed frogs is prepared.

STUFFED FROGS *(Palaman palaka)* / PHILIPPINES

Large frogs are skinned, eviscerated through an abdominal incision, and the body cavity stuffed with the following mixture: finely chopped stir-fried pork to which much crushed garlic, some brown sugar, salt, pepper, and a little vinegar are added. The openings of the stuffed frogs are sewed closed, the bodies are well rubbed with the same seasonings and hung in hot sun (or placed in the oven) to dry. They are deep-fried in hot oil until golden brown and thoroughly cooked through. Arrange them attractively on a platter with parsley or other garniture.

LEGS

THE universally used parts of frogs, however, are their large hind legs. The simplest method of preparation, and one of the best, is simply to grill them over charcoal, as is done in Spain and other Mediterranean countries.

GRILLED FROGS' LEGS *(Ranas parilladas)* / SPAIN

Paint some skinned legs with melted butter or olive oil, season them with salt and pepper, and grill over charcoal.

Restaurants in the little village of Chtoura in Lebanon's Bekáa valley are justly famed throughout the Arab world for grilled frogs' legs, which are invariably liked by all who try them.

GRILLED FROGS' LEGS *(Radjlin el dafatha maa el toum)* / LEBANON

Marinate prepared frogs' legs overnight in the refrigerator in olive oil containing *much* crushed garlic, salt, and pepper. Grill over charcoal, basting with the garlic and oil. Pour off any excess oil and serve the garlic-oil paste as a sauce with the frogs' legs.

Alternatively, season and lightly flour prepared frogs' legs and deep-fry them in hot olive oil. Serve with a sauce prepared by mixing 1 C TAHEENI with several tablespoons of lemon juice and enough water to make a mayonnaiselike consistency. Add crushed garlic, chopped parsley, and salt to taste.

FRIED FROGS' LEGS / UNITED STATES

Season prepared frogs' legs and roll them in fine cornmeal. Dip in beaten egg, in cornmeal again, and deep-fry until golden brown. Serve with tartar sauce and hush puppies.

I like the American treatment of frogs' legs when applied to catfish, but believe that it overwhelms the delicate flavor of frogs' legs. I feel somewhat the same about the two Mediterranean variations that follow, although their coatings are lighter and marination accents the meat.

BATTER-FRIED FROGS' LEGS *(Fritots de grenouilles)* / FRANCE

Instead of soaking them in water, marinate the seasoned legs, some finely sliced onions, chopped parsley, thyme, a bay leaf, and garlic in a mixture of olive oil and a little lemon juice. Dip marinated legs in a frying batter and deep-fry in olive oil. Drain on paper toweling, garnish with deep-fried parsley, and serve with a thin tomato sauce.

DEEP-FRIED FROGS' LEGS *(Zampe di rana fritte)* / ITALY

Seasoned legs are marinated in a mixture of white wine, chopped parsley, some sliced onion, and a little nutmeg. The legs are drained, floured, dipped in lightly beaten egg, and deep-fried in hot olive oil.

The most elegant deep-fried approach is, not unexpectedly, Chinese. Like the Filipino recipe for whole stuffed frogs, this recipe for stuffed legs should also stimulate further creativity in the kitchen.

STUFFED FROGS' LEGS *(Shiang wa twe)* / CHINA

Break the bones in large frogs' legs and carefully remove them. In their place insert pieces of ham of the same size. Salt and pepper and dip into a TEMPURA-type batter made with the beaten egg whites only and deep-fry in peanut oil. Serve with plum sauce.

Much more common are recipes for sautéing frogs' legs in butter. Here, first, is the classically simple but superb French treatment *à la meunière* followed by three equally famed French regional variations, each with its traditionally distinctive sauce.

FRIED FROGS' LEGS *(Grenouilles à la meunière)* / FRANCE

Season and flour frogs' legs and fry in hot butter until golden brown. Sprinkle with chopped parsley, some lemon juice, and browned butter.

FROGS' LEGS LYON STYLE *(Grenouilles à la lyonnaise)* / FRANCE

Brown the legs in hot butter as above, add some thinly sliced onions lightly browned separately in butter, sauté the two together a little, garnish with chopped parsley, and serve with a sauce prepared by warming some vinegar with the cooking butter.

FROGS' LEGS NICE STYLE *(Grenouilles à la niçoise)* / FRANCE

Substitute for the onions in the above recipe some roughly chopped, peeled tomatoes stewed with chopped and sautéed onions, chopped pimentos, garlic, and some tarragon.

Surely one of the best introductions of frogs' legs to the unbeliever is *à la provençale*, unless, of course, he also avoids the garlic that makes this great Provence cuisine. The always good Restaurant du Levant near the airport in Geneva does a great job with this recipe, using only very small, delicately flavored frogs.

FROGS' LEGS PROVENCE STYLE *(Grenouilles à la provençale)* / FRANCE

Season and lightly flour prepared legs and fry them quickly in hot olive oil or a mixture of butter and olive oil. Just before they are done, much crushed garlic and chopped parsley (sometimes also chopped chives and black pepper) are added to the pan. Brown butter is also sometimes poured over the legs on the serving plate, which is garnished with lemon wedges and fried parsley sprigs.

Last, I have also enjoyed this simpler variant of sautéed frogs' legs in Spain.

FRIED FROGS' LEGS *(Ranas con almendras)* / SPAIN

Sauté the prepared legs in butter in which a clove of garlic was fried previously. They are served with a simple garnish of chopped parsley and shredded almonds.

Another group of French recipes calls for sautéing the legs lightly, then simmering them in wine, and serving in a cream sauce. Here are three variations.

FROGS' LEGS IN CREAM *(Cuisses de grenouilles à la crème)* / FRANCE

Soak pairs of frogs' legs in milk. Dry them, season with salt and cayenne, and dust with flour. Sauté chopped onions, chopped mushrooms, crushed garlic, and a bay leaf in butter until soft and lightly brown the frogs' legs in this pan. Add a glass of dry white wine and simmer for 5 minutes or so. Discard the bay leaf and remove the frogs' legs to a warm platter. Add a thick, chicken-based béchamel sauce flavored with Madeira to the pan and stir the sauce until smooth. Serve it over the frogs' legs and garnish the dish with chopped parsley.

FROGS' LEGS WITH BROWNED SAUCE *(Grenouilles au gratin)* / FRANCE

The legs prepared as in the previous recipe are placed under the broiler and browned. Or, for a simpler version, legs simply browned in hot butter are placed on a platter coated with a cream sauce and surrounded by a border of sliced mushrooms. All are covered with more cream sauce, sprinkled with bread crumbs and melted butter, and browned under the broiler.

FROGS' LEGS WITH CHEESE SAUCE *(Grenouilles à la mornay)* / FRANCE

Place sautéed frogs' legs on a bed of mornay sauce, cover them with more mornay sauce mixed with some of the pan juices, and sprinkle with grated cheese and melted butter. A border of duchess potatoes brushed with egg yolk may also be added. The completed dish is then browned under the broiler.

Flavorful frogs'-leg stews are also eaten in a number of countries.

FRICASSEED FROGS' LEGS *(Zampe di rana fricassé)* / ITALY

Seasoned prepared legs and previously soaked dried mushrooms are added to some chopped onions and garlic that have already been browned in olive oil and then simmered in white wine. Water is added to cover and the stew is simmered for about an hour. It then is strained, reserving the broth. The legs and mushrooms are dried, lightly floured, and added again to the strained broth, which is then reheated. Some chopped parsley is added, the pan is removed from the heat, and the sauce is finished and thickened by mixing in lightly beaten egg yolks and some lemon juice. This dish is usually served over toast.

STEWED FROGS' LEGS *(Béka láb pörkölt)* / HUNGARY

Fry finely chopped onions in lard. Add a generous amount of paprika, chopped green peppers, chopped tomatoes, and a little water. Bring to a rapid boil. Add skinned frogs' legs, simmer for 10 to 15 minutes, and serve the stew over rice.

CURRIED FROGS' LEGS / SINGAPORE

Sauté frogs legs lightly and simmer in a sauce prepared as for the first recipe for goat meat curry. Serve with appropriate sambals and rice.

Escoffier gives a few recipes for frogs' legs (which he euphemistically calls "nymphs"), one of them for an elaborate hors d'oeuvre. This is a kind of recipe I never try to do, but perhaps it will really appeal to others.

FROGS' LEGS IN ASPIC *(Cuisses de grenouilles en gelée)* / FRANCE

Prepared frogs' legs are first poached in a white wine COURT-BOUILLON, cooled, dried, and dipped to coat in a white chaud-froid sauce. They then are laid in an attractive pattern on a previously poured and set layer of champagne aspic in a fancy silver or crystal dish. Chervil and tarragon sprigs are arranged between the legs; the whole is covered with more champagne aspic and served "set in a block of ice." (I am sure a bed of crushed ice would do quite well enough!)

Another example of flamboyant French *haute cuisine* is the frogs'-legs, crayfish, and truffle triple garniture, which seems to overwhelm the poor little omelet.

FROGS' LEGS OMELET *(Omelette Maxim)* / FRANCE

A plain omelet is garnished with alternating rows of crayfish tails cooked in a COURT-BOUILLON and truffle slices sautéed in butter. This all is surrounded by a border of frogs' legs *à la meunière*. It is, no doubt, very good.

Last, another of Escoffier's recipes is for a frog soup. This is more to my taste.

FROG SOUP *(Potage à la grenouille)* / FRANCE

Prepared legs are lightly sautéed in butter without browning, then simmered for about 10 minutes in a little added white wine and lemon juice. The legs are deboned, the meat pounded in a mortar and sieved (or blended in an electric blender) to a fine purée, and added to a thin but flavorful fish velouté. This hot frog soup is thickened by stirring in beaten egg yolks and finished with some added butter (and cream if desired).

All these recipes for frogs can also be applied to salamanders, another large group of amphibians that are less often eaten. The hellbender (*Cryptobranchus alleganiensis*), up to 27 inches in length, is found throughout much of the U.S. Middle West. It bites. Another excellent American food species is the mudpuppy *(Necturus maculosus)*, found throughout the Northeast and upper Midwest, where it reaches lengths of up to 18 inches. Other smaller species of salamanders are also edible.

14

Bony Fish & Mudfish

TECHNOLOGICAL IMPROVEMENTS in fishing by some countries, more effective controls on overfishing or in the use of destructive techniques, better protection of fast-diminishing estuaries, and coastal fish-breeding marshes—all could increase future yields, at least locally, of a number of species of highly valued marine fish.

We can also expect greater importance in the future of marine farming, or mariculture, though techniques have been reasonably perfected for only a few high-priced fish plus shrimp, oysters, mussels, and some other shellfish. Progress waits generally for the solution of a great many problems of marine disease, nutrition, and breeding. The countries of the Far East are much ahead of us in this whole field.

One thing we Americans can do while we strive to catch up is to begin to make better use of some abundant marine, as well as freshwater, species of fish we have but do not now eat to any great extent. Some edible marine fish, like menhaden, are harvested in appreciable numbers by our commercial fisheries, but then are made mostly into fertilizer because of the lack of a presumed food market. Many people do not know that sharks or common bottom fish like hake also provide good edible meat. Ironically, some of these species are not caught by our fishermen, yet are taken in American waters in enormous numbers by foreign fishing fleets, then resold to us, usually as overprocessed, breaded, frozen fish sticks for the fast-food trade.

Therefore, in this chapter I shall consider first some recipes that use as ingredients marine fish commonly referred to in the United States as "trash fish." Prejudices against eating such species are varied but tend to center upon their sometimes ugly or unusual appearance, the fact that some have venomous spines (and fishermen dislike handling them on that account), or that they may be bony and a little trouble to eat. Hake, a bottom fish, contains, for example, 16.5 percent protein and 0.4 percent fat and should be a more significant contributor to our dietary.

Marine Fish

TRADITIONALLY, throughout the whole Mediterranean region such trash fish are used for—are even essential ingredients of—highly flavorful and much prized seafood chowders or stews, the most famous of which is the Marseilles *bouillabaisse*. Its traditional ingredients include such fish as the rascasse (an ugly fish with poisonous spines), the anglerfish (another unattractive fish with a large flat head, narrow body, and no scales), and the conger eel. It is claimed that rascasse venom is, in fact, a flavor fixative (in the same way that musk and ambergris fix scents in the manufacture of perfume) and that this fact is responsible for the distinctively delicate flavor of a real Marseilles *bouillabaisse*. Rascasse are Mediterranean species of the fish family Scorpaenidae, *Scorpaena porcus*, *S. scrofa*, and *S. notata*, but other members of this family of fishes occur in North American waters (e.g., *S. guttata* on the Pacific Coast as far north as Monterey) and could be eaten in similar dishes by us. In Marseilles other fish often included in a *bouillabaisse* include chapon, St. Peter's fish (or John Dory, for which can be substituted Atlantic porgy or scup), red mullet, rougier, whiting, sea perch, hake, shark, spiny lobster, crabs, and other shellfish. The secret of any good *bouillabaisse* is a wide selection of fish. This is what helps give the dish its subtle flavor. One important thing to note, however, is that fatty fish are not used in *bouillabaisse*. Some recipes also add vermicelli, potatoes, green beans, or what have you.

Raymond Oliver devotes a whole very interesting chapter in his *Gastronomy of France* to the history and preparation of *bouillabaisse* and its many relatives, the original recipes for which he believes to have been Phoenician. This is one of several versions of the Marseilles stew that are regarded as authentic.

FISH CHOWDER *(Bouillabaisse)* / FRANCE

Use a large deep casserole. Put in a generous quantity of chopped onions, chopped, peeled tomatoes, crushed garlic, some sprigs of parsley, thyme, and fennel, some dried orange peel, and bay leaves. On these ingredients place the selected shellfish cut into regular-sized pieces, then similar-sized pieces of the firmer-fleshed fish indicated above or their relatives. Salt and pepper and add about a cup of olive oil and a little powdered saffron. (Other traditional ingredients could include carrots, leeks, potatoes, sea anemones, fish livers, or a tiny amount of vanilla extract.) Cover the fish with water, seawater, or fish stock, turn the heat high, and boil for several minutes. Add any softer-fleshed fish available and continue to boil vigorously for only about 5 minutes more. Serve the pieces of fish and the strained stock in bowls over fresh French bread and sprinkle all with chopped parsley.

Soups similar to *bouillabaisse* are prepared all around the Mediterranean with different combinations of seafoods and seasonings, usually using everything that is available. This alone is sufficient to encourage experimentation by Americans with almost any locally available marine fish.

Italian versions of *bouillabaisse* go by such names as *ghiotto* in Sicily, *cassola* in Sardinia, *cacciucco* near Livorno, *burrida* in Genoa, and *zuppa di pesce* in Naples. They often contain squid, mussels, and clams in addition to assorted fish and crustaceans. This is one variation our family particularly likes.

SEAFOOD CHOWDER (*Caccuicco*) / ITALY

Brown some chopped garlic, a little chopped onion, and a tiny red pepper in 1/2 C olive oil. Add whole unshelled shrimp or squilla, cleaned small squid, or a small octopus cut into rings plus their individual tentacles, and a small spiny lobster cut into pieces, shell and all. Boil about 15 minutes and add tomato paste, salt, some Marsala, and a glass of dry white wine. Simmer 5 minutes and then add scallops, mussels or cockles, codfish cut into pieces, and pieces of several of any other available fish. Cover the fish with water or fish stock (part canned clam juice is fine) and simmer 15 minutes. Salt to taste. Serve over toasted garlic bread.

And from Spain comes yet another favorite of ours.

FISH CHOWDER *(Zarzuela de pescado)* / SPAIN

Sauté some chopped garlic in olive oil in a soup kettle. Add a generous quantity of chopped tomatoes and chopped parsley and simmer for a while. Add slices of any available fish and also squid, whole shrimp, and a spiny or slipper lobster and/or squilla and cook for several minutes. Add a glass or so of white wine, some good, well-seasoned fish fumet, saffron, and paprika. Thicken with a ROUX made of flour and olive oil, add salt and pepper, and simmer until the fish is just tender.

One of many variations of this Spanish fish dish, *zarzuela a la Catálana* calls for an unthickened stock, with substitution of a paste of toasted almonds and garlic for the saffron and paprika. That is the way it is often served in the almond-producing part of Cataluña, where we have our farmhouse. Also good and somewhat unusual is *zarzuela a la Gaditana*, in which some sour orange juice (or orange plus lemon juice) substitutes for the saffron and paprika.

Another traditional French fish chowder is *bourride*, prepared originally as a sardine soup with an aïoli sauce added. *Bourride*, unlike *bouillabaisse*, usually contains sardines or some other type of fatty fish like the menhaden we now use largely for bait, oil, and fertilizer (although salted menhaden are much eaten in the West Indies).

FISH STEW *(Bourride)* / FRANCE

Prepare a light flour-and-butter ROUX. Stir in a hot stock made from an assortment of heads and tails of marine fish (e.g., flounder, conger eel, sardines) and seasoned with chopped parsley, thyme, bay leaf, fennel, watercress, and lemon peel, as well as peppercorns, cayenne, salt, a clove, and some saffron. Bring the slightly thickened stock to a boil, add sardines and fillets of cod, sole, turbot, sea bass, or other fish. Arrange the cooked fish on croutons in warm bowls. Stir into the stock a generous amount of aïoli sauce and strain the hot soup over the fish and croutons.

Preserved Marine Fish

Various marine fish, particularly small clupeids like anchovies, sprats, and herring, are caught in large quantities, and at times such fresh fish may be available abundantly at low cost. Their seasonal abundance would create for most householders the problem of preservation if sizable quantities are to be purchased. For this reason, greater attention in America needs to be paid to traditional means of fish preservation other than freezing, such as fermentation.

These recipes are for valuable fish products, some of which are used as seasonings. Fermented fish products are remarkably compatible with other foods. It is this fact that accounts for much of the distinctiveness of Italian and Filipino cuisine.

ANCHOVIES / MEDITERRANEAN COUNTRIES

Use clupeid fish (of which members of the genus *Engraulis* occur on our Pacific coast and *Anchovia* on all our coasts) to make anchovies. If you can find fat fish of a size so that 16 to 18 equal a pound, this is preferable.

Behead and gut them. Put a 3/16-in. layer of pure salt in the bottom of a wooden cask or other suitable container and cover this with a layer of the fish arranged parallel to one another. Add another layer of salt, a second layer of fish at right angles to the first, and so on until the container is full. The top layer should be salt. Place a weighted wooden disk on top of the mixture.

After 2 or 3 days the fish will have sunk. Then add alternating layers of fish and salt to the top of the container so it is filled again. "Curing" takes 6 to 7 months at room temperature during which time the water and fat will rise to the surface. You may add fresh 25-percent-strength brine if necessary to keep the fish well covered. After this the cured anchovies are ready to be repacked in small containers.

For commercial repacking anchovies are desalted, trimmed, filleted, and covered with olive oil. Some are not tinned, however, but are ground into a paste. If at least 90 percent of the paste is anchovies, one has *pâté d'anchois*; if at least 75 percent of the mix is anchovies and 10 percent oil, the result is *crème d'anchois*; and if at least 75 percent anchovies and 10 percent butter are ground, *beurre d'anchois* is the final product.

Of the following recipes that use anchovies, one is classically Swedish and the others are French. They were chosen to indicate something of the variety of ways such fermented fish are used in Western cooking. Other recipes using anchovies are listed in the index.

ANCHOVY AND POTATO CASSEROLE *(Jansson's frestelse)* / SWEDEN

Butter a casserole and put in it alternate layers of thinly sliced potatoes, sliced onions, and filleted anchovies. Bake in a 350°F oven for 10 minutes. Then pour in 2/3 C or so of cream and bake for 10 minutes more. Again add an equal amount of cream and bake another 10 minutes. Then reduce the heat to 300°F for a final 30 minutes in the oven.

ROASTED LAMB VISCERA WITH ANCHOVY SAUCE *(Abatis d'agneau aux anchois)* / FRANCE

Serve any roasted viscera of lamb with a sauce made by adding chopped, desalted anchovy fillets and pepper, chopped parsley, and lemon juice to the degreased pan drippings. Blend this sauce well over medium heat.

ANCHOVY FRITTERS *(Beignets d'anchois)* / FRANCE

Mix raw egg yolks with finely chopped parsley and a little butter. Spread this mixture on desalted and trimmed anchovy fillets. Roll them up, dip in a light batter (TEMPURA batter is excellent), and deep-fry. Drain and serve garnished with sprigs of deep-fried parsley.

The following is a provençal variant of a thick pizza with anchovies.

ANCHOVY TART *(Anchoïade)* / FRANCE

Press out pizza dough into a large, thin, round on a greased baking sheet. Allow it to rise about an inch. Coat the dough with olive oil and arrange on it desalted anchovy fillets and chopped tomatoes that have been sautéed in olive oil with lots of fresh garlic and basil. Bake the *anchoïade* in a hot oven and serve hot.

Anchoïades may also be prepared on halves of a split roll or loaf of bread.

ANCHOVY PÂTÉ *(Tapenado)* / FRANCE

In an electric blender, blend a generous quantity of ripe olives, washed anchovy fillets, and capers (2:1:1) with some lemon juice, dry mustard, a bit of thyme, a bay leaf or so, some cognac, and enough olive oil so that the mixture can be easily spread. You may add garlic and some tuna fish if you desire. Serve on pieces of bread.

In Scandinavia sprats, herring, salmon, and trout, as well as perch and other fish, are prepared as smörgasbord tidbits in a fermentative process similar to that for anchovies. This is one recipe.

PICKLED FISH *(Rokørret)* / NORWAY

Thoroughly wash small, fat river trout and soak them in salted water (1 t salt to 1/2 pt. water) for 3 hours. Scale and clean the fish well. Place a layer of fish with their bellies up in a wooden tub or earthenware crock. Sprinkle the fish with coarse salt and a little sugar. Repeat layering of the fish and the salt-sugar mixture. Cover this mixture with a well-fitting wooden disk and weight it down with stones.

Within a few days the liquid should cover the fish. At that point cover the container itself and store it in a cool place to ferment for about 3 months.

Another popular Scandanavian edible that goes somewhat beyond this in fermentation is *surströmming*. Choice small herring, or *strömming*, are used in northern Sweden to make a dish that, although it stinks to high heaven, is regarded by its devotees as pure gastronomic bliss. It is made this way if you care to try it.

PICKLED HERRING *(Surströmming)* / SWEDEN

Lay freshly caught herring in wooden vats and mix for 2 hours with 25 percent salt solution (4 parts herring to 1 part brine). This will draw the water from the fish. Leave in the brine for 48 hours. Then remove the head and intestines but not the hard or soft roes. Pack the fish in barrels, cover with fresh 17 percent brine, and close the barrels. Allow 6 to 7 weeks for fermentation to take place (at 30° to 35°F, May-June Swedish temperature). It is during this time that the odoriferous gas is produced in large amounts.

In Sweden most of the *surströmming* are canned in 12 percent brine, in which the botulism baccillus will not grow.

Similar things also are done to fish in many oriental cuisines. In fact, the "controlled spoilage" process may be allowed to go even further, with positive gastronomic results. In Vietnam this is done in *nuoc-mam*, which is basic to Vietnamese cooking. It is a salty, clear, brown liquid used rather like soy sauce. In Chinese grocery stores it is even labeled "fish soy."

Fermented Fish Sauce (Nuoc-mam) / Vietnam

Mix fresh, ungutted clupeid and carangeid fish with salt (4 to 5 parts per 6 parts fish) and place in a vat until it is full. Mound up the fish and cover with a layer of salt. In 3 days tap off the turbid and bloody liquid that has risen. Allow about a 2–1/2-in. layer of liquid to remain over the fish, which have settled in the vat. Put a wicker disk on top of the fish and heavily weight it.

After a few months the *nuoc-mam* prepared from small fish is ready to be drained off and used as a seasoning. For large fish, the time required may be a year or more. You may use the undissolved residue for fertilizer, as is done in Vietnam. A similar product, *nuoc-mam ruoc*, may be prepared from shrimp.

Variants of these sauces are made in all of the countries of Southeast Asia. In fact, *nuoc-mam* is also rather extensively used now in France, and this is not surprising. For it is likely that the common use of anchovies and anchovy paste in French and other Mediterranean cooking is a direct outgrowth of a *nuoc-mam*-like sauce called *garum* (or *liquamen* or *haimation*) that was used in the days of the Roman Empire. *Garum* was a liquid seasoning prepared by fermenting the intestines, livers, and other internal organs of scomber, mullet, and other fish. Sometimes various invertebrates, such as sea urchins, spiny lobsters, and oysters, were also used. *Garum* was added to almost all Roman foods, including sausages, and Pompeii was famous for its manufacture. According to D'Arcy Thompson, the use of *garum* in Mediterranean cooking survived at least to nineteenth-century Turkey. The historian Pliny noted, too, that much earlier *halec* (or *allec*), the sediment (or coarse lees) left over from *garum* preparation, was not only used in cooking but was also employed by Roman veterinarians as a drug to cure mange in sheep!

Today a *garum*-like material, which is called *pissalat*, is still made in Provence from larval anchovies or sardines. Mixed with onion purée and ripe olives, it is spread on bread dough and baked. Generically, it is like an *anchoïade*, but is is called *pissaladiera*.

In the Pacific the Filipinos are famous for a similar taste treat, *bagoong*. The preparation of *bagoong* differs from *nuoc-mam* in that the fish are first degutted. Much of the fermentation results from the enzymes of the fish itself, therefore, rather than from their intestinal bacteria. Filipino law sets a standard for *bagoong* of 40 percent solids, 13.5 percent protein, and 20 to 25 percent salt.

FERMENTED FISH SAUCE (*Bagoong*) / PHILIPPINES

Mix coarse salt with the fish (1:3) and pack in pottery vats. Allow to stand for several months until desirably "ripe." The resulting product is a paste with a cheeselike odor. You may also tap off during the fermentation process a liquid like *nuoc-mam* called *patis* and use it in cooking.

Drying and smoking are two other common ways to preserve fish. In Hawaii small fish are split open, gutted, salted, and hung until dry in the hot sun. Bigger fish are first cut into slices. Elsewhere, common forms of dried fish include *bacalao* (which is usually cod), *stockfish* (ling or cod dried only by the sun and wind and produced commonly in Iceland for export to West Africa), and *klippfish* (which is both salted and sun dried). Tuna, rays, dogfish, and octopus are all dried in Portugal, Italy, and Greece. Sun-dried conger eel is called *charquecito* in Peru. The Chinese, Japanese, and other Pacific peoples also sun-dry shrimp, sharkfin, squid, and sea cucumbers. In some instances they are first boiled. *Katsuwo-bushi* is a popular Japanese soup seasoning, prepared as hard sticks of skipjack by a combined drying, smoking, and fermentation process.

Smoking of fish is done less often than formerly as a means of preservation. Cold smoking of raw fish is now almost always very mild and merely adds a flavor which many Americans have grown to like. Salmon and herring (kippers) are probably the two fish most commonly smoked today. The temperature employed in the process is only about 86°F. Woods used in the smoking vary, but for salmon, oak sawdust is most often used with some juniper chips or dust added. Such cold-smoked fish are readily perishable. A useful guide is Sleight and Hull's *Home Book of Smoke-Cooking*.

FRESHWATER FISH

BESIDES such marine fish, other categories of neglected food fish are the very bony freshwater fish like carp and so-called mudfish, such as the catfish. Catfish are members of the family Siluridae, of which 34 species occur in the United States. Most commonly eaten are channel cats of the genus *Ictalurus*. *I. furcatus* is the largest species, the record specimen weighing 150 lbs., the average weight, however, being only a few pounds. Catfish contain 17.6 percent protein and 3.1 percent fat.

Outside of parts of the American South, where fried catfish is a regional specialty, catfish, carp, and other mudfish are usually also considered to be "trash" by most Americans and are rarely eaten. Despite the fact that their flesh is of high quality, flaky, and usually of excellent flavor, catfish are also subjects of prejudices in England, some of which were summed up in this verse from *Punch:*

> The Catfish is a hideous beast,
> A bottom-feeder that doth feast
> Upon unholy bait;
> He's no addition to your meal;
> He's rather richer than the eel;
> And ranker than the skate.

This avoidance situation is changing somewhat, however, as *Ictalurus* are being raised increasingly in commercial farm ponds throughout the United States as a cash crop. Pond-fish management in the United States started in the South, where a taste for the product already existed, and Auburn University took the scientific lead. From there it is slowly spreading.

To some, the acceptability of some mudfish as food is reduced by the flavor imparted by waters they may inhabit. For this reason some of the more delicately seasoned or simply prepared dishes given here may or may not meet with favor, depending on the quality of the local mud. Skinning the fish is sometimes a way to eliminate an otherwise strong and objection-able taste, and the flavor of many mudfish may be much improved if they can be kept alive in clean water for a few days before cooking. Mudfish are usually plentiful and can make good eating, so what I would suggest is quite a bit of local experimentation.

Of lesser potential importance for food than the channel cats are the bullheads, Great Lakes catfish, and the mud cat (or goujon or yellow cat), all of which reach considerable size. Although particularly strong prejudices exist against these species because of their ugliness, the meat is excellent, as this other verse quoted by Jordan and Evermann suggests:

> Don't talk to me o' bacon fat,
> Or taters, coon or 'possum;
> Fo' when I've hooked a yaller cat,
> I've got a meal to boss 'em.

Fish stews similar to *bouillabaisse* are made in Europe from catfish and other freshwater fishes. One of the best known is *pochouse*.

FRESHWATER FISH STEW *(Pochouse)* / FRANCE

Use several kinds of fish (e.g., eel, pike, carp, catfish), which should be skinned and cut into good-sized pieces. Place the fish in a kettle on a bed of chopped onions and carrots and add a BOUQUET GARNI, a generous number of garlic cloves, and enough dry white wine to cover the fish well. Boil rapidly at first and then continue to simmer for a total cooking period of about 25 minutes. Remove the fish with a slotted spoon and place them on croutons fried in butter and arranged in the serving dish. Garnish with diced lean bacon (scalded and fried in butter) and, if desired, mushrooms and small glazed onions. Some cream may be added to the sauce which, in any event, is strained over the fish.

In these two other mudfish stews from the Phillipines the fish are combined with vegetables or fruits.

GRILLED MUDFISH *(Pesang delag)* / PHILIPPINES

Clean and scrub mudfish, dip in boiling water and vinegar, and scrape off the dark skin with a knife. Cut into slices and salt. Sauté a thumb-sized piece of crushed ginger, 1 quartered onion, and the fish in oil. Add 2 C rice washings, 10 peppercorns, 1 small head cabbage, 2 heads Chinese cabbage, and 2 stalks of green onions, all cut into pieces. Boil briefly and season to taste. Serve with a MISO-and-tomato sauce.

For this one, however, the fish are first deep-fried.

MUDFISH AND BANANA STEW *(Pocherong delag)* / PHILIPPINES

Clean (as above) and slice mudfish and fry in deep, hot oil. Sauté 1/2 *head* of garlic, a thinly sliced onion, and a large, chopped ripe tomato. Add 1 C water and boil. Add 3 ripe bananas cut in halves, 1/2 small cabbage cut in 4 pieces, and 2 halved potatoes. Simmer in a covered pot until done. Add the fish, salt, and serve.

The classic American deep-fried preparation of catfish is also excellent and shows the good eating qualities of these fish to advantage. For several years while I was a veterinary student we haunted an Opelika, Ala., restaurant that specialized in this simple but good dish.

FRIED CATFISH / UNITED STATES

Roll cleaned catfish in fine cornmeal and deep-fry them in very hot lard or oil. Serve with hush puppies or other cornbread and a salad.

FRIED CATFISH *(Barbillon à la meunière)* / FRANCE

Small catfish may also be fried in butter *à la meunière*. See *Grenouilles à la meunière* (p. 272).

GRILLED CATFISH *(Barbillon grillé)* / FRANCE

Several diagonal incisions are cut in the sides of small- to medium-sized catfish. They are dipped in seasoned flour, painted with melted butter, and grilled (preferably in a special wire fish grill) over charcoal. The fish are basted with melted butter and turned only once. They may be served simply with chopped parsley and lemon wedges or any sauce for grilled fish.

A variation is to insert several anchovy fillets into the flesh of the fish before grilling.

American catfish can also be prepared by the great Iraqi recipe for *masgoof*. Lining the banks of the Tigris River at Baghdad are dozens of little outdoor restaurants that specialize in *masgoof*, a delicacy prepared from a large mudfish called *shabboot*. What makes these restuarants and this dish unique is that *masgoof* is prepared from freshly killed fish on order. The fish themselves are maintained alive, either in pens built out into the river or in old bathtubs sunk into the mud. The following recipe was given to us by Dr. Abdul Jabbar Al-Mashat.

GRILLED MUDFISH (*Masgoof*) / IRAQ

Split the fish down the *back*, spread it open, remove the backbone, clean it, and rub salt into the flesh. About 1 to 2 ft. downwind from an open fire impale the fish on two sharpened stakes so that the spread-open inner surface faces the fire. (It could also be planked or grilled over charcoal in a wire fish griller.) While the fish is cooking, fry some chopped or thinly sliced onions in oil, add some chopped tomatoes, salt, and pepper and cook for 10 minutes or so. When the fish is done, arrange it skin-side down on a platter and spread it with the onion-tomato sauce.

For variation, spread the internal surface of the fish with tomato paste or a lemon juice–curry powder paste before baking, or coat it after cooking with a mixture of chopped raw onions, raw tomatoes, parsley, and pickled mango.

The next two recipes are for baked catfish.

CATFISH MARINERS' STYLE (*Barbeau à la mode des mariniers*) / FRANCE

Lightly fry some chopped onions and shallots. Mix them with some chopped walnuts and chopped mushrooms and cover the bottom of a shallow baking dish with this mixture. Place on top of this bed a catfish seasoned with salt and pepper with several diagonal incisions made on each side. Add a few glasses of dry red wine and a generous amount of butter cut into small pieces. Bring to a quick boil and then bake in a 450°F oven for about 20 minutes, basting often. Sprinkle with bread crumbs and melted butter and return to the oven until the crust is browned and the wine has practically evaporated. Sprinkle with chopped parsley and serve.

CATFISH BURGUNDY STYLE (*Barbeau à la bourguignonne*) / FRANCE

Put a seasoned catfish in a buttered shallow baking dish (with a lid).

Surround it with small button mushrooms and small glazed onions. Add 2 C red burgundy and a BOUQUET GARNI. Cover and bake until tender. Remove the fish to a warm platter, surround it with the cooked vegetables, and prepare the following sauce: rapidly reduce the red wine stock to one-half its original volume, prepare a light butter-and-flour ROUX, and stir in the reduced stock to prepare a smooth sauce. Stir in several spoonfuls of butter and serve over the catfish.

A certain sign of its often delicate flavor is the fact that catfish can be simply poached to advantage.

POACHED CATFISH *(Barbeau bouilli)* / FRANCE

Poach the catfish in salted water containing lemon juice or vinegar, sliced onions and carrots, a BOUQUET GARNI, salt, and peppercorns. Drain well and serve with melted butter, hollandaise sauce, or caper sauce.

Catfish also may be prepared according to the recipes for *matelote* of eel.

Finally, this additional recipe for boned-out catfish meat is from the Ozark mountains.

CATFISH BALLS / UNITED STATES

Steam a catfish, remove the bones, and flake the meat. Add an equal volume of dry mashed potatoes, an egg for every 2 C or so of fish, and salt and pepper. Form into ping-pong–sized balls and deep-fry in oil.

Carp are another group of freshwater fish of the family Cyprinidae, which are not eaten commonly in the United States. In Japan carp are considered a courageous fish, which is the reason colorful paper carp are hung from Japanese homes on *tengo no sekku,* or Boys' day, the fifth day of the fifth month, to commemorate the birth of a son. Carp meat has about one-fifth more protein than T-bone steak and only about 2 percent fat.

Prejudices against eating carp primarily relate to their extreme boniness. In contrast to European species, most American carp are small, rarely exceeding a foot in length and often only a few inches; hence their common name in the United States of minnows. However, a few western species, like the squawfish, *Ptychocheilus oregonensis*, reach lengths of up to 4 feet! Carp have always been highly valued by American Indians for their excellent taste and surely deserve to be more widely appreciated. In fact, in most European countries they are holiday fare.

Carp may be deep-fried whole, as in the recipe for southern catfish, or pieces of skinned carp from which the large bones are removed may be deep-fried. Carp are also good grilled, or, if delicately flavored, they may be poached *au bleu*. In the latter case the whole fish can be served cold with mayonnaise or other dressing as one would a salmon. The soft roe or sperm of the carp also is good to eat.

These first three recipes are for very different approaches to baked stuffed carp. The first is poached in white wine and enjoys a typical Alsatian garnish of sauerkraut.

CARP ALSACE STYLE (*Carpe à l'alsacienne*) / FRANCE

Stuff a carp with a forcemeat made from a chopped, white-fleshed fish, bread crumbs soaked in milk and squeezed, chopped parsley and chives, butter, salt, pepper, and nutmeg, all mixed and bound together well with 2 lightly beaten eggs. Poach the fish in a dry white wine. Transfer it to a heated platter, garnish with sauerkraut and small whole boiled potatoes, and cover with a velouté sauce prepared from the reduced wine stock and a light butter-and-flour ROUX and finished with some more butter.

This Polish recipe (like many others) gives the lie to the incompatability of fish and red wine. It also illustrates the common Slavic use of fruits or other sweet ingredients with meats.

STUFFED CARP (*Karp fasherowany*) / POLAND

Lightly cover the bottom of a fish poacher with lightly sautéed chopped onions. Place a stuffed carp on this bed, salt and pepper it, and add on the side of the fish a BOUQUET GARNI and several pieces of gingerbread. Practically cover the fish with a mixture of fish stock and dry red wine (1:1) and poach it gently until tender. Transfer the fish to a heated platter, sprinkle it with lightly sautéed sliced almonds, and serve it covered with the following sauce: strain the wine-gingerbread stock, pressing the gingerbread through a sieve, add to this a sweet-sour syrup prepared by boiling 4 T sugar in 1/2 C vinegar, boil the mixture and finish by stirring in about 1/4 lb. of butter.

And German cuisine, like Flemish, shows the varied cooking possibilities of beer, a fact usually overlooked in the United States.

Stuffed Carp in Beer *(Gefüllter Karpfen in Bier)* / Germany

This is prepared as in the Polish recipe above, except that some chopped celery is added to the bed of onions and the poaching liquid is a light beer. The sauce is prepared by reducing the stock, straining it through a sieve, and finishing it with butter as above.

Carp may also be baked. An excellent dish is this Hungarian one in which the fish is finished with a generous amount of sour cream.

Baked Carp *(Sült ponty)* / Hungary

Cut a carp into slices, LARD them with slivers of bacon, and season them with salt and a generous quantity of paprika. Arrange the fish slices on a bed of sliced boiled potatoes in a buttered baking dish. Cover them with thin slices of onions, tomatoes, and green peppers and sprinkle with melted butter. Bake in a 450°F oven. When partly done, pour in a pint of sour cream into which had been stirred a tablespoon or so of flour.

Like catfish, carp is also excellent deep-fried, as in this simple holiday recipe.

Breaded Carp *(Gebackener Karpfen)* / Austria

For this traditional Christmas Eve dish, slices of carp are seasoned with salt and pepper, rolled in flour, dipped in beaten egg, coated with bread crumbs, and quickly deep-fried in lard. They are served usually with lemon wedges and potato salad.

Finally, two traditional carp soups, the first from Hungary, the second an elegant, whole, deep-fried fish in a delicate broth.

Carp Soup *(Ponty leves)* / Hungary

Boil the head and backbone of a carp, a small onion, and some celery leaves in salted water to produce a fish stock. Cut the rest of the fish into pieces and salt them. Sauté some chopped onions in a little lard until golden; add paprika and the strained stock. Then add sliced potatoes, simmer for 10 minutes, add the pieces of salted fish, some diced green peppers, and a cut-up tomato, and simmer for about 20 minutes more or until done.

This dish comprises the last two courses of a formal dinner. The fish is eaten first and the meal is capped off with the excellent soup.

CARP SOUP (*Di iu tan*) / CHINA

Cut several diagonal gashes in a cleaned whole carp. Dry it thoroughly and sprinkle the surface lightly with cornstarch. Deep-fry the fish until golden in hot oil and drain it well. In the meantime, stir-fry some sectioned scallion stalks and a little minced ginger in peanut oil. Add to them the fried fish, cover it with a well-flavored fish or fowl stock, bring to a rapid boil, and then barely simmer until the fish can be flaked with a fork (but remains firm and intact). During the simmering add a bit of sherry and fish "soy" sauce and 1 to 2 drops of sesame oil. Taste for salt.

Chop a couple of whole scallions and some Chinese parsley and sprinkle them in a long serving dish. Carefully place the carp on top and strain over it the hot soup.

HEAD

FISH heads, and often the tails, too, are cut off before most fresh fish reach American kitchens. This seems to represent principally a prejudice against eating fish that look like fish; yet some of the most beautiful and appetizing European and Far Eastern presentations of fish dishes involve the intact animal. Discarding the fish head is discarding in some instances a reasonable amount of good, edible meat. At the least it is throwing away the raw ingredient of fish stocks and FUMETS that are the very basis of creative seafood cookery. The least wasteful eaters of fish in America, as of other foods, have been black Americans. Out of necessity they have in the process combined various influences to create much of what is original and good in American cuisine. This is a simple, tasty, cheap, and nutritious example of a combination of available protein, vitamins, and carbohydrates.

Fish-head Stew / United States

Simmer assorted fish heads, onions, and green peppers until tender in water to barely cover. Salt and pepper and serve the stew over hominy grits.

Other poor people have all evolved similar no-waste meals such as this hearty Bulgarian peasant soup.

Fish-head Soup (*Chorba ot ribna glava*) / Bulgaria

Fry chopped onion in olive oil until golden, add a little cayenne, pepper, and flour and stir to make a soft ROUX. Add salted water and simmer. Add the salted heads of any white fish and simmer until the fish is done. Before serving, stir in beaten egg and chopped parsley and correct the seasoning. This also is eaten cold.

Such imaginative and nutritious uses of foods available have provided the foundation stones upon which all creatively adaptive and distinctive cuisines have been built. This next dish, for example, is, in some parts of England, regarded as a great delicacy. In the words of the musical, the French don't care what they say as long as they pronounce it correctly. A French wag once added uncharitably that the English don't care what they eat as long as they serve it properly.

Cod's Head and Shoulders / England

Gently poach the head and shoulders of a cod in salted water, drain well, and serve on a folded napkin. Traditional garnishes are parsley, lemon wedges, cod milt, cod roe, cod liver, and fried smelts. The dish is served with grated horseradish and a sauce prepared as follows, from cockles, mussels, or oysters.
Simmer the liquor from a dozen or so shellfish with a little mace and lemon peel. Add the shellfish and turn off the heat. After 10 minutes strain this broth into a cup of cream and prepare a thick smooth sauce with it and a butter-and-flour ROUX. Add the poached shellfish.

The principal use of fish heads, tails, and skeleton in cooking, however, is in the stock pot. These parts are rich in the gelatin and flavor that characterizes good stock.

FISH STOCK, OR FUMET

Gently sauté a MIRAPOIX of finely chopped vegetables in butter. Add a generous amount of heads, tails, and bones of delicately flavored fish plus water and white wine (3:1). Boil rapidly for a comparatively short time. In other words, reduce a fish fumet by not adding too much liquid rather than by prolonged boiling, which only diminishes its quality.

STOMACH

THE visceral organs are left intact in the fish for some of the recipes included in this chapter, but this is one in which the stomachs, or maws, of fish figure as a principal ingredient.

FISH'S-MAW SOUP *(Yu tu tan)* / CHINA

To a delicately flavored boiling chicken or fish stock add diced fish's maw, diced chicken, and diced water chestnuts. Simmer covered for a half hour. Add some spinach cut into 2-in. pieces and simmer until barely wilted. Stir in salt and white pepper to taste and a little light fish "soy" sauce. Sprinkle a little minced smoked ham on the soup as a garnish.

Similarly extolled in literature is the Italian dish *ventresco di tonno*, stomach of tuna, but I have been unable to find out how it is prepared. I have also heard of cod sounds (cod air bladders) stewed in milk, but again the details have not been available.

BLOOD

THIS unusual French shad-head, blood, and red-wine soup again pooh-poohs the purist who says fish and red wine don't mix. It emphasizes too that really fresh fish, like really fresh corn, is worth the effort.

SHAD BROTH (*Potage d'alose*) / FRANCE

Heat 1/2 bottle of dry red wine per person served until it is covered with froth but not actually boiling. The shad should be fresh caught, preferably still alive, and should not be washed or scaled. The head of the fish is cut off over the pan containing the wine because both the blood and the head are essential to the dish. The broth then is lightly salted and a clove added. Cooking is for no longer than 10 minutes with the stock kept just below the boiling point. The broth then is strained into a soup tureen or into bowls that contain slices of French bread, some thinly sliced garlic, salt, and a generous amount of freshly ground pepper.

15

Eels & Lampreys

MOST AMERICANS REGARD eels as slippery slimy water snakes. These
are recipients not only of all the emotional biases directed
against snakes but also those reserved for all furtive and seldom-seen crea-
tures of the murky deep. Probably most present-day Americans under 30
have never seen an eel except in an aquarium somewhere, yet even in my
boyhood live tanks of eels were still kept in our small-town fish market, and
my mother prepared eels at least a few times each year. For animals that are
such delicious eating and are prized in so many cuisines we generally admire
or at least respect, it is remarkable how little demand now exists in America
for eel meat. When, for example, despite their common availability in our
streams and coastal waters, have you seen an eel dish even offered in a good
restaurant?

I have said they are a prevalent animal. One species of true eel,
Anguilla chrisypa, populates coastal waters as well as all rivers of the
United States from Maine to Texas. It can even be found as far inland as
the headwaters of the Mississippi. In fact, their spawning pattern is exactly
opposite that of salmon. They go to the sea to spawn and spend the rest of
their lives in freshwater rivers, streams, and lakes. The average length of
the common American eel is 2–1/2 to 3 feet. In the spring thousands of
young eels are found below most waterfalls and dams on streams flowing
into the Atlantic or Gulf of Mexico.

Also on our Atlantic coast is found the conger eel, *Leptocephalus
conger*, virtually uneaten by us but highly prized in Europe. Moray eels of
the genus *Gymnothorax* also populate both of our coasts, reaching lengths

of 2 to 3 feet; they also make excellent eating. Eel contains about one-fifth more protein than T-bone steak and only one-fourth of its fat.

Basic Preparation

Stun the eel by hitting its head against a hard surface. Tie a string behind the head and suspend the eel. Incise the skin completely around the body below the string, peel it back, grab hold with a cloth or a pair of pliers and peel the skin off by inverting it in one piece. Eviscerate the eel through a ventral incision. Cut off the head. Large eels (1–1/2 lbs. or more) are sometimes poached whole or in pieces in a COURT-BOUILLON for 20 to 25 minutes before proceeding with the recipe.

Rather than follow my pattern of giving recipes for the whole animal first, let us begin our consideration of eels as food with several recipes for hors d'oeuvres or picnic snacks that, in my experience, are universally enjoyed and should easily convince noneel enthusiasts of what they are missing.

FRIED EELS (*Anguille*) / ITALY

Small prepared eels are cut into 2-in. pieces, rolled in flour, and fried in hot olive oil until evenly browned and cooked through. They are then drained on paper towels, sprinkled with salt, and served with lemon wedges.

Eel and whelk shops are found all over England for good reasons. Few animals are tastier.

FRIED EELS / ENGLAND

Skinned eels are cut into pieces, dusted with seasoned flour, and fried in butter and oil as in Italy, or coated with egg and bread crumbs and deep-fried. They then are served with a sharp bottled English sauce or with a sauce of fried crushed garlic and chopped parsley to which some lemon juice is added at the end.

As with most recipes, the French do it a bit fancier. All are equally good.

Fried Eels (*Anguille frite*) / France

Lightly score the backs of small prepared eels with a knife, form them into rings secured with a toothpick, soak in milk, dredge in flour, and deep-fry in hot oil. Drain and garnish with chopped parsley and lemon wedges. They may also be dipped in a light butter instead, deep-fried, garnished with fried parsley, and served with a tomato sauce.

Similarly enjoyable are grilled eels, particularly by this classical Japanese recipe.

Grilled Eels (*Kabayaki*) / Japan

Clean small eels, removing also the heads and backbones, but do not skin. Split each eel and cut them across into about 3-in. pieces. Skewer each with two well-soaked bamboo skewers inserted between the skin and meat. Prepare a basting liquid by boiling the backbones and heads in fish stock, remove them, and add some SHOYU and MIRIN to this stock. Grill the eels over charcoal (begin skin-side down), turning frequently and painting them each time with the basting mixture until crispy brown. They are served commonly on rice.

This is simpler but also good.

Grilled Eel (*Puhi uha*) / Hawaii

The Pacific conger eel (or other species) is cut into pieces, marinated in soy sauce, and broiled over charcoal.

Another fancier English grilled dish is for spitchcocked eel.

Spitchcocked Eel / England

Sauté pieces of eel fillets very lightly in a melted herb butter. Coat with beaten eggs and fine bread crumbs and grill until very crisp.

The Japanese also very much prize smoked eels, which are served in specially made lunch boxes. For those who lack home smoking facilities, custom smokers are found in many American cities. Smoked eels are relished in Scandinavia and elsewhere in northern Europe and provide the basis for open-faced sandwiches like these Norwegian ones or for a very good German salad.

EEL SANDWICH (*Ål smörbrod*) / NORWAY

On fancily cut slices of buttered bread arrange a few pieces of smoked eel and top with a thin slice from a grooved lemon. Or cover the bread slice with a layer of scrambled eggs and top it with a piece of smoked eel and a sprig of parsley.

SMOKED EEL SALAD (*Salat von geräuchertem Aal*) / GERMANY

Mix 1/2-in. pieces of smoked eel and chopped apples with some grated lemon rind and juice. Add to this some warm, diced, boiled potatoes that have been salted and tossed with olive oil. Stir in a dressing made by combining sour cream and mayonnaise (1:1) and chopped dill weed. Serve the salad in a nest of lettuce leaves. Sprinkle it with freshly ground black pepper and garnish with lemon wedges.

For a festive main course largish eels are roasted whole, as in this traditional English recipe or its Samoan counterpart.

ROASTED CONGER / ENGLAND

Clean the middle 12 to 18 inches of a conger eel. Rub the inside with onion juice and dry mustard and stuff with a good fish forcemeat. Sew it up and plug the open ends with small apples. Tie up, if necessary. Roast, basting frequently with the drippings and some cider. Serve hot with pickled red cabbage.

BAKED EEL (*Tuna tao i le ogaumu*) / SAMOA

Either prepared freshwater (*tuna*) or saltwater (*pusi*) eels may be used. They are generously coated with coconut cream, wrapped whole in banana leaves or moist corn husks, and baked in the ground oven, or *umu*, with *kalua* pig or other luau food. The cooked meat then is salted.

This next is a very good dish the Turks also prepare, omitting the bread crumbs and substituting lemon juice for vinegar. They then grill the eels.

BAKED OR GRILLED EEL (*Anguilla al forno o grigliata*) / ITALY

Mix olive oil, some wine vinegar, a few bay leaves, salt, pepper, and bread crumbs. Marinate a large prepared eel (cut in 4-in. pieces) in this mixture for about 3 hours, turning often. Alternate eel pieces on skewers with bay leaves. Bake in a greased dish at 375°F for 30 minutes, turning skewers and basting with marinade. These may also be barbecued over charcoal.

Eels in France are marinated as in Italy, with chopped watercress substituted for bay leaves and lemon juice for vinegar and then grilled.

This French recipe for a whole eel arranged attractively in a ring calls for poaching and then grilling.

DEVILED EEL (*Anguille à la diable*) / FRANCE

Poach a prepared eel in a ring in white wine to cover, with some chopped onions and carrots, crushed garlic, a BOUQUET GARNI, and salt and pepper. Allow it to cool in this stock. Dry it, paint it well with freshly prepared mustard, sprinkle with melted butter and a little cayenne, dust with fine bread crumbs, sprinkle with more melted butter, and grill carefully to avoid burning. Place the ring on a round dish, surround it with gherkins and fancily cut lemon slices, and serve with the following sauce diable: add 1 T vinegar, some pepper, a green onion, and a small *bouquet garni* to 3/4 C white wine and reduce to 1/3 the original volume. Strain and add an equal volume of the strained eel stock and thicken the sauce with a butter-and-flour ROUX. Finish the sauce with some chopped parsley and cayenne to taste.

This variant is poached only and attractively served.

POACHED EEL IN WHITE WINE (*Anguille à la bonne femme*) / FRANCE

Place a prepared eel as a ring on a bed of softly fried chopped onions in a sauté pan. Salt and pepper, add a cup of white wine and a BOUQUET GARNI, and gently poach, covered, for about 25 minutes.

Place the drained eel on a large round crouton fried in butter, fill the center with fried, diced potatoes, and sprinkle with chopped parsley. Serve with a sauce prepared by reducing the stock to one-half its volume and thickening with a butter-and-flour ROUX.

This is another instance of red wine with fish, but the eel in this case is first stuffed.

STUFFED EEL RING BORDEAUX STYLE
(*Roulade d' anguille à la bordelaise*) / FRANCE

Bone a large prepared eel and stuff it with the following: put meat of pike or other white fish through the fine blade of a food chopper, mix it with bread crumbs that were soaked in milk and squeezed, some soft anchovy butter, some BLANCHED chives, chopped parsley, salt, pepper, and nutmeg; bind this mixture with some beaten eggs. Place the eel in a ring in a pan, salt and pepper, add a BOUQUET GARNI, a crushed clove or so of garlic, and some chopped onions and carrots. Cover with a red wine and poach gently until done. Drain the eel and place it on a round serving dish and fill the center with a mound of sautéed mushrooms. Garnish with heart-shaped croutons fried in butter and serve with a sauce prepared by thickening the strained stock with a butter-and-flour ROUX.

Poaching liquids for eel vary greatly from country to country and, not surprisingly the Germans use beer.

EEL BERLIN STYLE (*Aal berliner Art*) / GERMANY

Simmer 2-in. pieces of eel until tender in ale and beer (2:1) with an onion, a bay leaf, some crumbled black bread, and a little lemon juice. Sieve the sauce over the eel.

In these next two Italian recipes eels are BRAISED with mushrooms or peas.

EELS GENOA STYLE (*Anguille alla genovese*) / ITALY

Soak a large prepared eel (cut in 4-in. pieces) in ice water for at least 15 minutes. Lightly brown a small sliced onion in 3/4 C olive oil. Add chopped anchovy fillets and cook 2 minutes. Add the eel and cook until the adherent water evaporates. Add a good quantity of sliced mushrooms, salt, and pepper and cook 5 minutes. Add a cup of dry white wine, crushed garlic, and several cups of fresh peas. Cover the pan and cook until wine is almost evaporated. Add a little tomato sauce and some water and cook about 30 minutes longer.

EELS ROMAN STYLE *(Anguille alla romana)* / ITALY

Cut some small, prepared eels into 3-in. pieces. Lightly brown some minced garlic and chopped scallions in olive oil. Add the eels, salt, and pepper and cook until the water from the eels has evaporated. Add some dry white wine, a little tomato sauce, a cup or two of fresh peas, a little stock and cook until the peas are tender. Add more stock if required.

Or eels may be prepared in rich cream sauces, sour cream in the first two, heavy sweet cream in the third.

EEL WITH GREEN SAUCE *(Aal grün)* / GERMANY

Cook 2-in. pieces of eel until tender in fish stock and white wine (2:1) to cover. Cook a generous amount of chopped parsley and some chopped chives, dill, and spinach in butter. Sprinkle with flour and stir until smooth. Prepare a sauce by whisking the hot stock into the herb-butter ROUX. Boil, add some sour cream, and serve the sauce over the poached eel.

This German dish is traditionally served with cucumber salad.

EEL WITH DILL SAUCE *(Aal mit Dillsosse)* / GERMANY

Poach an eel cut into 2-in. pieces in salted water until tender. Serve the pieces of eel covered with the following sauce: cook a butter-and-flour ROUX until golden; whisk in some of the hot eel stock and simmer to form a smooth, medium-thick sauce; stir in an egg yolk beaten with some sour cream and continue to simmer; add a few drops of lemon juice, a generous amount of finely chopped dill, and some chopped hard-cooked eggs.

EEL WITH PAPRIKA IN CREAM *(Paprikás angolna tejszinnel)* / HUNGARY

Cut a prepared eel into pieces and place in a sauté pan on a bed of chopped onions lightly fried in butter and mixed with a generous amount of paprika. Salt and pepper and add a BOUQUET GARNI. Cover with white wine, bring to a boil, cover, and poach for about 10 minutes. Add a number of large mushroom caps and simmer for about 10 minutes more. Place each piece of eel and a mushroom cap on a crouton fried in butter. Keep warm and serve covered with a thick sauce prepared by reducing the strained stock by one-half, thickening it with a little butter-and-flour ROUX, and adding a generous amount of heavy cream. Finish this sauce with a good amount of butter.

This classic fancy French eel stew is called a *matelote*.

EEL PLATTER *(Matelote à la canotière)* / FRANCE

Cut some prepared eels into thick slices. Put them in a buttered, deep frying pan on a bed of thinly sliced onions and crushed garlic. Add a BOUQUET GARNI and enough dry white wine to cover. Bring to a boil, add about 1/2 C warm brandy, light it, and when the flame has gone out cover the pan and cook the eel until tender. Remove the fish and reduce the stock to 2/3 its original volume. Place the eels, the reduced stock, which has been thickened with a butter-and-flour ROUX, a number of small glazed onions, and small sautéed mushrooms in a shallow casserole. Bring to a boil, correct the seasoning, and simmer for about 5 to 10 minutes. Traditionally this dish is served garnished with small river fish dipped (all except the head and tail) in beaten egg and bread crumbs and fried, and also with crayfish poached in a COURT-BOUILLON.

In a variant, *matelote à la meunière*, red wine is used and the traditional garnish is poached crayfish and triangular croutons fried in butter.

Of several main dishes once served to me in an Anglo-Indian home in Calcutta, most made use of inexpensive seafood.

EEL CURRY / ANGLO-INDIAN

Prepare small eels and cut them into 4-in. pieces. Half-cover them in a kettle with boiling salted water and cook until tender. Sauté chopped onions in butter and add flour and home-blended or prepared curry powder to form a smooth flour-curry-onion-butter ROUX. Add some hot eel stock to prepare a thick sauce. Serve this sauce over the cooked eels with rice.

One finds this Catalan classic in many Mediterranean restaurants from north of the French-Spanish border south to Alicante. It is very good.

EEL WITH GARLIC AND PEPPER *(All i pebre)* / SPAIN

Put a generous amount of finely chopped garlic and BLANCHED almonds in quite a bit of very hot olive oil. Add 1 t paprika and quickly stir-fry. Stir in pieces of several small, unskinned eels and water to cover. Simmer the stew for about 15 minutes, adding some hot red pepper.

A similarly traditional Spanish dish is fried *angulas,* the small larval eels that swarm in the spring and are taken in very large numbers. They provide a seasonal delicacy in many countries, as they could also in the United States.

FRIED BABY EELS *(Angulas)* / SPAIN

Young (less than 2–1/2-in.) transparent eels are washed in salted water, dried thoroughly, and fried very quickly in smoking hot oil. Drain and serve. They are also done in hot oil in individual serving dishes with chopped red pepper and whole cloves of garlic. These are served in Spain as excellent *tapas,* Spanish hors d'oeuvres.

In France the netted tiny fry of eels, herring, and other fish are called variously *blanchailles, poutina, melet,* or *nonats.* The English refer to them as whitebait.

FRIED BABY EELS *(Blanchailles frites)* / FRANCE

Spoonfuls of eels and other fry may be deep-fried in olive oil by first sprinkling them with lemon juice and then seasoned flour or by first mixing some with a little TEMPURA-type batter.

In England baby eels are often eaten for breakfast.

ELVERS AND EGGS / ENGLAND

Fry elvers (eels less than 2–1/2 in. long) in hot bacon fat until the transparent fish are white. Stir in a few seasoned beaten eggs and stir until they are set. Serve with crisp bacon.

Dill is an excellent seasoning and garnish for seafood and sees great use for that purpose in Scandinavia. This recipe is for cold eel in dill sauce.

COLD POACHED EEL (*Kokt kald ål*) / NORWAY

Cut a skinned, cleaned eel into 1-in. sections. Heat to boiling salted WATER ACIDULATED with vinegar. Add some peppercorns, dill weed, and the eel. Quickly return to a boil and simmer for 25 minutes. Transfer the pieces of eel to a bowl, skim the scum from the stock, strain it over the eel, and allow it to cool. Garnish with dill. Serve with boiled potatoes and a parsley sauce.

The Japanese also make a very popular pâté with eel meat.

EEL PÂTÉ (*Kamaboko*) / JAPAN

The raw flesh of conger eels is very finely ground. This is mixed with salt and sugar, shaped by packing in a mold, and then steamed. Starch is also sometimes mixed in with the fish. *Kamaboko* is also commonly prepared from lizard fish and croakers.

And this last is for an unusual eel soup in which pears are also a main ingredient.

EEL SOUP (*Aalsuppe*) / GERMANY

Chop a boned eel into small pieces, rub them with salt, and let stand for an hour. Simmer them until tender in salted water containing some white wine, a bay leaf, marjoram, and parsley. Arrange the pieces of eel in the bottom of a soup tureen with pear halves that have been previously steamed with red wine until tender. Strain the eel stock and add to it an equal amount of strained beef stock (in which some shallots and peas were cooked). Bring to a boil and cook in it some semolina dumplings. Thicken the soup, if desired, and pour it and the dumplings over the eels and pears.

LAMPREYS

THE lampreys, or cyclostomes, are primitive, smooth-skinned, eel-shaped cartilaginous fish with suckerlike mouths by which they attach to and feed on other fish. The completion in 1921 of the Welland Canal bypassing Niagara Falls permitted lampreys to enter the Great Lakes of North America, where they have played havoc with valuable commercial and sports fisheries. Lampreys, which also are distributed widely in rivers on both coasts of the United States, are themselves excellent eating, a fact that is little appreciated by Americans. The flesh of lampreys is particularly delicate, and they are prized highly in France. This is another instance where consumption at our dinner tables could help to keep a very destructive pest species under control.

Basic Preparation

Before cooking, lampreys often are bled first, then scalded briefly in boiling water, and skinned by scraping with a knife. The spinal cord is removed by cutting off the end of the tail, then hooking the cord through an incision behind the gills and drawing it out. Lastly, the animal is eviscerated.

Lamprey may be prepared by any recipe for eel, but here are three other special recipes.

LAMPREY BORDEAUX STYLE (*Lamproie à la bordelaise*) / FRANCE

Reserve the blood from a lamprey. Cut the fish into thick slices and place them in a pan on a bed of lightly sautéed sliced onions and carrots. Salt and pepper. Add a clove of garlic, a BOUQUET GARNI, and enough red Bordeaux wine to just cover the fish. Boil rapidly for 10 to 15 minutes and then remove the slices of lamprey. In a shallow casserole alternate the lamprey and some sliced leek sautéed in butter with chopped bacon. Prepare a sauce from the strained stock and a light butter-and-flour ROUX. Strain this sauce over the fish and simmer it until done. Remove from the heat, carefully stir in the reserved blood, and garnish the dish with large triangular croutons.

LAMPREY CASSEROLE *(Lampreda)* / ITALY

Fry thin slices of leek and some chopped thyme in olive oil in a deep casserole until golden. Add pieces of skinned lamprey lightly dusted with seasoned flour. Cook briefly and add enough beef stock to about half-cover the lamprey. Cover the casserole and simmer for about 15 minutes or until the lamprey is tender. Shortly before serving, add a wineglass of sweet vermouth or half a wineglass of white wine and half a glass of Marsala.

This or similar lamprey pâtés are among the most famous dishes of a number of Bordeaux restaurants.

LAMPREY PÂTÉ BORDEAUX STYLE
(Pâté chaud de lamproie à la bordelaise) / FRANCE

Cut lamprey fillets into thin slices and thread through each of them a desalted anchovy fillet. Marinate in a mixture of olive oil, white wine, brandy, salt, pepper, chopped parsley, chopped tarragon, and chopped chives. Fry the lamprey slices quickly in hot butter.
 Line an oval pâté mold with a pie dough. Coat the walls and bottom with a white fish forcemeat (put boned fish through the fine blade of a food chopper and mix with bread crumbs soaked in milk and squeezed, some finely chopped mushrooms cooked in butter, chopped parsley, chopped tarragon, chopped chives, salt, pepper, and beaten egg to bind).
 Put in a layer of lamprey slices, sprinkle with chopped shallots, add a layer of forcemeat, and continue until the mold is full. Pour in the marinade and cover with a final layer of forcemeat. Dot with some butter pieces, cover with a sheet of pie dough, and seal the edges. Decorate the top with rolled dough cut into various shapes and add some holes for the steam to escape.
 Bake in a 350°F oven for 1–1/2 to 2 hours. Before serving, add through a hole in the lid some fish velouté sauce to replace the liquid which has evaporated. (If the pâté is to be served cold, the velouté sauce is not added; but after the pâté has cooled, a fish aspic is poured in instead).

16

Sharks & Skates

SHARKS ARE very much underutilized for food in the United States. Their meat is of good quality, and it is unfortunate that prejudices against eating shark are so strong that, when it does appear as fillets in American fish markets, or on menus, it is most often deceptively, if not fraudulently, called "grayfish," "sea bass," "sea veal," or by some other euphemism. Prejudices arise from the appearance of sharks, the fear and loathing they inspire (and perhaps the remote possibility that, like crabs or other marine scavengers, they may have eaten someone). On the other hand, shark has always been much enjoyed in Japan and many other seafaring countries, and its popularity generally is increasing throughout the world. For instance, Mexico has already built several shark-freezing works, and when I was in Australia recently I was told that shark meat now accounts for a large portion of the wares of their popular "fish and chips" stands. From the nutritional standpoint the 23 percent protein and 0.2 percent fat of shark meat compares with 14.7 and 32.1 percent, respectively, for T-bone steak.

Shark fillets are also one of the cheapest fish meats available today, and they may be prepared to advantage by virtually any recipes suitable for firm-fleshed fish. The only shark recipes I have included, therefore, are just a few more unusual recipes, including two shark classics from the cuisines of Iceland and China.

MUSCLE MEAT

THE first recipe is for an unusual and especially tasty Spanish dish; the second is a locally famous and certainly *distinctive* shark recipe from

Iceland. First preparation of it would probably benefit from the guidance of a connoisseur!

SHARK WITH RAISINS AND PINE NUTS *(Tiburón con pasas y piñones)* / SPAIN

Shake small pieces of shark in a paper bag containing flour and fry them in very hot olive oil. Add chopped onion and brown it well. Throw in a chopped tomato, some raisins, pine nuts, crushed garlic, chopped parsley, paprika, and black pepper. Simmer a few minutes and serve.

FERMENTED SHARK *(Hákarl)* / ICELAND

Eviscerated sharks are buried in the sand or kept in an open barrel for three years to ferment. The resulting much prized product is rich in ammonia, and its taste resembles that of some ripe cheeses.

If that sounds weird, and you have already tried (and enjoyed) the classic Swedish salmon *(gravlax)* without perhaps knowing it is raw fermented salmon, the name "grave salmon" clearly suggests that it was originally made more or less like *hákarl*.

Should *hákarl* not strike your fancy, at least for starters anyway, you might reserve it for a future party to impress a new boss and begin your family experience with some good shark fillets *à la meunière* or another slightly less exotic dish like this excellent curry.

SHARK CURRY / MALAYSIA

Fry thinly sliced onions, crushed garlic, 2/3 t chopped dill, and 1/3 t mustard seed in 5 T coconut oil. Add 1-1/2 C salted water containing some tamarind (or grapefruit) pulp and the following paste: finely grind 25 dried chilis, 60 black peppercorns, 5 T coriander, 1 t cumin seed, and a piece of dry tumeric 1 in. by 3/4 in.; mix this with 3 crushed garlic cloves and onions crushed into a paste. Cook this sauce for 5 to 10 minutes. Add 2-1/2 C water containing a generous amount of tamarind (or grapefruit) pulp and boil for about 5 minutes. Add a pint of coconut cream and simmer for 5 minutes more. Add small sharks cut in cross sections and simmer until the fish are tender.

Coconut cream, a much used ingredient in Malaysian and Pacific island cuisines, complements fish nicely. This recipe is for a simpler creamed shark dish from Polynesia.

SHARK IN COCONUT CREAM *(Fai ai malie)* / SAMOA

A shark is eviscerated and cut into large pieces. These are boiled until nearly cooked. The pieces then are skinned and the meat cut into slices. They are again brought to a boil in coconut cream containing sliced onions and salt. Skate is also cooked in the same way in Samoa, as are fetal sharks.

I had these shark meat balls in an Australian home, but the recipe may have originated elsewhere in the Far East. These croquettes would be as good just plain with a tartar or other fish sauce, or in a curry or other fish stew.

SHARK BALL SOUP / AUSTRALIA

Put shark meat through a meat grinder, blend it with salted water and beaten egg, mix with finely chopped green onions, form into balls, roll them in cornstarch, deep-fry, and add to fish broth or a fish soup.

FIN

PROBABLY the best-known form of shark's meat among gastronomes is the fin. Shark's fin, which is salted and dried in the sun, is a Chinese delicacy chiefly because it is very rich in good-quality gelatin and makes an excellent stock. Because it sounds exotic and tastes so good, it is probably one of the best-known dishes in Chinese *haute cuisine*.

SHARK'S-FIN SOUP *(Iu che tan)* / CHINA

Rinse a dried, skinned shark's fin in cold water and soak it overnight in warm water. Remove the fin, rinse, and simmer it for about an hour in fresh water containing a clove of garlic and a piece of ginger. Rinse again and drain. Boil a good chicken stock, add the fin, and simmer, covered, for about 20 minutes. Add some shredded white meat of chicken (which has been lightly dusted with cornstarch) and flaked crabmeat in approximately equal amounts and simmer, covered, for 10 minutes more. Correct the seasoning and garnish with minced smoked ham and minced scallions.

LIVER

TUNA livers are the choicest fare on Japanese tuna fishing boats, and in some other cultures oil-rich and highly nutritious fish livers, including shark liver, are much prized. If you or any of your guests have fond memories, as I do, of the daily cod liver oil of your childhood, this is surely for you.

ROASTED SHARK LIVER *(Ate o le malie)* / SAMOA

A shark liver is wrapped first in taro or spinach leaves, then in breadfruit leaves or moist corn husks, and baked in the *umu*, ground oven, as luau fare.

DOG FISH

DOG fish are small, sharklike fishes, which many of us dissected in zoology class. They may be prepared by recipes suitable for sharks or rays.

SKATE, OR RAY

THESE relatives of sharks are especially prized in several European cuisines. Small skates, or rays, make the best eating. They contain 18.2 to 24.2 percent protein and scarcely any fat. Punched out circles of small skates' wings are sometimes fraudulently marketed in the United States as scallops. These can, in fact, be prepared by scallop recipes but at *much* cheaper cost than the real thing. This deception cannot occur in Europe, where scallops are almost always sold in the shell.

Basic Preparation

As an exception among fish, skate often is hung for 2 to 3 days, at which time it becomes quite ammoniacal. This is purely a matter of preference.

MUSCLE MEAT

A simple and tasty introduction to skate is as it is prepared in English fish-and-chip shops.

DEEP-FRIED SKATE / ENGLAND

Small, fresh skates are skinned, marinated in cold milk (or lemon juice and water), drained, dusted with seasoned flour, deep-fried in hot oil, and served with lemon wedges and deep-fried parsley.

Skate fillets may be prepared *à la meunière* as well.

Most frequently, however, skate fillets are poached and sauced in various ways.

POACHED SKATE / ENGLAND

The meat is cut into fillets, poached in ACIDULATED WATER, and served with sizzling brown butter to which a little vinegar is added at the end.

Poached skates also are served in France with hollandaise sauce or any other sauces or garnishes suitable for poached fish.

Elsewhere one also encounters a wide range of traditional garnishes and accompaniments.

POACHED SKATE WITH ONION BUTTER
(*Rochen gekocht mit Zwiebelbutter*) / GERMANY

Rub fillets of skate with salt and lemon juice and allow to stand for an hour. Put them in a pan with a bay leaf, peppercorns, a clove or two, marjoram, and parsley. Cover with boiling water and simmer for 30 minutes. Brown a generous amount of chopped onions in butter; add lemon juice, some chopped parsley, and a chopped mushroom or truffle. Pour this sauce over the drained skate.

Skate lends itself to baking, too, and accompaniment by such simple regional ingredients as sauerkraut.

SKATE WITH SAUERKRAUT (*Rochen mit Sauerkraut*) / GERMANY

Rub fillets of skate with salt and allow them to stand for an hour. Bring to a boil some milk containing sliced onion, a bay leaf, a clove or two, and some peppercorns. Add the skate, return to a boil, reduce the heat, and simmer for only 5 minutes. Drain the pieces of skate well, paint them with melted butter, and dredge with seasoned flour. Wrap the fish in foil and bake in a hot oven and serve with sauerkraut.

Or skate may be interestingly combined with a variety of sauces and then baked.

SKATE MALAGA STYLE *(Raya a la malagueña)* / SPAIN

Fry until golden brown some BLANCHED almonds, soft bread crumbs, and chopped parsley and set aside in a little olive oil. In another pan, fry in oil a generous quantity of sliced onion until golden and some crushed garlic. Add chopped tomatoes, salt, pepper, and a little saffron and stew for a while. Strain this mixture, return it to the pan, add the almonds, bread, and parsley and pour it all over salted fillets of ray, which have already been baked about 15 minutes in a 350°F oven. Continue to bake about 15 minutes more or until the ray is tender and most of the liquid in the sauce is absorbed.

Skate soups are traditional, too, in some cuisines. This is an unusual Italian combination of broccoli with seafood stock.

SKATE BROTH WITH BROCCOLI AND PASTA
(Pasta a broccoli col brodo d' arzilla) / ITALY

Cover a cleaned ray with an ample amount of cold water. Add a number of cloves of garlic, bring to a boil, and simmer until the meat of the ray completely falls apart and its cartilages dissolve. Filter this rich broth through double layers of muslin. Return it to a boil and add some tomato paste. Brown some cloves of garlic in olive oil in a soup kettle. Reduce the heat and add a paste prepared by grinding two desalted anchovy fillets with a generous amount of parsley in a mortar. Heat briefly and add salt, pepper, and the flowers from 3 or 4 heads of broccoli. Fry the broccoli briefly and add the boiling ray broth and a generous amount of small pasta. Cook only until the broccoli is still crisp and the pasta *al dente*.

LIVER

IN addition to the muscle meat of skates, their livers have enjoyed considerably more popularity than the livers of sharks, and a number of epicures have long extolled their virtues in many forms—poached, jellied, as fritters, and *en croûte*. Here are two classics.

POACHED SKATE LIVER ON TOAST / ENGLAND

The skate liver is poached in an ACIDULATED fish stock or water, cut into thick slices, and served on croutons fried in butter and sauced with either melted butter and lemon juice or browned butter.

SKATE LIVER FRITTERS *(Beignets de foie de raie)* / FRANCE

Skate liver is poached in a white wine COURT-BOUILLON. It is drained, cooled, and cut into slices. These are marinated in a mixture of lemon juice, olive oil, chopped parsley, salt, and pepper. The slices then are dipped in a fritter batter, such as for TEMPURA, and deep-fried in hot oil. They are garnished as is plain fried skate, above.

Part Four

SHELLFISH

SHELLFISH

*Few of us are adventuresome in the matter of food; in fact most of think
there is something disgusting in a bill of fare to which we are unused.*

WILLIAM JAMES

THE NEXT and most neglected category of potential animal-protein providers in the United States is the very large number of species of "animals without backbones," the invertebrates. I shall lump them all in this section under the conventional cookbook heading of "shellfish." Considered here, in addition to fairly familiar molluscs and crustaceans, will be the eating qualities of other invertebrate animals that inhabit water, like jellyfish and sea urchins, as well as those like insects and snails that also live on land.

Traditional cultural prejudices about eating invertebrate animals vary in the extreme and generally without rhyme or reason. Mosaic food laws, for example, ban all creatures of the waters without fins and scales to orthodox Jews yet consider locusts to be a valuable food item. Similarly, it is not unusual to encounter Americans who will eat oysters alive but consider the very idea of eating cooked squid or land snails disgusting. Shrimp may be prized, while freshwater crayfish are almost completely overlooked. We may be very fond of eating a sticky material secreted by bees, while thinking the bees themselves to be completely beyond the pale.

All shellfish should be eaten as fresh as possible. In fact, crabs and lobsters should be alive (or cooked) when purchased. Fresh shrimp, dead, are firm, shiny, and bright with bluish, gray color. Dullness or traces of pink color or softness are indicators of age in shrimp and of beginning spoilage. Open or broken molluscs should be rejected.

17

Molluscs

THE ONLY water-dwelling molluscs eaten fresh by many Americans are oysters. The fact that they survive relatively long out of water stimulated what Root and Rochemont have referred to as an "oyster cult" in most parts of this country beginning in the middle 1800s. The British consul in Boston in 1840 exclaimed on how "oysters are eaten in all ways, and in great quantities." These animals were so abundant then that New England cookbooks of the period called for up to 400 shucked oysters for a single recipe, and horse-drawn express wagons laden with oysters delivered them alive far into the Middle West, where the politician's oyster roast became an institution. To somewhat lesser extent comparatively, they still travel inland alive today and still are found there on restaurant menus. Our historical fondness of oysters, however, does not seem to protect us from present-day prejudices against even this "national dish." Among middle western and western university students queried, while only 3.9 percent had not tried oysters, an additional 19.3 percent had but reject them as food nonetheless.

Clams, while much enjoyed along our coasts, particularly the Atlantic, reach the rest of the country almost exclusively canned or as frozen clam chowder or minced clams. Twenty-seven percent of the university students surveyed in the study cited above had a strong aversion to eating clams. Beyond those species few Americans have experienced any other molluscs than scallops, half of the edible portions of which we waste entirely and increasingly reduce many of the parts we do eat to a prebreaded and frozen nonentity.

Where, oh where, for example, are even the "cockles and mussels, alive, alive, oh" that abundantly populate the tidal zones of all our coasts, much less whelks, limpets, or winkles? Or even the squid, which we also have in abundance and have now begun to export rather than eat at home? The conch is eaten only in Florida yet is distributed considerably more widely, and pen shells with scalloplike adductor muscles also range from Florida to North Carolina, to cite examples of other neglected species.

Let us start first with cockles and mussels, because we all know that others eat them. Like clams and oysters, they are both pelecypod, or hinged-shell, molluscs.

COCKLES AND MUSSELS

COCKLES, or heart shells, look rather like scallops with both half shells rounded. Called *bucarde* or *cocque* in French, they are the most valuable shellfishery in Great Britain, where boiled cockles can be found for sale in every fish stall. They burrow only a short distance into the sand and are easily collected. *Cardium magnum* and *Dinocardium robustum* are major species on our Atlantic coast. They reach a diameter of 5 inches, while *C. corbis, Clinocardium nutalli,* and other species on the Pacific coast are a bit smaller. Their protein content is 13 percent, or slightly less than T-bone steak.

Basic Preparation

Collected cockles and mussels should be placed in changes of clean seawater for at least several hours to give them a chance to expel ingested sand and bacteria. Discard open shells. If not to be shucked and eaten raw, they are scrubbed and placed in a saucepan with some green onions, parsley, some peppercorns, and water to a depth of about 1/4 inch. Cover the pan, bring to a boil, and cook only until shells open. Discard those that do not open and reserve the broth.

RAW COCKLES / ENGLAND

Sprinkle cockles on the half shell with a little lemon juice or vinegar.

BOILED COCKLES / ENGLAND

Arrange boiled cockles on the half shell and pour the strained broth and a little melted butter over them.

This Portuguese variation of boiled cockles is somewhat more flavorful because of the other ingredients added.

COCKLE STEW *(Amêijoas à bulhão pato)* / PORTUGAL

Put cockles in a kettle with cold, salted water, crushed garlic, black pepper, some olive oil, and a generous amount of chopped parsley and coriander. Bring to boil and simmer until the cockles are all open.

This is one of a number of other traditional English uses for boiled cockles.

COCKLE PIE / ENGLAND

Pepper a buttered deep baking dish and cover the bottom with a layer of brown bread crumbs. Add pieces of butter and then a layer of shucked cockles. Cover with a thick cream sauce containing a little nutmeg and anchovy paste. Repeat the layer of crumbs, butter, cockles, and sauce until the dish is full. Cover with a thin layer of seasoned mashed potatoes and bake in a moderate oven. Serve with lemon wedges.

One also finds them like this is many fish-and-chips shops.

FRIED COCKLES / ENGLAND

Shucked cockles, shaken in a paper bag with seasoned flour, are fried until golden brown in bacon fat or oil.

Or they are used as the basis for this very nice salad we once had in a Cambridge restaurant.

COCKLES IN SALAD / ENGLAND

On a bed of lettuce arrange shelled boiled cockles, sliced cucumber, tomato wedges, white asparagus spears, cooked beet slices, and crisp bean or alfalfa sprouts. Use a vinaigrette dressing.

Cockles are also a very popular garnish for other seafood or combine with others, as in this Spanish seafood casserole.

SOLE WITH COCKLES *(Lenguado con berberechos)* / SPAIN

Butter a shallow casserole and cover the bottom with lightly scored sole fillets. Surround the fish with prepared shucked cockles, salt, and pepper, dot with butter, and pour in some white wine to barely cover. Bake at 350°F for about 20 minutes and serve covered with the following sauce: lightly sauté chopped carrots, onions, and parsley in butter, add flour, stir, and cook to form a light ROUX. Stir in some of the cockle broth and cook to make a smooth sauce. Rub it through a sieve or blend in an electric blender and stir in beaten egg yolks and cream until thick.

As the next two recipes testify, cockles also provide an unexpectedly complementary garnish for roast meats.

ROAST LEG OF MUTTON WITH COCKLES / ENGLAND

Insert boiled cockles into slits cut all over a leg of mutton. Season and roast it normally and serve with a horseradish sauce.

COCKLE SAUCE MARINERS' STYLE *(Amêijoas à marinheira)* / PORTUGAL

Fry some cloves of garlic and sliced onions in a generous amount of olive oil until lightly browned. Remove the garlic and add peeled, coarsely chopped tomatoes, some flour, and black pepper. Simmer until the tomatoes are done and add cooked, shelled cockles, some mashed potato, and chopped parsley. Cook briefly and serve as a garnish for roast pork.

Finally, they readily substitute for clams or oysters in a New England style clam chowder or oyster stew.

COCKLE SOUP / ENGLAND

Put several dozen open cockles in a soup tureen. Pour over them a creamy soup prepared from a butter-and-flour ROUX, milk, pepper, ·nutmeg, and some anchovy paste, plus some cream. Serve hot.

MUSSELS

MUSSELS are cultivated in marine "farms" in parts of Europe. There, like here, they are also one of the most plentiful molluscs "in the wild." Yet this delicious animal is rarely eaten in the United States. As is the case with cockles, mussels seem to be shunned in the United States by many people who do eat clams and oysters. Whether it is their bearded shell, their attachment to rocks and pilings, or the brown to bright orange color of their flesh that is responsible is hard to know. Some people also describe their flavor as "coarse" or regard their texture as too soft. Part of the reason for the common prejudice against them may also be knowledge that a fatal poisoning has been associated with the eating of mussels on the West Coast of the United States. The cause of this sporadic poisoning is now very well understood, and, if the precautions indicated by your state's health department are observed, one should not fear to eat mussels. Note that this toxin is *not* destroyed by heat.

As in Europe, the bay mussel, *Mytilus edulis,* occurs on both of our coasts, as do other so-called horse mussels of the genus *Modiolus. Mytilus californiensis* also occurs on rocks on the open Pacific shore, where it reaches up to 8 inches in length. Their protein content is 10 percent.

Basic Preparation

The basic method of preparation is as given for cockles (page 322), except that the beards are trimmed from the shells.

RAW MUSSELS / ENGLAND

Mussels on the half shell are sprinkled with lemon juice.

Mussels are commonly boiled to open in liquids more varied and flavorful than those given under "Basic Preparation," as in this simple poached mussels in a wine broth.

MUSSELS IN WHITE WINE *(Muscheln in Weisswein)* / GERMANY

Fry some chopped onion in butter until golden. Add unopened mussels, salt, pepper, and a glass or so of white wine. Cover the pan and cook until the mussels have opened. Eat the mussels and broth in soup plates.

A variety of regional variations on the poached-mussels theme emphasizes that their taste is complemented by a wide variety of ingredients.

MUSSELS ON THE HALF SHELL *(Moules à la martégale)* / FRANCE

Fry chopped garlic in olive oil until light brown. Add some soft bread crumbs and tomato purée, stir, and add poached mussels on the half shell. Cover the pan and cook several minutes, sprinkle with chopped parsley and basil, and serve.

Some such dishes are usually served cold as part of a lavish course of mixed hors d'oeuvres, as in these next three recipes.

PLATE OF MUSSELS *(Midye plâkisi)* / TURKEY

Sauté chopped onion, carrot, and celery and some crushed garlic in olive oil. Add water to just cover and simmer until the vegetables are done. Stir in some chopped fennel, salt, and pepper. Place opened mussels removed from their shells on the bed of vegetables, sprinkle with chopped parsley, and serve cool with lemon wedges.

MUSSELS IN A SHARP SAUCE *(Mitili in salsa piccante)* / ITALY

Brown some garlic in olive oil, add mussels that have been opened, washed, and drained, some chopped anchovy fillets, dry white wine and white wine vinegar (2:1), and simmer over a low heat until the liquid is reduced one-half. Add chopped parsley and cayenne to taste. The mussels are kept in this mixture in earthenware crocks in the refrigerator for three days before serving.

COLD MUSSELS WITH ALMOND SAUCE *(Almejas con almendras)* / SPAIN

Open mussels and allow them to cool on the half shell. Serve them covered with the following almond sauce: in an electric blender, blend until smooth toasted almonds, some bread crumbs, a little vinegar, olive oil, salt, and a generous amount of pepper.

Alternately, the cold mussels may be dressed simply with blended olive oil and lemon juice (3:1) and coarse black pepper.

This cold first course is also a kind of mussel salad.

MUSSELS IN CELERY MAYONNAISE *(Moules tante gracieuse)* / FRANCE

Mix into some mayonnaise generous amounts of paprika and crushed celery seeds, a little lemon juice, and a little tomato paste. Fold in some stiffly beaten egg white. Gently stir in cooked mussels and a little mussel liquid and serve cold.

And here poached mussels are actually mixed with potato salad and sauced with a wine-laced broth.

MUSSELS AND POTATO SALAD *(Mexihões à francillon)* / PORTUGAL

Mix poached and shelled mussels in a dish with potato salad. Spoon over this some of the mussel broth mixed with white port wine and sprinkle with fresh oregano and parsley.

Mussels can also provide the meat for a wide variety of casseroles or other one-dish meals. Not unexpectedly, the English make a pie of them.

MUSSEL PIE / ENGLAND

Put shelled mussels in a buttered shallow baking dish and sprinkle them with white wine, some chopped parsley, chopped onion, salt, and pepper and cover with fine white bread crumbs. Dot with butter and add mussel liquid to moisten the crumbs thoroughly. Bake for about 20 minutes in a 325°F oven or until the top is well browned.

And, while I obtained this recipe from France, its inspiration is unquestionably the Near East, either directly or via Spain, where essentially identical rice and seafood dishes also abound.

RICE WITH MUSSELS *(Pilau de riz aux moules)* / FRANCE

Prepare a pilaf, but with some chopped onion and chopped tomatoes fried in the oil before the rice is added. As part of the liquid in which the rice is cooked, use the stock in which the mussels were boiled open. Also, incorporate a BOUQUET GARNI and a little saffron in the pot. When the pilaf is done, mix in the cooked mussels, heat through, pile high on a platter, and cover with grated cheese.

Instead of serving them on a bed of other ingredients, large mussels lend themselves very nicely to stuffing with many flavorful mixtures. This Turkish version is a classic encountered in some of the finest seafood restaurants of Istanbul.

STUFFED MUSSELS *(Midye dolması)* / TURKEY

Soak 2 dozen large, scrubbed mussels in cold water and poach them open. Fry several chopped onions in olive oil until golden. Add 1 C raw rice, cover, and cook over low heat for about 20 minutes. Add 1 C boiling water, some pine nuts and currants, cover, and cook until the water has evaporated. When cool, stuff the mussels with this mixture and tie each shut. Place them in a pan in layers, cover with boiling water, and weight the mussels with a plate. Cover the pan and simmer very gently for 1/2 hour. Drain carefully but allow the mussels to cool in the pan. Chill, remove the strings, and serve them with lemon wedges.

The French, like other Mediterranean peoples, prepare many regional variations on the same theme. Here are several excellent ones.

STUFFED MUSSELS *(Moules farcies)* / FRANCE

Prepare as above and stuff with any of the following:

1. Put some boiled and drained lettuce through a food chopper with some onion, parsley, and cooked liver. Simmer the tied mussels as above in a tomato, oil, garlic, and white wine sauce. Remove the strings and serve the mussels in the sauce.

2. Finely chopped cooked spinach seasoned with salt, pepper, and a bit of nutmeg and chopped leeks and onion fried in olive oil. Tie the

shells shut and arrange them side by side in a shallow casserole. Fill the spaces between the mussels with the spinach mixture, dust with fine, dry bread crumbs, sprinkle with oil, and brown well in a 400°F oven.

3. After opening mussels over high heat in white wine seasoned with pepper, thyme, bay leaf, and fennel, place them on half shells in a shallow casserole and cover each with chopped mushrooms and onions fried in olive oil, to which are added some white bread previously soaked in milk and squeezed dry, a generous amount of tomato purée, chopped parsley, pepper, and nutmeg. Dust the stuffed mussels with fine, dried bread crumbs, and some olive oil. Brown in a hot oven, sprinkle with lemon juice, and serve.

4. After initial preparation as in (3), cover the half shell with finely chopped garlic, shallots, parsley, tarragon, and thyme mixed well with some white bread previously soaked in milk and squeezed dry (into which is combined some soft butter blended with egg yolk). Then place the stuffed mussels on slices of French bread in a shallow casserole and bake at 350°F for about 8 to 10 minutes. Serve with lemon wedges.

Mussels are also especially delicious simply fried or grilled.

Fried Mussels *(Midye tavası)* / Turkey

Steam mussels to open, dip them in a light TEMPURA-type batter, fry in hot olive oil, and serve hot with lemon juice.

Mussels fried the same way also are eaten in Turkey with the following very good sauce: in an electric blender, blend into a smooth creamy sauce a mixture of walnuts and pine nuts, some olive oil, garlic, white bread crumbs, and lemon juice.

Grilled Mussels on Skewers *(Brochettes de moules)* / France

Alternate mussels on skewers (or presoaked rosemary branches) with thin squares of fresh pork fat. Bread them lightly and deep-fry in hot oil.

Alternatively, grill the unbreaded brochettes over charcoal and serve with grilled cherry tomatoes.

And a wonderful, very cheap dish for those who enjoy *escargots bourguignonne*, refuse to collect their own snails, and rebel at the cost of the tinned creatures from France is this one.

Mussels Burgundy Style *(Moules bourguignonne)* / France

Open mussels by poaching in well-seasoned wine. Cover each mussel on the half shell with "snail butter" (as for *escargots bourguignonne*) and put in a 350°F oven for only 5 to 6 minutes. Serve sizzling.

Like cockles, mussels provide surprisingly good accompaniments to other seafood and meats in several European cuisines. These are two fine examples.

Mussel Sauce *(Sauce de moules)* / France

Fish, such as sea bream, are baked covered and surrounded by this sauce.

Sauté some thinly sliced leek in olive oil, add coarsely chopped tomatoes, chopped parsley, chopped fennel leaves, crushed garlic, salt, and pepper. Cook until tender and well reduced. Add the strained liquid in which the mussels have been opened and simmer a bit longer. Remove from the stove and complete the sauce by stirring in a generous number of small mussels removed from their shells.

Veal Cutlet with Mussels *(Kalbskoteletten mit Muscheln)* / Austria

Score some veal cutlets lightly and dust them with seasoned flour. Fry them quickly in butter and remove from the pan. Add to the pan the strained mussel liquid and a little dry white wine. Stir well and bring to a boil. Return the cutlets and add the shelled mussels. Cover the pan and simmer a few minutes. Add butter and a little lemon juice and serve from the pan.

Last, whether one calls it mussel soup or poached mussels in their broth would be rather moot in this instance. For other soups, more liquid would be present.

Mussel Soup *(Zuppa di mitili)* / Italy

Lightly brown some crushed garlic in 1/2 C olive in a soup kettle. Add a little tomato sauce, salt, chopped red pepper, and about 36 mussels. Cook over high heat until the mussels open. Add some oregano and cook briefly. Serve the mussel soup over toasted bread.

SCALLOPS

I will not say anything at all about oysters and clams because both are well appreciated in America, and our ways of preparing them are among the best in the world. But before we leave the pelecypods, one word about scallops *is* in order—and that word is *unfortunate*! Unfortunate that for some odd but unforgivable historic reason only the adductor muscle of the scallop is sold in the United States. The at least equally good crescent-shaped, pink to orange-yellow "tongue," or coral, is thrown away. In Europe both parts usually are sold together on the half shell *(coquille)* in fish shops. Our custom readily allows the fraudulent selling of punched-out circles of skate wings as scallops.

RAZOR CLAMS

RAZOR clams are elongated like the case of a straight razor. Like other pelecypods, they are eaten raw or used any way that other clams and mussels are. The genus *Ensis* occurs commonly on our Atlantic coast.

One should be aware also that almost any of the very small bivalves easily collected along the shore or in tidal pools can also be the ingredients of good chowders or soups. They are simply held for a few hours or overnight in clean seawater, then rinsed several times, and cooked and served in the soup, shells and all. If they are big enough to make the effort worthwhile, the meat can be salvaged from each with a pick. If not, they still provide all their flavor.

The next group of marine molluscs to consider is the largest group, the gastropods.

GASTROPODS

THESE are the single-shelled molluscs, including the winkles or periwinkles, limpets, and whelks. As a group they are little eaten in America except in Hawaii. One exception is the ecologically threatened abalone on our West Coast.

WINKLES

THE periwinkle, *Littorina littorea,* occurs in abundance on both sides of the Atlantic and is harvested by the ton in Europe. *L. scutulata* and other species occur on the Pacific coast. *Opihi* are collected from seaweed in Hawaii and, with some of the latter as a garnish, are very good eaten raw out of the shell. After noting that for some rocky areas of our coastline, "one cannot walk about in such localities without crushing hundreds of [winkles]," Augusta Arnold, a marine biologist, has remarked that "in Great Britain they are used among the poorer classes for food." So much for such prejudices, for winkles are eaten poached, pickled, roasted, and as an accompaniment of other seafood by many nonpaupers. In fact, their 18 percent protein content is very high.

WINKLES *(Bigorneau)* / FRANCE

Boil some seawater containing a BOUQUET GARNI and some peppercorns. Place winkles in the pot and simmer them for about 15 minutes. Pick them out of their shells with a pin.

PICKLED WINKLES / ENGLAND

Boil winkles in salted water and then place them in cold water. Drain. Remove the animals from their shells with a strong pin and pickle them in cider vinegar. The English also roast winkles.

BAKED WINKLES *(Bodoletti)* / ITALY

Place the winkles removed from their shells in a shallow ovenproof dish. Salt them and add some olive oil and a bay leaf or two. Cover the dish and bake the winkles at 350°F for about 15 minutes.

FISH FILLET WITH WINKLES *(Filets de baudroie Raimu)* / FRANCE

Fillets of bass or other rockfish and a generous quantity of shelled winkles are poached in a clear fish stock. The poached fillets are placed on croutons fried in butter and olive oil on a heated platter. The stock is rapidly reduced and then removed from the heat. Some aïoli sauce and ROUILLE are whisked in and this sauce is ladled over the fillets. The winkles are arranged about the fish and the whole is sprinkled with chopped parsley and lemon juice. (This recipe was created by M. G. L. Panuel.)

LIMPETS

LIMPETS, or Chinamen's hats, as they are sometimes called, occur in abundance on most rocky coastlines. *Acmaea testudinalis* and *Crepidula* are common on our Atlantic shores, and *Lottia gigantea* of our Pacific coast grows up to 4 inches in diameter. The giant keyhole (volcano) limpet *Fisurella* is as large as 7 inches in diameter, but most are quite small. Like abalone, they clamp down tightly (somebody measured a force of 70 psi) but they may be pried loose with a screw driver or some similar implement. They are the puka shells of modern Hawaiian jewelry.

In Hawaii, limpets are most commonly eaten alive and raw out of the shell, sometimes with a soupçon of LIMU. Limpets can also be served as in any recipe for clams or oysters.

Basic Preparation

Wash well to remove sand.

LIMPETS ON THE HALF SHELL / HAWAII

To serve raw on the shell, loosen the animal from the shell with a thin knife and turn it over. Season with pepper or paprika and lemon juice. For fancier service the shells may be embedded in a bed of crushed ice and garnished with chopped parsley or seaweed and lemon wedges.

BROILED LIMPETS / HAWAII

Turn washed, medium- to large-sized limpets over in their shells, brush them with a little hot sauce and melted butter, and lightly brown under the broiler. Serve as is or with drawn butter.

FRIED LIMPETS / HAWAII

Shelled limpets are dusted with seasoned flour and deep-fried in oil.

LIMPET PIE / ENGLAND

This dish is made as for cockle pie. Sometimes hard-boiled eggs and diced bacon are added.

WHELKS

European whelks, *Buccinum*, also occur in North America, as do other genera of whelks, such as *Thais* and *Busycon*. They are all good eating and contain about 17 percent protein.

Basic Preparation

Put whelks in changes of clean, cold, salted water to rid them of their sand.

WHELK FRITTERS / ENGLAND

Drop whelks into boiling, salted water, remove the pot from the stove, and allow to stand 1 hour. Remove the animals from their shells, trim and drain them, roll in seasoned flour, dip in a light TEMPURA-type batter, and deep-fry. Serve with pickled red cabbage.

BOILED WHELKS / ENGLAND

Cook initially as for fritters and serve the unshelled hot whelks with parsley sauce or cold with an appropriate mayonnaise sauce, cocktail sauce, vinegar, or Worcestershire.

Steamed whelks are eaten the same way, and whelk stands are common in Britain, particularly in garish Victorian seaside resorts such as Brighton and Weston-super-Mare.

CHITONS

AMPHINEURANS, or chitons, are animals with light transverse plates which make them look something like little armadillos or large sowbugs. In the West Indies they are relished as "sea beef." Specimens of *Cryptochiton stelleri* up to 13 inches in length on our Pacific coast (called seaboots or gumboots) are eaten by the Indians. Other species on the Pacific coast, as well as *Acanthopleura granulata* of Florida and the Gulf, grow to 3 inches or more, but most Atlantic species are much smaller. They can be cooked like limpets and whelks.

Last, there are many good dishes that can use any of these marine molluscs that happen to be available. Japanese *tempura* is a classic example.

Some other gastropod molluscs are the land snails. Recipes for them follow those for insects in chapter 20. Before leaving aquatic molluscs, however, we must consider what are probably the most important food species worldwide—the cephalopods, animals that rarely grace an American table.

CEPHALOPODS

MANY persons who have not studied zoology do not realize that the squid, cuttlefish, and octopus are simply molluscs without external shells, and therefore close relatives of oysters, clams, and snails. Cephalopods vary enormously in size. Those used commonly for food range from thumb-sized cuttlefish to the *Loligo* squid of our two coasts, that reach lengths of up to two feet. Giant squid (*Architeuthis princeps*), with a total length of up to 48 feet and a body diameter of 5 feet, are the largest of invertebrate animals and are probably the sea monsters of legend.

American prejudices against eating cephalopods range from rejection of the unfamiliar to fear of octopuses, particularly, to squeamishness about their slithery, many-legged bodies and elusive habits, to objection to their tough and "rubbery" flesh.

SQUID

SQUID, in particular, are enjoyed throughout most of the world, and, especially among the Mediterranean countries and in the Orient, they contribute importantly to man's dietary. Squid now constitute about 8 percent of all seafood consumed in Japan, for example, with over 500,000 metric tons landed there in some years. Those caught in U.S. Pacific waters have begun to be exported in significant numbers to Korea and Japan. When are we going to learn what cheap, nutritious eating squid can provide? Their protein content of about 17 percent compares favorably, for example, with that of a T-bone steak's 14.7 percent.

Basic Preparation

Squid are cleaned and prepared for most recipes by removing their visceral organs and the skeletal cartilage. The pigmented skin then is peeled off and the animal washed well. The tentacles generally are eaten, while the head may be eaten or not, as preferred. The following recipes assume that the squid have been prepared this way unless they state otherwise.

About the simplest way to prepare squid, and one of the best, is to grill them.

Grilled Squid (*Calamari grigliati*) / Italy

Cut squid into several pieces each. Marinate them for about 1 hour in olive oil, salt, and pepper. Drain the squid and grill them over charcoal, brushing occasionally with oil.

I first had this very good dish in the Sardinian coastal village of Oristano. It was served simply in an earthenware frying pan and accompanied by nothing other than bread and plenty of good, golden Sardinian wine.

Fried Squid (*Calamari*) / Italy

Fry rings or pieces of squid alone or with some shrimp in a mixture of garlic, hot butter, and olive oil. Sprinkle them with chopped parsley and mop up the juices with bread.

Squid Roman Style (*Calamari alla romana*) / Italy

Small squid and cuttlefish, or rings of larger squid, are also delicious dipped in a TEMPURA-type batter and deep-fried in hot oil.

Around most of the Mediterranean, squid also are cooked slowly in a variety of sauces. Here are a number of possibilities.

Squid in Mushroom Sauce (*Calamari in salsa con funghi*) / Italy

Cook chopped anchovy fillets, chopped garlic, chopped parsley, and a little dry white wine a few minutes in a generous amount of olive oil. Add squid cut into pieces, a little tomato sauce, salt, pepper, and some water. Cover and cook 20 minutes. Add dry mushrooms (washed and cut into pieces). Simmer over low heat, adding more water if required, until the squid are as tender as desired.

Squid with Swiss Chard *(Calamari con bietole)* / Italy

Slice squid into rings and cut the tentacles into small pieces. Salt and pepper. Brown lightly in olive oil. Add well-drained, parboiled Swiss chard and dry white wine and cook 10 minutes. Add a little tomato sauce, a tiny hot pepper, and some chopped parsley. Cook until squid are tender, remove from heat, add lemon juice, and serve.

Squid and Artichokes *(Calamari con carciofi)* / Italy

Brown some garlic in olive oil. Add thinly sliced squid, salt, and pepper and cook about five minutes. Add a wineglass of water, cover, and simmer for 20 minutes. Add artichoke hearts cut into thin slices and simmer until artichokes are tender.

And almost every area of Italy as well as the other Mediterranean countries has its regional squid stew, of which these are but a few.

Squid Luciano Style *(Calamari alla luciano)* / Italy

Place large squid in a soup kettle. Add salt, black or red pepper, a few sprigs of parsley, quartered tomatoes, and about 1/2 C olive oil. Tightly cover the kettle with aluminum foil and put on the lid. Simmer two hours without removing the lid. Add lemon juice and serve hot or cold.

Squid Neapolitan Style *(Calamari alla napoletana)* / Italy

Brown sliced garlic in olive oil. Add some small squid, a medium can of tomatoes, salt, and pepper and cook 10 minutes. Add some pine nuts, chopped, pitted ripe olives, seedless raisins, and about 1/2 C water; cover the pan and cook until the squid are tender. Serve in soup dishes over toasted bread.

Squid Genoa Style *(Calamari alla genovese)* / Italy

Brown chopped onion in olive oil; add chopped parsley, garlic, rosemary, and sliced mushrooms and cook for a few minutes. Add a little tomato sauce, 1 C water, and cut-up squid. Cover and cook on low heat until squid are tender.

Squid Marche Style *(Calamari alla marchigiana)* / Italy

Brown sliced garlic in 1/2 C olive oil. Add cut-up squid, chopped parsley, salt, chopped anchovy fillets, and a small piece of red pepper. Cook until the water from the squid has evaporated. Add 1 C of dry white wine and cook until it nearly evaporates. Add 1/2 C of fish stock and cook over low heat until the squid are tender.

Squid with Wine *(Kalamarákia me krassí)* / Greece

Put small whole squid (or pieces of larger squid) into a heavy pan and heat them over a low flame while shaking the pan until most of moisture has evaporated. Add red wine and olive oil (1:1), a little sugar and water, and salt to taste. Simmer until tender, allow to cool, and serve from the pan at room temperature.

Cuttlefish with Raisins and Pine Nuts *(Globito con pasas y piñones)* / Spain

Fry pieces of cuttlefish (or squid) in very hot olive oil; add some chopped onion and brown it. Add chopped tomato and simmer until the cephalopod is tender. Add some raisins, pine nuts, crushed garlic, chopped parsley, paprika, and black pepper. Cook a minute longer and serve.

Stewed Squid *(Calmars à l'étuvée)* / France

Cut squid into rings and the tentacles into pieces. Fry them for a few minutes in olive oil in which some sliced onions and crushed garlic already have been lightly fried. Add some red wine, bring to a boil, and add a BOUQUET GARNI containing fennel, salt, and pepper. Cover the pan and cook over a low flame until the squid are tender. About ten minutes before serving, add some seasoned tomato purée.

Very different squid stews are eaten in the Orient and throughout the Pacific. This very good dish will give the idea.

Squid *Luau* and Coconut / Hawaii

Boil squid until tender and cut into pieces. Cook LUAU, drain, and chop finely. Add coconut cream and squid and simmer for 10 minutes. Season with salt.

The bodies of squid are perfectly made for stuffing, and the possibilities are really limited only by one's imagination. Here are a few starters.

STUFFED SQUID MARSEILLE STYLE *(Calmar farci à la marseillaise)* / FRANCE

Fry some finely chopped onion in oil; add the chopped tentacles and some finely chopped tomatoes. Salt and pepper. Add chopped garlic and parsley and a piece of bread dipped in milk and squeezed dry. Mix in a little hot water, remove the pan from the heat, and stir in several egg yolks. Fill the prepared squid bodies three-fourths full, sew them shut, and fry them in oil. Prepare a sauce with fried chopped onions, a bay leaf, and garlic. Stir in a little flour and then a wineglass of white wine and a wineglass of water.

Simmer and correct the seasonings. Strain the sauce over the fried squid, sprinkle with bread crumbs and oil, and brown in a 300°F oven.

The French also stuff squid with a mixture of highly seasoned sausage meat, mashed boiled anchovies, and spinach. Equally elegant regional variants come from elsewhere along the Mediterranean.

STUFFED SQUID *(Kalamária yemistá)* / GREECE

Squid are stuffed about half full with the following: brown a generous amount of chopped onions in olive oil, add the chopped tentacles, and, after they have colored, add uncooked rice, chopped parsley, chopped mint, and a generous number of pine nuts and stir-fry a few minutes. Add a little red wine to each of the stuffed squid, sew them shut, and pack them upright in a deep casserole. Add a little olive oil and then enough diluted tomato juice to just cover the squid. Bake in a 350°F oven until the squid are tender. Serve them hot or tepid with the sauce.

STUFFED SQUID *(Calamari ripieni)* / ITALY

Cut the heads and tentacles from some squid and put them through a meat chopper. Mix these well with chopped parsley, salt, pepper, a little uncooked rice, a very small finely chopped tomato, a chopped anchovy fillet, and 1 T or so of olive oil. Stuff the squid bodies with this mixture, place them in an oiled baking dish sprinkled with bread crumbs, and pour 1/2 C olive oil over all. Bake in a 400°F oven for about 35 minutes.

In another version, proceed as above with small squid. To the chopped head and tentacles add crushed garlic, chopped mushrooms, oregano, chopped parsley, some crumbled white bread, salt, pepper, and olive oil. Stuff squid with this mixture and sew them shut. Place squid in an oiled casserole, salt and pepper them, and pour over 1/4 C olive oil. Bake in a 375°F oven for 45 minutes and serve with lemon wedges.

STUFFED SQUID (*Calamares relleños*) / SPAIN

Stuff squid with a mixture of chopped smoked ham, chopped squid tentacles, chopped drained tomatoes, chopped parsley, salt, and pepper. Cook the squid until tender in a sauce prepared by sautéing chopped onions and garlic in olive oil and adding some wine.

Squid are included, too, as valued ingredients in many mixed seafood dishes, such as *paellas*.

Squid can even be stuffed simply with squid.

SQUID ROLL (*Ika no makini*) / JAPAN

Slit some squid open and flatten them out. Discard the heads. Put the tentacles and "vanes" on each opened squid, roll it up, and tie it. Cook the rolled squid until tender in a mixture of 4 T SHOYU, 3 T sugar, 1/4 t salt, 3 T sake, and a little AJINOMOTO.

In the Far East squid, like other seafood, are commonly dried so that they can be stored or eaten inland. Many oriental food stores in the United States stock these dried marine foods.

A Chinese steamer, also purchasable in most oriental stores, is a very handy kitchen utensil, not just for Chinese and Japanese dishes like this one, but for almost everyday use, particularly with seafood and vegetables.

STEAMED SQUID AND PORK (*Kan moi jiu tsao zo*) / CHINA

Cover 1/4 lb. dried squid with water for 30 minutes and then wash thoroughly. Mince 4 water chestnuts. Combine the squid and chestnuts with 1/2 lb. ground pork, 2 T soy sauce, 1/2 t salt, 1 t sugar, 1 T sherry, and 1 t ginger juice and mix well. Steam in a deep bowl for 30 minutes. Fresh squid could also be used. Serve with rice.

This next, more unusual, use for squid makes quite a nice hors d'oeuvre.

Squid Spread / Hawaii

Boil squid until tender and put them through the finest blade of a meat grinder (or blend in a blender with the mayonnaise). Add some chopped celery, chopped parsley, chopped olives, mayonnaise to moisten, salt, and paprika. Serve on crackers and garnish with watercress.

The following is also a somewhat uncommon use for squid.

Squid Sauce for Pasta *(Salsa di calamari)* / Italy

Cut the body and tentacles of squid into very small pieces and add them to some chopped onion, garlic, and chopped parsley that have been sautéed in olive oil. Cook about 15 minutes and add salt, pepper, some well-drained chopped tomatoes, and a little tomato paste and simmer the sauce until the pieces of squid are tender.

Last, this tasty soup may be prepared from either fresh or dried squid. The other ingredients are available in oriental stores. Or, like any Chinese cook, substitute.

Squid or Cuttlefish Soup *(Moi jiu tan)* / China

If dried squid or cuttlefish are used, they must be presoaked for 24 hours, washed well, the viscera and cartilages (and, if desired, the head) removed. They then are cut into convenient pieces. Some pork neck bones are parboiled for about 5 minutes, the water discarded, and the bones washed in cold water. The bones then are covered with fresh water, brought to a quick boil, the heat reduced to very low, and any scum and fat skimmed. Add the presoaked molluscs, a piece of presoaked dry tangerine peel, a few Chinese red dates, and a generous quantity of peeled lotus roots that have been split and cut into slices. Simmer, covered, for about 2 hours, restore the water to the quantity needed, correct the salt, bring again to a quick boil, and serve.

In Japan dried squid is also reconstituted in water and eaten as one does fresh squid. Alternately, it is seasoned first with a mixture of MISO, SHOYU, and sugar. In addition, Japanese make a special fermented dish from squid.

FERMENTED SQUID *(Shiokara)* / JAPAN

Mix salt and an inoculum of the rice mold *Aspergillus oryzae* with the raw muscles and liver of squid. Allow to ferment.

This uniquely flavored dish can also be prepared from sea urchin gonads or from intestines and stomachs of the skipjack tuna.

OCTOPUS

OCTOPUS and squid are closely related molluscs, and many recipes for one are suitable with little, if any, modification of the other. The common octopus of our Atlantic coast is *Octopus vulgaris*, that of the Pacific *O. hongkongensis*.

Basic Preparation

Octopus usually is cleaned and prepared for cooking by turning the "head" inside out and removing the internal organs and ink sacs. The raw octopus is then pounded until tender. (In the Pacific islands they rub it with coarse salt, hold it by the "head," and pound it in a wooden bowl. They continue this with more salt and pounding until the skin can be easily torn off.) It is then washed thoroughly.

RAW OCTOPUS *(He'e)* / HAWAII

Cut pounded raw octopus into bite-sized pieces. Mix in a bowl with some chopped LIMU, grated onion, and crushed red pepper.

Almost as simple is this Japanese recipe.

BOILED OCTOPUS *(Yude dako)* / JAPAN

Cut pounded octopus into pieces and boil it until tender. Serve in a MISO sauce thinned with SHOYU.

In the Orient, as well as in Europe, octopus is also simply fried.

FRIED OCTOPUS *(Tsa tsan iu)* / CHINA

Stir-fry a clove or so of garlic in peanut oil and discard. Quickly stir-fry thin slices of pounded octopus in hot oil until they curl. Serve with soy sauce containing grated ginger.

FRIED OCTOPUS *(Poulpe frite)* / FRANCE

Parboil pieces of prepared octopus, drain, deep-fry in oil, and serve with spinach.

Or fried octopus can be the principal ingredient for a number of interesting main dishes like these three from the south of France.

OCTOPUS PROVENCE STYLE *(Poulpe provençale)* / FRANCE

BLANCH and drain pieces of prepared octopus and fry them lightly in oil with chopped onions. Add a generous quantity of dry white wine, an equal volume of water to cover, a BOUQUET GARNI, and some garlic. Cover the pan and simmer until the octopus is tender. Dust with chopped parsley and serve.

OCTOPUS TOULON STYLE *(Poulpe à la toulonnaise)* / FRANCE

Marinate pieces of pounded octopus in dry white wine, a BOUQUET GARNI of fennel, parsley, thyme, and salt and pepper. Fry chopped onions, carrots, and bacon in olive oil until lightly browned. Add chopped tomatoes, an onion stuck with cloves, the octopus, the strained marinade, the *bouquet garni,* and enough white wine and water (1:1) to barely cover. Cover the pot and simmer until the octopus is tender (2 to 4 hours). Heap the meat in the middle of a deep platter and surround with slices of French bread spread with aïoli sauce and moistened with a little of the octopus sauce. Serve with additional aïoli sauce.

This *niçoise* version is colorfully prepared at table.

OCTOPUS NICE STYLE *(Poulpe à la niçoise)* / FRANCE

Fry some chopped onions, crushed garlic, and chopped parsley in olive oil until golden. Add well-dried strips of prepared octopus and a BOUQUET GARNI and fry until the octopus strips are golden. Add warm cognac and light it. When the flames have gone out, stir some flour into the oil, add a generous amount of chopped tomatoes, and, when they are soft, enough white wine to cover the octopus. Salt and pepper, cover the pan, and simmer the octopus until it is tender.

Octopus is also a commonly served dish at Pacific island feasts. Here are two variations of octopus with coconut cream from insular America.

BAKED OCTOPUS *(Fai ai fe'e)* / SAMOA

An octopus is tenderized by wrapping it in papaya leaves and leaving it in the shade for a day (the same could no doubt be accomplished by using purified papain or some other enzymatic meat tenderizer). The flesh of the animal is then hardened by placing it on the hot stones of the *umu*, or ground oven, for about 5 minutes. The meat is cut into small strips and put in a sauce of the octopus ink mixed with coconut cream. This mixture is wrapped in banana leaves (or corn husks) and baked with other foods in the *umu* for a luau.

OCTOPUS WITH *Luau* AND COCONUT CREAM / HAWAII

Put a pounded octopus in cold water and bring to a boil. Add salt and cook until tender. Add some LUAU and cook a little longer. Drain, add coconut cream, and heat through.

18

Crustaceans

C RUSTACEANS, the closest relatives to insects, are by far the most frequently eaten invertebrate animals in America. One might even say that crustaceans are our *only* really commonly eaten invertebrates. Frozen shrimp tails enter many of our kitchens, crabs are appreciated along our coasts, and flown-in live Maine lobster can be had for a price practically anywhere in this country. These several species we know quite well, yet of West Coast university students surveyed, 13.9 percent avoided shrimp, 17.5 percent crab, and 21.3 percent lobster. Since World War II frozen spiny, or rock, lobster tails have also been shipped to the United States all the way from Australia or South Africa. What a real pity that from this really large group of animals the variety of species eaten by most Americans is so small.

Equally sad is the fact that comparatively few American cooks inject any variety into their methods of preparing even these few species. It is probably a safe guess that a good 40 percent of shrimp tails consumed in this country (how many people even know this animal actually has a head and thorax too?) are boiled and drowned in some variant of catsup. Another 50 percent of them, at least, are deep-fried in a coating or batter which, more often than not, because of its thickness, stage of under- or over-doneness, or the quality or temperature of the cooking oil, bears about the same resemblance to a delicately prepared Japanese *tempura* as a drive-in hamburger does to steak tartar.

For space reasons, and because we do eat *some* of them, I have decided to say relatively little about other saltwater crustaceans. I particularly regret not including recipes for spiny lobsters (marine crayfish, langouste) because they are the one marine animal on which I have personally done research, some studies in Hawaii many years ago on their hormones. In the process I learned to cook them by virtually every recipe man could devise—and then some.

With this expertise I can urge those who have only tried American restaurant-style versions of frozen spiny lobster tails (often boiled before they are frozen) to try to obtain the fresh animals, which compare very favorably with their majestic cousin, the North Atlantic lobster. In several European countries, fish markets (indeed, even supermarkets), as well as many restaurants, keep spiny lobsters from the Mediterranean alive in tanks, just as they always do trout. In my experience, however, even the better restaurants in places like Honolulu or Miami never do this. What a pity, for locally caught live spiny lobsters are available from North Carolina on south, as well as on our Gulf and Pacific coasts, and there certainly are people with sufficient interest in eating them in most American cities to make the effort worthwhile.

First, a few words about other edible marine crustaceans available on our shores because they can be cooked to advantage by almost any recipes for crab, shrimp, or lobster.

BARNACLES, HERMIT CRABS, SLIPPER LOBSTERS, AND MANTIS SHRIMP

MANY crustacean species are wasted by American commercial fishermen, who discard them as animals for which they feel there is no market. What a crime. Crustaceans in this class include the several genera of slipper lobsters, the moderate-sized relatives of the North Atlantic and spiny lobsters, which range through the Pacific and Indian oceans into the Mediterranean Sea. The French call them *cigale*, the Spanish *cigarra*. These brownish, mottled, smooth-carapaced fellows occur in Hawaiian waters, where they are usually 5 to 8 inches long but sometimes grow to 12 or more inches. Whatever their size, they make *very* good eating.

Other usually wasted crustaceans include stomatopods, or mantis shrimp, hermit crabs, and barnacles. Virtually any recipe for the Maine lobster can be applied with good results to any large specimen of any of them. As an example, here is a good Italian recipe especially for mantis shrimp, or *Squilla*, which grow as long as 10 inches on our Atlantic coast. *Pseudosquilla* of our Pacific coast is much smaller but still good eating.

Mantis Shrimp *(Cannocchia)* / Italy

Poach the mantis shrimp in barely boiling water until they are firm all through (some species will not get very firm). Shell them (this is not easy for the small ones because of the spines on the edges of their abdomens) and dip the meat into a light, runny batter (made of beaten egg, flour, olive oil, a little white wine and water, salt, and pepper). Fry until golden brown in deep, hot olive oil.

We also use small ones in Spain sometimes just to prepare fish stock because they are so cheap.

Barnacles also are good eating. They look like molluscs but really are sessile crustaceans. One finds them attached to rocks on most coasts. They are eaten in many countries. Street vendors in Chile, where a particularly large species occurs, offer them for sale along with sea urchins. The acorn barnacle *(Balanus)* is particularly prized. Specimens of *Balanus nubilus* of our own Pacific coast may reach almost a foot in diameter. Species on the Atlantic coast are much smaller. Barnacles have a delicate flesh that may be prepared by most recipes for crab.

Hermit crabs are decapod crustaceans, but more or less commensal ones. They appropriate the cast-off shells of whelks, winkles, and other gastropods to live in. That is why they come in such a wide array of shapes and color. Called "Bernard l'Ermite" by the French, this animal can be eaten like any other crab after it is extracted from its pilfered cave. The genus *Pagurus* is common on our east coast.

Another crustacean, the horseshoe crab, *Limulus polyphemus*, is a rather plentiful living fossil on our Atlantic seashore. It could be harvested in limited numbers and can also be prepared and eaten like other crabs. In fact, it used to be enjoyed very much by the coastal Indian tribes of North America.

When any marine crustacean has shed its old shell and its new one has not hardened, it is particularly vulnerable and usually remains well hidden. If eaten in this soft state, crustaceans just need to be cleaned, as for the ordinary hard-shelled animal, and can be eaten whole, shell and all. Small animals are the most tender and flavorful. Soft-shelled crabs were choice items of diet on much of the Atlantic coast when I was a boy, where *Callinetes sapidus* is the most commonly eaten species. An excellent way to do them or other soft-shelled crustaceans is to dip them in a mixture of melted butter, lemon juice, and cayenne and broil them over charcoal. A good Japanese way to do them is to dip in a SHOYU, MIRIN, and sugar mixture and broil.

Mention should also be made of ways of preserving and using seasonally abundant crustaceans, particularly those too small to handle individually. Small shrimp are pounded with salt into a thick brine and then sun dried in both Vietnam (where it is called *nukemum*) and South China. Dried shrimp powder can be purchased in oriental stores and makes a flavorful stock. Similar products are fermented seafood pastes and sauces, some of which were discussed in chapter 14. Here is one other.

SHRIMP PASTE / BURMA

Dry shrimp in the sun. Pound them with much salt and leave them spread in the sun for several days. They become a grey-black pungent paste. Store this in unglazed pottery jars and use for flavoring any compatible meat or vegetable dish.

MIXED SEAFOOD MEALS

THIS is probably as good a place as any to include a few recipes in which almost any crustaceans or molluscs or other marine invertebrates available can be incorporated. Unlike many American cooks who are used to following recipes in cookbooks literally, really creative cooks worldwide test their skills by using what ingredients are at hand according to "generic" cooking rules for that class of foodstuff. Thus regional sauces, seasonings, and methods of cooking characterize *niçoise*, Cantonese, or Cajun cookery more than specific main ingredients or specific proportions.

Seafood soups, chowders, or bisques provide notable examples of imaginative and good uses for hearty, one-dish meals. Some recipes were given in chapter 14; here is another.

SHELLFISH SOUP / ENGLAND

Simmer some onion, carrot, and saffron in a tasty fish stock. To the strained stock add any or all of the following: whelks, mussels, winkles, cockles, and scallops. Shrimp, lobster, and crab also may be added, if desired. Simmer for a few minutes, salt and pepper, add some sherry, and serve.

The same goes for *tempura*, another great way to cook various seafoods as well as vegetables.

BATTER-FRIED SHELLFISH AND VEGETABLES *(Tempura)* / JAPAN

Most molluscs and crustaceans are excellent for a mixed *tempura*. Dip them individually in TEMPURA batter, deep-fry in a bland oil until golden, and drain well. Pieces of vegetables (eggplant, sweet potato, cauliflower, parsley, asparagus, green beans, etc.) are all excellent too for a *tempura*. Some must be parboiled. Serve tempura with a SHOYU-WASABI sauce or another preferred sauce.

The name of this other "party-mover" refers, of course, to the classic aïoli sauce of Provence.

MIXED SEAFOOD *(Le aïoli)* / FRANCE

Typically, an aïoli consists of a large bowl of aïoli sauce surrounded by boiled cockles and winkles, pieces of boiled octopus, poached fish, whole cooked artichokes, boiled potatoes, green beans, hard-boiled eggs—in fact, almost anything that goes well with aïoli—and most things do. Americans would quickly add *raw* vegetables, too. Cauliflower, cucumbers, others. You just sit around, dip, and eat.

The New England missionaries and whalers who went to the Pacific in the 1800s must have felt completely at home with the Polynesians' luau. They had earlier taken wholeheartedly to the American Indians' clambake, another festive meal to which all creatures of the sea can contribute.

CLAMBAKE / NEW ENGLAND

For a clambake, prepare an *imu* on the beach. When the stones are red hot, remove the excess ashes and cover the stones with a thickish layer of seaweed. Cover this with chicken wire and another thin layer of seaweed and then cockles, mussels, clams, and other molluscs. Cover these with more seaweed, add large crustaceans, more seaweed, a layer of unshucked sweet corn, and more seaweed to carefully cover all. Then spread a tarpaulin or wet burlap over everything and cover it with sand.

About an hour, sometimes less, sometimes more, is what it takes to steam everything. Clambake food is eaten with lots of melted butter (to which some add lemon juice and cayenne) and cold beer.

FRESHWATER CRAYFISH

WHAT I really intend to devote most of this chapter to is that very great *freshwater* crustacean that is available in relative abundance throughout much of the United States, the crayfish. These miniature lobsters, whose common English names (crayfish and crawfish) are merely mispronounciations of French *crevice*, can be found, as I did as a small boy in Virginia, by turning over rocks in a local creek. I suspect that most young fishermen have met crayfish in similar spots, but how many have taken them home for dinner? For some inexplicable reason, crayfish are little eaten by Americans. This cannot be prejudice, I feel, because we do eat their marine brothers and sisters. It seems to be almost completely a question of ignorance that we have such a really choice food animal at hand yet avoid it. In fact, outside of Louisiana, where 18 to 20 million per year are caught (and almost all locally consumed), crayfish are not even served in most of our very best restaurants.

In contrast, European restaurants keep live crayfish on hand in tanks or ponds. In France there is a tale, probably true, that these animals are the *only* item of fresh food that the Savoie's great three-star restaurant, the *Auberge du Pere Bise*, imports. The preparation of them by the Bises is so delectable that the late oil-rich Armenian mystery-man Gulbenkian used to drop by about once a month from wherever in the world he might be just to partake of this crustacean delight.

No people enjoy freshwater crayfish more, however, than do the Scandinavians. For them it was a tragedy when their formerly vast populations of crayfish were decimated several years ago by an epidemic of an infectious disease, *kräftapest*. Recently the Swedish government sent a biologist to our campus of the University of California to study California crayfish and to explore the possibility of introducing disease-resistant animals from Lake Tahoe into Swedish lakes and streams for restocking purposes. His wife, who was herself a microbiologist, worked in my department during the time they were here. It was from them we learned how easy it is to trap *écrivisse* for the table. Two genera of crayfish, *Cambarus* and *Astacus*, thrive in streams, lakes, and ditches throughout much of the United States. Our county in California is first in the United States in rice production, and it is really sad that hundreds of thousands of crayfish die uneaten here every year when the rice fields are drained. But enough lamentation for those not eaten.

Crayfish have about the same protein content as T-bone steak and only about 0.6 percent fat.

Basic Preparation

To prepare crayfish for any recipe, wash them well and place them in a tray in the freezer for a few minutes to anesthetize them (this should be done for all crustaceans). Quickly remove the intestine by locating the anus at the middle of the tail segment on the ventral side, picking the intestine up with the point of a sharp knife inserted just in front of the anus and, by pressing it between the point of the knife and your thumb, withdrawing it without breaking it off. This "deplumbing" also may be done by carefully twisting off the middle tail segment and withdrawing the attached intestine that way. Unless otherwise indicated in the recipe, the chilled crayfish then should immediately be plunged headfirst into a boiling COURT-BOUILLON of white wine and water or water and lemon juice or, alternatively, *court-bouillon* containing a cooked MIRAPOIX of chopped onions and carrots, a small crushed garlic clove, some cayenne, and a BOUQUET GARNI. Whatever, boil the crayfish for 10 minutes or less, depending on their size.

BOILED CRAYFISH *(Ecrevisses à la nage)* / FRANCE

Merely allow the prepared crayfish to cool for 5 minutes in the cooking stock and serve them in the stock in an attractive bowl.

CRAYFISH LIÈGE STYLE *(Ecrevisses à la liègeoise)* / FRANCE

Drain the boiled crayfish and arrange them in a deep dish. The strained stock then is reduced by boiling to 1/4 the original volume. Beat into it much butter and pour the resulting sauce over the crayfish. Garnish with chopped parsley and serve.

Because, in Sweden, eating crayfish could literally become a way of life, conservation demands that their season be strictly limited to a part of August. On August 7, at the firing of the gun, the Swedish economy grinds to a halt as the whole country sits down to eat crayfish and dill with the fingers and drink aquavit by the liter—a Norse orgy they call *kräftskiva*. I spent one August in Stockholm so I have seen just how it is done.

If you are interested in holding a *kräftskiva* of your own, here is how to proceed.

BOILED CRAYFISH *(Kokta kräftor)* / SWEDEN

Boil a bunch of fresh dill in a large quantity of salted water for about 20 minutes. Remove the dill, keep the water at a brisk boil, then add live chilled crayfish and more fresh dill. Boil for about 7 minutes. Remove the crayfish and cover them with additional fresh dill. When the stock has cooled, pour it over the crayfish. Keep them refrigerated for 1 to 2 days and serve with a garnish with further fresh dill—and lots of aquavit.

The Austrian version of the same substitutes parsley and caraway for dill and, not unexpectedly, beer for the water.

CRAYFISH IN BEER *(Krebsen in Bier)* / AUSTRIA

Boil enough light beer with a big sprig of parsley, some caraway seeds, and salt to cover the amount of crayfish you have. Plunge the crayfish into this boiling stock and cook until done (about 7 or 8 minutes). Place the crayfish in a tureen and then strain the stock over them through a double layer of muslin. Serve in soup plates.

Crayfish poached in these ways may be used for any other use boiled shrimp or lobster are put to—in these two good salads, for example, or the other French classics that follow.

CRAYFISH SALAD *(Rapusalaatti)* / FINLAND

Remove the meat from crayfish that have been boiled in salted water with dill (as in the Swedish recipe). Handle several of the shells carefully so as to keep them intact for a garnish. Cut the meat into pieces. Line a salad bowl with crisp lettuce leaves and attractively arranged shredded lettuce, sliced hard-cooked eggs, and the crayfish meat. Dress with the following: blend olive oil and some dry mustard and blend into this mixture wine vinegar, sugar, salt, white pepper, and finely chopped chives. Garnish the salad with crayfish shells.

CRAYFISH ASPIC *(Aspic de queues d'écrevisses)* / FRANCE

Coat a plain mold with a fish aspic. Arrange cooked shelled crayfish tails in an attractive pattern. Pack the mold with a Russian salad (diced and crisply cooked mixed vegetables bound with a thick mayonnaise). Chill well and unmold.

The bodies of crayfish can be salvaged even after the tails have provided their own good eating in this crayfish sauce and crayfish butter.

CRAYFISH MAYONNAISE *(Sauce à l'huile d'écrevisses)* / FRANCE

In an electric blender, blend seasoned cooked crayfish torsos with some olive oil until creamy. Pass through a fine sieve. This may be used as is, heated, or it may be blended into mayonnaise or any other hot or cold sauce.

CRAYFISH BUTTER *(Beurre d'écrevisses)* / FRANCE

In an electric blender, thoroughly blend the shells and trimmings of poached crayfish with an equal amount of melted butter. Strain this hot crayfish-butter mixture through a cloth, wringing out as much as possible, and solidify it over ice or in the refrigerator.

CRAYFISH IN NANTUA SAUCE *(Queues d'écrevisses à la nantua)* / FRANCE

Shell the tails of cooked crayfish. Put the remainder of the crayfish (from which the stomachs have been removed by opening the ventral thorax) through a food grinder with the vegetables from the cooking stock. Add this purée to a simple milk béchamel sauce. Add an equal volume of the strained stock in which the crayfish were boiled and reduce this mixture to 1/2 its original total volume. Press it through a very fine sieve or a cloth and reserve. (Or use a traditional béchamel sauce prepared from a crayfish FUMET.) In either case, this then is called nantua sauce.

Heat the shelled tails in butter and sprinkle them with a little flour to take up most of the butter. Mix well. Add a little brandy, a generous amount of heavy cream, and simmer, stirring until thick and smooth.

Add the nantua sauce and mix. Remove from the heat and stir in several tablespoonfuls of butter. This dish may be used to fill vol-au-vent, crepes, or tart shells. It may also be used as a garnish for other dishes.

CRAYFISH IN BROWNED SAUCE *(Gratin de queues d'écrevisses)* / FRANCE

Use the crayfish nantua (prepared as above) and put it in a buttered earthenware dish. Sprinkle with Parmesan cheese and melted butter. Brown in a medium oven. Prepared and served in a baked flan shell, this dish is called *flan aux écrevisses.*

Or, again, crayfish may be sautéed as in recipes for shrimp or in variants like this, devised especially for them.

CRAYFISH PROVENCE STYLE *(Ecrevisses à la provençale)* / FRANCE

Fry chopped onion in olive oil until golden. Add chilled crayfish and cook until pink. Ladle ignited warm cognac over the crayfish and let the flame burn out. Add a generous amount of white wine, a BOUQUET GARNI, some tomato purée, salt, pepper, and cayenne. Simmer for 5 to 6 minutes, sprinkle with crushed garlic and chopped parsley, simmer a moment more, and serve.

Far from the sea crayfish have provided the makings for elegant "seafood" dishes by central Europeans like the Hungarians (with a soupçon of paprika, of course).

PANCAKES WITH CRAYFISH *(Folyami rák palacsinta)* / HUNGARY

Dice cooked crayfish meat. Chop a generous quantity of mushrooms and parsley and fry all ingredients in butter. Soak some pieces of bread in milk. Squeeze them and pass through the fine blade of a food chopper. Mix the bread well with the other ingredients. Add salt, pepper, a generous amount of paprika, and a little cream. Fill salted, unsweetened crepes with this mixture, fold the sides in, and roll them carefully. Dip each in beaten egg, then fine bread crumbs and fry in hot lard. Serve with crayfish sauce, such as nantua sauce.

Crayfish filling can be used effectively for other foods as well. This next recipe is for one of the richest roast chicken dishes imaginable and fully rivals Austria's famous, equally rich pastries and cakes.

ROAST CHICKEN WITH CRAYFISH STUFFING (*Gefüllte Krebshühner*) / AUSTRIA

Prepare a generous amount of melted crayfish butter. Work beaten egg yolks into some of it. Next prepare a thick panada of bread rolls and cream. Mix in some of the crayfish butter and egg yolk. Allow this panada to cool and then beat it into the rest of the crayfish butter–egg mixture. Salt. Fold in some stiffly beaten egg whites. Stuff a roasting chicken with this mixture. While roasting, baste the chicken often with crayfish butter. Serve with a sauce made with a (crayfish) butter-and-flour ROUX, some chicken stock, cream, salt, pepper, and pieces of crayfish tails.

And, of course, crayfish can be stuffed with crayfish.

STUFFED CRAYFISH (*Coquille d'écrevisses*) / FRANCE

Cool crayfish that have been poached in a COURT-BOUILLON. Remove the meat and chop it, keeping one shell per serving intact. Prepare a sauce by frying some chopped prosciutto in butter, stirring in and cooking some flour and then adding milk, salt, pepper, and nutmeg, and cooking further until smooth and very thick. Stir in the crayfish meat. Allow to cool somewhat and then stir in some beaten egg yolks. Fill the reserved crayfish shells or some scallop shells with this mixture, sprinkle with bread crumbs and pieces of butter, place in a shallow pan, and bake until light brown in a very hot oven.

Last, crayfish provide the makings of superb soups. These three very different examples should give the idea.

CRAYFISH CHOWDER (*Folyami rák halászlé*) / HUNGARY

Boil crayfish in salted water containing parsley and chopped caraway seeds. Remove the tail and claw meat from the shells. Sauté some chopped onions in butter and add chopped mushrooms, paprika, chopped green peppers, and salt. Cook for about 10 minutes. Add the crayfish meat and enough light veal stock to make a very meaty chowder. Thicken this slightly with a little butter-and-flour ROUX.

CREAM OF CRAYFISH SOUP *(Bisque d'écrevisses)* / FRANCE

Prepare crayfish nantua sauce and simmer it with an added mixture of crayfish stock and cream (enough to produce the consistency desired). Season with a little cayenne and some paprika. Add diced, cooked crayfish tails. As a garnish put in each plate a crayfish body that has been stuffed with a fish forcemeat and poached.

CRAYFISH SOUP *(Krebssuppe von frischen Krebsen)* / GERMANY

Boil the crayfish in a fish stock and then cool them in the stock. Separate the tails and cover them with brandy. Blend the remainder of the crayfish with some of the stock in an electric blender. Add this purée to a generous amount of melted butter and cook for about 10 minutes. Strain the purée and put the liquid aside. Add the purée to a mixture of boiling beef stock and the crayfish stock (2:3) and simmer for about a half hour. Pass the soup through two layers of muslin. Thicken with cornstarch and water and add some white wine. Stir several egg yolks beaten with cream into the soup and remove from the stove. Heat the crayfish tails and some asparagus tips in the butter liquid, add the brandy marinade, and stir this mixture into the soup. Serve immediately.

19

Other Aquatic Animals

MOST PEOPLES who live by the sea have, over the centuries, experimented in the kitchen with many of the sea creatures that abound therein. But nowhere has this been more the case than in countries surrounding the Mediterranean Sea and in the Far East. Despite the fact that American Indians taught our earliest colonists from Europe how to eat much of our tidal fauna, our present use of this potential food resource is disgracefully inadequate.

Some of the animals discussed in this short chapter are easily available only to Americans fortunate enough to live close to one of our country's three extensive shorelines, but modern refrigeration and transportation could permit the broader dissemination of many. Moreover, modern freezing technology or old preservation methods, such as drying, could also widen their distribution substantially. Even now a few abundant forms, such as the sea cucumber and jellyfish, can be obtained in dried form in almost any store handling oriental groceries.

Probably the most important food animals of the seashore we do not eat are the edible members of the phylum Echinodermata. Together with the ubiquitous starfish, various edible sea urchins and sea cucumbers comprise this animal group.

SEA URCHINS

SEA urchins are those pincushionlike animals found in abundance on most of the world's coasts. Some have very sharp and even poisonous spines and must be handled with respect. The Spanish aptly called them *erizos de mer*, or hedgehogs of the sea. The edible parts are the gonads. Naturally, they're supposed to be a potent aphrodisiac.

Sea urchin gonads (five masses of yellow to orange to pink, rounded follicles) are eaten raw right out of the shell in parts of the world as scattered as Chile, Samoa, and France. With a little lemon juice, they make an excellent "poor man's" caviar. In the British West Indies the urchin *Tripneustes ventricosus* is called a "sea egg," and its gonads are eaten various ways, including fried in butter.

Two North American species that are excellent eating are the green urchin (*Strongylocentrotus droehbachiensis*), found on both of our coasts, and the big purple or red urchin (*S. franciscanus*), which grows up to 7 inches in diameter only on our Pacific coast.

Since we do not eat them ourselves, an urchin fishery for export to the Orient is now developing on our West Coast. Off Santa Barbara, Calif. some individual divers collect 2 tons of sea urchins a day!

BOILED SEA URCHINS / MEDITERRANEAN COUNTRIES

Boil washed sea urchins briefly in saltwater. Drain them and open the concave side with scissors or a special French urchin cutter. (Leave it to the French!) Discard the digestive system and dip buttered pieces of bread into the shell. Urchins also may be roasted in hot wood ashes and served the same way.

The gonads also add excellent flavoring to hot or cold sauces.

SEA URCHIN GONAD PURÉE (*Purée d'oursins*) / FRANCE

The gonads of sea urchins are rubbed through a sieve and mixed with an equal volume of thick béchamel sauce (or the two are blended in an electric blender). The purée is simmered for about 5 minutes and some butter is stirred in. For hors d'oeuvres this purée may be spread on croutons fried in butter, sprinkled with grated Parmesan cheese, and browned under the broiler. It can also be used to fill small VOL-AU-VENTS or the like.

SEA URCHIN GONAD SAUCE (*Crème d'oursins*) / FRANCE

The gonads of sea urchins are mashed with a little olive oil and blended into a hollandaise sauce or mayonnaise. This sauce is served over poached fish.

Related is this French Mediterranean classic.

EELS WITH SEA URCHIN GONAD SAUCE *(Oursinado)* / FRANCE

Poach fillets of conger eel or any firm white fish in white wine containing some grated onion and carrot, salt, pepper, and a BOUQUET GARNI. Prepare a purée of the gonads of poached sea urchins, a mixture of soft butter and egg yolks, and a little of the fish stock. Whip with a wire whisk over hot water until smooth and thick. Cover the bottom of a shallow casserole with 1/2-in. slices of French bread, add only as much fish stock as the bread will readily absorb, pour the urchin sauce over the bread, and bake at 350°F only until heated well. Serve the poached fish and pass this sauce dish separately.

In fact, the variety of dishes into which sea urchin gonads can be incorporated to advantage is limited only by the cook's imagination. Here is a simple omelet to start.

SEA URCHIN GONAD OMELET *(Omelette d'oursins)* / FRANCE

Mix sea urchin gonads with eggs (about 6:1), salt, and pepper and prepare as an ordinary omelet.

SEA CUCUMBERS

SEA cucumbers, or holothurians, are strange, fleshy, sausage-shaped animals that, like sea urchins, are in the phylum Echinodermata. Their eviscerated bodies, boiled and then dried or smoked, are the great Chinese delicacy bêche-de-mer, or trepang. Trade in this valuable product is associated historically with the spread of pidgin English throughout the Pacific.

One of the oddest things about sea cucumbers is that a type of small fish live within their cloacas and can be seen protruding from or darting in and out of cucumber's anus. When John Steinbeck and "Doc" Ricketts took their famous fishing and beer-drinking trip into the Gulf of Lower California (commemorated in their fascinating book *Sea of Cortez*), they thought they had discovered a new species of this peculiar commensal fish which over a few drinks one afternoon they playfully decided to give the scientific name *Proctophilus winchelli*. Probably no other news columnist has been so honored in perpetuity.

My former graduate school roommate Sidney Townsley, who is now professor of zoology at the University of Hawaii, believes sea cucumbers could be raised in large quantities by mariculture techniques and thus have considerable potential as an underexploited protein source. They contain about 7 percent protein.

Basic Preparation

Dried sea cucumbers, if not purchased presoaked, must be treated by a fairly involved process. First soak them for 4 hours in cold water and then scrub them with a brush. Place them again in cold water, bring to a boil, cook 5 minutes, and allow to cool in the water again. Repeat this process 10 times. The meat then is swollen and soft and ready to use in the following recipes.

This first is for a common Chinese preparation of this delicacy.

STEWED SEA CUCUMBERS *(Dun hoi sum)* / CHINA

Place 8 prepared sea cucumbers in cold water. Bring to a boil, simmer 5 minutes, and drain. Then simmer them for about 20 minutes in about 3 C chicken stock and cut the drained meat into large pieces. Discard the stock. Stir-fry the meat for about 2 minutes with a little light soy sauce in some hot oil in a WOK. Remove the meat. To another *wok* add some fresh oil, heat it, add 2 green onions cut into 1–1/2-in. lengths, about 6 thin slices of ginger, 2 T sherry, and the sea cucumbers. Stir-fry a bit and add 3 T light soy sauce, dashes of pepper and AJINOMOTO, 1/2 t sugar, 1/2 T dark soy sauce, and 1/2 C fresh chicken stock. Cook on high heat 2 minutes. Add 1 T cornstarch dissolved in 2 T cold water and 1/2 T sesame oil. Stir well and serve.

Sea cucumbers have the interesting habit of shedding their respiratory and reproductive tracts and portions of their intestines when they are annoyed. These organs (particularly the ovaries) are sold in Samoan markets in cola bottles filled with seawater.

FERMENTED SEA CUCUMBER *(Se'a)* / SAMOA

Cucumber entrails are eaten raw with other foods or made into soup. Their flavor is said to improve if they are kept in the bottle for a few days in order to ferment. The skinned body of the sea cucumber also is eaten raw in Samoa.

A far fancier dish, a Chinese classic in fact, has sea cucumber as a ₊ principal ingredient.

TEN PRECIOUS SOUP *(Sup bo tan)* / CHINA

To some very hot peanut oil in a WOK add and momentarily stir-fry some small shelled shrimp tails and shredded bamboo shoots. Add shredded prepared bêche-de-mer, a bit of sherry, and stir briefly. Add hot chicken stock and bring to a quick boil. Stir in some cornstarch* mixed with cold water until the soup is slightly thickened. Last, stir in quickly a finely chopped scallion, a drop or two of sesame oil, a little vinegar, and a couple of beaten eggs. Remove from the stove and serve at once.

This is another famous Chinese dish seldom encountered even in China except in the best restaurants.

HAPPY FAMILY *(Tien tia fo)* / CHINA

Put some pieces of lean pork through the electric blender. For each pound of pork add 3 t soy sauce, 3 t sherry, and a little sugar and salt. Form this mixture into 1-in. balls, brown them well in a WOK in hot peanut oil, and remove them from the pan. Add to the sauce pan some chicken stock and bring it to a boil. Add some presoaked black mushrooms cut into convenient pieces, some sliced bamboo shoots, and the pork balls. Cook, covered, over a moderate heat and then add some diced white meat of chicken, some diced smoked ham, and prepared bêche-de-mer cut into short sections. Correct the content of salt and sugar and simmer, covered, for a few minutes. Thicken as required with cornstarch and cold water and stir in some snow peas just before serving.

Probably the next most important phylum of marine invertebrates neglected as food animals in the United States are the coelenterates, which include the corals, anemones, and jellyfish.

ANEMONES

SOME of the beautiful, flowerlike anemones of the sea, like other coelenterates, are commonly eaten, particularly about the Mediterranean and the Pacific. They taste something like crab or lobster. Called variously *tomate de mer, rastègne,* and *orties de mer,* species such as *Anemonia sulcata* and *Actinia equina* are relished by Frenchmen. Dahlia anemones *(Tealia)* are among the edible species found on both coasts of the United States.

Basic Preparation

The tentacles are removed and the animals are scrubbed and scraped in running water to remove embedded sand. They are then marinated in vinegar.

FRIED ANEMONES *(Anemoni di mare fritti)* / ITALY

Either deep-fry anemones in hot oil or marinate them in olive oil, lemon juice, and garlic and fry them in a pan until golden.

ANEMONE FRITTERS *(Beignets de pastègues)* / FRANCE

Dip prepared sea anemones in a light batter and deep-fry them in hot olive oil.

ANEMONE OMELET *(Omelette d'anémones de mer)* / FRANCE

Chop anemones and sauté in butter. Salt and pepper and fill an ordinary omelet.

ANEMONE SOUP *(Soupe d'anémones de mer)* / FRANCE

Sauté lightly in olive oil in a deep casserole a mixture of prepared anemones and cleaned winkles or other molluscs in their shells. Add chopped onion and brown it. Then add water, salt, pepper, and a BOUQUET GARNI and simmer until done. Cook some pasta in the soup at the end and serve it with grated Parmesan.

JELLYFISH

PARTICULARLY in China and Japan jellyfish are dried and prized as food. In the Gilbert Islands even highly venomous jellyfish called sea wasps are considered a delicacy. Their ovaries are dried and deep-fried and are said to taste rather like tripe.

Basic Preparation

Soak a sheet (approximately 4 oz.) of dried jellyfish (purchasable in oriental stores) in cold water in the refrigerator for a week, changing the water daily. Wash it thoroughly under running water to remove all adherent sand or dirt.

PICKLED JELLYFISH *(Alu alu)* / SAMOA

Fresh jellyfish are cut into pieces, marinated briefly in lemon juice or vinegar, and then eaten raw.

JELLYFISH *(Sueh tin yue)* / CHINA

Cut well-drained, presoaked jellyfish into long, thin strips about 1/8 in. by 4 in. Add a little light soy sauce, 1 T sesame oil, a dash of sugar, and a dash of AJINOMOTO. Mix well and serve cold.

Shredded cucumbers may be added as a variant.

JELLYFISH AND WHITE TURNIP SALAD *(Sueh tin yue lopo sala)* / CHINA

Cut the jellyfish as above. Peel and chop into a fine JULIENNE 2 medium-sized Chinese white turnips (or Japanese DAIKON), sprinkle them with salt, let stand an hour, and squeeze them dry between paper towels. Mix the turnips, the jellyfish, and a little coarsely chopped green onion. Pour over this about 4 T of hot vegetable oil. Mix and add 3 T light soy sauce, 1–1/2 T sesame oil, 1/2 t sugar, and a dash of AJINOMOTO. Mix, chill, and serve.

20

Insects & Other Land Invertebrates

Hᴏᴡ strange that we think it natural to eat *some* arthropods—*even* crabs, which are notorious scavengers of the deep, but just the idea of eating any of our really beautiful bugs and caterpillars, which feed on clean vegetation, makes us shudder. Yet virtually all arthropods, including insects, are excellent sources of animal protein, and insects occupy an important place in the diets of a number of peoples today, particularly in Africa, Australia, and Southeast Asia.

Insects were eaten, too, by most Indian tribes of the western United States, and insect foods, such as *ahuahatl*, still are relished in Mexico. Also in parts of Europe, locusts, cockchafers, and sage galls are eaten today, and many insect dishes feature prominently in the sophisticated cuisines of Canton and Szechuan in China.

As with most other edible animals, the French amd Chinese have experimented extensively with insect eating, both at home and abroad. And why not? Honey is merely a kind of "bug juice" that Americans eat without a second thought. Biblical manna was a secretion of aphids found on certain desert plants. And, like his contemporaries, John the Baptist lived well on locusts and honey. In fact, Moses specifically excepted locusts and grasshoppers from his list of taboo foods for Jews! They have remained to this day as particularly enjoyed foods of various peoples in North Africa and the Middle East.

Besides honey, who of us has not inadvertently consumed his share of cabbageworms, lettuce worms, or fruit fly larvae without noting any unusual taste? Is it not time, then, that we honestly face up to our farcical customs of regarding as good food pigs, which will eat practically anything, while refusing favor to other animals which feed solely on vegetables and fruits we too enjoy?

To tempt us to begin to correct such irrational behavior, I have gathered for this chapter an assortment of good-sounding recipes. They are from cuisines familiar to us, cuisines that, I believe, people already respect and enjoy. These recipes hardly exhaust the possibilities, however. In fact, an Israeli ecologist, F. S. Bodenheimer, has written a whole book about insect eating, and for first knowledge of some of these recipes I am indebted to him.

Locusts and Grasshoppers

Locusts and grasshoppers are essentially the same. In some parts of the world some species reach a length of 4 inches or more The Bible reader knows too that these insects caused devastating plagues in ancient times— as they still do in parts of the world today. The U.S. West has had its share of their depredations. Both their size and the ecological impact are good reasons not to neglect them as items of diet. Over 1,000 species of orthopteran insects occur in North America, but the most important grasshoppers, economically, are the clear-winged, differential, two-striped, red-legged, migratory, and American.

Basic Preparation

Locusts and grasshoppers are prepared for cooking by removing the wings, the small legs, and the distal portion of the hind legs. Then pull off the head, withdrawing any attached viscera. Most species of locusts and grasshoppers contain 46 to 50 percent protein, as compared to 14.7 percent for T-bone steak.

This first is an indigenous American recipe that substitutes well for peanuts on a cookout.

ROASTED GRASSHOPPERS / NAVAJO NATION

Put prepared grasshoppers in the hot wood ashes of the cooking fire until well browned.

Locusts are merely skewered, roasted, and nibbled as hors d'oeuvres in several countries.

Locusts can also be dried and stored as a protein-rich powder. Here is one flavor not yet discovered by Howard Johnson *or* Baskin-Robbins.

DRIED LOCUSTS AND MILK *(Jourad yabes bel mille)* / ARABIC NORTH AFRICA

Dry prepared locusts by putting them in the hot sun for several hours; then grind them into a flour (the blender can be used to do this). Mix with milk and drink as is.

They can also versatilely add good-quality protein as starch-dish substitutes.

LOCUST DUMPLINGS *(Jourad mtayeb)* / ARABIC NORTH AFRICA

Knead dried locusts (see above) with flour, salt, and a little water or milk. Form into dumplings and cook in boiling water to which salt and butter have been added until the dumplings float. Serve in place of rice or COUSCOUS with any Arabic meat dish.

Probably the most common way grasshoppers are eaten is fried. Here are several variations to help convey the idea that "everyone is doing it" but us.

FRIED GRASSHOPPERS *(Tsa ku meng)* / CHINA

Fry prepared grasshoppers in sesame oil until they are crisp. Serve and eat like roasted nuts.

FRIED GRASSHOPPERS / THAILAND

Coat prepared grasshoppers with a layer of salt and then fry them in oil.

Prepared the following way, grasshoppers are available canned in American gourmet shops, and even my Norwegian-American father-in-law has pronounced them excellent. It is far cheaper to prepare your own, however.

FRIED GRASSHOPPERS *(Inago no kara age)* / JAPAN

Marinate prepared grasshoppers in SHOYU and then fry them in a little oil.

In Arabic countries a proverb says, "A locust in the hand is worth six in the air." They are fried there in a variety of ways. Here are two.

FRIED GRASSHOPPERS *(Jourad)* / ARAB COUNTRIES

Boil prepared locusts and then fry them in oil or butter. Or fry the prepared insects without boiling and serve in a little vinegar.

Pioneers crossing the American desert learned another recipe from friendly Indians. They fried prepared Rocky Mountain locusts in their *own* oil until crisp and seasoned them with salt.

More elaborate dishes for grasshoppers, as for their marine cousins, shrimp, are in such stews as the following three. A locust gumbo, for example, would probably be superb.

LOCUST STEW / PIONEER AMERICA

Boil prepared Rocky Mountain locusts in salted water. Add assorted cut-up vegetables, butter, salt, and vinegar to the broth and cook until the vegetables are tender. Serve as a thick soup or over boiled rice as a main dish.

BOILED LOCUSTS WITH RICE *(Nâú chau-chau vói gao)* / VIETNAM

Boil prepared locusts in salted water to which lemon leaves and spices have been added until the water is almost evaporated. Salt to taste and serve over boiled rice.

BOILED LOCUSTS WITH *Couscous (Couscous bel jourad)* / ARABIC NORTH AFRICA

Season prepared locusts with pepper and nutmeg and then boil them in salted water until the protein coagulates (about the same time you'd boil a similar-sized shrimp). Serve with COUSCOUS. Grilled locusts also can be served in this way.

Last, here are two clear broths with different seasonings.

LOCUST SOUP *(Chorba el jourad)* / ARABIC AND JEWISH NORTH AFRICA

Season and boil locusts prepared as above. Pound them in a mortar (or blend them in an electric blender) with pieces of bread fried in butter and garlic or a purée of rice. Return this mixture to the locust stock and simmer very gently. Strain the soup and add croutons fried in butter.

This last has been described as "quite palatable and can scarcely be distinguished from beef broth."

LOCUST SOUP / PIONEER AMERICA

Prepare a locust broth by simmering the larvae or adults of Rocky Mountain locusts *(Melanoplus spretus)* in salted water for about two hours. Strain, add some butter, and season with pepper and wild mint or sage before serving.

CRICKETS

CRICKETS, which are closely related to locusts, are also eaten by a number of peoples. Prevalent and costly pest species in the United States include the Mormon cricket, *Anabrus simplex,* and the field cricket, *Acheta assimilis.* Crickets often were eaten by the American Indians, but today they are particularly relished in Southeast Asia. Probably the best-known cricket dish is Vietnamese *con-de-com,* which is prepared from mole crickets.

Basic Preparation

Prepare as locusts (page 366).

FRIED MOLE CRICKET *(Con-de-com)* / VIETNAM

Wash mole crickets well. Mix with shelled peanuts and fry in lard.
Serve as a condiment.

BEETLES

BEETLES, both adults and grubs (larvae) of various types, are probably eaten
as commonly as locusts. One favorite in several countries is the
palmworm, which is the grub of *Rhynchophorus palmarum*. Other species
of snout beetles occur in the United States, where they are costly pests.
Their grubs are certainly worth a try, too.

The culinary adaptability of the French is world-renowned. Here they
have imaginatively combined two local ingredients.

ROASTED PALMWORMS WITH ORANGE JUICE / FRENCH WEST INDIES

Skewer the palmworms and roast over charcoal. Roll in a mixture of
fine bread crumbs, salt, pepper, and nutmeg and sprinkle with orange
juice. Return to the fire to brown.

This one sounds really delectable, too, no?

FRIED PALMWORMS *(Chiển bo gôi)* / VIETNAM

Dip the grubs in *nuoc-mam* sauce and fry in lard. Wrap in pastry and
refry. Or simply roll in flour and fry in butter.

This dish was described by Masuji Ibuse in his book *Black Rain* as
"savory and rather nice."

BROILED BEETLE GRUBS *(Kabuto mushi no yochu)* / JAPAN

Grubs of longhorn beetles, species of which occur in the United States,
particularly those associated with figs, are marinated in SHOYU and
broiled.

Cockchafers are scarabaeid beetles. The European species *Melolontha melolontha* is a forest pest. A banquet featuring them was once held at the Café Custoza in Paris. Here are two recipes.

FRIED COCKCHAFER GRUBS *(Larves de hanneton sautées)* / FRANCE

Place the live grubs in vinegar for several hours. Then dip in an egg, milk, and flour batter and fry in butter. Or fry the live grubs in butter or oil to which chopped parsley and garlic have been added.

Scarabaeids are the largest beetles, and many other species, including the Japanese beetle *(Popillia japonica)*, June beetle or white grub *(Phyllophaga drakei)*, and rose chafer, are pests in the United States.

ROASTED COCKCHAFER GRUBS IN PAPER *(Larves de hanneton en papillote)* / FRANCE

Salt and pepper the grubs and roll in a mixture of flour and fine bread crumbs. Wrap in parchment baking envelopes well-buttered on the inside or in aluminum foil. Bake in the hot ashes of a wood fire.

Or the adults can flavorfully enhance an otherwise insipid or mundane broth.

COCKCHAFER SOUP *(Soupe de hanneton)* / FRANCE

Remove the heads and wings from adult cockchafers. Pound in a mortar (or put in an electric blender) and sieve into a hot bouillon.

Although in American Samoa larvae of cerambycid beetles are often eaten raw, for non-Samoans this recipe might be more palatable until beetles become a less squeamish part of your cuisine. Many species of cerambycids, the long-horned borers, are found in the United States.

ROASTED BEETLE GRUBS *(Afoto)* / SAMOA

Feed the larvae on coconut shavings for a day. Then wrap them in a banana or other suitable leaf and roast over charcoal.

Water beetles (Dytiscidae and Hydrophilidae), usually called diving beetles, are common in the United States. They are also a very special delicacy in the Orient, where they are prepared many ways. Besides being enjoyed, they are believed to combat diarrhea. Here are a few samples.

Basic Preparation

Remove the hard wing covers, wings, legs, and head.

ROASTED WATER BEETLES *(Nu'ố'c nâú bọ hung)* / VIETNAM

Roast the beetles on a pan in a hot oven and serve with *nuoc-mam* sauce.

Species of *Cybister* and other water beetles are prepared in this way. These may sometimes be found in Chinese shops in San Francisco if one's local supply of water beetles is low. In addition to serving these as nuts, it is worth noting that in Indonesia they are served as a sambal with curries.

FRIED WATER BEETLES *(Tsa tia tan)* / CHINA

Fry in oil, salt, and eat as one would nuts. Or boil the beetles and eat in the same way.

Prepared this next way, water beetles are said to taste like Gorgonzola.

WATER BEETLES IN SHRIMP SAUCE *(Mang daar nah)* / LAOS

Steam water beetles *(Lethocerus indicus)*. Then marinate in shrimp sauce and eat as hand food.

For those of you who are as tired of the usual cocktail dips as I am, why not try this one next time? Your guests will surely remember you!

WATER BEETLE COCKTAIL SAUCE / LAOS

Pound together boiled shrimp and water beetles. Mix well with sufficient lime juice, garlic, and pepper to use as a sauce for dipping raw vegetables.

BUTTERFLY LARVAE (CATERPILLARS)

EDIBLE caterpillars subjected to nutritional analysis have shown a composition of 37 percent protein an 13.7 percent fat.

FRIED CACTUS CATERPILLARS *(Gusanitos del maguey)* / MEXICO

Caterpillars of skipper butterflies, which live on the maguey cactus, are toasted or fried and eaten with mescal as "caterpillar pretzels." They are even sold canned in Mexico. Since the maguey is the source of pulque and tequila, these *should* be great!

There are examples, as with grasshoppers, where pest species could be eaten under control. We have probably all eaten this next insect already since U.S. Food and Drug Administration quality standards for coffee and other foods do not usually specify *absence* of contamination from insects but the allowable *proportion* of coffee beans that can contain insects. Many of us would possibly not like coffee if it was *not* partially a decoction of bugs like this. It would taste flat.

ROASTED COFFEE-BORER CATERPILLARS / LAOS

Roast caterpillars of the coffee-borer *(Zeuzera coffeae)*. Salt and eat with rice.

The most eaten butterfly, however, is the silkworm, *Bombyx mori*, after it has pupated. It is a domesticated species that has been introduced into the United States from time to time. The potential for eating native lepidopteran pupae is suggested in this variety of dishes. Silkworm pupae contain 23.1 percent protein and 14.2 percent fat. T-bone steak has 14.7 percent protein and 37.1 percent fat.

SILKWORM OMELET *(Fu yung sui)* / CHINA

After reeling the silk from the cocoon, bake and salt silkworm pupae. Then soften them in water. Mix with beaten chicken eggs and fry in oil as a flat omelet.

European visitors have commented on the very pleasant smell of silkworms cooking.

FRIED SILKWORM PUPAE *(Chiên tằm con)* / VIETNAM

First boil the pupae and then fry them in fat. Season with lemon leaves and salt.

FRIED SILKWORM PUPAE AND ONIONS *(Tsa tsen jon jan tso)* / CHINA

Soak baked or salted pupae in water. Drain and stir-fry in a little oil to which sliced onions and a little soy sauce have been added.

SILKWORM PUPAE SOUP *(Canh tằm)* / VIETNAM

Boil pupae with cut-up cabbage, *nuoc-mam* and other seasonings in salted water until both are tender. Serve as a soup.

BEES, WASPS, ANTS, TERMITES, AND OTHERS

HYMENOPTERID insects are widely enjoyed as food. Honey ants, like big yellow currants, are a must at country weddings in Mexico.

A former student of mine, Dr. Manuel Torres, used to import delicious ants from Bogota coffee trees for hors d'oeuvres. Understandably, his cocktail parties were the rage of Davis, Calif. His delectables had been either roasted or fried, but here are other ways of preparing these kinds of insects.

RED ANT CHUTNEY *(Chindi chutney)* / INDIA

Ants are collected in leaf cups and put directly into the hot ashes of the fire for a few minutes. The ants then are removed and ground into a paste. Salt and ground chilis are added and the mixture is baked. It is said to have "a sharp clean taste" and is often eaten with alcoholic drinks or used with curries.

WASP PUPAE *(Hachi no sanagi)* / JAPAN

Pupae of vespulid wasps (yellow jackets) are available canned from Japan, but I am not sure how they are prepared. They usually are served as hors d'oeuvres. We, of course, have them in the United States.

BEE GRUBS IN COCONUT CREAM *(Mang non won)* / THAILAND

Marinate bee grubs, sliced onions, and citrus leaves in coconut cream containing some pepper. Wrap in pieces of linen and steam. Serve as a topping for rice.

Bee grubs also are eaten fried in Thailand and sometimes used as an ingredient of curries.

Termites are commonly called "white ants," but they are not hymenopterans; they are isopterans. Forty species are found in North America.

This termite dish is said to be a delicacy in Zanzibar, but although I kept my eyes open and palate prepared, I failed to encounter it there, or on neighboring, little-visited Pemba. Fried termites contain three times the protein of T-bone steak and approximately the same amount of fat.

WHITE ANT "PIE" / ZANZIBAR

Termites, sugar, and banana flour are ground together to form a kind of honey-nougat paste.

CRISP ROASTED TERMITES / SWAZILAND

Swarming termites are drowned in water, sun-dried, and roasted to a "delicate crispness." They will keep this way for a year.

FLY LARVAE / CHINA

Maggots of *Chrysomyia* flies similar to American screwworms are raised on meat baits in China, collected, washed, and sun-dried. They are eaten this way both as food and medicine.

And finally, dragonfly larvae can be served any way one would boiled shrimp. Three hundred species occur in the United States. Nymphs are found on the bottom of streams and ponds. At maturity, when they reach a length of 1 to 2 inches, they leave the water and crawl onto a stick or stone.

DRAGONFLY NYMPHS *(Mang por)* / LAOS

Boil dragonfly nymphs. Eat them.

ANNELIDS

I include only one recipe for earthworms, invertebrate animals which are nationally abundant and which are now raised on many worm farms, chiefly as fish bait. However, Gaddie's North American Bait Farms, of Ontario, Calif., have for several years sponsored earthworm recipe contests that anually produce about 500 recipes! Gaddie says, "Worms [presumably dried] taste like shredded wheat. I like them best in oatmeal cookies, but I've eaten them with rice, sprinkled on top of salads . . ., with scrambled eggs and with steak and gravy." Another devotee describes the taste of salted earthworms as like jerky; they are said to be 72 percent protein and less than 1 percent fat.

The Chinese discovered this cheap, nutritious meat long ago. In China earthworm broth is said to be a good treatment for fever, but it probably would not be a bad first course for any meal, if one is sick or not.

EARTHWORM BROTH *(Tio in tin tan)* / CHINA

Slit open some earthworms and wash them well to remove particles of soil. Simmer them in water until the broth is reduced by half.

SNAILS

As in the sea, the main classes of food-providing invertebrates are not annelids but the arthropods we have already considered and the molluscs. There are many different kinds of land snails which are almost all edible. They are one of the very oldest known foods of man, *Helix salomonica* having been a part of the diet of people in the Mesopotamian river valleys between 15,000 and 70,000 years ago; *H. prasinata*, a closely related species, was eaten in Neolithic Jericho. *Helix* snails contain more protein than T-bone steak and only 1.4 percent fat, and the population of France alone now consumes over 16 million pounds of them each year!

I used to collect *Helix aspera*, the familiar *escargot*, on the campus of the American University of Beirut, and here in Davis, Calif., a budding entrepreneur could easily strike new gold by canning the beggars available in any local garden. Of course, snails may also be purchased at a very high price in the can from France. The French raise them on farms, as have other Europeans back at least to Roman times. I read recently that one *escargot* farm has, in fact, been started here in northern California. Wild-caught live snails may be brought to the same condition as canned snails, but better, by the following procedure.

Basic Preparation

Use operculated snails (hibernating snails with a white membrane over the opening of the shell) or purge actively feeding snails of possibly noxious plants by feeding them for several days on lettuce or greens of choice. Wash snails in several changes of tap water and then place them a few hours in water to which vinegar, salt, and a little flour has been added. This helps get rid of the mucus. Wash again and BLANCH for 5 minutes in boiling water, drain, and cool under running water; remove them from the shells and snip off the greenish black tip of each snail.

Simmer the snails in an appropriate stock (see below) and proceed as in the particular recipe.

The shells are prepared for use by boiling in a bicarbonate of soda solution, washing, and draining dry. They may, of course, be reused.

The only way many Americans have tried land snails is in the style of Burgundy. And that is hard to improve upon, I admit.

SNAILS BURGUNDY STYLE *(Escargots à la bourguignonne)* / FRANCE

After the first step above, put the snails into a saucepan and add equal parts of a light stock and white wine, or water containing a generous quantity of cognac. Then add carrots, onions or shallots, a large BOUQUET GARNI, and 1 t salt per qt. of liquid and simmer about 4 hours.

Prepare the butter as follows: cream butter with some finely chopped parsley, chives, shallots or green onions, salt, pepper, and much crushed garlic.

Put a small piece of butter in each shell, replace the snails, and plug the shell with additional butter. Sprinkle with bread crumbs (if desired), place the shells in serving dishes, and heat in a 400°F oven for a few minutes or until sizzling. Serve with a good crusty bread to mop up the butter.

The following is a slight modification.

SNAILS IN CHABLIS *(Escargots à la chablaisienne)* / FRANCE

Prepare as above, but instead of some of the compound butter put in the shell some finely chopped shallot and parsley cooked in Chablis and a little meat extract. Replace the snail. Salt and pepper. The snail shells are then plugged with burgundy butter as above and cooked in the same way.

An interesting *French* restaurant, the Imperial Dynasty, which is run by two Chinese brothers, Ernest and Richard Wing in Hanford, Calif., prepares a tasty variation of *escargots à la chablaisienne* with a bit of Dijon mustard added to the chablis sauce. In doing this myself, I have also marinated the snails in chablis in the refrigerator for 24 hours before replacing them in their shells.

For another variation, simply add a little lemon juice to each snail and use a plain parsley butter to seal the shells. Or try one of these other French versions. They omit the shells.

CREAMED SNAILS *(Escargots à la mode de l'abbaye)* / FRANCE

After the first step above, simmer snails in the same stock as for *escargots à la bourguignonne* and drain. Sauté some chopped onions in butter until golden, add the snails, and stir in a little flour. Gradually add some scalded cream, stirring constantly, and simmer for about 5 minutes. Beat some egg yolks, mix with more cream (4 egg yolks per C of cream), add to the snails, and stir until thickened. Do not boil. Season with salt and white pepper. Serve them in patty shells.

SNAILS BORDEAUX STYLE *(Escargots bordelaise)* / FRANCE

Simmer prepared snails in stock as in *escargots à la bourguignonne* in an earthenware casserole on a bed of finely chopped salt pork, chopped onions, chopped parsley, chopped celery leaves, crushed garlic, thyme, salt, and pepper. Cover with red Bordeaux. Cover the casserole and cook for 2 hours in a slow oven. Thicken as required with some butter kneaded with a little flour. Add some cognac and serve.

SNAIL STEW *(Escargots à la poulette)* / FRANCE

Simmer prepared snails for 1-1/2 hours in a COURT-BOUILLON with thyme, bay leaves, parsley, salt, and pepper and then drain. Brown some chopped onions, add a little white wine and water, and when the mixture boils add some allemande sauce. Return the snails to the sauce and simmer for about 7 minutes. To finish this dish, blend in some butter and egg yolks and a little lemon juice and correct the seasoning.

In this Italian recipe the flavor of mint adds an interesting complement to a snail stew.

SNAILS ROMAN STYLE *(Lumache alla romana)* / ITALY

Brown some sliced garlic in olive oil. Add chopped anchovy fillets and brown, then several chopped, skinned tomatoes, salt, and pepper and cook 15 minutes. Add some fresh mint, a little red pepper, and 3 to 4 dozen prepared snails that have been replaced in their shells. Simmer for 1/2 hour.

Here also the snails (but in their shells) are central to a good, spicy stew.

SNAILS LANGUEDOC STYLE *(Escargots à la languedocien)* / FRANCE

Replace prepared snails in their shells and simmer them gently for about an hour in the following sauce: In a generous amount of rendered goose fat, brown some finely diced ham, chopped onion, chopped parsley, and crushed garlic; add flour, stir, and cook until a smooth golden ROUX is produced; add enough water and cook to produce a creamy sauce; then add salt, pepper, a few cloves, grated nutmeg, juniper leaves, slices of lemon, and some saffron.

This rich soup recipe is from Swabia, the Black Forest country.

SWABIAN SNAILS *(Schwäbische Schnecken)* / GERMANY

Replace prepared snails in their shells and seal each with a generous plug of soft butter mixed with finely minced onion and chopped basil. Mix some beef gravy and red wine (2:1) in a pan. Add the snails to the pan, bring to a boil, cover, and simmer for 5 minutes. Serve the snails in a soup plate with the sauce and a sprinkling of chopped parsley.

Snails also can be used to make a tasty clear soup.

SNAIL BROTH *(Bouillon d' escargots)* / FRANCE

Purge snails and wash as indicated above. Remove the snails by care-fully cracking the shells. Do not wash. Put the snails in a saucepan with water (10 snails per qt. of water). Add lettuce (1/3 head per 10 snails), some purslane leaves, and salt. Boil and skim, reduce the heat, and simmer for 3 hours. Add gum arabic (10 grams in 1/3 C of warm water per 10 snails). Strain the broth through a fine cloth.

Last, they make excellent hors d'oeuvres.

SNAIL PASTRIES *(Schnecken in Brotteig)* / GERMANY

Cut rolled pie crust dough into 3-in. squares. Put a prepared snail and a piece of parsley and onion or garlic butter in the center of each, fold over, and seal. Bake in a 425°F oven until the pastry is golden and serve hot.

This is also very good with puff pastry or *fila* dough.

The familiar large *Helix* is not the only edible land snail, however. In Europe, particularly in the south, small land snails that occur in abundance are also eaten. Large baskets of them are available in most Spanish markets and any day we can collect enough from our own trees to make a meal. Preparation is the same as for *Helix*.

There are also land-snail species so large that a whole family can dine on one individual. Here is one example with a restricted U.S. distribution.

The Giant African Snail

Man has intentionally or inadvertently spread many animals and plants far beyond their original habitats. Many of these introductions have been of great value. In the face of food prejudices and the usually slow adoption of new foods by all peoples, we tend to forget some of these great successes. This has been the case particularly with food plants native to the western hemisphere, such as corn, potatoes, sweet potatoes, cassava (manioc), peanuts, tomatoes, and certain beans. These plants have become dietary staples in many parts of the world within only the last few hundred years. In fact, can we even imagine what the English or German diet was like without the potato, or the Italian without the tomato, or the African without corn and cassava? It is almost impossible now to conceive that "no plant cultivated by the American Indians was known to Asia, Europe, or Africa prior to the white settlement of America and that the introduction of these plants more than doubled the available food supply of the older continents" (Vaillant, 1950).

Many other introductions of animals and plants, however, have been ecological disasters. Hosts and vectors of diseases, disease agents themselves, agricultural pests, other noxious species, undesirable competitors of valuable species—all have been spread by man far beyond their original homes. The starling, the English sparrow, the water hyacinth, and the Argentine fire ant are several examples for the continental United States, while Hawaii has the prickly pear cactus, the mongoose, the ornamental lantana—and the giant African snail, *Achatina fulica*.

This huge land snail, whose shell sometimes reaches a size of 6 inches or more, is a living juggernaut that proliferates madly and devours practically everything green in its path. It can be a disaster! The story goes that one day in 1936 a farmer in Hawaii was pleased to receive a parcel from Japan that contained a number of living *Achatina*. But the neighbor to whom he showed these new animals was aghast—did his friend not know that the giant African snail was a banned species and that it was illegal to introduce it into the United States? Startled, and perhaps fearful to possess his now unwanted gift, it is said that the farmer quickly tossed them out! True or not, Hawaii now has this "awful" beast in abundance.

Achatina then entered the mainland United States in 1966 when an eight-year-old boy walked through customs in Miami with a box of new pets he had acquired in Hawaii. Since then foci have popped up around the Miami area in Florida, the latest in 1971. So far each newly discovered focus has been "wiped out"—but obviously not so. What its future is in Florida no one knows.

But *need Achatina* necessarily be such an ecological disaster? Malacologists believe that it is perhaps a native of Madagascar. During the 1800s it had spread from there, often by man's intentional efforts, throughout much of Africa, through the islands of the Indian Ocean and out into the Pacific. In some places it played havoc, but in the islands of Japanese-mandated Micronesia it was very successfully held in check because the Japanese valued it as food! Only when the Japanese colonial population was repatriated following World War II and replaced in part by *American* administrators and technicians did the giant African snail really become a pest and begin to eat everyone out of house and home. And why? Because, unlike the Japanese, the Micronesians and the Americans did not regard land snails as proper food.

What more appropriate recipes to end this chapter, then, than a few for giant African snail? Some of them were kindly supplied by Peter van Weel, professor of invertebrate physiology at the University of Hawaii. Despite the fact that the van Weels were introduced to this item of diet while prisoners of war in Indonesia in World War II, they still prepare them for themselves and their more broad-minded friends. "But I must confess," he writes, "that, given the choice between a tender and rare broiled beef, or *Achatina*, I would prefer the former." Anyhow, ecologists, "Up and at it," because the giant African snail contains a nutritious 9.9 percent protein and only 1.4 percent fat.

Basic Preparation

Purge the snails by allowing them to feed on lettuce or other nonnoxious greens for 48 hours—or, better still—don't feed them at all. Try to keep their container, and the snails, clean by washing both several times during this purging process. Then, according to Professor van Weel, you "smash the shells with a hammer and wash them free of shell fragments under a jet of tap water." The mucus then is removed by boiling snails for 30 minutes in a large quantity of water to which some salt and lemon juice or vinegar has been added. (The water must be quite acid.) The adherent coagulated mucus is then rubbed off each snail by hand under flowing tap water.

Now, van Weel says, one can prepare the muscular foot according to any recipe for *escargots*. *Achatina* resemble our much prized abalone in texture and taste. The visceral organs also are edible, if you wish, although batches of ready-to-lay eggs should be removed and discarded.

Peter van Weel recommends *Achatina* as basis for a curry or grilling them *teriyaki*.

The Ashanti people and others of West Africa actually value giant African snails equally with goat, mutton, and beef in preference to pork, chicken, or fish. They usually kill the snail by heating it in water; then they remove it from the shell, wash the fresh soft parts, and use them immediately in local dishes. They also skewer a number on a stick and smoke them over a wood fire (first at high heat and then for several hours at low heat) until they are well dried. They then are kept for up to three months and, for cooking, are first soaked in water for about half an hour.

Snails provide about half of the daily animal protein consumed by many West African peoples.

CONGO MEAT / NIGERIA

Break the shells of 4 large African snails, trim them, cut each snail in two, wash them with water and then with alum and lime juice to remove all of the slime. Chop some tomatoes, a red pepper, and some onions and fry them together in hot palm oil until they are well browned. Drain the snails, add them to the vegetables, salt to taste, and simmer the mixture for about 1 hour. Serve over rice.

In Ghana snails prepared this way are then skewered and served as hors d'oeuvres.

DEVILED SNAILS *(Ngwaw nkwan)* / GHANA

In this somewhat similar recipe, the cleaned snails are covered with water in a kettle, some chopped onions and cloves are added, and the meat is simmered until tender. Then fry some sliced onions in peanut oil until they begin to brown. Add cut-up tomatoes to the pan and fry over a low heat for several minutes. Add these vegetables to the snails, season with white pepper, and serve the mixture over rice.

Finally, an excellent-sounding soup.

SNAIL AND BITTER-LEAF SOUP *(Lgbin ati ǫbę ewuro)* / NIGERIA

Prepare and clean giant African snails as above. Salt them and grill them over charcoal until tender. Fry chopped onions in palm or peanut oil, add tomato paste, salt, pepper, some shrimp or prawns that have been put through a food chopper, washed spinach, sorrel, kale, or Swiss chard leaves (in place of unavailable Nigerian bitter leaves), and the cut-up snails and simmer for about 10 minutes. Add a generous quantity of chicken stock and simmer the soup for another 1 to 2 hours. Cooked rice, ground rice made into a paste, or boiled and pounded yams may also be added to the soup before serving.

Part Five

NONFLESH FOODS

of Animal Origin

NONFLESH FOODS
of Animal Origin

One man's meat is another man's poison.

T HOUGH IT might seem odd to conclude a book dealing with American food avoidances with topics like milk and eggs, to omit consideration of these foods would be to overlook the very narrow range of animal species from which we obtain such foods and the limited variety of ways we eat them. In fact, we do have some strong milk and egg prejudices, but before considering them, we may profitably see how others look upon these reproductive and metabolic products of other animals.

An important and unique human discovery in antiquity that has received surprisingly little comment from historians is that the females of various *other animal species* could assume a supplementary maternal role for man by wet-nursing him and his young. And little note has been taken of the fact that perhaps one-third of mankind has rejected, for various reasons, establishment of this unique maternal or parasitic bond to other species than its own. For example, animal milk is not used as human food throughout large areas of China, in Thailand, Vietnam, Cambodia, and Laos or among specific indigenous populations of India. Little milk is drunk either in Burma or in the Malayan peninsula. Some African tribes also observe milk prejudices generally, or they restrict milk to certain classes of people. Among Zulu, use of a particular cow's milk is restricted to the family of the cow's owner. Moreover, because consumption of milk by pregnant or menstruating women is believed harmful to cattle, Zulu women beyond the age of puberty seldom drink milk. Though imported sweetened canned or powdered milk has found some slight popularity among some of these milk avoiders in recent years, this has seldom stimulated any local interest in dairying.

Much of the region of present milk prejudices in Asia coincides with the extent of Buddhist influences, particularly of certain Mahayana sects. Therefore, milk drinking today is confined largely in Southeast Asia and China only to those fringe areas historically influenced by the Mongols, Tibetans, and Hindus, the former two largely Buddhist peoples, but ones with long prior histories of milk usage.

Some milk avoidances have been explained locally in terms of not wishing to harm the calf by depriving it of needed nutrition, and there is some foundation for this idea in early Buddhist teachings. Others, however, raise the issue of the inappropriateness of the maternal bond established between animal and man through milk drinking. Still other peoples regard milk as a body fluid not unlike urine, or for other reasons object strongly to its smell and taste. The very idea of drinking milk or eating milk products may make some Southeast Asians vomit, and cheeses are especially repugnant to them. Of course, many Americans share this aversion to ripe cheeses, and probably a good portion of our countrymen also now find unchilled milk unappetizing or curdled milk disgusting.

Prejudices in both the milk and egg spheres often reflect, too, the perceived textures or consistencies of these foods. The sense of touch in eating is very important, and American prejudices against a number of foods discussed in this book can be attributed to perception of consistency. Most people have remarkable abilities to distinguish between such qualities of foods as their being solid or soft, pliable or crisp, sharp or dull, thick or thin, dry or moist, rough or smooth. Individuals have greater and lesser sensitivities or subjective reactions to these qualities, but abilities to detect minor gradations of each are commonly highly developed. The use of sauces in many cuisines probably results, for example, from common preferences for smooth rather than grainy, lumpy, or rough qualities in foods. While milk and cream often provide these qualities to the foods of Indo-European peoples, these "smootheners" are unused in the cuisines of China and nearby countries. At the other extreme, many people also object to too smooth or "slippery" foods or to the related sensation of "thinness" in foodstuffs. For them the skin on boiled milk products and certain fruits or the membranes covering various meats, as examples, may stimulate the gag reflex. Few Americans like raw egg whites. The complexities of these touch sensations, particularly prominent in many milk and egg foods, are affected by other qualities of foods, such as their temperature, taste, or smell. For example, some cheeses much enjoyed by one people may smell so nearly like vomit that persons to whom they are foreign readily sicken in their presence.

Of interest with respect to milk prejudice is modern evidence that many individuals in such milk-avoidance areas, particularly as adults, are now biologically intolerant of milk because of a relative inability to properly digest lactose, or milk sugar. Limited studies suggest that lack of the enzyme lactase, which digests milk sugar, now occurs more commonly among individuals of oriental or African extraction than it does among Caucasians. The only European population which shows a higher than average level of lactose intolerance is the Greek.

Despite our "melting pot" origins and the fact that the most highly educated and wealthy segments of our society probably experiment more with recipes of diverse nationalities than any group in the world, American food preferences in general continue their rapid decline to a lower and lower common denominator. Nowhere is this clearer than with respect to milk products, where the making and enjoyment by most of our ancestors of smelly and sharp cheeses of many kinds, and of curds and the like, has now given way to their almost universal replacement by the blandest of cheeses or so-called cheese products. Dairy products are perhaps man's most valuable foods, yet milk and butter usage in the United States are on the decline. While pizza and cheeseburger crazes have accounted for a recent increase in total per capita cheese consumption in the United States, it is almost all in the form of what Clifton Faddiman has rightly called "solidified floor wax," those rubbery, synthetically colored, processed abominations that J. H. Kraft was inadvertently responsible for when he innocently began to retail uniform-sized pieces of genuine cheeses wrapped in foil.

Most of the space in our supermarket cheese cabinets today is occupied by these homogeneous molds of something that would not pass as cheese anywhere else in the world. The potential for rebirth of small cheese factories or home cheesemaking in the United States is great.

Besides being superb sources of highest-quality protein, dairy products in many cultures normally provide most of man's needs for calcium. Recent studies on older Americans on low cholesterol diets warn of the associated risk of calcium deficiency leading to osteoporosis, a degenerative condition of bones that is a particular problem in females over 60.

21

Milk, Eggs, & Sperm

A NUMBER of present-day pastoral peoples still live largely, and well, on the milk (and blood) of their animals. Milk and blood puddings are prominent in the backgrounds of many of us, and the Irish in the area of Cork still eat an ancient dish called *drisheen*, of coagulated milk and blood.

A notable exception to the American trend away from milk and other dairy products generally is the recent interest in yoghurt on the part of many young Americans. While their discovery of yoghurt began mostly as a low calorie dessert fad, the potential for far more imaginative American yoghurt use now exists than our mostly fruit-flavored, *expensive* store varieties permit. For yoghurt and its relatives, which in their pristine, white, and unadulterated form could readily be made cheaply in any American kitchen, occupy a prominent place in a number of the world's cuisines and are surely great to eat, drink, or cook with. Because the whole subject of our present utilization of dairy products is too large for exploration here, yoghurt can well illustrate another possibility for better protein exploitation that is now foreign to us.

YOGHURT AND YOGHURT DISHES

MY children were born in Lebanon and grew up on yoghurt (or *leban*, as it is called in Arabic). They have craved it since. Making it is simple, but, as for any fermented dish, the key to quality in yoghurt is the starter.

MILK CURD *(Yoğurt)* / TURKEY

Boil whole or skimmed milk and cool it to 106°F to 109°F. Put it in a bowl and beat in a few spoonfuls of a good batch of previous yoghurt. (Use only 1 teaspoon of starter per qt. of new yoghurt.) Wrap the bowl well in a blanket or small eiderdown. The room temperature should be more than 65°F. Do not disturb the setting yoghurt for at least 8 hours.

The resulting product then may be used for many purposes, including this refreshing summertime drink.

YOGHURT DRINK *('Ayraan)* / MIDDLE EASTERN COUNTRIES

Beat or blend yoghurt, salt to taste, and enough cold water to make a milklike drink.

There are also excellent cold yoghurt soups that we often serve our family in hot weather.

CUCUMBERS AND YOGHURT *(Cacık)* / TURKEY

Mix 1 quart of yoghurt, 1 large, finely chopped cucumber, and 6 to 8 crushed garlic cloves. Salt to taste.

(For variants, add chopped mint, chopped dill weed, or chopped walnuts.) Refrigerate. To serve as a cold soup, dilute to the desired consistency with cold water.

COLD YOGHURT SOUP *(Ash-e-mast)* / IRAN

Add to some yoghurt a little cream, some onions and cucumber cut in very thin slices, some previously soaked raisins or fresh grapes, chopped, hard-cooked egg, salt, and pepper. Thin the soup to the desired consistency with chicken stock.

The following is more a stew.

COLD YOGHURT STEW *(Okroshka)* / RUSSIA

Dilute yoghurt with cold water to a soupy consistency. Add a generous amount of diced cucumbers, some diced cucumber pickle, cooked shrimp or other fish or shellfish cut into pieces, diced cooked chicken or cooked Polish-type or garlic sausage, and a little each of chopped fennel leaves, green onion tops, parsley, and hard-cooked eggs. Salt and pepper, chill well, and serve with an ice cube in each bowl.

SPINACH AND YOGHURT *(Ispanak yoğurtlu)* / TURKEY

Sauté a generous amount of chopped onions in butter until golden. Stir in some finely chopped lamb and cook for a few minutes. Add a lot of well-drained, BLANCHED, chopped spinach, a handful of uncooked rice, a little tomato purée, and some lamb stock. Bring to a boil, cover, and simmer over very low heat for about 35 minutes or until the liquid is absorbed and the rice is tender. Spread on a serving platter and spoon uncooked yoghurt over the center of the spinach mixture.

Similarly, plain yoghurt is an excellent sauce for shish kebabs, pilaf, or many other meat or rice dishes.

COOKING YOGHURT

Yoghurt often curdles when used in cooking. To avoid this, put 5 C of yoghurt through a fine strainer. Stir in 1 T cornstarch (previously mixed in a small amount of cold yoghurt), 1 egg white, and 1 T salt. Cook over high heat, stirring constantly. When the mixture just begins to boil, lower the heat and continue to stir and boil gently until the yoghurt is the consistency of heavy cream. Do not cover. Yoghurt in this form may then be used in preparation of cooked dishes like these hot soups.

CHICKEN YOGHURT SOUP *(Chootyen māstoni)* / ARMENIA

Cook thin noodles or vermicelli and drain. Beat some yoghurt and sour cream (1:1) until smooth (or use cooking yoghurt as above) and gradually add a boiling, rich chicken stock (just off the stove), stirring constantly. Add the noodles. Stir in lemon juice to taste. Season with some cayenne and finely chopped mint. Serve immediately. Do not reboil.

DUCK AND YOGHURT SOUP *(Yoğurtlu ördek çorbası)* / TURKEY

Fry chopped shallots in butter until golden. Add the finely chopped meat from a small duck and a generous amount of grated lemon rind and cook for a few minutes. Stir this mixture into boiling duck stock to which some red currant jelly and a generous cup of red wine have been added previously. Remove from the stove.

Beat together yoghurt (1/4 as much as the duck stock), an egg, and an extra egg yolk (1 each per 2 C of yoghurt used) and stir this into the soup. Reheat but do not boil. Salt and pepper to taste and sprinkle the surface with finely chopped lemon verbena.

Yoghurt is also a prominent ingredient in many cheap and nutritious one-dish meals.

Barley and Yoghurt Soup *(Yayla çorbası)* / Turkey

Soak about 1/2 C pearl barley overnight. Drain and boil it in 3 to 4 C chicken broth until tender. Chop 2 large onions and cook them in butter until soft. Add to the broth 1/4 C chopped mint, 1/2 C chopped parsley, the cooked onions, salt, and white pepper. Simmer about 1 hour. Add 2 C well-beaten yoghurt just before serving.

Meat Ball and Yoghurt Curry *(Kofta curry)* / India

Make walnut-sized balls of finely chopped mutton, chopped mint, finely chopped onions, crushed garlic, grated ginger, salt, chili powder, and powdered cloves. Fry additional chopped onions in oil until they are golden, add a coarsely chopped tomato, 2–1/2 C cooking yoghurt, 1 t coriander powder, and simmer 15 minutes. Add crushed garlic, some grated ginger, 1/2 C water, and the meat balls; cover and simmer for about 45 minutes. Serve with rice.

Minced Lamb Balls with Yoghurt *(Kibbeh bi leban)* / Lebanon

Blend lamb in small amounts in an electric blender. Blend in about an equal amount of BURGHUL, some onions, ice water, salt, and pepper. Make this *kibbeh* into small balls the size of a walnut and deep-fry them. Combine the meat balls with about 1 C cooked rice, 5 C cooked yoghurt, crushed garlic, salt, and chopped mint (the last lightly fried in butter). Simmer until the sauce is thickened and serve with more rice.

The following is a relatively uncommon Arabic recipe introduced to our family by our longtime friend and maid Afifi Shweifati. We and our friends love it.

Eggplant with Yoghurt (*Batanjan bi leban*) / Lebanon

Peel and slice 2 large eggplants, sprinkle them lightly with salt, and allow them to sit 30 minutes or so on paper toweling in the hot sun. Dry with paper towels and fry the slices individually in olive oil until they are soft and lightly browned. (They will absorb much oil in the process.) Allow the excess oil to drain off in a strainer. Add to the cooked eggplant slices about 1 quart of yoghurt, 6 to 8 crushed garlic cloves, and salt to taste. Serve either tepid or cold.

Salmon with Yoghurt Sauce (*Yoğurtlu somon balığı*) / Turkey

Poach a whole salmon in water containing chopped carrot, chopped onion, 1 to 2 cloves, several peppercorns, and a BOUQUET GARNI. Drain the fish, skin it, and place it on a bed of chopped cooked spinach in a flat casserole and keep warm. Reduce the stock to 1–1/2 C over a high heat. Strain the stock and thicken it with a butter-and-flour ROUX. Add a pinch of nutmeg and salt and whisk in a cup of beaten yoghurt. Cover the salmon with this sauce, sprinkle with grated Parmesan, and brown in a 475°F oven.

As yoghurt ages it becomes more acid. What you do with it then is make *labneh*. This is the equivalent of cream cheese, and it is particularly good for breakfast with olive oil, ripe olives, and Arabic bread.

Soft Cheese (*Labneh*) / Arabic Countries

Add some salt to *leban* and hang it overnight to drain in a cheesecloth sack in a cool place.

Similar to Arabic *labneh* is Icelandic *skyr*.

Soft Cheese (*Skyr*) / Iceland

Boil milk and cool it until a finger can just be held in it to a slow count of ten (or about 98°F). Pour it into a bowl. Thoroughly mix in some well-beaten sour cream and rennet tablets dissolved in cold water (1 tablet per 2 gal. milk). Mix well, cover the bowl, and allow to stand at room temperature for 24 hours. The curd then is hung in a sack of 4 to

5 layers of cheesecloth until the whey has drained. The *skyr* then is beaten well; it should be thick and smooth. It is served with sugar and cream as a dessert.

And if you have a horse of the right sex, you could also try *koumiss*. My introduction to *koumiss*, an alcoholic fermentation of mare's milk, was in a Kazakh shepherd's comfortably carpeted and pillowed round felt tent not far from the Chinese border. A bowl of *koumiss* ladled out of a large crock is traditionally the first thing offered to visitors throughout much of Turkic and Mongolian Central Asia. It was already the drink of many of the Asiatic "barbarians" who invaded the Roman Empire, but somehow its use in Europe died out. A pity, for *koumiss* is, in fact, a most pleasant and refreshing drink, being lightly carbonated and of quite low alcohol content (1–1/2% to 3–1/4%)

FERMENTED MARE'S MILK *(Koumiss)* / CENTRAL ASIA

To prepare *koumiss*, you must first milk a mare. After that a starter may be made by blending 1/2 lb. of brewer's yeast, 1/4 lb. of flour, a little honey, and 1 C of the mare's milk. This is covered, set in a warm place, and the next day 3 qts. mare's milk are added to it and allowed to ferment. Traditionally the container is a skin bag, but other things will do. Subsequently, the old batch of *koumiss* is the starter for the next. *Koumiss* is also distilled in Central Asia to make something stronger. Alcoholic "wines" also are made from other milks; that from camel's milk, for instance, is called *kephir*, and from yak's milk *airan*. If those sound intriguing, the Chinese also make "snake wine" and "dog wine" in which the meat of these animals is added to milk before it is fermented. These milks are said to have special "medicinal" properties. So after the novelty of acupuncuture wears off, who knows what else we'll discover from the Mysterious East?

GERM CELLS

THE unfertilized or fertilized female germ cells of several animal species are also relished by man in some parts of the world and avoided like a plague in others. The animal eggs that are eaten are almost all relatively large ones, like bird and turtle eggs. Exceptions are caviar, some insect eggs, and the like. Being deposited by the female externally, bird eggs and turtle eggs possess quite a bit of yolk material to sustain the developing zygote, and this is what some of us particularly like to eat.

Prejudice against eating bird eggs, however, is even more widespread and more strongly held than that against eating chicken meat. Some hill peoples in Assam in India do not eat eggs but do use them for divining purposes. Other peoples who avoid eggs as food live elsewhere in India, in Sumatra, Malaya, the Philippines, parts of Arabia, and throughout much of Africa.

Many of these taboos are associated with beliefs about sex and fertility. Among one African tribe, for example, if a woman offers to cook eggs for a man, it means she is ready to go to bed with him. Others, like the Navajo, also hold that eggs possess aphrodisiac properties. Other strongly held beliefs are that eggs are harmful to the fetus or cause barrenness, all of which may be reasons why they are prohibited to women more than men. The Nuer tribe of Africa, on the other hand, regards egg eating by men as effeminate.

Other peoples share a strong aversion to or disgust for eggs. Some Somali and Ethiopian peoples regard them as excrement of chickens, and Indians and others may disdain them because they come from an animal with carnivorous or filthy eating habits. Simoons cites a report of a Brahman becoming violently ill when he saw eggs being cracked open and beaten into an omelet. Some Americans would share this aversion to raw eggs or to eating the uncooked white of an egg. Some peoples of the Arabian peninsula and Africa also find it sickening just to see someone eat eggs.

Some beliefs in the harmfulness or undesirability of eggs have been overcome by convincing the person that they are not fertile, that is, not alive, as among some Indians, or by cooking them, as in parts of Africa.

CHICKEN AND OTHER EGGS

WHILE we Americans are undoubtedly the world's greatest consumers of chicken eggs, we rarely eat eggs of other animals. And despite the fact that chicken eggs can be prepared in so many different ways, whole cookbooks being devoted to them alone, we in this country seem to eat almost all of them simply fried "sunny-side up" or "once over light" or scrambled.

I have included just a few "interesting" recipes for birds' eggs to show that we lack versatility in egg cookery generally and that we do have *some* egg prejudices. While I do not advocate the collection for food of wild birds' eggs, unless they are of pest species like starlings, one thing to remember, if you do, is that eggs of wild birds that build relatively exposed nests generally have an unpleasant taste. Birds that ordinarily more or less camouflage their nests lay really palatable eggs.

For one thing, eggs are good deep-fried.

EGG IN OLIVE OIL *(Bayd)* / ARABIC COUNTRIES

Break fresh chicken eggs individually into a saucer and gently slip each into deep, hot olive oil. Eat them sprinkled with fresh mint or marjoram and green onions.

The Arabs also do eggs in another interesting and good way.

EGGS IN PUFF PASTRY *(Brik)* / ARABIC NORTH AFRICA

Beat some eggs with black pepper, cinnamon, and chopped parsley. Put several spoonfuls of this mixture (or an unbeaten egg) on a square of puff pastry or similar dough. Cover with another square of pastry and press them together along the edges to thoroughly seal. Tunisians then fry this *brik* in hot olive oil; Algerians use peanut oil.

While temporary seasonal surpluses of chicken or other birds' eggs in the United States usually are solved by reducing them to a dried powder, they can be preserved in better form by salting.

SALTED BIRDS' EGGS *(Sien tan)* / CHINA

Eggs, preferably duck eggs, are placed in concentrated brine and gin (supersaturated saltwater prepared by dissolving 1 lb. coarse salt in a gallon of boiling water, then allowing it to cool to room temperature, and adding one cup of gin) for at least 30 days. Alcohol is definitely the secret of good salted eggs! The brine coagulates the yolk and makes the whites taste salty. Salted eggs are eaten cooked either by hard-boiling or steaming, or they may substitute for fresh eggs in omelets or other dishes. Another way to salt them is to leave them in the brine for only a week and then to coat them well with a mixture of mud, salt, and chaff. In either case, salted eggs are kept no longer than several months.

For longer preservation, the procedure is a little diffferent. So-called hundred- (or thousand-) year-old eggs are usually not quite *that* old, but they are at least 1 to 2 years old—in fact, the older the better!

One-Hundred-Year-Old Eggs *(Pi-tan)* / China

Soak chicken, duck, or other bird eggs in a special brine (prepared by boiling more salt than will go into solution with some lime, lye, and tea leaves) for about 3 months. They then are dried and coated with a paste of clay, lime, ashes, and salt and buried in the ground. They are perceptibly altered by this process in appearance, texture, and taste. The yolks turn an attractive green and are cheeselike, while the whites become gelatinous and yellow. Sort of the Brazilian flag in reverse. They usually are eaten raw, often with a vinegar and shredded ginger sauce, and are highly prized. *Pi-tan* would certainly be no stranger to the American palate than a ripe limburger or even a bleu cheese or Camembert would be to a Chinese.

Preserved Eggs and Ham *(Yien tan huo twe)* / China

Shell some preserved eggs and with a sharp knife cut each crosswise into 1/4-in. slices. Cut some smoked ham into a JULIENNE. Toss 1–1/2-in. sections of endive with a sauce made by mixing peanut oil, vinegar, and soy sauce (3:1:1) with crushed garlic and a generous amount of dry mustard. Cover a flat serving dish with a bed of the tossed endive and arrange over it the eggs, ham, and some watercress sprigs.

The Filipinos shell them first.

Pickled Eggs *(Pinoy)* / Philippines

Hard-boil fertile or nonfertile chicken (or duck) eggs, cool, and peel. Drop them into a boiling mixture of vinegar and sugar (2:1), salt, and some allspice (in a cloth bag). Simmer 5 minutes. Put into sterile jars and sterilize for 25 minutes. Seal. The longer these eggs are kept the better.

Filipinos, Chinese, and a number of other peoples like to keep fertilized eggs a while, to wait "until there is something in them to eat." In the Philippines their production is a $10-million-a-year industry.

FERTILE EGGS *(Balut)* / PHILIPPINES

Chip a hole in the top of a 15- to 18-day-old fertilized duck egg and suck out the liquid. Then break the shell and eat the embryo. They can be coddled first.

The one sauce made from eggs that is mentioned in other recipes in this book is the great garlic mayonnaise of the French Mediterranean coast.

AÏOLI SAUCE / FRANCE

Quick aïoli sauce may be made by beating thick mayonnaise until smooth, then whisking in crushed garlic. Mayonnaise is prepared using olive oil, egg yolks, and lemon—*all at room temperature*. Put two egg yolks, 1/4 t dry mustard, and 1/2 t salt in the jar of an electric blender and blend at top speed. Add 1 T lemon juice and blend a little more. Uncover jar and with the blender at high speed very slowly trickle in 1 C olive oil.

Other kinds of eggs are much more neglected by us.

TURTLE EGGS AND SNAKE EGGS

LIKE bird eggs, reptile eggs contain fairly large amounts of yolk. Turtle eggs are relatively abundant in some places and can be subjected to controlled harvest. In other areas, the pressure upon particular species is already excessive. In a few parts of the world they are trying to do something about this. To help prevent the further dwindling of some of its valuable species, the Malaysian government has recently planted 47,000 giant sea turtle eggs in protected hatcheries. Some hatcheries with controlled release also have been established in the Caribbean.

Turtle and snake eggs usually are simply boiled or used in some of the recipes included under turtle meat. Iguana eggs are prized in Mexico and Latin America and are eaten fried, pickled, and dried.

FISH EGGS

THE other most commonly enjoyed animal eggs are those of certain fish. Throughout much of the Western world the hard roes of fish have been eaten and prized from at least Roman times. Caviar, the eggs of different species of sturgeon and popularly called the dish of kings, is certainly the best known of these. The recent decline, however, of the sturgeon fisheries of the Caspian Sea has made it an even more high-priced delicacy than ever before. In some parts of the United States you could consider making your own caviar. Our Davis friend Julia Sadler makes a very good product from immense sturgeon caught right in our own Sacramento River.

As the sturgeon is being threatened ecologically in its principal Old World fisheries and fancy caviar recipes are easy to come by anyway, I will consider here only some of the uses for other very good but less "snobbish" fish eggs. (And to think the Russians used to squash caviar and use it to clarify fish stock!)

"Caviar" also is made from the roe of sevruga, salmon, shad, herring, sterlet, keta, dog salmon, pike, mullet, tuna, lumpfish, and other fish. "Red caviar" is really salmon roe and is also excellent food, as is herring roe. In addition, in Mediterranean countries mullet or tuna eggs are pickled in brine or vinegar and then pressed. This preparation is known as *poutargue, botargo, botarga,* or *boutargue.* Its making is said to have been learned from the Persians by Alexander the Great.

The roes of carp, cod, herring, and shad are about 23 percent protein and a little over 2 percent fat, while those of salmon and sturgeon have about 10 percent fat.

RAW HERRING ROE / JAPAN

Thinly slice a well-washed raw herring roe and sprinkle the slices with sake. Marinate them for 1 to 2 days in the refrigerator in the following mixture: boil and then cool equal volumes of SHOYU and MIRIN with a few shavings of *katsuobushi* and a little AJINOMOTO.

SCRAMBLED EGGS AND HERRING ROE / UNITED STATES

Poach the roe in ACIDULATED WATER for about 15 minutes, drain, remove the membranes, and mash it. Beat some chicken eggs with a fork, stir in some cream, salt, white pepper, and the mashed roe. Scramble in butter to a soft creamy consistency and sprinkle with chopped parsley.

CARP ROE ON TOAST (*Croûtes aux laitances*) / FRANCE

Poach carp or herring roe in lemon juice and butter. Put them on rectangular slices of bread that have been fried in butter. Top with bread crumbs that also were fried in butter and sprinkle with lemon juice. Heat in a hot oven and garnish with some chopped parsley.

MULLET ROE PASTE (*Poutargue*) / FRANCE

The eggs of the gray mullet in their membranes are salted, washed, pressed, dried in the sun, and sold throughout the Mediterranean encased in wax. They are sliced thinly and eaten with lemon juice, oil, and pepper. But *poutargue* (also called *boutargue* in Arabic, *avgotaracho* in Greek, and *bottargo* in Italian) is *most* famous as the chief ingredient of *taramosalata,*.

MULLET ROE DIP (*Taramosalata*) / GREECE

Blend together into a smooth paste some desalted *poutargue* (or smoked cod roe) with bread that has been soaked in water and squeezed dry, olive oil, and lemon juice. Garlic and cayenne pepper are among a variety of possible additions.

CREAMED FISH ROE / HAWAII

Wash the roe, heat slowly to a boil in salted water, and simmer for 1 minute. Remove the dark membranes and veins and cut the roe into pieces. Make a cream sauce with nutmeg added and cook the roe in it in a double boiler for 20 minutes. Serve on toast.

SHAD ROE CURRY SIDE DISH (*Telow terubok sambal*) / MALAYSIAN INDIAN

This curry sambal is prepared by frying shad roe in oil and mixing it with finely chopped onions and chilis, a little white vinegar, lime juice, and Worcestershire sauce.

FISH SPERM

SPERM, or soft roes, of fish are called variously, milt, *laitance*, and *laite*. Those of the carp, herring, and mackerel are much prized in Europe. Catfish sperm are also good. Before they are cooked, fish sperm are washed in cold water and the membranes that contain the blood vessels are peeled off. No matter how they are prepared ultimately, sperm then are poached quickly in a mixture of lemon juice, water, butter, and salt.

The most common ways to cook poached sperm include *à la meunière*; or served as is, with a sauce of browned butter and lemon juice and a garnish of capers and chopped parsley; or as fritters (cooled after poaching and marinated in lemon juice, oil, and chopped parsley, then dipped in batter and deep-fried); or in scallop shells (with a poached oyster, some cooked mushrooms, a few shrimp and/or mussels, and covered with a Normande sauce and garnished, if desired, with a bit of truffle); or in tartlets or on croutons, covered with lemon wedges; or as a milt butter for canapés or other hors d'oeuvres (ground in a mortar or blender, blending in equal weight of butter and 1 t dry mustard per 4 oz. sperm, sieved, and chilled before serving). In Russia, sturgeon milt also is canned in tomato sauce or with vegetables.

Fish Sperm Crepes *(Pannequets aux laitances)* / France

Spread unsweetened crepes with a mixture of chopped fish sperm and mushrooms bound with a fish-based béchamel sauce. Roll them, place in a buttered dish, sprinkle with grated Parmesan and melted butter, and heat in a 350°F oven until the top is brown.

Herring Sperm with Cream / England

Poach some herring sperm for 4 minutes in salted water containing a bay leaf and juice of a lemon. Simmer a chopped shallot in a half-wineglass of dry vermouth until the wine is almost entirely reduced. Stir in a wineglass of heavy cream and bring almost to a boil. Salt and pepper, add the poached sperm, and heat through. Chill and serve the roe with crisp diced cucumbers.

Epilogue

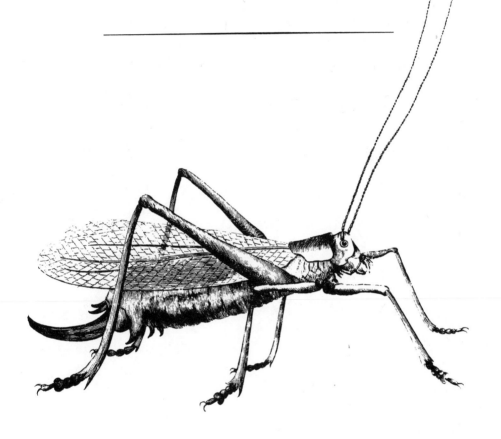

EPILOGUE

De Gustibus?

Food preferences, like language, are obstinate cultural traits.
NAOMI BLIVIN

A S THE VARIETY of sources for high-quality proteins in the American diet becomes ever more restricted, beef alone accounts for a higher and higher proportion of our total protein intake. Neither the extent to which this pattern of increasing dependence upon a single protein source has recently and rapidly evolved in the United States nor the problems it may create for us in the future have received much public comment. Moreover, not only do we eat many fewer species of animals today than in times past, but rarely do we eat anything more than the muscle tissues of even those animals. A quick survey of meat recipes published by *Good Housekeeping* magazine shows these trends early. For example, while its 1908 and 1909 volumes included 5 recipes for mutton and 6 for rabbit, the 1968 and 1969 issues contained no recipes for mutton and only 1 for rabbit. Similarly, there were 11 recipes for liver, 6 for heart, 3 for tripe, 2 for sweetbreads, and 1 for kidneys in 1908 and 1909, while the later volumes included only 5 for liver and *none* for any other visceral organ. Stated differently, though over 25 percent of all *Good Housekeeping* recipes nearer the beginning of this century used these several kinds of meats, less than 3 percent of their recipes now suggest using such foods.

The true extent of these profound changes in the American diet becomes even more apparent when we realize that 40 percent of all the *beef* we eat is in the form of the mechanically ground, homogeneous paste we call hamburger. While 4.6 percent of the recipes in the 1908-9 issues of *Good Housekeeping* used chopped beef (7 of 10 recipes for beef chopped by the cook), 11.7 percent of 1968-69 recipes called for ground beef. The average American now eats four-fifths of a pound of hamburger weekly, and this bland mince of uniform appearance, texture, and taste constitutes the main protein course in the average American home twice a week. In fact, a recent study of food purchasing in one urban community in the U.S. Middle West showed that, besides hamburger, the *only* meat or fish items commonly eaten were other fresh beef meat, hot dogs and other processed luncheon meats, chicken, and bacon.

Despite the fact, therefore, that U.S. grocery stores now stock an average of 7,525 different food items versus only 867 in 1928, the implication with respect to dietary variety is clearly deceptive, since a vast majority of currently available food items are expensive, prepackaged, and often precooked and processed foods. The actual variety of fresh protein foods readily available to the average consumer is far narrower today than in 1928. Present marketing and advertising policies of food manufacturers are designed to promote these trends ever futher.

Unless they can be reversed by an aggressively directed reeducation of our palates, it is not difficult to predict some of the consequences of our growing food-prejudice and food-avoidance patterns. A survey by *Scholastic Magazine* in 1978 of 66,000 American adolescents aged 11 to 18 showed that their favorite foods were hamburgers, steak, and pizza and we can easily imagine what family "dining" in America will be like when *they* grow up and buy their own microwave ovens.

REASONS FOR OUR CULINARY DECLINE

A number of explanations have been offered for this rapidly contracting range of sources for proteins eaten by Americans. One is that American immigrants from poor economic backgrounds abroad were particularly prone to discard as quickly as possible food items they thought were associated with their former poverty and distinguished them from "regular Yankees." However, Margaret Mead has perceptively pointed out some ethnic differences in this regard, mentioning that "societies where children are fed lovingly, and where food is a great pleasure and delight, [are] . . . very resistant to change. The food habits of Italian immigrants to the U.S.A., for example, were very difficult to change, whereas those of certain Germanic groups, where food was treated as one element of a rigid system of discipline, were changed easily." It would seem, therefore, that while the culturally homogenizing influences of the American "melting pot" have contributed to a narrowing of our food choices, they have not been the primary factor. Indeed, as Paul György has stressed, the food habits of immigrants were probably among the last of their distinctive habits to change. "When Europeans came to the U.S.A. as small children, they did not want to be conspicuous. They first changed their clothes, then their languages, but they did not change their food habits because they could enjoy those at home without being seen."

Most evidence suggests, in fact, that many of our growing meat prejudices and avoidances are considerably more recent than the great waves of immigration to this country. A study not only of American homemakers' magazines but of cookbooks published in the last century clearly supports that idea and demonstrates an accelerating pattern of such avoidances. This deterioration of the American diet can best be attributed, therefore, to a complex combination of affluence, laziness, and parental permissiveness, the biggest encourager of which probably has been a rapidly accelerating concentration of ownership and management in the food-producing, processing, and marketing industries, with increasing integration of operations, beginning in the 1930s. This has led to aggressive promotion of the idea and the products of "agribusiness" as superior to those of the traditional American pattern of farms and retail food stores owned and run as family enterprises.

Efficient exploitation of "convenience-laziness" considerations, often in the partially false guise of household economics, by these growing food–producing-processing-marketing industries, particularly as they have become increasingly merged into giant financial conglomerates, has pressured and cajoled the American consumer into a dietary conformity and mediocrity of taste rarely matched elsewhere in the world. Brewster and Jacobson (1978) have concluded similarly that the "nation's mammoth food industry plays a major role in influencing food habits . . . [and has] encouraged a trend [in America] toward a diet composed of relatively few different foods." "The American appetite is [now] worth over $300 billion a year," and our food industry spends $6 billion a year, or 3 percent of our total food bill, directly for advertising and promotion of specific processed foods. McDonalds alone spends $100 million per year mostly to promote a simple "beef paste" sandwich any child could make in five minutes at home at much less cost—and so successfully that this single fast-food chain's sales have increased twentyfold between 1964 and 1976.

WHAT ARE THE LIKELY CONSEQUENCES?

How critical are such questions about our own diets likely to be for the foreseeable future? Surely we Americans now obtain, on the average, more than enough total protein and more than enough high-quality protein well balanced in amino acids (i.e., protein from animal sources). Those are not *our* local problems now although they will become more so if several food trends of more immediate concern continue as they are. One is the continuing promotion of meat-production methods that are ecologically imbalanced and needlessly expensive in energy inputs. Another is the increasing transfer of ownership of our animal-protein–producing capacity to predominantly nonagricultural investors who are sometimes most interested in taking calculated losses for tax purposes or solely in maximizing shareholders' profits. The third is the factor with which this book is concerned, the rapid narrowing of our preferences in foods and especially animal-protein foods. If these trends are not reversed, their future result will very surely be the failure of our domestic supply of commonly eaten proteins to keep pace with demand, a dramatic rise in the price of these animal proteins, and a decline in our national role in helping to alleviate serious food deficiencies in other countries, perhaps in exchange for some of *their* resources.

Recent projections disagree somewhat on how large the world's 1978 population of 4.2 to 4.4 billion will become by the year 2000. Some independent demographers say 5.8 billion, the World Bank says 6 billion, the U.N. projection is 6.3 billion, and the private Environmental Fund believes 6.5 billion! Give or take 700 million, that is a lot of people, and despite the fact that virtually all such growth projections for some years past have picked A.D. 2000 as the magic year, the world's population growth presumably will not stop then.

The lessons seem obvious. Some things must give. We Americans preserve the myth that we have a green thumb that gives us the unique ability to produce more and more food almost at will. We do not. A recent report of a National Academy of Sciences committee on agricultural-production efficiency in the United States warns that our producing potential for some major foods may already be leveling off or actually declining.

At the same time, the research support that might help prevent this is declining too. One thing we must realize in these connections is that development of our much-boasted-about labor-efficient agriculture (i.e., the ability of only 4 percent of our population to produce a surplus of food) has been at the expense of greatly increased energy consumption, most of it of irreplaceable fossil fuels, and of displaced, unemployed people. For these and other reasons, we should probably have substantially *more* Americans on our farms in the future.

The extent to which these patterns have changed is seldom realized. Between 1940 and 1970 on-farm energy consumption in the United States actually increased 400 percent, and the amount of energy required to produce an average food calorie rose from 4.5 to 9 calories. Some of these changes were caused by the fact that between 1947 and 1972 the percentage of U.S. beef cattle being grain-fed rose from 35 to 75 percent and the weight at which grain feeding was initiated dropped from 740 to 800 pounds to 450 pounds. The principal results were shorter time to reach slaughter weight and a higher proportion of fat in beef. The late E. F. Schumacher has rightly queried whether "an industrial system which uses forty percent of the world's primary resources to supply less than six percent of the world's population could be called efficient [unless] it obtained strikingly successful results in terms of human happiness, well-being, culture, peace and harmony."

Our agriculture is not only energy-inefficient, it is land-inefficient when compared with many labor- and animal-intensive crop-rearing systems elsewhere. Moreover, the family farms in which we have taken such justifiable pride in our past, through which diverse crop-animal systems have efficiently recycled energy and nutrients without leaving polluting plant and animal wastes to accumulate unused, become fewer and fewer. Sixty percent of California's agricultural production, for example, now comes from only 2,774 very large farms with sales of over $500,000 per year and an average value of 2.4 million dollars. Between 1929 and 1964 the percentage of U.S. livestock produced on very large farms rose from 2.1 to 46.8 percent and by 1972, 58 percent of U.S. fattened beef came from just 2,204 immense feedlots, with 168,843 smaller lots supplying the remainder. The trend is for even greater concentration of ownership in fewer and fewer farms, much of it in the hands of corporate conglomerates rather than farmers. Moreover, a recent California survey showed an annual turnover in ownership of its grazing rangelands of 4.4 percent with

68 percent of sales to buyers whose main income also was not agricultural.

Most of us must be prepared to alter our life-styles unless we are prepared to risk conflicts over the world's resources in the future that could leave us almost alone in the world. One not so small change we could begin to make now is to expand our palates, to diversify our diets more, and to use our available overall food resources, particularly our protein resources, more efficiently and wisely.

FOOD AVOIDANCES AND INTERNATIONAL DEVELOPMENT

THOUGH American food prejudices have now reached the proportions indicated, this problem of food avoidances and associated waste is certainly not ours alone. A book like this one could be written for each of the world's peoples. Aside from what this subject says about people's individuality, creativeness, taste, and general level of culture, the important questions about food prejudices anywhere are how much they help create situations of want amidst relative plenty or otherwise widen the world food-population gap. This is now impossible to assess with any accuracy. Many indicators suggest, however, that food prejudices are important, underestimated, and largely neglected contributors to human hunger worldwide. And, as I have tried to show, not only do we not know enough about them in others, but also scarcely recognize them in ourselves. *Each* society needs to examine its own food customs and habits in order to recognize its own irrationalities, particularly where these irrationalities may threaten its own or some other people's well-being.

Our current lack of information about food habits generally, the specific reasons different peoples have adopted some of them, the tenacity with which they are held, the untoward effects they may now have and their real possibilities for modification put us all on the horns of a dilemma. On the one hand are those who say "do nothing" about this problem. These include died-in-the-wool romantics who would preserve the food habits of every human community—and all other aspects of people's lives—undisturbed, like so many exhibits in a museum of human experience. In a similar vein biological, environmental, or social determinists tell us that (for different reasons) each human population is necessarily evolving its own "right pattern" of food consumption and related practices. Some ideologically uncommitted planners believe too that food prejudices are factors that are particularly insusceptible to voluntary change and for that reason alone must persist as unmodifiable elements even in the face of increasingly unbalanced equations of resources and wants.

More radical planners, on the other hand, would impose what they perceive as a "better life" on other peoples, overturning by force those food habits and other vestiges of "unenlightened cultures" that stand in their way. Many people who have worked in the developing world are aware that this latter approach is adopted not only by totalitarian regimes but far too often in national and international development efforts generally. Small groups of persons who are in a position to determine national and international policies—particularly money and development policies—may in their "wisdom" simply decide what is best for a people and proceed to finance and implement a plan designed to achieve it. They usually have not explored adequately a people's real preferences, why they exist, and their often vastly different cultural perceptions of what constitutes "the good life." They rarely have given adequate consideration to those non-quantifiable, noneconomic variables that historical experience has distinguished as humane values. In forcing such widespread changes they may also trample the reasonable and the cherished.

In such areas as food planning, as elsewhere in development planning, policymakers thereby run a substantial risk of replacing long-established practices with whose *merits* they may be completely or partially unfamiliar with other superficially attractive practices and systems about whose undesirable trade-offs and long-term effects they may also lack sufficient information. For planners, like others, are enveloped in their *own* cultural and historical cocoons—their biases—to the extent that they cannot view alternative practices and beliefs objectively. Elsewhere, I have used the apparently simple case of man's relationships to cattle to illustrate this general problem—the effects of a culturally and technically narrow-minded approach to development.

The whole problem of trade-offs involved in making protein and other food-production policies worldwide is an extremely complex one. From our past successes and failures, what now appears most likely is that interacting problems of food, health, population, environment, and humane values will be most readily solved by identifying the *different combinations of local actions that will produce the most desirable total effects locally*, rather than by some widely applied but almost inevitably too simplistic national or regional master plan.

Planning is at least as vital in government as in any other human activity, but if we do not want blanket decisions for our future and that of others that are based too completely upon opinions with only partially identifiable biases, upon computer printouts from economic models, or upon other, too narrowly perceived "benefits," then we clearly require more information on an area-to-area basis. The argument, of course, is that action is required in many areas like food policy *now*, and we cannot afford to wait until we know all the answers.

CORRECTING THE PRESENT SITUATION

WITH respect to variables such as food prejudices, therefore, it is important to realize that there is already considerable evidence that *certain* food customs *are* irrational for life today and tomorrow, and we should not delay trying to do something about them. Further, history suggests that some of them may be more susceptible to voluntary changes, given favorable circumstances and proper tactics, than is often believed. For example, at several points in history peoples have adopted relatively large numbers of completely new foods in relatively short periods of time. One such occasion followed the introduction into Europe by the Arabs through Portugal, Spain, and Sicily of a large number of completely new dietary items. An even more profound influence on the eating habits not only of Europe but also of Africa followed rapidly upon the exploration and colonization of the Western Hemisphere. In fact, as I have already indicated, it is difficult for us today even to conceptualize a northern European cuisine without the white potato, a Mediterranean cuisine without tomatoes or most beans, or an African cuisine without maize or cassava.

While all the national examples cited in this book can provide lessons to Americans for changes *we* can make personally, none is in a position to influence us more constructively in this regard than the single example of south China, whose cuisine most of us already respect and enjoy. For, as Anderson and Anderson (1977) have so well pointed out, "no culture on earth, not even the French, is so concerned with gastronomy as the Chinese," and none have developed such an unprejudiced approach to what is edible. Shedding our biases need not produce a pauper's diet, as the Chinese experience clearly demonstrates. "There is continual concern with the quality of food, [yet] . . . food taboos are foreign to south China. Similarly, there is little commitment to a certain diet. . . . South Chinese are usually quick to experiment with new and different foods."

What, then, if, given better information about *our* food habits and prejudices—as influenced by 40 years of food-industry advertising—we were to *redirect* through government this propaganda effort to the discouragement of irrational and potentially harmful food habits? If the American public could be persuaded so effectively in such a short period to adopt an inferior diet, could it not be persuaded by similarly aggressive efforts to adopt a more enlightened view of what is edible, nutritious, and good to eat? And could others not be influenced by a similar approach to voluntarily shed *their* food prejudices and avoidances?

All the world's people *must* begin to overcome in themselves—and even more so in their children—senseless taboos about what is edible and what is not. Only then can we stop today's universal animal-protein wastage. How ironic it would be, in this scientific age, for mankind to starve largely because of a bunch of old wives' tales, irrational beliefs, silly associations, and the lack of a sufficient spirit of culinary and gustatory adventure.

Glossary

Selected Bibliography

Indexes

Glossary

ACIDULATED WATER. Water containing a small quantity of vinegar or lemon juice (approx. 10:1)

AJINOMOTO. Japanese name for monosodium glutamate

ANATTO. South American red-orange food dye from the waxy pulp surrounding the seeds of *Bixa orellana*; also called *achiote*

BARD. To make lean meat fatter by tying thin sheets of fat on its surface before cooking

BLANCH. To boil in water a short time but not enough to cook completely

BOUQUET GARNI. Unless other ingredients are indicated, a tied bouquet consisting of a sprig of thyme, a sprig of parsley, and a bay leaf

BRAISE. To sauté in fat or oil and then cook *in very little liquid* (compare with stew); a way to thicken sauces by reduction or evaporation

BURGHUL. Finely cracked wheat

CHILIS RELLENOS BATTER. Light Mexican batter made by beating until stiff whites of 2 eggs and carefully folding into them first the 2 beaten yolks, then 2 T flour

COURT-BOUILLON. Any aromatic liquid in which to boil meat or fish; often water containing white wine or a little lemon juice or vinegar; *nage* is virtually a synonym

COUSCOUS. Cracked millet (or wheat) grain boiled and eaten in North Africa as a carbohydrate staple

DAIKON. Japanese radish

DASHI. Japanese seafood stock; substitute fish or chicken stock

DEGLAZE. To pour some liquid in a pan where meat, game, or poultry was cooked to dissolve the caramelized pan juices and to reduce the mixture over high heat

FIVE-SPICE. Chinese spice mixture of star anise, anise pepper, fennel, cloves, and cinnamon; available in oriental groceries

FUMET. A stock, particularly of fish or shellfish; sometimes one boiled down until it is much reduced

GARAM MASALA. Indian mixed spices, made, for example, as by grinding together 2 oz. black peppercorns, 2 oz. coriander seeds, 1–1/2 oz.

caraway seeds, 1/2 oz. cloves, 20 large cardamon seeds, and 1/2 oz. cinnamon

GARUM. See *Halec*

GHEE. Clarified butter

HALEC. The paste residue left after making Roman fermented fish sauce, or *garum*; substitute anchovy paste

JULIENNE. Food cut into thin strips

KIM CHEE. Korean pickle mainstay of Chinese cabbage cut into pieces and fermented with ginger, garlic, and hot red peppers; available in oriental groceries

KONBU. Edible seaweed, sold in dried sheets in Japanese food stores

LARD. To make lean meat fatter by inserting strips of pork fat into it before cooking

LIMU. Hawaiian edible seaweed; substitute soaked *konbu*

"LONG RICE." Transparent, cellophanelike noodles made from rice flour

LUAU. A leafy Hawaiian vegetable; substitute spinach or Swiss chard

MIRAPOIX. Finely diced vegetables sautéed in butter until tender

MIRIN. Japanese sweet rice wine; substitute sherry

MISO. Japanese soy bean paste; available in oriental groceries

QUATRE-ÉPICES. Commercial powdered mixture of spices, containing white pepper mixed with nutmeg, cloves, and ginger (and, sometimes, thyme, bay leaf, basil, sage, coriander, and mace)

ROUILLE. Hot pepper sauce

ROUX. Melted butter or other shortening into which flour is stirred with a whisk to make a smooth paste, a light *roux* being cooked only long enough to eliminate the raw flour taste

SHOYU. Japanese soy sauce

STEW. To cook by simmering in water to cover (compare with braise)

TAHEENI. Arabic sesame seed paste available canned in Greek or Middle Eastern stores

TEMPURA BATTER. A light Japanese batter made by lightly beating 1 egg and then beating into it with chopsticks 1 C flour and 1 C water (it should be a bit lumpy)

TOFU. Oriental bean curd cake; available in oriental groceries

VOL-AU-VENT. Puff pastries shaped to contain certain other food

WASABI. Japanese hot horseradish; available dry in cans

WOK. A Chinese round-bottom cooking pan

Selected Bibliography

Anderson, E. N., and Anderson, M. L. 1977. Modern China: South, *in* Chang, K. C., ed. *Food in Chinese Culture.* Yale Univ. Press, New Haven.

Arnold, A. F. 1940. *The Sea-Beach at Ebb-Tide.* D. Appleton-Century Co., New York.

Arnott, M. L., ed. 1975. *Gastronomy, the Anthropology of Food Habits.* Mouton, The Hague.

Bodenheimer, F. S. 1957. *Insects as Human Food.* Junk, The Hague.

Borgstrom, G., ed. 1961. *Fish as Food.* 4 vols. Academic Press, New York.

Brewster, L., and Jacobson, M. F., 1978. *The Changing American Diet.* Center for Science in the Public Interest, Washington, D.C.

Brothwell, D., and Brothwell, P. 1969. *Food in Antiquity.* Frederick A. Praeger, New York.

Brown, E., and Brown, B. 1961. *Culinary Americana; Cookbooks Published in the Cities and Towns of the United States of America during the Years from 1860 through 1960.* Roving Eye Press, New York.

Burgess, A., and Dean, R. F. A. 1962. *Malnutrition and Food Habits.* Tavistock Publications, London.

Clark, F. L. 1968. Food habits as a practical nutrition problem. *World Rev. Nutr. and Dietetics* 9:56-84.

Dumont, R. 1975. *Croissance . . . de la Famine.* Le Seuil, Paris.

Flower, B., and Rosenbaum, E., transl. 1958. *Apicius' the Roman Cookery Book.* Harrap, London.

Food Facts and Findings (vol. 1, 1976–). Newsletter of the International Committee for the Anthropology of Food and Food Habits, Wilson Museum, Castine, Maine 04421, U.S.A.

Giammattei, V. M. 1976. *Raising Small Meat Animals.* Interstate Publishers, Danville, Ill.

Gibbons, E. 1962. *Stalking the Wild Asparagus.* David McKay, New York.

Hall, I. S., and Hall, C. S. 1939. A study of disliked and unfamiliar foods. *J. Amer. Diet. Assoc.* 15:540-550.

Harris, M., and Ross. E. B. 1978. How beef became king. *Psychol. Today* 12:88-94.

Hoffman, W. E. 1947. Insects as human food. *Proc. Entomol. Soc. of Washington* 49:1-5.

Jordan, D. S., and Evermann, B. W. 1920. *American Food and Game Fishes*. Doubleday, Page, Garden City, N.Y.

Kyle, L. R., Sundquist, W. B., and Guither, H. D. 1972. Who controls agriculture now?—The trends underway, in *Who Will Control U.S. Agriculture?* Univ. of Illinois Cooperative Extension Service Special Publ. 27.

Lasnet de Lantz, H. 1967. *La Characuterie à la Campagne*. La Maison Rustique, Paris.

Leverton, R. M. 1944. Freshman food likes. *J. Home Econ.* 36:589-590.

Lyon, N. 1963. *Meat at Any Price*. Faber and Faber, London.

Mittaine, J. 1962. Milk other than cow's milk, in *Milk Hygiene*. World Health Organization Monograph 48, Geneva.

Montagné, P. 1961. *Larousse Gastronomique*. Crown Publishers, New York.

Moore, H. B. 1957. The meaning of food. *Amer. J. Clin. Nutr.* 5:77-82.

NAS. 1975. *Agricultural Production Efficiency*. National Academy of Sciences, Washington, D.C.

Oliver, R. 1967. *Gastronomy of France*. World Publishing, Cleveland.

Orrington, J. D., ed. 1963. *The Better Use of the World's Fauna for Food*. Institute of Biology, London.

Page, L., and Friend, B. 1978. The changing United States diet. *Bioscience* 28:192-197.

Price, J. F., and Schweigert, B. S., eds. 1971. *The Science of Meat and Meat Products*. 2d ed. W. H. Freeman, San Francisco.

Pyke, M. 1968. *Food and Society*. John Murray, London.

Renner, H. D. 1944. *The Origin of Food Habits*. Faber and Faber, London.

Romans, J. R., and Ziegler, P. T. 1977. *The Meat We Eat*. 11th ed. Interstate Printers and Publishers, Danville, Ill.

Root, W., and de Rochemont, R. 1976. *Eating in America, a History*. William Morrow, New York.

Schultz, G. 1964. Food taboos. *Today's Health* 42:28-32.

Schumacher, E. F. 1975. *Small Is Beautiful*. Harper and Row, New York.

Schwabe, C. W. 1978. The holy cow: provider or parasite? A problem for humanists. *Southern Humanities Rev.* 13:251-278.

Schwabe, C. W., and Ruppanner, R. 1972. Animal diseases as contributors to human hunger: problems of control. *World Rev. Nutrit. Dietetics* 15:185-224.

Seifrit, E. 1961. Changes in beliefs and food practices in pregnancy. *J. Amer. Dietetic Assoc.* 39:455-466.

Simoons, F. J. 1961. *Eat Not This Flesh: Food Avoidances in the Old World*, Univ. of Wisconsin Press, Madison.

Sleight, J., and Hull, R. 1977. *Home Book of Smoke-Cooking*. Stackpole Books, Harrisburg, Pa.

Syckle, C. 1967. Some pictures of food consumption in the United States: Part I. 1630 to 1860, *in* Beeuwkes, A. M., Todhunter, E. N., and Weigley, E. S., eds. *Essays on History of Nutrition and Dietetics*, Amer. Dietetic Assoc., Chicago.

Tannahill, R. 1973. *Food in History*. Stein and Day, New York.

Titcombe, M. 1969. Dog and man in the ancient Pacific, with special attention to Hawaii. *Bernice P. Bishop Museum Special Publ.* 59, Honolulu.

Toupin, E. A. 1967. *Hawaiian Cookbook and Backyard Luau*. Silvermine Publishers/Grosset and Dunlap, New York.

Vaillant, G. C. 1950. *The Aztecs of Mexico*. Penguin Books, Middlesex, England.

Yadkin, J., and McKenzie. J. C. 1964. *Changing Food Habits*. Macgibbon and Kec, London.

General Index

Abalone, with pork stomach, 105
Abomasum, 138
  beef, 56
  tripe, 53
Afromchemoyle, 139
Agneau de lait (paulillac), 124
Agouti, 203-4
Agribusiness, 409
Agriculture
  development planning, 413
  draft power, 3
  energy for crop production, 3
  international development, 412-14
  nonagricultural investment, 410-12
  nonarable land, 2
  research decline, 411
  tractor-powered, 3
  U.S. production efficiency, 411
Aïoli sauce, 400
Air bladder, cod, 295
Allemande sauce, 33
Alligator, 259
Americans
  appetite, 409
  diet, 407-8
  dietary restrictions, 408
  food prejudices, 412
    see also Food prejudices
Amino acids, essential, 2
Amphibians, 269-76
Anchovy, 280, 281
  with beef heart, 42
  with beef lung, 42

cured, 281
fritters, 282
pâté, 282-83
with pork liver, 100
and potato casserole, 282
tart, 282
Anchovy fillets
  with beef heart, 38
  with beef kidney, 65
  with grilled catfish, 288
  in hare fillets Provence style, 193
  in liver pâté, 100
  in small birds in casserole, 250
Anchovy paste
  in cockle soup, 325
  in stuffed hare, 184
Anchovy sauce, for roasted lamb
  viscera, 282
Anemone, 362
  fried, 362
  fritters, 362
  omelet, 362
  soup, 362
Anglerfish, 278
Animal eggs, 396-97
Animal fat, 3-4
Animal food consumption, 2
Animal protein, 1, 206
  cost of, 40
Anisakis worm infection, 268
Annelids, 376
Ant, in red ant chutney, 374
Aorta, beef, 51

Cholesterol, 3-4, 82
Chorizo, with beef tongue, 21
Chowder
  crayfish, 355-56
  fish, 278-80
  seafood, 278, 279
Christianity, 157
Christmas liver sausage, 102
Civet, 147, 192, 233
Clam(s), 321
  razor, 331
  in rice with rabbit and shellfish, 188
Clambake, 349-50
Clostridia, 9
Cockle(s), 322-25
  boiled, 323
  with clambake, 349
  with cod's head and shoulders, 294
  fried, 323
  with mixed seafood, 349
  pie, 323
  raw, 322
  with roast leg of mutton, 324
  salad, 324
  sauce mariners' style, 324
  in seafood chowder, 279
  in shellfish soup, 348
  with sole, 324
  soup, 325
  stew, 323
Cocks' comb, 221
  in pigeon pupton, 242
Cod air bladder, 295
Cod head and shoulders, 294
Cod liver, in cod head and shoulders, 294
Cod milt, in cod head and shoulders, 294
Cod roe, in cod head and shoulders, 294
Cod sounds, 295

Colon, pork, 109
Conger eel, 278, 297
  in fish stew, 280
  roasted, 300
  with sea urchin gonad sauce, 359
  sun-dried, 285
Congo meat, 383
Consumer protection, 161
Corned beef, 16-17
  with garnished sauerkraut platter, 109
Cornish game hen, 218
Cotton rat, 205
Cottontail rabbit, 180
Cougar, 176
Cow, *see* Beef *entries*
Cow heel, 29
Cowboy soup, 39
Crab
  with chicken livers, 225
  soft-shelled, 347
Cracklings, 79, 88-89
Crayfish (crawfish), 350-56
  aspic, 353
  in beer, 352
  boiled, 351, 352
  in browned sauce, 354
  butter, 353, 355
  calalou, 201
  chowder, 355-56
  cream soup, 356
  with eel platter, 304
  Liège style, 351
  mayonnaise, 353
  in nantua sauce, 353-54
  with pancakes, 354
  Provence style, 354
  in roast chicken stuffing, 355
  salad, 352-53
  soup, 356
  stuffed, 355

fritters, 334
  in shellfish soup, 348
  steamed, 334
White sausage, 141
Whitebait, 305
Whitetail deer, 155
Whole carcass
  dog, 171-72
  frog, 270
  goat, 150-51
  hare, 182-85
  lamb, 127-28, 150-51
  opossum, 199-200
  rabbit, 182-85
  raccoon, 199-200
  small bird, 246-51
Wild boar, 82
Wild cervids, 154-56
Wild duck, 219
  burgoo, 198
Wild geese, 219
Wild hog, 209
Wild ruminants, 154-56
Wild swine, 82
Wildcat, 176
Wildlife, ecologically threatened, 3
Wing
  chicken, 224, 259
  goose, 220
  poultry, 222-23
  turkey, 220, 221, 223
Wing tips
  duck, 234
  goose, 234

Winkles, 332
  baked, 332
  with fish fillet, 332
  in mixed seafood, 349
  pickled, 332
  in shellfish soup, 348
Wood rat, 205
Woodchuck, 201-2
Worm infestation, fish, 268

Yaks, 3
Yak's milk, 396
Yoghurt, 391-95
  and barley soup, 394
  in chicken soup, 393
  cold soup, 392
  cold stew, 392-93
  cooking, 393
  and cucumbers, 392
  drink, 392
  and duck soup, 393-94
  with eggplant, 395
  with lamb tongue, 130
  in meat balls, 127
  and meat ball curry, 394
  with minced lamb balls, 394
  with rabbit, 189-90
  sauce for salmon, 395
  with sheep feet, 133
  with sheep kidney, 145
  and spinach, 393
Yorkshire sausage, 57
Yrchins, 104

REGIONAL INDEX: RECIPES BY COUNTRY

Fish
  Di iu tan, 293
  Yu tu tan, 295
Fly
  Fly larvae, 375
Frog
  Shiang wa twe, 272
Grasshopper
  Tsa ku meng, 367
Jellyfish
  Sueh tin yue, 363
  Sueh tin yue lopo sala, 363
Octopus
  Tsa tsan iu, 343
Pig
  Hon tsao tsu tu, 104-5
  Jao hwa, 116
  Jiu feh tan, 98
  Ju tiao, 92
  Nan chow sin, 96
  Po tsai tsu kan, 99
  Siu yu jiu, 79
  Tsu tsa so, ue pi, kan, 112
  Tsu tu pao pi, 105
  Wen to jao hwa, 116
Pigeon
  Hung tsai kuh zon, 243-44
  Jiu pi kuh, 237
  Shang kan kuh, 238-39
Sea cucumber
  Dun hoi sum, 360
  Sup bo tan, 361
  Tien tia fo, 361
Shark
  Iu che tan, 311-12
Small birds
  Tsa huang chu, 248
Snake
  Shuh zo tan, 261
  Tsuh zo fan, 260
Squab

Jo kuh ton sen kan, 239
  Su tsa nen kuh, 237
Squid
  Kan moi jiu tsao zo, 340
  Moi jiu tan, 341
Turtle
  Kwe zo tan, 258-59

Colombia
  Beef
    Sesos en tomate, 38

Cuba
  Pig
    Chicharones, 88

Denmark
  Beef
    Tunge salat, 20
  Pig
    Dyrelägens natmad, 101
    Sylte svine labber, 90

England
  Beef
    Baked marrow bones, 35
    Beef gravy, 52
    Beefsteak and kidney pudding, 68
    Brain cakes, 24
    Cow heel, 29
    Headcheese (oxhead brawn), 18
    Mock goose, 38
    Neat's-foot brawn, 29-30
    Ox palates and chicken, 23
    Oxhead brawn, 18
    Roasted ox, 15-16
    Stuffed sweetbreads, 61
    Tripe sausage, 55
    Yorkshire sausage, 57